Sister
Aimee

ALSO BY

DANIEL MARK EPSTEIN

POETRY

No Vacancies in Hell
The Follies
Young Men's Gold
The Book of Fortune
Spirits

PROSE

Star of Wonder
Love's Compass

PLAYS

Jenny and the Phoenix
The Midnight Visitor

Daniel Mark Epstein

Sister
Aimee

THE LIFE OF
AIMEE SEMPLE McPHERSON

A Harvest Book

Harcourt Brace & Company

SAN DIEGO   NEW YORK   LONDON

Library of Congress Cataloging-in-Publication Data
Epstein, Daniel Mark.
Sister Aimee: the life of Aimee Semple McPherson / Daniel Mark
Epstein. —1st Harvest ed.
p. cm.
Includes bibliographical references.
ISBN 0-15-600093-8
1. McPherson, Aimee Semple, 1890–1944. 2. Evangelists—United
States—Bibliography. I. Title.
BX7990.I68M274 1993
289.9—dc20 92-23324

Designed by Trina Stahl
Printed in the United States of America
First Harvest edition 1994
A B C D E

For my daughter,
Johanna Ruth Epstein

ACKNOWLEDGMENTS

The author wishes to record his thanks to many people who contributed to this biography through research activity, by providing documents, and by sharing their memories and impressions of Aimee Semple McPherson and the events of her life, both on and off the record, for attribution and for background. He wishes first to thank Rolf McPherson and Roberta Salter for their generosity in submitting to many hours of interviews; he is also grateful for lengthy interviews granted by Nathaniel Van Cleave, Leland Edwards, Charles Duarte, Howard Courtenay, and Jean Gulick in Los Angeles, and Mary Young, A. B. Teffetteller, Modena Teffetteller, Edythe G. Dorrance, Elmer McCammon, Margery McCammon, Ruth Baker, and Edyth Campbell of Hemet, California. Everett Wilson, a local historian in Salford, provided many essential documents, rare news clippings, photographs and census records, as well as hospitality. Doug Carr and J. C. Herbert of Salford were very helpful there, as were the librarians of Salford. In Los Angeles, I was fortunate in having the kind and energetic cooperation of Leita Mae Steward and the heritage department of Foursquare International. They generously provided workspace, copying facilities and unconditional access to the archives of the Church, and helped arrange interviews. Marc and Alice Davis provided generous hospitality in Los Angeles, and Alice Davis, who once acted on the stage at Angelus Temple, shared many anecdotes. The enormous task of obtaining and organizing most of the news articles, books, and periodical essays from the years 1918–1944 was accomplished by researcher Catherine Martin, who was resourceful in finding answers to difficult historical and medical questions. Dr. William Waldman, M.D., helped to answer medical questions, as did Dr. Jackson Eyeliff. My father-in-law, Julian Hartt, professor emeritus of religion at the

University of Virginia, answered many of my questions about the origins of the charismatic movement. The staff of the library at Union Memorial Hospital provided important medical articles concerning arthritis, cancers, disorders of the immune system, and spontaneous remission, as did the Institute of Noetic Sciences. Robert Bahr donated his entire file of primary resources from a book that he wrote about the evangelist more than a decade ago. My daughter Johanna Ruth Epstein helped organize the footnotes, and provided helpful editing suggestions. Rosemary Knower helped trim the manuscript and reorganize many sections—once again her wise editing has been an invaluable aid to clarity. The head of research at The Enoch Pratt Library, Eleanor Swidan, discovered hundreds of documents, old news articles, and references to Aimee Semple McPherson in contemporary literature; without her imaginative and painstaking detective work, this book would be much narrower in scope.

CONTENTS

1. THE EARLY YEARS

2. HER RISE TO FAME

3. THE HEALING TOUCH

It happened not in the misty, nebulous long ago, to white-robed men and women in a time we cannot quite visualize as ever having had reality, but to children and men and women who had street addresses and telephone numbers, who came in automobiles and not on camel-back by caravan, as it was said they did long ago. The blind saw again; the deaf heard. Cripples left their crutches and hung them on the rafters.

—LOUISE WEICK,
The San Francisco Chronicle, 1921

1

THE EARLY YEARS

MOUNT FOREST, ONTARIO, 1915

Somebody must have seen her marching up Main Street from the direction of the bank and the barbershop, a very young woman in a white dress, carrying a chair.

Her auburn hair was swept up from her temples into a loose chignon, revealing the cameo perfection of her profile. She had set the chair down firmly against the curb on the street corner and jumped up on it as though she were about to sing or give a speech to no one in particular; at that hour of the evening in Mount Forest, Ontario there were few people around—some after-dinner strollers, an occasional carriage or automobile, a kid on his bicycle.

Standing on the chair, she raised her long hands toward heaven as if calling for help in whatever it was she had undertaken to do. And then she did nothing. Given her unconcealable nervous energy, this was probably harder for the young woman than anything. She closed her large, wide-set eyes and just stood there with her arms straight up, like a statue of marble invisibly vibrating.

That had been quite a while ago. A man stopped to admire her, and another. A little boy was tempted to toss a pebble at her to make sure she was alive, but his mother caught his wrist. Once people saw her, they could not pull their eyes away, partly because she was so beautiful in the intensity of her concentration, partly because they had to see if she would move.

Now the crowd that gathered around the shapely young woman began arguing over how long she had been standing there, on the chair, at the corner on Main Street in Mount Forest, Ontario, with her hands up. Some said it was no more than twenty minutes. But one old farmer claimed he began watching her when the sun was above the pines. That had to be an hour past, because now it was well on toward dusk. And still he could scarcely detect the rise and fall of her breast as she breathed in and out.

It was not hard to draw a crowd in Mount Forest in 1915. A new motorcar or a dogfight would do it. But this was probably the only time a person ever drew a crowd there, and held it, just by standing still in silence.

They fell to speculating and arguing over what could be the matter with the little woman on the chair—whether she was crazy, possessed by the devil, or catatonic. She certainly was not a native of Mount Forest. Someone in the crowd said he had seen this young woman around the Victory Mission just up the street. Someone else offered the information that the rigid madonna on the chair above them was Sister Aimee Semple McPherson.

While we have Sister Aimee Semple McPherson squarely in our sights and she is standing still (like the hummingbird), let us seize this opportunity in the summer of 1915 to take a long hard look at her. She has not stood still this long since she began to walk, and she will not stand still this long again while she is breathing. Aimee is twenty-four years old. She is in the bloom of health, quite beautiful by any standards, with pointed features that are curiously both angelic and foxlike. She is particularly beautiful now in repose, her full lips concealing rows of long, even teeth. Later, when she smiles her dazzling smile, or laughs, the upper lip will draw back over the slightly protruding teeth with an effect that might be described as . . . horsey. This is the single defect, a minor one. There is an almost terrifying symmetry in the face, as if it were a half-face folded over. Now with her eyes and mouth closed we may admire the brow, high and broad, the straight hairline, the Hellenic nose. Most of us have a light and dark hemisphere to our faces—Aimee's is one oval of light.

After hundreds of thousands of photographs the face will merely seem (particularly in profile) a period piece. It will conjure up the style of the teens and twenties, long, angular, Greek revival influenced by art deco. Hers was one of the faces that expressed for millions the character of an era: passionate, ironic, tragic.

Her body, as the white cotton dress displays it, comes as something of a surprise. The long, graceful neck leads to broad shoulders and muscular arms now upraised, the arms of a laundress. Her breasts and buttocks are ample and roundly proportioned—it is a buxom peasant body upon sturdy legs. From the neck down she looks like the farmer's daughter of a thousand bawdy stories, the girl you hitch to the plow when the horse gets tired. Standing on a chair above the crowd, her raised arms pulling the dress hem up over her calves, Aimee Semple McPherson has the head of a Renaissance angel and the solid ankles of an Ingersoll milkmaid.

Now we are going to consider how she got herself into this position and what, in her animated stillness, she is doing. As the first question is easier to answer than the second, we will begin with the story of Aimee's past before trying to explain what precisely she was doing to cause a scene in Mount Forest, Ontario in the summer of 1915.

AIMEE'S PARENTS

She was born in a farmhouse near Salford, Ontario. Aimee Elizabeth Kennedy was the only child of the improbable and scandalous marriage of James Morgan Kennedy to his young housekeeper, Mildred "Minnie" Pearce.

The groom was three decades older than his bride. He was born of second-generation Irish-American stock, with a dash of Dutch blood on his mother's side, in 1836. Minnie Pearce, a descendant of English and Irish immigrants in flight from one famine or other, was born around 1870.

So Aimee Elizabeth Kennedy's parents were just barely contemporaries. It was more common then for men to marry much younger women, but the age gap between this couple had an

almost Biblical aura, like the patriarch and his handmaiden.
Photographs of James Kennedy reinforce the impression: the
dignified farmer and road engineer, a tall, well-proportioned
old man with white hair and beard trimmed carefully above his
bow tie, who looks remarkably at ease in a dress suit, for a
farmer. He has a strong, mystical Irish face, and his eyes twinkle
with humor. He will need it, to live with his child bride, and
later, to manage the outbursts of his youngest daughter. He can
follow a plow for ten hours, or plan a river bridge. At the age
of eighty James will be able to get down on all fours, at his
grandson's bidding, and make a fine play horse for the boy to
ride.

His marriage to Minnie Pearce was his second. James was
married for the first time in the early 1860s, to Elizabeth Hoag.
It is little known that there were three children of that marriage,
Aimee's half siblings Mary, William, and Charles. The death
of Elizabeth Hoag closed the door forever on any discussion of
James Kennedy's former life; neither Minnie nor Aimee would
ever mention it. Mary had begun her own family, in Salford,
giving birth to the first of her six children in 1882. The fate of
Aimee's half brothers is vague. One is believed to have died
young, of consumption; the other, rumored to have been born
with a mental defect, was sent away and never heard of again.

In 1886 Elizabeth fell ill. James Kennedy placed an ad in the
newspaper requesting the services of a live-in nurse. In reply to
the ad, the fourteen-year-old orphan Minnie Pearce traveled to
Salford to the Kennedy Farm. Minnie was judged satisfactory,
evidently; she was engaged as nurse to the fatally ill Elizabeth.
A few months later the wife was dead. The little nurse helped
the widower with the burial and stood by him in his grieving.
He found her indispensable, and she stayed on.

The neighbors began to talk. The energetic nurse-cum-house-
keeper was nubile, marriageable, and extremely attractive, with
her wide-set eyes and sharp, square features. Men were envious.
Women were shrewdly critical of the "arrangement" the old
man had made. He let them talk. On October 3, 1886, he took
Minnie Pearce across the border to Michigan, where the two
were unknown. He was fifty, she fifteen. Giving their ages as

forty-two and twenty-two, they became Mr. and Mrs. James Morgan Kennedy.

While he may not have been the man of her dreams, the handsome old gentleman farmer was surely a comfort to the little orphan Minnie.

Her father had died when she was an adolescent. With the whimsy of an abandoned child, she entertained the fantasy of being captured. Returning home from school one day, Minnie read in the paper of an "Army" that was to come to town and "take prisoners for the King." This sounded grand. Pleading with her mother to risk the danger, Minnie persuaded Mrs. Pearce to take her to the heart of downtown London, Ontario, where the two waited in the downpouring rain for this army of occupation.

At last on the street corner the crowd whispered that the army had arrived. Three women uniformed and cloaked in blue marched into the square and knelt, silently praying. Army women! They began to sing. Their song explained that they were bound for the land of the pure and the holy, the home of the happy, and their chorus ended with the warm invitation: "Oh! say—will you go to the Eden above?"

And a little voice within Minnie said yes.

This was the most brilliant, glorious proposal she had ever heard in her life. Her mother was a "shouting Methodist" of the old school; she had talked of God's mighty power in the days of John Wesley, when men and women were slain upon God's altar. Now, she said, the glory had come again in the blue uniforms of the Salvation Army. Minnie decided then and there to pledge herself to the service of the King.

Soon thereafter Minnie's mother fell ill. In Aimee Semple McPherson's autobiography, called *This Is That* (1919), she gives this account of her mother's childhood. Upon her death-bed Mrs. Pearce offered her daughter a choice: she could go and live with her uncle Joseph Clark, a rich lumber dealer, or journey to Lindsay, Ontario to live with the Salvation Army captain and his wife, who had become Minnie's spiritual god-mother.

Minnie chose the Army. Upon her mother's death, Minnie

packed up her few belongings and set off for the Salvation Army
quarters in the distant town.

There in Lindsay, for the next year, Minnie's life was taken
up with missionary service: visiting "the sick and sinful," selling
the Army periodical the *War Cry*, and praying. She adored the
long prayer meetings and the godly life of her leaders, particularly the captain, who would spend whole nights on his face
before God "in intercession for precious souls."

But within a year Minnie got "sick." She was stricken with
an unspecified illness at the age of thirteen, somehow infected
during the month of praying and hawking papers and visiting
the sick and sinful. Her illness required her to be sent away
from Lindsay and her devoted Salvation Army guardians, and
to convalesce on a farm near Ingersoll.

There she would learn of James Kennedy's advertisement for
a live-in nurse. Minnie cared for the dying Elizabeth Kennedy,
and soon thereafter married the widower—too soon, said some
of the neighbors; not quite soon enough, according to others.

Their marriage made lively conversation in Salford as well
as in Ingersoll, the larger farm town six miles distant. But it
soon was evident that the "child bride" was every inch a woman
and the emotional equal of her patriarchal husband. The Ingersoll natives found her strong and determined as she drove
the buggy or bicycle or walked the road from Salford to the
Salvation Army division in Ingersoll twice a week. Minnie
headed the fund drive at Christmas. She got contributions at
every door she knocked upon. And when the Army barracks
needed a Sunday school superintendent, the young woman volunteered. A great reader of the Bible and other books, Minnie
became, without schooling, an eloquent speaker at religious
meetings at the mission and in people's homes all around the
town.

James Kennedy was a pillar of the Methodist church. He sang
the old hymns quite beautifully and directed the choir.

Meanwhile his young wife threw herself into the grass-roots
evangelistic campaigns of the 80's. The Salvation Army with
its drums and bells and tambourines arrived from England in
1880, under the commission of George Railton and seven

women officers. Within a decade it had swept the continent. The Army won thousands of converts among the poor and degenerate by its martial and boisterous methods. Yet the established churches regarded the Army with distaste or ridicule. After all, these Christian soldiers held out their hands to sinners fallen beyond the reach of conventional ministries, most notoriously to "loose women" and alcoholics.

James Kennedy, whose father and grandfather were pious Methodist preachers, must have been troubled to find his wife in the clamorous ranks of the upstart Salvation Army. Yet there is no evidence he ever tried to stop her. From all accounts, he appears to have been a kind and patient husband. So it is curious that Minnie described those years to her daughter as years of misery, of imprisonment amidst the strenuous and strange duties of farm work.

"She was compelled to acknowledge that she was caught in the devil's net," her daughter recalls. A curious phrase. James Kennedy was an altogether unlikely devil. He provided little orphan Minnie with security and affection she had never known from any man. It is certain he did not kidnap the girl to Michigan or force her to marry him. She could have returned to the holy captain and his wife in Lindsay, Ontario to continue her religious pursuits.

But she did not. She chose, rather, to marry the man she would later describe as her jailer, in a personal legend that cast her as a holy martyr.

"Shorn of her usefulness, fettered by circumstances, she truly did grind in the prison house; but, strange as it may seem, during all that time that her body was fettered, her soul was turning heavenward." Thus Aimee paraphrases her mother's recollections. Every hour of every day Minnie's longing became more intense. She wanted to continue the missionary work for which God had ordained her, for which she had left her home and extended family. Finally she could think of nothing else; it "became her one dream in repose—she *must* make good her belated pledge," the pledge she had made as a girl to serve the King.

Early in January of 1890, eighteen-year-old Minnie Kennedy walked up the stairs of the farmhouse and shut herself in her room. It was a cold and cloudy afternoon, and the room was dim. She had been reading the Bible story of Hannah, over and over. Hannah, as described in the first book of Samuel, was tormented in marriage because she was childless, though her kind husband consoled her with the famous line "Am I not more to you than ten sons?" He loved Hannah barren or not. But his other wife teased and made fun of her. So at last Hannah prayed to the Lord to give her a son, and she would in turn dedicate him to the Lord, and see that no razor ever touched his head.

Minnie Kennedy got down on her knees beside the bed and prayed in imitation of Hannah, but with a difference. She confessed to God that she had failed to go and preach the Gospel and save souls as she had been called, and that she was truly sorry for it.

"But if You will only hear my prayer, as You heard Hannah's prayer of old, and give me a little baby *girl*, I will give her unreservedly into your service, that she may preach the word I should have preached, fill the place I should have filled, and live the life I should have lived in Thy service. O Lord, hear and answer me; give me the witness that Thou has heard me . . ."

She got up. She swept the curtains away from the window that overlooked the orchard, the valley, and the hills against the dark clouds. While she was watching, the clouds opened as if a hand of sunlight were parting the cloud curtains. A ray of sunshine spotlit the hill before moving down through the orchard toward the house itself. Then the light shone full upon her face, momentarily blinding her as it illuminated the bedroom where she had been praying.

———

And so it came to pass that a baby was born in that upstairs room of the farmhouse with scrollwork under the eaves, Minnie Kennedy's requested daughter. The child was born under Libra (a water sign) on October 9, 1890, and they named her Aimee Elizabeth.

Later Minnie claimed she never doubted for a moment that

the child she was carrying was a girl. With great care she had designed, sewn, and embroidered the gowns and pink receiving blankets for the unborn daughter. And before anyone had time to describe the squalling newborn, the mother, semiconscious, had cried out with confidence:

"Where is *she*? Bring *her* here."

The delegation who came from the mission to visit the baby also brought news of the death of Catherine Booth, the sainted wife of their general. They were not above the pagan notion that this baby might be the vessel for Catherine Booth's spirit.

For the child of the Salvation Army mother there would be no christening. On October 30, when the Canadian wind is already too cold for a baby, Minnie Kennedy rose up. She announced to the household, which included a nurse and a neighbor or two and James Kennedy's younger sister Maria, that there was a Jubilee that night at the Salvation Army mission in Ingersoll, five miles down the road. It was Minnie's intention to go and take Aimee Elizabeth with her.

Snowflakes were falling. Minnie had hung the child's blankets on a chair before the open oven. The nurse and Aunt Maria Kennedy advised against the excursion, while Minnie was dressing and bundling up the baby. They told her to keep the child home by the fire, while Minnie was heading for the door. Someone suggested that little Aimee might get pneumonia. And as Minnie climbed to the buckboard with the baby in one hand and the whip and reins in the other, Aunt Maria, holding her lantern, shouted that Minnie would kill the baby; that any woman who did not know how to take care of a baby better than that shouldn't ever have one. And Aunt Maria went back into the house.

Kerosene lanterns shone through the windows of the barracks on Thames Street in Ingersoll. Minnie sat with her daughter on the front bench of the mission as a band in braided uniforms played. They listened to the tambourines and handclapping, the prayers and the testimony.

There would be no baptism for Aimee Elizabeth Kennedy, because Minnie was going to consecrate her daughter to the holy orders of the Salvation Army. The Army believed that sacraments like baptism were not necessary for the soul's salvation. In place of baptism the newborn child would be welcomed into the Army's Christian ranks with a ceremony of dedication. They placed Minnie Kennedy's infant daughter on a chair on the barracks platform, and the corps commandant recited the following prayer:

"In the name of the Lord and the corps of the Salvation Army, I have taken this child, who has been fully given up by her parents for the salvation of the world. God save, bless, and keep this child. Amen."

The majority of Christians in Ingersoll of 1890 could not have approved. What was this Army to which Minnie was so fiercely dedicated that she would deny her daughter the sacrament of holy baptism?

The founder of the movement, William Booth, had been a Methodist clergyman in England. But his early experience as a pawnbroker in Victorian London convinced him that the established church had become inaccessible to the people who needed it most: men and women of the streets, alcoholics, prostitutes, orphans, and unwed mothers. There was no religion for the underclass. Booth, who had the passionate eyes and flowing beard of our own zealot, John Brown, began to envision the world's salvation as a holy war between evangelists like himself and the suffering masses of the unconverted. He declared war upon the body of humankind that resisted the principles of Protestant Evangelism. General Booth mustered troops on the model of the British Army, with blue gold-braided uniforms, titles, brass bands, with knee drills and marching orders and garrisons.

The General ordered his troops to march upon the London streets with their drums and bugles and tambourines, and win souls for Christ. He could not have predicted the enemy would be so fierce. More than half his soldiers were women. Believing in the absolute equality of the sexes in religion and combat, the General did not foresee the horror of the public confronted with this brazen image: an Englishwoman in military twills preaching the Gospel.

It was outlandish, it was heretical, it was disgusting. The polite as well as impolite observers denounced the clanging, boisterous manners of the street-corner evangelists, especially the manly women. But the Army simply turned up the volume. They paid their critics no heed above the clamor of brass and drums and vociferous voices. They preached on. To get the evangelists' attention, mobs started to push and shove the foot soldiers. Ruffians began to pelt them with stones and raw eggs, to run away with their drums and tambourines.

As the fighting increased in the early 1880's, more and more of the crowd joined the lists of the Army. The battlefield widened. Mobs forcing platoons of Salvation Army soldiers off the London streets became increasingly physical. If the women persisted in masquerading as men, said the outraged critics, they did not deserve to be treated with the respect due the fair sex. So the Salvation Army women were subject to brutal sexual assault. The law would not defend them. Members of the judiciary held opinions even more conservative than the brutes charged with assault. Many local magistrates allowed their own distaste for religious enthusiasm to sway their judgment. In the year 1884 alone, at least six hundred Salvationists received prison sentences for "disturbing the peace" with their preaching activities. Only by fanatic persistence and the change in public opinion brought about by the Army's achievements as a social welfare agency did the movement win its freedom at the end of the century.

The Salvation Army is not so much a religion as a utopian social community. From the beginning, the Army's views were those of denominational evangelism. But it disdained customs and institutions. They would have no priests, no altar, no liturgy. Meetings would be held in a hall with joyous singing and hand clapping and a brass band. There would be free prayer and Bible reading and personal testimony, and an open invitation to repentance. For anybody who made a commitment to the Lord and signed the Articles of War the old sacraments would not be necessary. The General expected his converts to become soldiers and work as missionaries in religious and social causes, soup kitchens, and maternity homes. The Army's officers agreed to marry within the "family" and serve at their posts for life.

Most important to Minnie was the equality between men and women. This was thirty-five years before American women won the right to vote.

Minnie Pearce, orphaned at eleven and as ripe for victimization as any girl-child lost in a crowd at Marrakesh, got into the Salvation Army on the ground floor. It was father and mother to her, home and sanctuary. Among these revolutionaries the budding woman would find not only succor, protection, and companionship. She would find, in the pioneering egalitarianism of the Christian Army, a thing of increasing value to her as she grew independent—she would find empowerment.

Knowing the character of the Movement, we no longer wonder at Minnie's dedicating herself and her infant daughter to it. Rather we remain perplexed as to why she ever left it to toil as nurse and housekeeper for James Kennedy on a farm so far from Lindsay. Her granddaughter has said that Minnie left Lindsay because she did not wish to burden her Salvation Army parents, and that she remained with James Kennedy for the same reason.

CHILDHOOD MEMORIES

The beautiful young woman standing on the chair in Mount Forest in 1915 had vivid and delightful memories to entertain her. An enthusiastic and romantic chronicler of her own past, she would recall a great deal of her "happy childhood" on the farm in images so precise we cannot mistake their meaning, a certain bittersweetness in the recollection. She will not be reduced to a porcelain happy shepherdess, even in her own words.

She remembered her mother rocking her in the big armchair

at twilight, singing hymns, and lulling her to sleep with Bible stories: Daniel in the lion's den, Shadrach, Meshach, and Abednego in the fiery furnace, Joseph and his coat of many colors, Moses leading the Children of Israel through the desert—all thriller-tales of the soul in peril. More vague were her early memories of the Gospels, except the refrain that Jesus has gone ahead of us to prepare a wonderful place called Heaven. All her life she would boast that by the age of four she could stand on a drumhead on the street corner and draw a crowd by reciting the best Bible stories.

Sunday school, of course, provided her earliest entrance into society. On the dark field of the chalkboard shone a huge eye under a sinuous eyebrow, its pupil precisely centered. The teacher pointed to a sentence written above the shining eye, and had the children read aloud: "Thou God seest me." The tiny girl who had been standing next to the door crossed to the other side of the room under the window while keeping her eyes upon the great eye that shone on the blackboard. It frightened Aimee. While the older children got on with their lessons and the teacher spoke, the eye of God kept watching her. It seemed to see not only her body as she moved around the schoolroom. It seemed to peer into her mind as well.

As she and Minnie rode homeward behind the sorrel mare, Aimee looked up at her mother and asked if God could see her. Minnie said that God could see her very well. "Even through the hood of the buggy?" Aimee asked, thinking that God might be limited to a sky-view. "Yes, dear," said Minnie.

Back at the farmhouse, the child looked high and low for a hiding place so remote and dark that she might escape God's intrusive scrutiny. Finally she hid herself under the steel kitchen range. From there, she startled her mother, as Minnie walked by, with the tiresome question, "Can He see me now?"

"Anywhere and everywhere," her mother answered.

Aimee went down into the cellar where she had been told she might help cut potato sprouts for the spring planting. She worked with unusual industry for a small child. In the half-light of the root cellar she felt that the Eye of God was still watching her every movement and divining her thoughts.

She had no sister or brother to distract her from such reflections. On the farm they were far from neighbors; she had no playmates. So she developed a preternatural communication with animals. She loved horses and dogs and cats and frogs and dragonflies. This affinity she shared with her father, who as a working farmer had the farmer's fascination with beasts. James regarded them with humor and respect but without sentimentality.

One night he brought home an owl, which requires a delicate hand, and set it upon the back of a kitchen chair. The owl blinked and blinked in the lamplight, looking at Aimee Kennedy, whose eyes grew wide in response. The old man told his daughter to walk to one side of the owl and watch what happened. The owl turned its head so its eyes followed the girl, not unlike the Lord's insistent Eye. "Keep walking," said James Kennedy, and little Aimee could hardly believe what she saw; the owl turned its head full circle as she moved around it.

"Go round and round the owl, Aimee," said her father with a twinkle in his eye. He told her that if she circled the owl long enough, it would wind its neck up like a spring in a clock and unwind in a whirl. But though she walked round and round until the room spun, with the owl's unblinking yellow eyes following her, the owl's head stayed on straight. She could not understand why the neck did not wind like a clock spring, as her father said it would. She could not see that the bird was snapping his head from one side to the other faster than the eye could see, so fast that it truly appeared to be winding full circle.

She befriended the owl, and the dogs and cats. When visitors came to the house, she would hover, frantic, over her guinea pigs, to prevent clumsy hands from reaching into their cage. Her father said that if someone picked up a guinea pig by its tail, the creature's beady eyes would fall out.

Her earliest extended memory, which she would tell again and again, is so early, it lies on the borderline of self-awareness. Aimee was small enough to fit easily into a water bucket, so the world then seemed to her titanic. This story of her adventure with the "windlass well" she would tell and reinterpret according to the changes in her life and moods: it would become an emblem of her psyche.

Though she had been cautioned against it, Aimee's favorite place to play was the artesian well. On tiptoe she could just barely see over the square wooden structure that boxed the well, and look down into the darkness beyond the rows and rows of moss-covered stones that walled the shaft. Across the casement that guarded the mouth of the well reached a wooden windlass. The little girl loved to turn the iron crank handle, coiling the rope on the thick wooden roller. More than once, when she let go of the handle, it flew back and whacked her on the head. And when she howled in pain, the dark well filled with answering echoes.

The lonely child was drawn to the well by the sound of voices in its depths, voices like her own.

One afternoon, when the sun was overhead, she got her chin up on the casement. Looking deep into the well, she saw a circle of light that framed the face of a girl her own age. She realized this was where the voices were coming from. "Yoo-hoo!" she called to the girl, and "Yoo-hoo!" the girl replied.

Day after day the dialogue continued. Though her parents called her away from the well, Aimee would return; and in her most charming voice she invited the girl in the well to come and play. Though the girl down below repeated Aimee's suggestion with equal enthusiasm, she stayed put. So Aimee made up her mind that someday she would go down to her.

Feeling that Mother and Father would not approve, Aimee bided her time, waiting for a moment when no one would be watching except God. There were few such moments. But one evening the minister came to dinner, and while the adults were all lingering over dessert, the excited girl, in her pink dress, excused herself from the table.

Confident that they had forgotten her, little Aimee went out to the yard toward the well to visit her lonely playmate. She climbed up on the casement and stepped into the bucket.

The windlass snapped free and the crank began to spin; the child felt herself plummeting weightless into the darkness. Minnie Kennedy, having seen the tail of her daughter's pink skirt disappearing into the well-shaft, ran, leaped for the crank, and, breathless, hauled her up.

One may search in vain for a more resonant image of this yearning and adventurous soul. Aimee would plunge into the earth's depths if that would bring her into communion with a soul mate. At the time her mother rescued her, she did not realize that the object of her mission, which might have drowned her, was simply an image of herself. Years later, Aimee would interpret the incident in many ways, mostly as a metaphor for the descent into sin and the sinner saved by Grace. But for all her interpretive powers, she never saw the windlass well story for what it was: a variation on the theme of Narcissus, the soul's apprehension of itself.

There is another wonderful story that, taken with the one above, gives us a clear picture of the girl's courage and determination: it is the story of Aimee and the Gentleman Cow. She may have been a little older, old enough to be assigned the chore of bringing in wood chips for the breakfast fire.

James Kennedy built bridges. Behind the barn stood an old-fashioned circular bench saw the old man used for cutting the timber for his bridges. All around the bench were piles of fresh cedar chips.

Aimee was drawn up with pride in her new dress, a white frock covered with large red moons. Why the moons were red, or how anyone but Aimee knew that the shapes on the white frock were moons she does not tell us. Perhaps the pattern showed the moon in its various phases. In any case it is an obvious feminine symbol she wore, or recalled wearing, as she left the farmhouse with her bucket in hand. She turned the corner of the barn on the way to the woodpile about the same time the cattle were returning from the fields to gather around the watering trough.

And just as she had her bucket almost filled with the sweet-smelling cedar chips, she spied near the open gate the "gentleman cow."

Head down, nostrils flared, his furious eyes ablaze, the bull bellowed and pawed the earth as he advanced.

The girl was terrified. Until now the bull had always been silent and slow and gentle, so it never occurred to her to expect danger from this quarter. Perhaps the red moons on her new dress had enraged him, the dress she thought was so beautiful.

"Boo-o-o!" bellowed the bull as he headed toward the girl.

"Boo yourself," cried Aimee, and threw a wood chip at him.

She must have been all of four and a half years old, her eyes level with the brisket of the advancing bull. The detail of the story you would not believe—if the child's boldness had not flowered so famously in the legend of the woman—is the hurled wood chip. The bull, stunned by the missile, towered over the child for an instant before butting her, rolling her in the mud of the barnyard. Luckily her father had sawed off the bull's horns, so she was not gored.

Aimee got to her feet, still holding the bucket of wood chips, trapped between bull and barn. The furious animal bunted her again, sending her sprawling. Her new dress was smeared with mud, and there was blood on her chin. It is a wonder the bull did not trample the girl to death before she found an avenue of escape. Aimee knew the corner of the barn was too far, so she headed for the hollow space under the lumber her father had stacked over a sawhorse. She scrambled into one end of the tunnel of wood. While the bull stuck his muzzle in that end, she escaped out the other end and ran for the house.

Her hand, as she ran, still clasped the half-empty bucket of cedar chips. It never occurred to her to let go of the bucket. She stumbled toward the farmhouse door with the taste of dirt and blood in her mouth. Minnie first thought the sound of the child's crying was singing, but when she saw her distress, she gathered her up in her arms. Carrying Aimee to the windlass well, she sat and bathed her with cold water until the child fainted dead away, only then releasing her frozen grip on the bucket of cedar chips.

As with the parable of the windlass well, the grown woman would recall this drama time and again to illustrate a moral or two that would be better served by David and Goliath or St. George and the Dragon. But we can read this story, with its vivid details—the girl in the white frock with red moons, the bucket of kindling, the polled bull—as an elegant and precise sexual allegory. She was a child whose femininity would some-day drive men mad, for a variety of reasons; polled and emas-culated, the furious men would never quite manage to trample her. She would always escape with her precious fuel.

SCHOOL DAYS

These signature memories tumbled from a cornucopia of charming recollections of farm life: horses, goslings, and chick-ens; the dragonflies skipping on transparent wings; the "darning needles" (a colloquial name for the prince dragonflies) the little girl fled from because the hired man told her they might sew her ears closed; the blue flags (a cathartic herb) she gathered for an old lady's ailments; pussy willows, cattails; turtles that snapped at fireflies. She remembered spending hours asprawl in the ribbon grass because her father had told her he would give her a dollar if she could find two blades exactly alike.

She remembered Jenny the pet pigeon who once disguised herself as a dove by falling into a pan of milk in the kitchen cabinet, and then disgraced everyone by flying into the parlor where she perched, dripping milk, upon the shoulder of the preacher who had come to tea.

Aimee was such an outdoor girl that when she got pneu-monia, practically every pet on the farm had to be brought to her room: the Newfoundland dog, the guinea pigs, owls, geese, doves. Whitetail, the family cat, who never allowed herself to be touched until Aimee got pneumonia, came to her bed. The cat sat patiently on the blanket as Aimee dressed her up in doll clothes and petted her by the hour. When Whitetail could stand it no more, she would run away to the cellar, still dressed like a doll, to nip a mouse "daintily through the neck" and lay it on Aimee's pillow as her "love offering." When the cat repeated this performance, the child began to think Whitetail believed she was starving; only when the hunter saw that Aimee was not eating the mice did Whitetail cease, with wounded dignity, to serve that meal.

The hired man put his head in at the door to ask if there was anything he might do for the bedridden child.

"I would like to hear the frogs sing," sighed Aimee. "Do go down to the swamp," she commanded, "and bring me three or four frogs and put them in a pail of water by my bed."

Here is a child who could never complain that her slightest wish went unheeded. About an hour later the hired man came sloshing in wet boots up the stairs under the weight of an overflowing bucket that contained four frogs, and a few lily pads to make the quartet feel more at home. He set the bucket down next to the bed, tipped his hat, and was gone, away to a far field. There he could not hear Aimee call for him to round up the frogs, which had jumped out of the bucket and were now playing leap frog under the child's bed. Minnie, puffing and muttering, had to crawl under and catch them, as Aimee watched her mother's legs.

These stories and others of early childhood she would tell with humor and with flair for the pungent detail. She delighted in her memories and always found them regenerative. She was not a graceful writer, but she might have been, with a year or two of leisure in the right library with a good syllabus. Her narrative powers, turned loose upon a live audience, would be staggering but resolutely archaic, for her literary education (until her middle age) began and ended with the King James version of the Bible, Shakespeare, Voltaire, and Thomas Paine.

Her mother read to Aimee and told her stories from the Bible. James Kennedy, driving his daughter to school on her first day in September of 1896, asked her if she knew the first letters of the alphabet. When she told him no, he said he would get her started with the first three: Letter rip, letter tear, and letter fly.

"I wonder if I can remember them," she wondered.

"Better say them over a few times," said James Kennedy, driving the carriage horse. And as they rode along through the fields, the child said the letters over to herself, letter rip, letter tear, and letter fly, until she got them by heart. She leaped proudly out of the buggy when they arrived at No. 3 Dereham School, on fire to impress the teacher, Mr. W. R. Bloor, with her scholarship.

Mr. Bloor, a soft-featured, hollow-eyed young Canadian with insufficient humor for a schoolmaster whose ears stuck out, must have thought this new student was making fun of him. When Aimee recited her letters, there was such an uproar in the classroom that he felt there was no recourse for his authority but to make an example of Aimee Elizabeth Kennedy, in the nineteenth-century manner. So the child, on her first day of school, was fitted with a pointed dunce cap and exiled to a high stool in the corner.

This was the beginning of a singular career in the Canadian public school systems of Dereham, Salford, and Ingersoll. There are no surviving academic records. But various news clippings, class photographs, and stories passed down for generations in Ingersoll make it clear that little Aimee did not attend school for the pleasure of W. R. Bloor or any other teacher. Aimee Elizabeth Kennedy was willful, bright, and devastatingly funny. It is fair to say she was subversive.

She went to school because she was supposed to, and she did her lessons, mostly. But when the program got dull in the classroom, Aimee would rise to the occasion and do whatever needed to be done to liven things up.

She was a blond, angelic minx, with her pointed features. She had wide-set brown eyes and a slight, charming overbite typical of beautiful faces in their early development. Other children found her attractive but did not know quite what to make of her. Aimee was unfamiliar with children, having had no brothers, sisters, or neighboring playmates. And then her classmates' parents told them that Aimee's family was in that peculiar Salvation Army whose noisy barracks was in town, flying the banner with the blood and fire.

The children knew what to do then. They would make fun of Aimee Kennedy, the only Salvation Army brat in a school of Methodists, Episcopalians, and Presbyterians. They buzzed her on the schoolyard, in twos and threes, chanting "Salvation Army, Salvation Army." This only frightened her a little, and then it made her angry. Anger prompted the thought: I will make them understand.

She took a cheese box, a ruler, and a red tablecloth from the classroom. She drafted Fatty Peck as the standard-bearer to wave the tablecloth, and began singing at the top of her voice and banging on the drum as she marched around the school, the woodshed, and the horse stable. Boys fell in behind her, mimicking, and eventually the girls too; everyone loves a parade. Around and around they marched, beating on shingles, the girls using their mufflers for Army bonnets, singing

> Glory be, we've got him on the run,
> Shot the Devil with the Gospel gun.

After that Aimee's classmates didn't tease her anymore. She was still strange, of course, but her unyielding strangeness had elevated her in their esteem. She was *with* them if not *of* them —she was the captain.

Very early she seems to have seen herself in authority. Her mother held the imposing title of junior sergeant major in the Salvation Army, which means that Minnie was superintendent of the Sunday school. She would bicycle, her daughter on the handlebars, to the Army barracks. Aimee so loved the Sunday school meetings and her mother's role in them that she could not wait for Sundays to come. So she would carry chairs from all over the house to an upstairs bedroom which she arranged like a meeting hall, and then address the invisible Christian soldiers.

"Now Sergeant Major will lead in prayer." With this, she knelt.

"Now Sergeant Major will sing a solo." Aimee sang. And so on and so forth, till the commander had led her phantom army to the penitent form.

The most revealing evidence about her academic career at No. 3 Dereham is the school photograph taken on September 9, 1898. There are forty-one children in four rows standing and

sitting, against the white-board schoolhouse, children ranging
in age from five to thirteen.

The older boys stand in the back row, looking like a juvenile
police lineup in their Sunday best, most with low foreheads and
amazing ears. Their mothers must have cut their hair with sheep
shears. They are gazing over the heads of the older girls, who
look a little more civilized in their high collars. Below them
sits W. R. Bloor, his pale hands on his knees, in a long row of
the younger girls and boys. The schoolmaster sits in the center
of the picture. And, just in front of him, in the forefront of the
row of girls cross-legged on the grass, Aimee Kennedy holds
the slate sign: SS NO. 3 DEREHAM, SEPT. 9TH, 1898.

The girls on either side of Aimee are furious. So are the small
boys to the right of W. R. Bloor. He can scarce contain his
anger at the scene that preceded the click of the camera's shutter.
A boy to the teacher's right has a black eye. The story that has
come down to us is that all the little children wanted to hold
the class sign, until Aimee Kennedy jumped and grabbed it.
Aimee's competition quickly dwindled as the screaming girls
and boys fled from her with barked shins and bloody noses.
Two or three brave ones who persisted she led a merry chase
around the schoolyard, whacking them with the blackboard
when they came too close, until W. R. Bloor intervened. Then,
looking around him at the fallen and wounded, and staring into
the ferocious brown eyes of Aimee Elizabeth Kennedy as she
wielded the piece of slate, he turned and ordered the class into
the ranks now immortalized in the photograph. Aimee sits between his knees, holding the blackboard.

The other children are sullen in defeat; Aimee, her beautiful
bee-stung lips drawn into a pout, is proud, triumphant. There
is absolutely no question who is in charge here, and on that
morning she was a month shy of her eighth birthday.

Her career at No. 3 Dereham under the tutelage of W. R.
Bloor seems to have gone from bad to worse. She put
glue on his chair. She locked him in the gymnasium. We have
no record of the dispute that finally led to a parting of the ways
between the schoolmaster and his strong-willed student. All we
know is that years before Aimee's scheduled graduation from

No. 3 Dereham she enrolled at No. 2 Dereham. The transfer was accomplished by Mr. and Mrs. Kennedy at great expense, no less than the price of purchasing acreage in the neighboring school district so the student would qualify for enrollment. Which fact supports the local legend that nothing, in the opinion of the Kennedys, was ever too good for Aimee Elizabeth, including the schoolmaster. Whatever success they had in modifying this child's behavior at home did not suit W. R. Bloor's purposes in the classroom. No one, evidently, could make her fit the mold that he had available for her. So Aimee Elizabeth chose to go elsewhere, where she might be properly appreciated.

In 1950 W. R. Bloor was honored by the University of Rochester, presumably a belated recognition for valor, having outlasted and outlived his famous pupil.

How a child who will become a great woman regards authority is of critical interest. There is hard evidence from this early date that Aimee Kennedy, like her mother, had a sportive attitude toward authority of all kinds—parents, grownups, gentlemen cows, teachers, even God at first, as we shall see. It was not so much that Aimee was disrespectful. She just had so much innate authority of her own that she was not going to accept adventitious authority without first giving it a run for the money.

In this audacity, some say, she met with limited resistance from her parents. There are folks in Salford who say the child was spoiled rotten; the evidence suggests rather that the high-spirited daughter simply wore her parents out, the old father, the young mother who saw her as the answer to a prayer.

Here is the earliest recorded instance of Aimee's being addressed by the Devil: One afternoon, as she was playing with thirteen kittens she had saved from drowning, her Aunt Elizabeth baked cookies. She gave Aimee six to eat, putting away the rest in a round tin in the pantry. "No more for you until supper," said Aunt Elizabeth, and went off for her afternoon nap.

While the rest of the family was napping, Aimee thought of the cookies. The sweet smell of them in the kitchen was almost more than she could bear. "I'll just go into the pantry and have a look at them," she thought. The tin was on the top shelf, high above shelves of flour cans, sugar, baking powder, baskets of eggs, corn meal, butter, lard, wheels of cheese, fruit preserves, and marshmallows. The Kennedys ate well. She began climbing the ladder of shelves with the utmost care, placing her feet in spaces between the soups, chips and vinegar, currants and artificial flavorings. She grabbed hold of the shelf board beneath the maple-sugar patties with one hand and lifted the lid of the cookie tin with the other.

The Tempter whispered to Aimee that she ought to hold one of the cookies in her hand just to have the feel of it, that she really didn't need to eat it. She agreed.

No sooner did she reach into the tin than the shelves collapsed under her weight and she fell in an avalanche of lumber and groceries.

"My father entered with a birch switch and went to work," she would recall.

If the girl was spoiled or wrought havoc in school, it was not because James Kennedy, or his wife Minnie, spared the rod. Aimee tells how "after similar outrages to the dignity of the household, I would be banished to my room and told that in exactly one-half an hour I would be spanked."

Weaned on stories of heavenly intervention, little Aimee would drop to her knees in prayer.

"Oh God, don't let Mama *whip* me!" she prayed, loudly, earnestly. The house rang with the sound of the child's pleading. And when the door at last opened, she kept praying pathetically until Minnie lost her resolve. Reprieved, the girl ran from the room and slid down the banister, delighted with the knowledge that the worst sinner might find mercy upon her knees.

————

She entered the Ingersoll Collegiate Institute (an upper school) in 1905, one of six girls in a class of eleven. As the institute drew upon all the area surrounding the town of Ingersoll, we know it was a privilege to be in the class.

Despite an ankle sprain that kept her home for weeks, she passed the examinations at the head of her class, and came in second for the scholarships. At night, when Aimee left her books to go to bed, Minnie would study them.

Fortunately, a photograph of Aimee's 1905 entering class is preserved. The photo is just as revealing in its way as the turbulent scene at Dereham in 1898, though less dramatic. The young gentlemen and ladies surrounding their lovely teacher, Blanche Riddel, appear dignified and affluent, the men in their three-piece suits (and knickers), the women in their fine dresses and lace collars. Young Blanche, quite attractive herself, appears to have things under control.

These are the future magistrates and matrons of Ingersoll, all but Aimee. She stands in the back row toward the left, in a magnificent dress with a deep white tippet, a large satin bow at the back of her neck, her auburn hair swept back from her temples. Eyelids drooping, her sultry lips slightly parted, she looks for all the world like a Russian countess, beautifully, unostentatiously arrogant. By some trick of the light there is a sort of sunburst over her left shoulder.

She will not be with them for very long.

She appears to be looking into a camera beyond the one set up to photograph her classmates. If any young woman ever had a glorious self-image, and small challenge to that image, it was Aimee Elizabeth Kennedy. Many men and women achieve greatness in reaction to feelings of inferiority. She was not one of those. Whenever she said she felt "unworthy," it was wise to test her rhetoric—either she wished to charm us with her humility, or she had sided homiletically with all humankind, fallen from grace. Someday she would develop real humility, but only as the result of suffering beyond the capacity of most people to comprehend. At age fourteen she had unassailable confidence in her superiority—basic equipment for a tragic heroine.

Naturally she began to compete in areas where her confidence fed upon applause. Her expressive voice and talent for mimicry had made her a popular comedienne in village entertainments while she was still in grammar school. She began going to the nearby Methodist church across from her school, where James Kennedy led the choir. The Methodists had pageants, plays, and variety entertainments for oyster suppers and concerts. They had teachers of elocution and drama, who quickly recognized the girl's gifts: her flair for comedy, her booming voice, her ability to hold an audience just by standing there. She could make them laugh with an improvised monologue or a recitation in an Irish brogue—Pegeen the washerwoman chasing the black pig through the fresh linen.

At twelve years of age she had put on a black dress and drove herself in a buggy to Ingersoll to enter a public speaking contest sponsored by the Woman's Christian Temperance Union. No one in the crowd that gathered in the basement of the First Baptist Church could recall the speech that Aimee delivered there—presumably a standard homily with a Christian moral. What several people did recall is that from the moment the long-haired girl in the dark dress got up to speak, it was obvious who the winner was going to be. "This girl was very sure of herself. There was more animation in her presentation than in all the other speakers put together." She won the silver medal, and so was invited by the City of London to compete for the gold medal, which she won too.

By the time she was thirteen, Aimee was a celebrated public speaker. Churches all over Dereham invited her to entertain at church suppers and picnics and strawberry festivals and Christmas-tree auctions. Organizers always knew folks would come for miles around and buy tickets to hear little Aimee.

Her life for the next few years centered on the Methodist church in Salford. There she got training in speech, music, and drama. Evidently these Methodists accommodated a confusing range of morals. She discovered that novels had strayed somehow into the church library and began guiltily reading them. "And when I had devoured them, I learned where more could be obtained," she recalled, like a recovered addict. She felt the novels were the first step on a downward path that led to the moving picture theater. A fellow choir member invited Aimee to the movies. She decided to go without telling her mother, because Minnie regarded movies as more sinful even than novels. Sitting in the glow of the silver screen, Aimee felt much better when she recognized several church members and a Sunday school teacher in the crowd.

Naturally the young performers at the Methodist church, particularly their star, Aimee Kennedy, talked of going on the stage, though it was forbidden. Sarah Bernhardt was the most famous actress of the time; so the legend has arisen that Aimee idolized Bernhardt, and wanted to follow her until she got religion. In fact Aimee never mentioned the divine Sarah. She did mention in passing that the applause was very alluring, and that the church provided the youngsters with excellent theatrical training. This must have been confusing if not actually disillusioning to the child actors. Methodist doctrine in those years frowned upon all "entertainment" in concert halls and theaters; meanwhile Methodists were mounting comic revues at the church social. The young performers, groomed to shill for the church, could see plainly, as Aimee wrote, that "there was not much difference whether a play or concert was given in the church or the theater."

REBELLION

She had a keen eye for cant and hypocrisy. Like other bright teenagers, she was eager to expose them—but with something more than a smirk and a clever remark in the lecture hall. Aimee wrote an open letter to the largest newspaper in Montreal. That letter produced a flood of responses from around the world, and a controversy that raged in the Canadian papers for weeks afterwards.

The subject was evolution and the Bible. Charles Darwin published his *Origin of Species* in 1859, and by the dawn of the twentieth century his ideas had found their way into Aimee's textbook. Surely Aimee Elizabeth Kennedy was not the only farm girl to detect the disagreement between Darwin and the Bible. But no one ever made more of it, in private or in public, than this child of a Salvation Army orphan and a Methodist choirmaster. By nature and nurture she was inclined to deep faith in God and belief in the Bible. So she was at once more susceptible to a crisis of belief, and far more horrified by it, than other children.

The offending textbook was *High School Physical Geography*, which she read during her first year at the Ingersoll Collegiate Institute, 1905. The book explained the origin of life on earth, how insect life first appeared from the sea, out of slime and fungus. From insects, animals evolved, and by the process of natural selection at last man appeared, a higher form of life but still a cousin to the chimpanzee.

Aimee was stunned. In her travels from church to church she had occasionally heard preachers say there were mistakes in the Bible. This was the "higher criticism." Her fundamentalist background had put her on guard against it. But this textbook presented a frighteningly logical attack upon Genesis. "Science was arrayed against the Word of God, evolution against Genesis, and mundane chance against the miraculous," she recalled.

She cornered a professor in the school laboratory.

"I have been brought up to believe that my Bible is infallible. I find my new textbook diametrically opposed to its teachings. Would you please tell me which to believe?"

The professor explained to his troubled student that her Bible was a wonderful classic of literature. As such it warranted her notice and study. But as far as its scientific value was concerned, well . . . concerning the early history of the human race the Bible was bigoted and full of error. Biological research had superseded ancient superstition, and Darwin's amoeba had replaced the mud man of the Pentateuch.

Aimee felt that the ground had opened up and swallowed her. "I was falling down, down, down, down into a black coal chute where leering specters jeered, 'There is no God! There is no heaven! There is no hell!' If the Scriptures tell one lie, they must leak like a sieve!"

Like someone long deceived, Aimee became fascinated with the awful truth. She demanded from the cornered professor more proof as he rambled on, searching for some avenue of escape. At last he begged her pardon, he had to go and teach a class. He sent her off to the library with a list of references: Voltaire, Ingersoll, Paine, in addition to Darwin.

The girl's response revealed the character of the woman. Already Aimee's attitude toward authority was well established. She would go to the library. And when she had done reading Voltaire, Ingersoll, Paine, and Darwin, there was nobody in the town, perhaps nobody in the province of Ontario, to argue with Aimee Kennedy for or against the Bible or Darwin. She began, with an aching heart, to take Darwin's part against her parents, preachers, and God Himself if He should dare to debate her. In all subsequent discussions of evolution she displayed an understanding of science that seems inconceivable in one who finally rejected it. She would end as the most famous opponent of Darwin ever to thump a Bible, before William Jennings Bryan entered the lists in 1925 as prosecutor in the Scopes Trial.

Aimee Elizabeth went home and started on her mother. Minnie was coming up the cellar stairs with a pan of milk. Or perhaps it was her father coming up the stairs with a pan of milk—when she first tells the story (1919) it is her mother; years later (1930) it is her father bearing the milk. In both versions Aimee's question is the same: "How do you know there is a God?" Her mother (or father) was astonished. He (or she) nearly fell backwards down the stairs, milk and all, before launching into the age-old defenses of the Bible. The parent quoted Scriptures, and pointed out the kitchen window at the glories of God's creation as evidence of His existence.

And in both versions Aimee Kennedy delivered the modern arguments against Genesis and the existence of God with devastating force. Aimee's later accounts of the dialogue with her father are fascinating. In his mouth she placed the arguments she would adopt later in defense of the religion she now attacked.

"All my life," she began, "you have spoken with assurance

of an all-seeing, all-knowing Father." This sentence has two
meanings, grammatically: it says that he has spoken with assurance *about* God, and that he has spoken as if he *were* the deity.
Never in Aimee's recollections will the old man so resemble
the wry God of Moses as in this argument, which he does not
seem to see any need to win. He seemed delighted to make her
think: Who made the constellations, the moon and stars? When
she told him these once consisted of molecules drawn together
by the law of gravity, he replied:

"Who was the Lawgiver back of the law of gravitation?"

Her schoolbooks had not explained this.

"If there was no Creator, who made man?"

She told him man just happened, accidentally. The lavalike
ball of earth grew cool on the outer surface, and salty oceans
formed. Then our great, great-grandmother, the amoeba, appeared.

The old man asked, politely, for the venerable amoeba's family tree. Aimee told him that spontaneous generation was the
most popular hypothesis. When she could not define "hypothesis," he sent her off to the dictionary, so they might agree that
spontaneous generation was a "supposition, a conjecture."

"Now go on," said the old man, "tell me more of this con-
jectured antecedent."

And when Aimee told him the amoeba was the oldest, sim-
plest, and lowest form of life, he asked, "And the amoeba set
the clock of life ticking which later evolved all the greater mam-
mals?" Aimee looked at the bridge-builder and told him that
was what she had learned.

Whereupon he smiled and burst into song, a variation on the
ancient lullaby:

> Poor little Amoeba,
> Don't you cry.
> You'll be an elephant
> By and by.

Which just about ended the discussion, except that the old
man couldn't resist casting some manure on the idea of spontaneous generation by asking his daughter if her professors

claimed to be able to create something out of nothing. He mentioned Louis Pasteur—how the scientist had disproved, through the use of a vacuum and hermetic sealing, that exposed meat created maggots. You have to admire the old man, James Kennedy, real or imagined by his daughter. While he did not win the argument, he did put it into perspective; he made his daughter laugh and put her in her place with the final words: "There'll be no agnostics in this family."

Sometime between the autumn of 1905 and the spring of 1906 Aimee read her *High School Physical Geography* and had the discussions just recounted. When she had studied the problem from all angles, she wrote a letter to the editor of the biggest newspaper in Montreal, the *Family Herald and Weekly Star*. On July 18, 1906 the letter was published. Like everything else the writer would ever do in public, Aimee's letter had the immediate effect of selling quantities of newspapers:

> As a Collegiate (high school) pupil, I have for some time been an ardent student of the High School Physical Geography. All my life I have been trained in unwavering confidence in the teachings of the Holy Scriptures and God as Creator of all things, and that man God created in His own image, a living soul. The teachings of the high school geography tend to undermine and destroy this faith in God as Supreme Being and Creator. Its doctrine is at direct variance with that taught in our Holy Bible. It leads us to believe that neither earth nor man were created by God, but by a process of evolution, man being a product of the animal kingdom.

She told how the textbook tested her faith, and then she wrote:

> Just in the nick of time I had my eyes opened to the awful position one must be in who accepts the teachings of this book. If need be, I will be willing to sacrifice science rather than religion.

It is a long letter. She closed with a call to arms:

> Let me appeal to every student to rally and stand by the sacred old truths which right away through the ages have withstood every storm, and risen triumphant above every blast in spite of all the

cold-blooded reasoning of scientists. "For what shall it profit a man if he gain the whole world and lose his own soul?"

"Just in the nick of time," she wrote, "I had my eyes opened." It is hard to say who opened her eyes—surely it was not her teachers, her parents, or any of the clergy whose advice she sought. This is why she was forced to deliver her problem to a public forum. It was a big problem of international interest, too big for Ingersoll. The response was staggering. Letters poured in for months from all over Canada, from England, New Zealand, Australia, and America, from ministers, teachers, scientists, even from an Archbishop Hamilton. There were good arguments both for and against the textbook. Many of the letters criticized the student's naivete. This must have sent her back to the library to reopen the case she had considered closed in the spring. She had tasted fame.

––––––

After another year of entertaining at church suppers and strawberry festivals, observing Christians who sat in the pews on Sunday and played cards and watched movies during the week, the sixteen-year-old girl was more skeptical than ever.

Next she attacked the minister who came to call.

Minnie was in the kitchen preparing dinner. Aimee led the minister to the parlor. There, on the pretext of showing him the family photo album, she began to harangue the innocent cleric on the subject of James 5:14 concerning the healing of the sick. Once Aimee began to distrust the Bible, she wanted folks, especially preachers, to know the whole vessel was as full of holes as a swiss cheese. It must, inevitably, sink.

"Now what about this passage here in James," she asked. "Does the Lord ever perform miracles or heal any sick folks now?"

He told her that the day of miracles was over. This is the doctrine of the "cessation of charisms," which has dominated theology since the time of Augustine. The gentleman had no idea that at that moment, in a little mission in San Francisco, a movement was afoot that would challenge the doctrine as it had

not been challenged since Augustine. And the blond child ha-
ranguing him on the passage from James would someday become the most eminent leader of that movement.

The minister looked at her in astonishment and sympathy.
He said: "People are expected to use the intelligence and wisdom
the Lord has given them along medical and surgical lines—these
are really miracles, you know."

But this was no answer to Aimee's question. She pointed to
the passages "Jesus Christ is the same yesterday, and today, and
forever," and "He that believeth in Me, the works that I do
shall he do also . . ." and read them aloud to the restless preacher,
who was wondering what had happened to dinner. She asked:

"How do you reconcile that the Lord no longer does miraculous things, with these Scriptures?"

The preacher did not know what to say. So he suggested that
these issues were beyond a young woman's comprehension.

Clearly, this was not the problem. At sixteen, Aimee knew
the Scriptures well enough to be intrigued by their contradictions. She was thoroughly prepared for Bible analysis on a
rabbinical level—not just prepared, she was hungry for it. Who
could she talk to in Dereham County? She was ripe for vigorous
wrangling over a text, the life and joy of the spiritual intellect
—and she had no one to play with.

Her recollection of the scene she made at a church meeting,
the next evening, is pathetic. Aimee had agreed, reluctantly, to
attend a revival meeting when she was done with the fancy
dress carnival at the skating rink. She was scheduled to lead the
first ice waltz.

The rink was whirling with clowns and kings and snow
queens. A band played waltzes as the skaters laughed and glided
and fell on the ice. Regretfully she said her goodbyes. She
slipped out, removed her skates, and in a sleigh drove her horse
Fritzie to the church door.

The church was packed. She entered still humming a new
tune the band had played at the skating rink. She was dressed
like the evil queen of the Ice Capades.

"There'll come a day of reckoning!" shouted the preacher,
"a day when sinners will be obliged to pay for their neglect."

Aimee had the feeling he was looking right at her. If he wasn't, he was probably the only man in the room who wasn't.

"This is ridiculous," she thought. "He can't mean me."

But he did. Next to Aimee in the entry stood the preacher's daughter. By some filial telepathy, she felt inspired to lay her hand upon Aimee's shoulder; and as the evangelist went on preaching, the young girl asked the ice skater softly if she was a Christian.

"Oh no," said Aimee Kennedy, "I go to high school."

When the evangelist's daughter asked Aimee what high school had to do with it, she got an earful of Darwin and Thomas Paine. Then the sharp-tongued ice skater charged that these were not Christians, who built churches with one hand while with the other they paid school taxes to train atheists.

The evangelist's daughter realized she had gotten in water over her head.

"Wait here till I go get my mother."

"I'll wait," said the ice queen. Aimee's parents were down in front listening to the end of the sermon. She couldn't leave without them. The preacher's daughter reappeared leading a sweet-faced, middle-aged woman. She did not last five minutes in conversation with Aimee, but with her brow furrowed she whispered: "Stay here till I fetch my husband."

They met somewhere between the altar and the church door, man and maid. They debated Scripture, Darwin, and Genesis. Men and women gathered around them, shaking their heads, nodding, sighing, and whispering to each other that they had never heard the like. Aimee's parents stood on the edge of the crowd, mortified. The preacher knew his Bible as well as Aimee, but he was no match for her on the broad battlefield of debate. Beaten back to her "last remaining trench," she let fly with a verbal brickbat for which the preacher was completely unprepared: "If the Bible is true, why do our neighbors pay good tax money to tear down our faith?"

And neither he nor anyone else in Ingersoll could answer her.

She had the last word, but she was not satisfied. Like other adolescents in rebellion she might have found a certain security in defeat, particularly if somebody had proved himself wiser upon this point. Remember, the girl was weaned on Bible stories, and taught to believe her very entrance upon the stage of life was God's answer to a prayer. In attacking the Bible, Aimee Kennedy was not only challenging her society's principles, she was sawing a hole in the stage under her feet.

She recalled a deadly silence in the buggy as she drove back to the farm with her parents on that cold winter night. Her mother and father were embarrassed, and deeply wounded. Minnie and James Kennedy had not, so they believed, raised their only daughter to carry on like that in public.

When she got home, Aimee ran upstairs to her room. Without pausing to light the lamps, she went to the window and threw it open wide. A blast of cold air swept over her as she gazed "at the starry floors of heaven . . . the silvery moon sailing majestically toward me from the eastern sky."

The farm girl wanted answers, and she wasn't getting them from anyone in authority. Now she grabbed a comforter from the bed and gathered it around her as she studied the sky. Looking out upon the snow-covered landscape, Aimee turned these questions over and over in her mind: Is there really a God? Who is right? What is the truth?

These are essential questions of mysticism. The scene that occasioned them, and the woman's response as she recalled it throughout her life, provide a fitting prelude to a religious biography. The scene reminds us of similar awakenings in the lives of John Wesley, David Brainerd, and others described in William James's study of the "conversion phenomenon" in *The Varieties of Religious Experience*. Like many another bright adolescent, Aimee Kennedy came to question her parents' faith. The peculiar circumstances of her birth and upbringing, and the passionate nature of her intelligence, raised the stakes higher for Aimee than for most teenagers—it was a matter of desperate importance that she find firm ground for her faith.

And where could she look for it? She started by asking her

teachers, parents, ministers, and the far-flung readers of the
Montreal *Family Herald and Weekly Star*. Having come up
empty-handed, now she would appeal to the only authority that
would ever mean anything to her, the "Master Musician," the
Authority of authorities.

She was ripe for a classic "conversion experience," and her
state of mind on the eve of conversion remains interesting to
the psychologist of religion. Her genius, we will see, was a
natural wellspring for metaphor, and now it began to bubble
up, providing us with a rare insight into the workings of the
mystic intelligence:

> The entire atmosphere seemed stretched taut in the clear, cold
> air, like the strings of an overstrained violin. The very stars were
> singing in a high-pitched tremolo. Upon the gem-arched Milky
> Way the radiant moon was gliding lazily. Venus winked at Saturn.
> The Big Dipper ladled out stardust in the bowl of its smaller sister.
> The Dog Star swung warily away from the Big Bear.
>
> How magnificent they were . . . those lofty, luminous bodies
> that topped our tiny earth! How precisely they moved and swung
> and sang! It was as though a Master Musician beat exacting time
> with a directing baton and the orchestra of the universe moved and
> played, chimed and swayed in unison. Surely there must be a Divine
> Hand back of so much precision, order and splendor!

Thus Aimee Kennedy saw the heavens upon the eve of her
conversion: thoroughly animated, transformed into a divine
orchestra, as musical instruments and players. "Venus winked
at Saturn." There are famous monks and nuns who frustrate us
in their vague accounts of mystical experience. They lack Aimee's gift of poetry, which is sensual, transformational, based
upon keen observation and a delight in the resemblances of the
physical world: dragonflies and darning needles, bulls and
gentlemen cows, constellations and orchestras. Overwhelmed
by the music of the spheres yet still in anguish over her crisis
of faith, she stretched her arms out the window and, "looking
past the stars," whispered:

"O God—if there be a God—reveal yourself to me!"
An answer would come within forty-eight hours.

———

By now it may seem that Aimee Kennedy, with or without
faith, had everything else a seventeen-year-old girl could wish
for. She had beauty, brains, a celebrated gift for elocution, and
devoted parents. They were financially comfortable, if not rich,
by local standards. She had horses, dogs and doves, and beautiful dresses. And when the weather did not permit her to drive
Fritzie to the Collegiate Institute in Ingersoll, Aimee took the
train from Salford.

An article with her picture in the *Woodstock Sentinel Review*,
August 31, 1907, announced she was a winner in the newspaper's subscription contest. The prize was a trip down the St.
Lawrence and Sanguenay rivers. Within the oval frame the only
photographed winner peers out at us. Aimee is a study in relaxed
determination, in her ruffled collar, under a bonnet covered with
flowers—a young woman most likely to succeed in any contest
she enters. The news article includes the intriguing sentence:
"Miss Aimee Kennedy of Salford was the last girl to enter the
fight, but she finished among those who were the highest."
Out of the corner of her eye she glimpsed the prize and knew
she would have it, though she had given everybody else a head
start. This is confidence bordering on bravado.

What Aimee Kennedy lacked, beyond a teacher who could
match wits with her, was a clear purpose in her life. So she
drew crowds at church suppers and made them laugh; and she
sold newspaper subscriptions (how prophetic!) with a facility
that would have done credit to Horace Greeley. She never had
a real calling to act upon the stage. Nor did she remember any
ambition to write for the papers, despite her famous letter to
the *Family Herald*. And nowhere does she record an opinion
about the vocation favored then by farm girls: becoming a wife
and mother. Strange, because every picture of Aimee Elizabeth
Kennedy, from teenage minx to bride, breathes the aura of a
woman made for worldly love. Her superiority was not the

sort that lifts a woman above her body: at seventeen she could upset the meditations of most gray-bearded saints. She was not fit for a nun's habit.

At seventeen she went the rounds of costume skating carnivals, play rehearsals, and college balls with the air of some royal child whose pedigree has been concealed from her. She brought home an engraved invitation card to a dance. Her mother flatly refused to let her go, then relented. Minnie bought her daughter a dress and dancing slippers. Aimee went to the ball excited, though conscience-stricken, knowing her mother was sad at home, praying for her. But Aimee discovered, to her relief, that the dance hall (a den of sin?) was full of church members, and the first person who whirled her around the floor was . . . the local Presbyterian minister.

She had a purpose she could not recognize until the time was ripe. It should have surprised no one that at seventeen years of age the willful young woman would discover a teacher, a lover, and her life's purpose all in the matter of a few days. Yet she shocked her parents and scandalized the whole community as she went about it.

FIRST LOVE

Minnie, more than anyone, should have understood how her daughter could fall in love with a penniless stranger, an itinerant revivalist from Ireland. But Minnie was not prepared. At first her daughter's involvement with Robert Semple looked to her like sheer delinquency.

For Minnie, the sun truly did rise and set in her daughter's eyes. The child was loving, but willful—sometimes unmanageable. She would rebel against everything except her mother's original prayer for her—the destiny which she would realize beyond a mother's wildest dreams. From the day Minnie got down on her knees and prayed for a child until the day Aimee fulfilled her mother's spiritual promise, decades later, the two women practically functioned as a unit; yet during the daughter's adolescence, she was as incomprehensible as teenagers have been since the dawn of time.

The night Aimee Kennedy argued with the preacher about evolution, and made a fool of him, and embarrassed her parents, was in December. Aimee had been rehearsing her parts in several plays and concerts scheduled for the Christmas season. The next day, her father was driving her from school along Main Street, past store windows dressed in red and green tinsel. They saw a sign in a storefront window that said HOLY GHOST REVIVAL and ROBERT SEMPLE, IRISH EVANGELIST.

Now Aimee had heard about these meetings where the congregation shouted Amen, and where people sometimes fell down on the floor and babbled under the power of the Holy Spirit. She was curious.

"It would be loads of fun," said Aimee the atheist, "to go and see them."

So the next evening, before Aimee's rehearsal for the Christmas program in the town hall, James Kennedy took his daughter to the little mission. He sat with her in the back row.

She was amused to see the milkman and the dry-cleaner with their hands lifted, singing hymns enthusiastically. She also noticed that none of the wealthy or well-known citizens of Ingersoll appeared in this lively middle-class congregation. They sang and prayed and shouted testimony with a freedom she had only seen, from time to time, in the Salvation Army barracks up the street. On one side of the room was an "Amen corner" and on the other was a "Hallelujah echo." Aimee thought this was a splendid show. If she had not so recently blown the whistle on religion and its hypocrisies, she might have done some shouting herself. As it was, she was enjoying the spectacle of these naive and earnest Christians, as from an intellectual tower.

That was before Robert Semple entered the room.

Robert James Semple was at least six feet two inches tall (six feet six by some accounts), loose-limbed, with chestnut-brown hair parted slightly off-center and a curl that kept falling over his right eye. He would brush it back with his delicate fingers in a gesture that drew attention to his handsome, intelligent forehead. His blue eyes, Aimee observed, had the light of Heaven in them, and wonderful humor.

There is much in his Irish face to remind us of Oscar Wilde, if Wilde had ever been handsome: a certain devil-may-care frankness overlaying the depth of Celtic mysticism. Of his wit, very little has survived. Once, in China, it grew so hot, and he was perspiring so heavily, the evangelist told his young wife he "could feel the Presbyterians rolling down his back." It was his kind of humor exactly, droll, linguistic humor with a philosophical edge. Robert Semple was born in 1881 and raised in a Presbyterian family, on a farm near Magherafelt, Northern Ireland, thirty miles from Belfast.

He had sailed to New York in 1898. Driven by desire for adventure, he left the family farm and general store in Magherafelt to wash dishes and sweep the streets of New York, Toronto, and Chicago.

He was a sales clerk at Marshall Field's in Chicago at the beginning of 1901, when a young woman in a Kansas Bible school had a kind of seizure. That distant event would alter the course of Semple's life, as it transformed American Christianity in ways that still defy rational understanding.

———

The school was actually a missionary training center, housed in a fantastic Victorian mansion on the outskirts of Topeka. Local wits dubbed it "Stone's Folly." Mr. Stone's mania kept him from ever completing it as he added another tower here, another gable or cupola there. At last it resembled an abandoned drawing of Piranesi or Escher, fit only for ghosts or brave and adventurous Bible students.

Agnes Ozman at thirty was just such a student. Like many in the avant-garde of American Christianity, she was influenced by the passionate John Wesley and the Holiness movement. She believed in marks of sanctification such as prophecy, and the power of healing. The last was of particular interest to Agnes, as she was dying of tuberculosis.

Charles Parham, her teacher, believed he owed his life to the divine power of healing. Stricken with encephalitis as an infant, and then with rheumatic fever, he never outgrew the clothes of his boyhood. A severe attack of rheumatic fever in 1891, which he survived by praying, confirmed his belief in the doctrine of divine healing. Parham left his pastorate in the Methodist Church in 1895, when he was twenty-two, and in 1898 he and his wife founded the Beth-el Healing Home in Topeka. His ministry there also included editing the Holiness journal called *Apostolic Faith*.

In the spooky chambers and corridors of Stone's Folly, Charles Parham was systematically educating young missionaries upon a principle which was extremely bizarre if not insane. He had thought this up during the summer of 1900, while visiting Frank W. Sanford's Holiness commune in Shiloh, Maine. Shiloh was one of the many Christian communities prepared for the Second Coming. They believed that Christ's premillennial return would follow upon a worldwide revival. The Holiness Christians spoke of the approaching "latter rain," an outpouring of the Holy Spirit which would fall upon people as it had in the Church's earliest days.

Parham was intrigued. He looked into his own mind and heart for a manifestation of this power. Frank W. Sanford told him how he heard reports from far-flung missions that here and there an inspired evangelist, as in a trance, had burst into the speech of his foreign hosts. These missionaries could speak the native language without study. Sanford called the wonder "xenolalia."

Parham became convinced that this xenolalia was proof the Holy Spirit was returning to the earth to accomplish an "end-time" baptism. Xenolalia offered a practical method for global revival: if Parham could train an army of spirit-filled missionaries, they could cover the world and preach the Gospel without the painstaking process of learning new languages.

He knew what people would think of his brainstorm. So he

made no public announcement of this "missionary xenolalia"
when he returned to Topeka in September of 1900, gathering
a few students by word of mouth. He rented the Gothic halls
of Stone's Folly and set up his Bible school. It was a perfect
Halloween setting for ghosts, holy and otherwise. In October,
he taught his thirty-four students the principles of Holiness
theology, millennialism, and faith healing.

In late December of that year he challenged the class to search
for true evidence of the spiritual outpouring that would come
at the end of time. He opened his Bible to Acts II, where the
apostles were gathered in a house, and tongues of flames appeared to them, and they were all filled with the Holy Spirit
and began to talk in other tongues as the Spirit gave them power
of utterance.

At their New Year's Eve service, Agnes Ozman asked her
teacher to lay his hands upon her head. She asked him to pray
that she might receive the baptism of the Holy Spirit with the
"Biblical sign." Parham's students had all agreed independently
that speaking in tongues would be the only indisputable proof
of the end-time Holy Spirit baptism.

Parham did as he was asked. He laid his hands upon Agnes
Ozman and prayed for a sign. A halo immediately appeared
around her head. This must have been an unsettling experience.
But the halo was not nearly so unnerving as what came out of
her mouth, an eerie and at first unrecognizable singing. Someone at length identified it as Chinese.

Agnes Ozman had grown up in rural Nebraska. She went to
Bible school in St. Paul and New York and served as a missionary in Kansas City before coming to Topeka. She had not
heard ten words of Chinese in her life. But for the next three
days the poor woman would not speak a word of English,
nothing but Chinese. It had to be translated by a local citizen
who had some familiarity with the language. Invigorated by
this experience, the dying woman would live almost to the age
of seventy.

About the time Agnes Ozman regained her command of
English, Charles Parham and a dozen of his students were likewise empowered with the gift of tongues. At a prayer service

they began one after another to cease praying in English. They launched into discourse which was unfamiliar and mysterious to the speaker, but which in some cases a witness could translate. This time the outbreak attracted a great deal of local attention, then publicity, when a frightened student named Dorothy Riggins defected, denouncing the strange new doctrine in the newspapers.

Reports of the revival in Topeka spread as far as St. Louis. In late January of 1901 Parham and a band of spirit-filled students headed for Kansas City. There they planned to establish a circuit of missions in major cities all over the Northeast.

Stone's Folly, on the outskirts of Topeka, Kansas, happens to lie precisely dead center of the contiguous forty-eight of these United States. Both the location and the date of Agnes Ozman's conversion are wonderfully coincidental, or providential, depending upon your religious belief. Anno Domini 1901 is the same year as Max Planck's discovery of quantum theory, four years before Einstein's special theory of relativity, which in turn precedes the decisive Azusa Street Pentecostal Revival in Los Angeles by a few months. Historiography delights in drawing connections between seemingly unrelated events. If Darwin created a crisis of faith in Genesis, Max Planck and Albert Einstein were laying the groundwork for Armageddon, for which no one could claim to be better prepared than Charles Parham, the acknowledged founder of Pentecostalism.

Historians describe Pentacostalism's rapid spread as a clockwise spiral, a native cyclone that erupted in Topeka, twisted toward Kansas City and in ever-widening circles toward Galena and Baxter Springs, Kansas before invading Missouri and Oklahoma and reeling down into Texas. There, early in 1905, Parham established a string of Apostolic Faith churches. By 1906 the movement had blazed through Los Angeles and across the northern Rockies toward Canada.

In Chicago, Illinois it swept up the young Irishman Robert Semple, who was walking the floor as a salesclerk in Marshall Fields.

———

His timing could not have been better. Robert James Semple arrived on these shores the year Charles Parham founded the Beth-el Healing Home. By the time Semple was old enough to assume a man's role in the American revolution of Pentecostalism, the movement had achieved critical mass. Semple was baptized in the Holy Spirit and spoke in tongues, and had established a reputation as a rousing evangelist in Toronto. His reputation preceded him to Ingersoll in December, 1907.

Now the handsome blue-eyed evangelist stood at the head of the congregation in that little mission off Thames Street. He opened his Bible to the second chapter of Acts. Putting his whole heart and soul into two syllables he called to the people the simple command: Repent. Repent . . . Repent. He said it over and over, as if the word could find its meaning only in his soulful repetition.

And Aimee Kennedy, sitting in the back row next to her father, wished that the tall young man would stop and say some other word. For that word did seem "to pierce like an arrow through my heart." The allusion to St. Theresa is wholly unconscious, and erotic as Bernini's famous statue. Aimee's description of his effect on her, from the instant she saw Robert Semple and heard his voice, will blur the distinction between the religious and the sexual. Cold shivers ran up and down her back.

"I had never heard such a sermon. Using his Bible as a sword, he cleft the whole world in two."

She means that Robert Semple divided humanity into two categories: Christians and sinners. There were those, like Aimee, who loved the theater, dancing, novels, ragtime music, and skating rinks. These folks were on the way to hell if they did not renounce the world right speedily.

Aimee sat up straight in her seat.

"Why, it just looked as if somebody had told him I was there, so vividly did he picture my own life and walk . . . His words seemed to rain down upon me, and every one of them hurt some particular part of my spirit and life until I could not tell where I was hurt the most."

The preacher saw no middle ground between sinners and

those who were saved. If the love of the world was in you, the love of the Father was not: it was as simple as that. He explained the meaning of salvation, the death, burial, and resurrection you would know as you became identified with our Lord; and he began to preach the baptism of the Holy Spirit, how the message of salvation and the incoming of the Spirit went side by side.

Then he closed his eyes, and his face began to glow with an inner light. Suddenly, Robert Semple changed voices. It was as if somebody had turned a radio dial to an international band, except that the vocabulary the young man was using had no earthly grammar or lexicon.

But his meaning, however confusing it may have been to the rest of the congregation, was perfectly clear to Aimee Kennedy. It was the voice of God thundering into her soul.

"From the moment I heard that young man speak with tongues to this day I have never doubted for the shadow of a second that there was a God, and that he had shown me my true condition as a poor, lost, miserable, Hell-deserving sinner.

"My very soul had been stripped before God—there was a God, and I was not ready to meet him."

CONVERSION

It is fair to say that Aimee's conversion experience was one part religion and nine parts falling in love. By this I do not mean to cast doubt upon the authenticity of her belief, only to describe its nature. She fell in love with Robert Semple at first sight, madly in love. Aimee's feeling for the young man whose voice pierced her heart like an arrow would color her sense of his theology. Her ministry would forever be infused with the spirit of eros.

A common early symptom of falling in love is the feeling of

unworthiness. The lover measures everything by a new
standard—the beloved appears on an impossibly lofty plane, to
which the lover at first hardly dares to aspire.

"No one," Aimee recalls, "had ever spoken to me like this
before. I had been petted, loved and perhaps a little spoiled: told
how smart and good I was . . . Oh how could I have looked
down upon the dear people and felt that I was better than they?
Why, I was not even worthy to black their shoes."

She and her father slipped out before the service was over so
she could attend her rehearsal in the town hall. Aimee went into
a tailspin. For the next seventy-two hours she could not study
or concentrate on her role. Whenever she closed her eyes, she
saw Robert Semple. His words "Poor, lost, miserable, Hell-
deserving sinner" rang in her ears. She decided she could not
possibly be a Christian and recite those silly Irish monologues.

Yet it was too close to Christmas to get someone to take her
place. At first she prayed to God that she might just live until
after Christmas, when she would give her heart to Him.

"Oh, don't let me die until after Christmas," she begged.

Driving home from school on the third day after hearing
Robert Semple, it seemed to Aimee the whole winter landscape,
the clouds, trees, and fields were all frowning at her. She
thought the sky was going to cave in. She stopped the carriage
in the middle of the lonely road, threw up her hands, and
screamed at the heavens to have mercy upon her.

It came instantly. Darkness passed away and light entered.

"The sky was filled with brightness, the trees, the fields, and
the little snow birds flitting to and fro were praising the Lord
and smiling upon me.

"So conscious was I of the pardoning blood of Jesus that I
seemed to feel it flowing over me." It was her own tears.

This was the first step in the conversion process that would
close the gap between Aimee and Robert Semple. All the way
home she sang hymns in praise of the heavenly father she had
found at last. When she got home, she announced that she would
not be taking part in the Christmas entertainments. She burned
her ragtime music, novels, and dancing slippers in the wood
stove.

This was the easy part. During the next weeks she was in ecstasy, despite the criticism of the folks in town. At last she had found a friend, a brother.

"I, who had never known brother or sister, had an Elder Brother with whom I could talk. Not a moment of the long miles to and from school but he was right beside me."

Robert Semple had gone back to Stratford, but not before she had him underline her Bible. He was present, as was Jesus Christ, in the words of the New Testament, in the Bible she concealed within the covers of her *Algebra and Geometry*, where before she had hidden her novels. Her heart became so full, right there in the classroom, she had to excuse herself. Aimee would run down to the basement, fall on her knees, and pray for the Lord to baptize her with the Holy Spirit.

She had found God, but God had not exactly found her, at least not in the way He had found Robert Semple. The hours she spent on her knees turned from ecstatic praise to thanksgiving, then to a bittersweet yearning which expressed itself thus: "O Lord, what can I do for Thee in return?" Kneeling by her bed, she closed her eyes tightly and concentrated. She saw a wide black river rushing past with millions of men, women, and children being swept to destruction in the current over a waterfall.

"Become a winner of souls," came the answer.

Now this could only mean one thing. It seemed impossible that she should become an evangelist like Robert Semple. Women did not become evangelists: St. Paul had cautioned against it. Eve, the mother of all living, had been the first transgressor. Yet there was Evangeline Booth, and Catherine Booth, who died a few days before Aimee came into the world. Perhaps a farm girl was just as likely to preach the Gospel as Peter the fisherman, or Matthew the tax collector. Studying her Bible, Aimee discovered the only strict requirement for becoming an evangelist was the baptism of the Holy Spirit.

Against her mother's wishes, Aimee began attending the "tarrying" meetings at the storefront mission where she first heard Robert Semple. A tarrying meeting is just a prayer session devoted to baptism in the Holy Spirit. This can have a number of peculiar manifestations—speaking in tongues (glossolalia), automatism, prostration—depending upon the individual who receives it. Some do and some do not.

In 1908, this was radical behavior. It says a great deal about the liberality of that Canadian province that the Pentecostals were not run out of town on a rail. Even the Salvation Army officers, in their barracks up the street, took a dim view of the newcomers. They paid a call on Minnie. The officers told her that Aimee's association with the Holy Rollers made them all look bad, because Minnie had for so many years been active in the Army. Her daughter should show better sense.

Nice girls in 1908 did not smoke cigarettes or go to cockfights or seek baptism in the Holy Spirit. As a stimulant it might lead to conduct unbecoming a lady.

Aimee Kennedy, of course, did not much care what anybody thought of her except Robert Semple. She was appealing to a higher authority, which was the Authority of authorities. We do not know how much time Robert Semple spent in Ingersoll during the winter of 1908. Probably he traveled back and forth between Stratford and Ingersoll. This would help explain Aimee's open defiance when Minnie told her to stay away from the mission. The high-school principal had sent a letter that said that Aimee had fallen so far behind in her studies, she would likely fail. The lovesick student had been cutting classes to attend the tarrying meetings.

———

The Monday morning after her mother forbade her to go to the tarrying meetings, Aimee took the train to school. Looking out the window at the snow falling, she prayed the Lord might fix things so she could get on with her spiritual quest without mundane interferences like school and parents.

Walking to school from the station, she had to pass the mission, and then the home of the sister who held the tarrying meetings. It dawned upon Aimee that the Holy Spirit was more important than school examinations. The phrase she uses to recall this impulse sounds like a line from a barrelhouse torch song. "You need oil in your vessel with your lamp."

So she turned back to the house, rang the bell, and went in.

When she told the Pentecostal sister of her conflict, the sister suggested they "tell Father about it." They kneeled. The older woman prayed for Aimee either to be baptized then and there, or for things to arrange themselves so Aimee could tarry until she was.

The snow that had been falling in light flakes began to come down in billows. A blizzard was on.

After a day on her knees, Aimee trudged to the railroad station, where the ticket agent told her the snow had stopped the trains. And when she tried to telephone her mother, the operator told her the lines were down on account of the storm. Leaping and shouting Hallelujah, she ran back to the sister's home to continue her vigil.

"Time was precious, for while man was working so hard to shovel out the snow, and God had His big clouds all working to shovel it in, I must do my part in seeking with all my heart."

Now we must consider what exactly Aimee Kennedy was doing on her knees from Monday to Saturday, snowbound in the home of the Pentecostal sister. She was praying, but what does that mean? As snow fell and water froze in the pitcher and the washbasin, she prayed. Rising at whatever hour she awakened, she would slip out of bed with the blankets wrapped around her. Watching the ghosts of her breath, she prayed for the baptism of the Holy Spirit. At noon she would come to the table for a bowl of potato soup, drain it, and go back to her solitary work.

Most of us have had no experience to which we can compare Aimee's. It is a rare gift of the intellect and the will to be able to concentrate on anything for more than a few minutes. The mind naturally wanders. As a child, you may have wished for something: a horse, a signet ring. You wished first upon a star, or upon the birthday candles before you blew them out. You closed your eyes tightly and, directing your will to an image in your mind, for a few seconds you wished with all your might. That is not prayer exactly, but it is a voluntary effort resembling one aspect of prayer.

Students of meditation study for years to gain some control

over the mind's antics, so that they will not be distracted by a cold draft under the door or a fly on the forehead. Aimee Kennedy was born with prodigious powers of concentration, altogether remarkable in a child of such explosive energy; when the young woman got down on her knees, it would take dynamite to shake the pattern of her prayer.

Prayer is far more than an act of will. It is a disposition of spirit with respect to the world. At some point in the process of exhaustive prayer the individual's will dissolves in the solution of spirit, right along with the boundary between the pilgrim and the rest of the world.

From Monday until Friday, as the snow fell, Aimee prayed to be emptied of self and filled with the Power promised from Heaven. She prayed for the baptism of the Holy Spirit, the true evidence of which she understood to be the gift of tongues. Considering her physical strength and her skeptical intellect, Aimee's inner resistance to the baptism must have been great, as great as her faith would become. A striking feature of Aimee's baptism is that she achieved it in solitude—speaking in tongues is usually a group phenomenon, an emotional chain reaction.

She spent more and more hours praying, and ate and slept less; at last it seemed there was little difference between waking and sleeping, and all her hunger was for the Lord. Her physical stamina was enormous. She felt as if she were battering her way "through a thick stone wall that was growing as thin as tissue paper."

"Lord, I'll never eat or sleep again until you fill me with this promised Spirit of power."

"I am more willing to give than you are to receive," said the Bible open before her.

The effect of such labor over a period of days has been described in the literature of psychology. The strongest man or woman under the strain of this type of concentration begins to suffer. The fatigue has specific symptoms: weakening of the critical faculties, visual and auditory hallucinations, automatism. Whether one calls it religion, hypnosis, or brainwashing, the fatigue's effect is the same: the subject enters a trance state, a twilight between sleeping and waking where the will relaxes and subconscious thought flows freely into the waking mind.

If you are a charismatic Christian, you believe the trance is the working of the Holy Spirit. This does not make it any less a trance; and all the psychiatrists in Christendom cannot disprove that the trance is the working of the Holy Spirit.

On Friday Aimee waited upon the Lord until midnight. Saturday morning she rose before anyone in the house was awake, crept downstairs to the parlor, and took up her vigil kneeling by the Morris chair in the corner.

It was there she heard God's voice: "Now child, cease your striving and your begging; just begin to praise me, and in simple childlike faith, receive ye the Holy Ghost."

Aimee did what she was told. She whispered, "Glory, glory," and each time the word seemed to come from a graver source within her and in a deeper voice. At last the words of praise came thundering out of her, resonating from her feet to her diaphragm and out the top of her head.

Her hands and arms began to twitch and tremble, gently at first and then more violently, and then her whole body was shaking with the power of the Holy Spirit. She recalls that this seemed altogether natural; she had seen how the storage batteries she experimented with in school hummed and shook and trembled under the power of electricity. Her image is precise, and weirdly modern. How much was her automatism influenced by the scientific model? She trembled, and she quaked, until at last she slipped to the floor and "was lying under the power of God, but felt as though caught up and floating upon the billowing clouds of glory."

The cords of her throat began to twitch. Her lungs filled and began to heave. Her chin quivered, shook violently, and then her tongue began to move in her mouth, first up and down, then sideways. Vowels came howling and then a distinct syllable, and another, stammering, until they flowed in a sentence Aimee could not understand. This led to another slowly formed sentence, and several more that followed, each more swiftly.

"Then suddenly, out of my innermost being flowed rivers of praise in other tongues as the Spirit gave utterance" (Acts 2:4). By now she had awakened the whole house. Soon her solitude was broken by fellow "saints" shouting and rejoicing in Aimee's hard-won triumph, and one of them was Robert James Semple.

At last she had broken through to him.

MARRIAGE

Six months later, on August 12, 1908, Aimee Kennedy married Robert Semple at Kosy-Kot, which the newspaper describes as "the charming country home of Mr. and Mrs. James Kennedy near Salford." You would think that Minnie had convinced the journalist there was no barn behind the house, no cows or chickens in residence.

Lieutenant-Colonel Sharpe of the London Salvation Army officiated in the presence of fifty guests. He stood with the bridegroom beneath an evergreen cedar bower interwoven with golden glow blossoms. And while Rosie Mitchell of Ingersoll played the wedding march on the piano, James Kennedy led his daughter from her room, across the lawn, and under the bower. There she stood, in a white silk gown trimmed with lace, holding a bouquet. She vowed to love Robert Semple, honor and obey him forever and ever, until death.

The reception, held afterwards on the lawn, was catered by Brooks Brothers of Ingersoll. This was an unheard-of extravagance. The wedding cake came as a gift from a Chinese confectioner in Toronto whom Robert Semple had converted to Christianity.

The sun shone on the wedding and most of the marriage feast. But as the cake was cut, rain clouds gathered over the farm, and the party rushed for the house in a downpour. Indoors they passed the time in music, laughter, and conversation, until the newlyweds left for their honeymoon in Toronto.

How Aimee spent the winter, spring, and summer before her

wedding was a subject of gossip. School records show her attendance was irregular. By the second semester she must have made her decision not to graduate. She had found a real teacher in Robert Semple.

"He was my theological seminary, my spiritual mentor, and my tender, patient, unfailing lover."

After her conversion she spent long hours in Bible study, arming to defend herself against her parents, the Salvation Army, and the Methodists. All of them believed the Devil had hypnotized or possessed their fair-haired child. Aimee relied heavily on the text that "He who asks for bread shall not be given a stone" (Matthew 7:9) and "If your earthly fathers knew how to bestow good gifts upon their children, how much more shall your heavenly father give the Holy Spirit . . ." (Luke 11:13). So she and the charming Robert Semple persuaded the Kennedys that Pentecostalism was not wicked, nor was their engagement, though the young revivalist had little to offer their daughter in the way of worldly goods.

The courtship period piques our curiosity. Aimee is vague about her lover's comings and goings in Ingersoll from winter to summer. She received the baptism, and her call to preach, in the dead of winter. Semple then left for Stratford, where he began a correspondence with the beautiful convert. The letters are lost. In the spring she volunteered to nurse two children stricken with typhoid fever, in that same sister's house where she received her baptism.

Late at night the door opened, and in walked Robert Semple.

He told her he had come to sit up with the sick children. She told him *she* had been called to sit up with the sick children. So they decided they would both sit up with the sick children— this is how Aimee would tell the love story years later, with lusty humor. And the audience would laugh aloud, and weep, knowing the story's end.

They sat down side by side and read the Bible in the lamplight. He told her of the great fields of golden grain, of the need for laborers in the final days, the many souls yet to be saved, and what a life of faith really meant—the sacrifice, the reward. Taking Aimee's hand in his, he told her of his love. He asked her to marry him and enter the work as a helpmate by his side. He had been called to go soul-winning in China and wanted her with him.

Before she could answer, Robert Semple led her to kneel with him by the sofa, and pray about it. Years later this too would seem funny, as she told the story of the curious proposal, and her lover's quaint manners. At the time it was not at all funny, as things transpired in the same charmed space where the Holy Spirit first possessed her. As she knelt with her lover, and her heart was pounding, the room filled with the blinding light of angels. These lined a golden road that stretched away into the future toward the Heavenly City, and she and Robert were walking the road together. This was the visible answer to her prayer. Startled, she opened her eyes and looked about her to find no angels and no road, only flowered wallpaper faded in spots. Closing her eyes tight to get another look at the angels, she saw the golden road again. But this time she was walking alone. Wanting to see him again, she opened her eyes wide and told Robert she would marry him and follow him to China or anywhere else God wanted them to go.

God wanted them to go to Hong Kong. This saddened Minnie, and frightened her a little, as the man her only child had married seemed blessed with more inspiration than common sense. Their wedding notice reports the newlyweds' plan to embark for China, before they had the slightest idea how they would cross the ocean.

First he took her to his three-room flat in downtown Stratford. Smoke from nearby foundries drifted over the roof.

Semple supported his evangelism by working in a locomotive boiler factory. All day he wormed his way through the tubing with a trowel, scraping away carbon deposits. At night he preached. The bride labored in a tiny backyard, over a washtub. She would scrub and rinse, but as fast as she washed the clothes and hung them up to dry, the soot came along and smudged them. Her biscuits were golden and the evangelist praised them after his hard day's work in the boiler factory.

After a little while in Stratford the couple was called to London (Ontario), where they stayed at the home of a Sister Armstrong. There the evangelist preached in private homes. Aimee cleaned house, played piano, sang at the meetings, and prayed with the converts. Within several months a hundred people had received the baptism of the Holy Spirit "with the Bible evidence," many more were saved, and Aimee recalls several remarkable healings.

Late in 1908 they went to Chicago, where on January 2, 1909 Robert Semple was ordained by William H. Durham, pastor of the Full Gospel Assembly. Robert and Aimee stayed at the North Avenue mission in Chicago for several happy months, preaching and saving souls in the working-class Italian neighborhood before they went on the road with Brother Durham, to Brother Leonard's mission in Findlay, Ohio.

———

It was in Findlay that Aimee first experienced a miraculous healing.

There are four major charismata, or gifts of the spirit, defined by the Pentecostalists: glossolalia (speaking in tongues), prophecy, interpretation of tongues—and the power of healing. The power of healing, which Aimee exercised with reluctance and spectacular results, presents an overwhelming problem to historians, who largely ignore it.

In her late twenties Aimee would become a healer of such documented genius that a major church would be built upon it. The Church stands. But the documents that attest to Aimee Semple McPherson's healing ministry are so baffling, they have been buried in the Church archives for almost seventy years. The few surviving eyewitnesses of that ministry, including the evangelist's son and daughter, discuss the healings hesitantly, brimful with emotion, like veterans of a battle too horrible to recollect.

It started in 1909, when Aimee tumbled down the stairs at the mission in Findlay and broke her ankle. She could hear the bones crunch as she fell, bending her ankle under so that her toes turned toward her heel.

The ankle swelled rapidly and turned blue from the fracture. A doctor who was at the prayer meeting said that not only was the metatarsal cracked; she had torn four of the ligaments that move the toes, all but the largest toe. The outside of her foot had been pulled around and backwards. When they rebandaged the swelling, Dr. Harrison and his son, local physicians, drew the bent foot back into place. They put on a plaster-of-Paris cast. Those doctors lacked the expertise to suture the torn ligaments; they explained that while the bone would heal, the torn cords would never grow together. Her healed foot would be straight but stiff. They gave Aimee crutches, advising her to put no weight on the foot for a month.

So off she hobbled, in excruciating pain, to the train that would take her back to Chicago. The afternoon she arrived, Aimee attended a service at the North Avenue mission, resting her feverish limb on the platform in front of her. Every footfall on the hollow wooden floor of the mission sent a shock of pain through Aimee's leg. Finally she couldn't take it anymore. She limped back to her room a block away from the hall.

While sitting there, staring at her black and swollen toes sticking out of the cast, she heard a voice.

"If you will wrap the shoe for your broken foot, and take it with you to wear home, and go over to North Avenue Mission to Brother Durham and ask him to lay hands on your foot, I will heal it."

Aimee looked around her to see that she was alone. Then she laughed. The idea of wrapping up the shoe, which had pinched even before she broke her foot, was hilarious; but while she laughed in the half-delirium of her pain, she heard the voice again, "Wrap up your shoe to wear home, take it with you as you go to be prayed for, and I will heal you . . ."

She was eighteen years old. Since she had received her baptism a year before, she had heard voices several times. But they were Bible echoes, passages she had read and memorized. This was different. It was the same tone as the voice in her head that quoted Scripture in answer to her prayers; but now the voice of the Lord was issuing to Aimee a specific and disturbingly irrational command.

She searched for her crutches, hobbled over to the loose shoe, and wrapped it up. Tucking the parcel under her arm, she made her way down the winding staircase to go to the mission for prayers. Once her crutch slipped into a hole in the sidewalk, and as she stubbed her toes, the sweat stood out in beads on her forehead. Two men carried her on a chair up the stairs and into the meeting.

When she told them what the Lord had told her, all twelve of the assembly but one began to pray for her; that man, the brother of Pastor Durham, was a skeptic, but he would not be one for long. As William Durham strode up and down the room calling upon the powers, he stopped suddenly, and laid his hands on Aimee's ankle. After a few sentences in an unknown language he said, "In the name of Jesus, receive your healing," and Aimee "felt as if a shock of electricity had struck" her foot.

It flowed through her whole body, causing her to shake and tremble. Again she uses the precise electrical image to describe the trauma, and we cannot help but wonder how much the transformation owed to its scientific metaphor.

The darkness faded from the skin of her foot. Aimee felt the ligaments ease into place as the bone was made whole, and a strange coolness there in the absence of pain. She asked for help to cut away the cast.

"Don't be foolish," said the skeptic. "You will only have to pay a doctor three dollars to replace the cast."

But his eyes grew wide and he joined the others in praise as the plaster was removed from the healed foot, and Aimee laced on the shoe that she had brought. She leaped and began to dance and jump on her new foot.

That night the mission was packed, and the pastor asked Aimee to come to the platform and tell of the healing. She recalls that the faithful rejoiced with her. The doubters were thereafter divided geographically: the Chicago doubters did not think the foot had ever been broken, and the Ohio doubters, when notified, did not believe it had been healed. Only she and the twelve on North Avenue knew the truth. All they could do was swear to it.

This would serve as the core of her faith in faith-healing. The "wounded healer" is a common figure of literature and psychology, in keeping with the notion that the physician must know illness from the inside out. Aimee could heal because she had been healed. Whether or not her ankle was miraculously healed is of some concern to us. But we must live with our curiosity, because we have no account of the experience but hers. She told the story in 1918, when her career as a healer had just got under way, and at a time when she was not given to bold deception. We have observed her gifts of metaphor and narrative; yet this story has the eerie ring of authenticity—and it will be a triumph of her career to enlarge the dimensions of possibility. The significance of this story is that she believed it. She believed in healing so deeply, she would convince others of it on a scale that would make the little repair of her ankle a miracle hardly worth remembering.

———

In the late winter of 1910, Robert Semple told his young wife they would be leaving for China in six weeks. He was about to announce it to his congregation.

The couple had not begun to raise money for the passage. Cheerfully Robert Semple explained that when the Lord calls you to a certain place, He provides transportation.

That night, as he said goodbye to the crowd in the Italian church, he made no mention of his need for money. But afterwards the signors and signoras formed a long line that went up one aisle and down the other, so everyone could shake Robert Semple's hand or give him a hug or pat on the back while Aimee stood away from him on the platform. She saw they were pressing folded banknotes into his hands, and then into hers, between kisses, and dropping gold and silver into her purse until the coins spilled over onto the floor, so she began collecting money in her hat until that too was full.

At home they counted more than enough cash to pay the boat fare.

It was a hard crossing to Liverpool, through a famous storm that swept the wheelhouse from the *Lusitania*. Aimee, who was pregnant, spent most of the voyage in her cabin, seasick. From Liverpool they sailed to Belfast, where Robert's father, mother, two sisters, and two brothers met them and took them by car to Magherafelt, twenty miles distant.

Magherafelt is a beautiful old country town set in emerald hills. Aimee described Robert's home as "that quaint, glorious stone house among the shamrocks."

Surely she was never happier than during those weeks in Magherafelt. Robert did some preaching in Belfast, where the Lord Mayor presented him with the key to the city, but the time in Ireland was foremost a holiday. She and Robert spent days walking the hills and sheep pastures, and sightseeing in the castles and ancient stone quarries. This was the closest they ever came to a real honeymoon. A photograph taken by Abernathy Studio in Belfast shows Aimee leaning back against a cardboard crescent moon, with stars over her left shoulder. She wears a radiant smile and a white carnation in her hair.

Everywhere she went, she purchased postcards, a few photographs of tourist sights but mostly the humorous postcards popular then. Each day she mailed one to Minnie, with affectionate and humorous notes, full of details, puns, and the dialect she was learning from her in-laws. Minnie mounted the cards in an album which has survived. These and the photographs are rich souvenirs of a young woman blissfully in love but who still missed her mother.

At the magical stone quarry in Magherafelt there were huge and oddly shaped wishing stones. What should she wish for? She was young, beautiful, and in love with a great man who shared with her a glorious ideal. Soon she would be a mother. There was a legend that down in the depths of the lake at Magherafelt there was a cathedral, and if true lovers stood beside the lake, they could hear the bells ringing. When she stood by the lake with Robert Semple, she was not sure if she heard the bells ringing or if it was the sound of her own heart.

She might have wished the time in Ireland could last forever. Robert's mother, a wizened, strong-jawed old woman dressed in black taffeta, prayed aloud that the couple would stay until the child was born. Her eyes shone behind wire-rimmed spectacles. She had a premonition that when her son sailed for China, that would be the last she would ever see of him.

The parting was difficult.

They sailed from London, where the Christian millionaire Cecil Polhill put his mansion and chauffeur at their disposal. He sent them in his limousine to Big Ben and the Tower of London and introduced them to the growing Pentecostal community. And he had a surprise for Aimee. Polhill took it into his head that the pretty young woman should "bring the message" at a meeting the night before she left London.

Aimee had never preached. But she did not want to tell the millionaire, for fear of discouraging his patronage. He informed her in the afternoon. The car would come for her at seven. Robert was away at another meeting, and during those anxious hours of waiting Aimee was so nervous, all she could do was pray and ruffle the pages of the Bible. The limousine, with Aimee terrified in the back seat, pulled up to a building that covered an entire city square. Aimee was ushered to the crowded rostrum of Victoria and Albert Hall, where she looked up at fifteen thousand faces rising in tiers to the auditorium's fifth balcony.

A minister turned to her and said, "Our lady missionary is a few minutes late, but she has now arrived and will speak immediately." It had been more than a year since she faced an audience of any size.

She was not yet twenty, but her destiny was fully formed within her. Panicked, she opened her Bible and looked down: the passage which seemed to stand out in boldfaced type was the surrealistic verse from Joel 1:4: "That which the palmer-worm hath left hath the locust eaten; and that which the locust hath left hath the cankerworm eaten; and that which the can-kerworm hath left the caterpillar eaten."

A current went through her body and she trembled. The sensation went beyond panic. It was somehow connected to the fifteen thousand people in the hall, as if the book in front of her were the positive pole of some enormous electric generator and she was the wire conducting the voltage to the audience as ground. Her eyes closed, her tongue began to move as it had the morning she was baptized in the Spirit. But this time the sentences came in pure prophetic English.

The Spirit spoke through her in prophecy. And as she spoke in that deep melodious voice for more than an hour, she did not know from moment to moment what the next word would be. In the center of the hall she envisioned a great circle composed of ten smaller circles, the topmost of which touched the sky. It was the dispensation of the Holy Spirit from the day of Pentecost to the date of the Second Coming, visualized as a tree in stages of bloom and decay: in full leaf and flower in the topmost circle, declining by depredation of palmerworm, locust, and cankerworm till it was a blasted trunk in the lowermost circle of the Dark Ages before rising again to luxuriance as it began.

The beautiful prophetess simply described what her bright eyes saw as plain as day in the air before her. Now and then she would pause to look down and read from the Bible open at Joel: "And I will restore to you the years that the locust hath eaten, the cankerworm, and the caterpillar, and the palmerworm, my great army which I sent among you." And she interpreted the images as they came to her; how the tree with its perfect fruit was the early Church; how the palmerworm destroyed the fruits of the Spirit, and miracles waned; how the locust wrought up the leaves and there was no more speaking in tongues, and then the cankerworm went to work upon the Church's limbs, and so on till the Dark Ages. But then Martin Luther crawled up the cathedral steps on his hands and knees over broken glass. And John Wesley came a-preaching on street corners, Charles Finney, William Booth, and the saints of the latter Rain. "In the last days, I will pour out my Spirit upon all flesh."

People were leaning forward in the crimson velvet-covered chairs, and now and then a volley of amens or hallelujahs thundered through the hall, or they would stop her for a moment with their applause. They could see at once when she was done, because all of a sudden the light in her went out, as though someone had pulled a switch.

She was uncertain of exactly what had happened as she looked out upon the sea of people clapping and wiping their eyes. Robert had arrived in time to hear her. He put his arm around her shoulders and led her back to the car, as mystified by the performance as the preacher herself. She would never do it again in his lifetime.

CHINA

The crowd on the street corner in Mount Forest in 1915 who watched the woman standing on her chair was held by an emotional resonance she had gained through tragedy. Her devotion to Robert Semple had almost killed her.

She and Robert arrived in Hong Kong by way of the Suez Canal and Ceylon, in early June of 1910. The sun beat mercilessly upon the parasols and pith helmets of the white-suited missionaries who awaited them on the pier. Under the cloud-wreathed hills the round harbor swarmed with sampans, houseboats by the thousands, and black junks with sails like bat wings. The narrow streets of the bannered city teemed with jinrikisha men in wide-brimmed hats, jostling for fares to and from the busy docks.

Ten years after the Boxer Rebellion, China was on the verge of revolution. The Manchu dynasty, critically weakened, could neither deal with internal dissent nor resist the encroachment of foreign powers. Although less than one percent of the people had been converted to Christianity, its influence had been decisive. Roman Catholic and Protestant missionaries had opened the Great Wall to Western literature, education, and medicine, not to mention Western capital.

The Boxers' violent reaction against Western and Japanese interests meant death for scores of missionaries and hundreds of Chinese Christians. This did not discourage the imperial evangelists of Robert Semple's generation; it inspired them. The populous shores of Canton and Yangtze seemed sweetened with the fresh blood of Christian martyrs. War between Japan and Russia over Manchuria had further destabilized the vulnerable nation. At the moment Robert and Aimee Semple arrived, Hong Kong was a happy hunting ground for soul-winners.

Aimee's recollections of her months in China show a struggle to conceal her horror of the brutal heat, revolting foods, and "demonic" habits of the superstitious natives. We have no account of this adventure but Aimee's guilt-ridden and incredible memoir; it suggests that Robert Semple was driven to this foreign land by a death wish that his bride could not dispel.

From the day they arrived, Robert spent more and more time in solitary prayer. He used to walk through the graveyard at Happy Valley reading the inscriptions on the Christian martyrs' tombstones. Later in life, she would recall Robert's humor as he watched the natives consume live worms in the market, or as he teased her about her fear of the rats and mice and huge centipedes in their house. It is grim humor, which thinly disguises her memory of living on the edge of hysteria.

As soon as they arrived, Robert began preaching the Gospel through an interpreter. Aimee went house hunting. Houses tended to be either too cheap or too expensive. When at last she found a whole street of vacant apartments on the road that led to the cemetery, she could not figure out why they were so inexpensive and so freely available. She rented the flat next door to the Hindu temple, where the priests kept up a constant chanting and thumping of drums.

Aimee had not lived there for long before she discovered that the street was deserted because it was haunted. At all hours of the day and night she heard weird tappings, howlings, footsteps, and ghostly conversations in various languages. She did not know if it was her imagination or the spirits being worshiped at the neighbor's.

"Certainly the powers of hell seemed to hover over that heathen land whose flaming sky burned like the lid of a burnished copper cauldron."

One of the most revealing passages in all of Aimee's writing is an open confession of hysteria. This occurred several weeks after their arrival in China. She had followed Robert to the end

of the earth as she had promised, enduring seasickness, home-
sickness, rats, centipedes, and the reek of rotten eggs and putrid
dog meat in the torrid heat. But when her Hindu neighbors
began burning one of their cousins upon an altar outside her
window, this was more than she could bear. She had thought
it was one more stew of old meats she had forbidden the cook
to prepare. She was about to fly into a rage at him over the
noisome odor when she saw the flaming pyre outside and the
Hindus dousing it with kerosene. The victim drew up his knees,
sat up, and showed signs of mortal distress.

Making a valiant effort not to scream, Aimee closed the windows. She ran to her bedroom and threw herself on the bed.
When Robert asked what was troubling her, she quietly told
him the Hindus were burning a man alive in the backyard. She
would not be convinced that the man was dead before the burning, that his contortions had been caused by the effect of heat
on the sinews and muscles.

"Don't touch me," she hissed at her husband. "Don't touch
me or I'll scream."

He moved to comfort his frightened wife, and the instant he
touched her, she screamed and would not stop screaming. Her
recollection of this response is such essential autobiography, it
must be quoted verbatim:

> His sympathetic caress touched the match to the pent-up powder
> keg of my emotions, and immediately I was in the grasp of violent
> hysterics. It seemed as I listened to the high-pitched wails and wild
> laughter that came from my heart that the screams came from
> another person entirely.

From another person entirely. Aimee has the classic disposition
for ecstasy, religious in some, demonic in others. When Robert
had calmed her hysteria, he forgave her outburst. Yet he might
have sensed that his wife's great gifts came with a price tag.
The psychoanalytic explanation for miraculous healing as well
as miraculous conversion is that both these phenomena are clinical indications of hysteria; great mystics, from John the Baptist
to St. Theresa, have owed more or less of their accomplishment

to fits of ecstasy which psychoanalysts prefer to call "hysterics."

Aimee Semple hated China nearly as much as she loved her husband. Her memory of it sharpens the edge of her irony: "I knew I would never live through the ordeal. But somehow I did. Lived to come down with a fine case of tropical malaria."

Malaria was epidemic in Hong Kong and Kowloon, and down the coast of Macao, where the Semples migrated hoping to escape the heat. Against everyone's advice Robert Semple would go out preaching to dazed Chinese in the noonday sun, wearing his cork sun helmet and carrying a white parasol lined with green.

In August of 1910 malaria and dysentery struck both Semples. They grew so feverish and weak they could no longer move from bed to bed to nurse each other. Man and wife were returned by steamer to Hong Kong, where coolies carried Robert in his hammock on bamboo poles up the mountain to Matilda Hospital. When the attending physician asked Aimee what she had been feeding her husband, she told him a careful diet of market produce. The doctor shook his head in dismay. Had no one explained to the young wife how Chinese fields were fertilized with the excrement of the families who tilled them? Malaria was the least of Robert's problems.

Robert James Semple died in Matilda Hospital on August 17, five days after their second wedding anniversary.

One month earlier, two maiden ladies in Chicago had been awakened in the dead of night by a voice saying: "Sister Semple is in trouble. Rise up and send her sixty dollars." The two old women got out of bed and posted the check, which arrived in the afternoon mail the day of Robert Semple's death. It was just enough money to bury him decently. He was laid to rest in the Happy Valley cemetery, among the tombstones whose inscriptions he had so greatly admired.

For the next month, as she opened her eyes morning after morning to the horror of Matilda Hospital and what had happened to her, Aimee Semple would sit up and scream at the white walls.

———

She gave birth to a daughter on September 17, 1910, and this seems to have calmed her. She named the girl Roberta Star, as the baby represented the only star of hope in a dim and forbidding future. The child at birth weighed only four and a half pounds.

Six weeks later they sailed to Shanghai en route to San Francisco. Minnie had sent money for the fare in installments; by the date of embarkation not all the checks had caught up with Aimee, not enough to get her across the continent to New York, where Minnie was now living. As Aimee stepped off the steamer in San Francisco, the purser overtook her with an envelope containing sixty-five dollars—the passengers' collection for the missionary widow and her miniature baby. This should not have surprised her. All along the voyage she had only to wish for a thing and it came: a blanket, a baby bottle, a shawl would be brought to her door and handed over just as it was needed. Thus, she recalls, the Lord "tempers the wind to the shorn lamb."

A snapshot speaks eloquently of this dark passage in the young widow's life: a flawed madonna out of focus, the baby just a blur on the mother's lap. But Aimee is so proud and pathetic, one can hardly look into those shining eyes without weeping, because they are the emblem of weeping. There is no other picture so unaffected and affecting in the vast photobiography, nothing so candid. The hair is pulled back, showing premature wrinkles in the wide brow. The eyes are swollen, dark-rimmed. She looks like a child who has discovered her womanhood in a sea of tears. The death of her husband will become a dominant note on the instrument of her fulfillment, but she is not yet aware of this. She may have believed, at age twenty, that she was irreparably broken.

Meanwhile her mother had a curiously "modern" arrangement with James Kennedy. Shortly after Aimee's wedding Minnie had the farm transferred to her for the price of five hundred dollars. This was to avoid inheritance taxes upon James's death. Guaranteeing the old man a lifetime tenancy, she left, in 1908, to resume at last her own missionary work with the Salvation

Army in New York. She also ran a boarding house, to support her mission.

Minnie was not yet forty; James was in his seventies. Though nothing is known about his feelings in the matter, the separation cannot have been easy for him; yet the door was always open to Minnie when she wished to return to the farm, and she did return to help with the harvest. He continued to treat Minnie, who had deserted him, with the same paternal solicitude most men reserve for their daughters.

Minnie urged her forlorn daughter to work for the Salvation Army. They would give her half the money she caught in her tambourine on street corners. But Roberta was only thirteen weeks old and still so frail, she needed Aimee's constant care. Besides, Aimee had the feeling that her only happiness lay in carrying on the Pentecostal work of her martyred husband.

She found the Glad Tidings Mission of Reverend Brown in the heart of New York. There she gave her testimony, which was not wholly cathartic.

Her mourning was complicated by feelings of shame and guilt, even in the presence of those whose comfort she most needed, the dear "saints" who had sent her on her fateful od-yssey. Aimee had the feeling that they questioned the authen-ticity of her call to Hong Kong, that somehow Robert's death had been a punishment for her misguided inspiration.

Yet they took up a collection for her, which helped Minnie buy her daughter a train ticket to Chicago. Aimee wanted to work in the churches where Robert had preached.

Her old friends found her a furnished room, where they left her, in her black dress and veil, to care for the sickly infant by day and rejoin them at night for the meetings. She helped out as before by playing piano, and singing as much as her sadness would allow, and praying with converts. She was terribly lonely and confused during that autumn of 1911. The nocturnal sched-ule and the noise and smoke of Chicago did not agree with the baby. Roberta became more and more frail, her complexion "like transparent wax." When the child stopped eating during the winter, Aimee wired her father and returned to the farm.

Minnie took a leave of absence and returned to Salford. When
she had nursed Aimee and Roberta back to health, they returned
to Chicago, briefly. But Aimee was not able to go it alone.
When a doctor examined the baby, he told her that Roberta
would never be well without "a good home and plenty of fresh
air, warmth, and care."

Aimee returned to New York. There she met Harold
McPherson, a young accountant for a Fifth Avenue restaurant.
He had ambitions.

This was a dark and bewildering period of her life. The exact
circumstances of her meeting the accountant, only six months
her senior, and marrying him, are shrouded in mystery. She
gives three different dates for the marriage, the most likely being
February 28, 1912. Whenever it began, there is no question but
that the marriage ended in bitterness.

Harold Stuart McPherson ("Mack") came to New York from
Providence, Rhode Island, where his mother owned a boarding
house. As far back as anyone could remember, his father and
forefathers had been merchant seamen, and Harold had plenty
of salt in his blood. He was the kind of unflappable, clear-
thinking bruiser to whom you would entrust the life of your
family in any emergency. Square-shouldered, ham-handed, a
solid middleweight, Harold McPherson made Robert Semple
look like Ichabod Crane. Mack was not exactly handsome, with
his prominent jaw, large nose, and straight line for a mouth,
but he exuded a magnetic strength as well as an unmistakable
kindness.

Mack fell in love with Aimee Semple and wanted to marry
her at a time in her life when she was loaded with baggage most
men of twenty-one would not have dreamt of taking on: a sick
daughter, a stubborn passion for her martyred husband, a touch
of malaria. Yet Mack pursued her. And she, with her unerring
instinct for motherhood, ran from Mack until she turned and
caught him. Then she had him for as long as it took to provide
a father for her son and get her career under way.

As a creative thinker he was no match for Aimee. He became,
under her influence, a competent if not an inspiring preacher.
Subsequently he would make his living in the world of business,

as he had promised her when they met. Aimee's daughter Roberta, who knew this man long after Aimee had put him out of her life, insists that he went on loving her mother until the day he died.

But we are getting far ahead of the story. By the spring of 1912 Aimee Semple had become Mrs. Aimee Semple McPherson. She would never acknowledge she married Mack out of any sentiment besides desperation and loneliness. But the photographs of the couple, Roberta's recollections, and their history contradict this. He was lovable, and devoted, and she loved him. Aimee, in her entire life, was never "forced" into anything so serious as a marriage. She went with him to Providence, where Anna McPherson, "Momma Mack," gave them a second-floor bedroom in her boarding house on Claverick Street, overlooking the convent of St. Francis Xavier Academy. Mac got a job as a bank messenger.

In July Aimee was pregnant.

The next three years of her life with Harold McPherson in Providence, as she recounts them, are darkened by her bitter memory of their divorce and her growing tendency to self-dramatize and turn her life story into parable. From now on she identifies the major passages of her life with Bible stories. According to her son Rolf this was not just a historical exercise: she called the first three years of her marriage with Harold McPherson "Nineveh to Tarshish." She saw herself as Jonah who fled "unto Tarshish from the presence of the Lord." Like Jonah, she had an obligation to preach the word of God. When she fled from this and went to live in the shelter of the McPherson boarding house, she wound up, like Jonah, in the belly of the whale. She describes this period as a three-year depression. It was punctuated by tantrums, real and psychosomatic illnesses, and, toward the end, a full-blown nervous breakdown, all because she had turned her back on the Lord.

The truth is more complex, interesting, and credible. Surely she must have yearned for the adventure of the missionary life, as she gazed out upon the greensward of St. Francis Xavier and the young novices going to and fro in their devotions. She has said that she married Mack upon the condition that "if, at any time in my life, He (the Lord) should call me to go to Africa or India, or to the Islands of the Sea, no matter where or when, I must obey God first of all."

The truth is that this woman *never* did for very long what she did not want to do. She wanted to have children, and she was beyond any question an excellent mother. Both her children, Roberta and Rolf, give her the highest marks, without a shred of sentimentality. Aimee Semple McPherson was a first-rate mother who would have had good excuses for being a neglectful mother, if she had wanted them. Those who observed her in the role were frequently amazed she found time for it.

But Aimee's instincts were unerring when it came to these major decisions. If she was ever going to have children, this was the time for it; if there was ever to be a perfect father for Rolf McPherson (who would achieve distinction in his own right), it was the solid, compassionate, and practical Harold McPherson. From Mack the boy inherited a level-headedness and self-possession he would never have got from Robert Semple.

Aimee would never tell the world that her business, during these three years, was child-nurturing, which gave her the emotional maturity to become what she was to become. She would never admit that her efforts to make a home for herself and her children and Harold McPherson were often joyful. But that was true according to those who knew them at the time.

He wanted an old-fashioned housewife and was pleased, for the most part, with her efforts. The mother-in-law was not so pleased. She clearly saw that this was no old-fashioned housewife, but a flamingo in the chicken coop. Aimee sang as she mopped, too sweetly perhaps. She played the piano in the parlor, somewhat to the distraction of the male guests. When out of humor, she sulked, or lost her temper altogether in a voice that could crack a sherry glass.

In the early morning hours of March 23, 1913 Mack took Aimee to the nearby Providence Lying-in Hospital. After giving birth to her son Rolf, Aimee entered a postpartum depression which was at least partially physical in origin. According to her own accounts she would sit on the floor in the corner behind her bed, weeping and trying to pray. When she could shake off her lethargy, she attacked the housekeeping chores with such fury, she wore the polish off the furniture. Then she would fall to weeping and praying again.

Anna McPherson advised her son to rent and furnish their own home for Aimee, thinking that might lift her spirits. With the help of Minnie and Anna, the young family of four was able to move into a lovely house at 34 Benefit Street. But Aimee was no better off in the new house. She addressed herself thus, in the looking glass:

"Now see here, my lady, this will never do! What right have you to fret and pine like this? Just see those shining, polished floors, covered with soft Axminster and Wilton rugs. Just look at that mahogany parlor furniture and the big brass beds . . . Why aren't you glad to have a home like this for the babies, as any mother would be?"

Mack would say: "Well, Aimee—I don't see what more you want. I don't believe anything could make you happy. It must be your disposition."

Her nerves grew so delicate, she could not bear the singing of the tea kettle on the stove, or the sound of voices. She begged the children to speak in whispers. She hated the sunshine and wanted to keep the shutters closed and the shades drawn tightly.

"The doctors said I would lose my reason if something was not done."

Sometime after Rolf's birth she began hearing the voice of God. At first it sounded like the promptings of her own conscience telling her gently to return to the work she was born to do. The more she made excuses, the louder the voice became and the more insistent. It took on a life of its own, became what you might call an auditory hallucination: "Preach the Word! Preach the Word! Will you go? Will you go?" The voice talked to her constantly, like Jiminy Cricket, as she cleaned, or cooked, or fed the children. It was always there, rising from a whisper to a shout and then echoing back into whispers.

In the spring of 1914 she began working the Wednesday night prayer meetings and Sunday night services in the Pentecostal churches in and around Providence. She led Bible study classes and gave talks on her missionary experiences in China. But this did not satisfy the voice. "Go! DO THE WORK OF AN EVANGELIST, Preach the Word! The time is short; I am coming soon." Whether this was an auditory hallucination or the voice of God is known only to Aimee and to God, and God has remained silent upon the matter. Aimee writes that she heard the voice of God until she could not bear it anymore; that it commanded her to do a thing no honorable wife and mother could do in the face of American society of 1914.

So she became deathly ill. Along with her neurasthenia she developed "heart trouble." She began to hemorrhage from her stomach.

In those days the treatment of choice for hysterical women with internal bleeding was a hysterectomy. The surgical techniques were haphazard. Aimee went under the knife several times during this period, the surgeons extracting one organ and another, here an ovary, there an appendix. Each time she returned from the hospital a little worse, more nervous, more depressed. The scalpel so crisscrossed her abdomen, she would never fully regain control of her lower stomach muscles. She became convinced that God had sentenced her to a slow execution because she had strayed from His way.

So she begged God to let her die.

It is well known the human body cannot survive in direct opposition to the will of the spirit. Harold McPherson was no jailor. He hadn't the will to hold her for five minutes. Aimee was her own guard in the stronghold of traditional marriage, a structure so despotic that she nearly died in it.

In her memoirs she makes high drama of the deathbed scene. Her mother had been summoned by telegram. The doctors and nurses gathered in a conference room to explain to Minnie the scientific reasons her daughter had to die. Remarkably, she does not recall the presence of any other family member, as if this scene was a private matter for the Kennedy women alone.

Something in Minnie refused to let go of the promise God had made concerning her daughter.

"Brokenly she wept and prayed, reviewing and doubling her vows to God to help in every way to get me back into the work and keep me there . . ." The nurses wept. The doctor cleared his throat as Aimee came out of the ether, muttering he had never witnessed such a scene: the dying woman was preaching, calling souls to her in the weird falsetto of patients under gaseous anesthetics which tighten the vocal cords. Three interns carried her "into the separate room where people were taken to die."

At two o'clock in the morning the attending nurse took fright. The patient could not catch her breath; the air seemed to stop high in her throat. Aimee recalls that the white-robed nurse holding her hand seemed to be receding. Then there was the utter darkness she was certain was death's passageway, in which she heard someone, maybe her mother, maybe the nurse, say:

"She's going."

And then she heard that other voice, the insistent voice that had given her no rest since the birth of her son, saying:

"NOW WILL YOU GO?"

And Aimee knew she had to go one way or the other.

With what she believed to be her last breath, the would-be corpse whispered that she *would* go, and blacked out for a few seconds.

When she opened her eyes, the pain was gone. Aimee took a deep breath, and then another, and another. The patient was able to turn over in the bed without pain, much to the nurse's alarm.

In two weeks she was up and well. "That great white whale, the operating table, had thrown me up on the shore. The Lord had spared my life under a definite promise that I would serve Him."

In the spring of 1915 Mack was transferred to the night shift at the Industrial Bank and Trust. Minnie was back on the farm in Canada, and Aimee wired her for money.

One night while Anna McPherson slept, her restless daughter-in-law called a taxi, bundled the children in warm clothes, and sped away to the train station. There they boarded the 11:55 train to Toronto, where they met the connection to Ingersoll.

Harold McPherson returned in the morning to find his wife had left him.

THE OLD-TIME POWER

No matter what the world thought of Aimee Semple Mc-
Pherson, she took comfort in the thought that God, and Minnie
Kennedy, were on her side. As soon as Aimee arrived at the
farm, Minnie informed her she was to leave the next day for a
Pentecostal camp meeting in Berlin (as Kitchener was called
before World War I). Minnie had given up her place to her
daughter as soon as she received her telegram. Now she planned
to stay at the farm and take care of the children. It had all been
settled.

Soon Aimee would be whole again, but not until she was
actively "on the path." Before leaving for Kitchener the next
morning, she dispatched this extraordinary telegram to her husband: "I have tried to walk your way and have failed. Won't
you come now and walk my way? I am sure we will be happy."

She had tried; and he would try, but not just yet. Harold
McPherson would not pursue his wife until she had got to
Mount Forest in the summer of 1915, where we left her standing
on the chair. By that time Aimee was so far along "her way,"
Mack would never catch up.

On the way to the little city of white tents under the forest
trees of Kitchener, Aimee was full of doubts and misgivings.
She felt "leaked out" and conscience-bound to explain to her
old friends why she was not where she once was, spiritually.
It seemed to her she might never regain the power she had
known in partnership with Robert Semple.

The folks' welcoming smiles and handshakes, the sight of
their enthusiasm as they worshiped, immediately ignited the
passion that had been smoldering in her. Toward the end of
the prayer meetings there is always an altar call when people
seeking baptism, or with special needs, move to the front. There
the ministers pray with them, or lay hands upon them.

Aimee bowed at the altar. And when the brother in charge told her to lift up her hands and pray aloud as she had once told others to do, she felt that first she must beg for forgiveness. But no sooner did she begin to beg than she heard the voice of God. He was telling her, very clearly, to forget it.

"Such love," she recalls, "was more than my heart could bear. Before I knew it I was on my back in the straw, under the power."

Aimee was restored. The next thing she knew, she was speaking in tongues, laughing and weeping and shaking. A crowd gathered around her. A brother from London had a message in tongues, and Aimee was inspired with the interpretation. An old Mennonite preacher, who had been seeking baptism for years, was kneeling at the far end of the altar. Aimee recognized him. She had known his brother, and "prayed him through" to the baptism before she left for China.

Now she felt drawn to the old Mennonite. Walking upon her knees, her hands outstretched, Aimee invoked the power of the Spirit. The man fell over and was speaking in tongues as he hit the ground.

"The old-time power and anointing for praying with seekers rested upon me," she recalled.

This is a peculiar gift, difficult to understand if you are not Pentecostal. We may compare it to the power to induce hypnosis, as long as we respect the distinctions: we must not profane the sacrament we cannot understand. The hypnotist works at breaking down conscious defenses in order to introduce a suggestion to the subconscious mind. This is an act of individual will. The evangelist sees himself as a medium of God's will. He draws upon his own faith to inspire faith in others. The gift for inducing automatisms, tongue-speaking, and trembling in the seekers of baptism, is emotional and histrionic. Believers will explain it as a wealth, a richness of faith which spills over into other lives. Aimee surely had wealth of this sort. But she had another thing, the powerful will of a great hypnotist, which acted like a step-up transformer for God's will. And then, she was a beautiful vessel, a harmonious medium.

By and by we will look closely at her eyes and hands which

have become, at age twenty-five, the perfect instruments of a sorceress for the faith.

During the weeks that followed at the camp meeting in Kitchener, those upon whom Aimee laid her hands received the baptism of the Holy Spirit, right and left. Sometimes she attended the altar services until two in the morning, then arose again at dawn for the morning meeting. When she was not praying, she washed dishes and waited tables. She played the piano, she led the choir. When the visiting ministers went home, and the local preacher lost his voice, Aimee did the preaching. She had not been so happy since the day she married Robert Semple.

Elizabeth Sharpe of Mount Forest heard Aimee preach in Kitchener. Later she watched the young evangelist praying in a tent with five teenage girls who were driven to religious ecstasy. And God spoke to Elizabeth Sharpe (according to her letters), saying, "There is the one for your work, the one I shall use in the revival I promised you." At once she invited Aimee to Mount Forest, and "the next day she [Aimee] received the assurance and confirmation from the Lord that she was to come."

These women were operating and communicating through a spiritual "ground of being" well described by Julian Jaynes in *The Origins of Consciousness in the Breakdown of the Bicameral Mind*. Before the Renaissance, and in primitive cultures, men and women did not rely upon a conscience to make moral choices. They simply appealed to the voice of God within them. With the decline of religion and the rise of individualism, the voice of God fell to a whisper. Then it grew silent altogether, except in the minds of a few saints and schizophrenics.

Yet in 1915 Aimee Semple McPherson was hearing the voice of God loud and clear whenever she listened for it. She had recaptured the primitive inspiration of the "bicameral mind." For the next decade she would not make a significant move without a command from God.

God told her to go to Mount Forest.

At home she found letters from Providence. Mack demanded she return "to wash the dishes," "take care of the house," and "act like other women."

"I had put my hand to the Gospel plow," she remembers, "and I could not turn back."

MOUNT FOREST, 1915

Robert Semple once told her, "Whenever in doubt, pray." The crowd that gathered at the street corner, waiting to see if and when the beautiful woman would come down off her chair, was held partly by her visible will, which had taken the form of prayer.

With arms uplifted she was praying that God might give her the power to summon enough people to fill the Victory Mission down the street. Aimee understood she could not save souls one or two at a time. Her brand of conversion required a dozen or more people in a closed space.

Aimee was praying that her own life might be justified ultimately by the number of lives she saved. The prayer pumped from her heart and into her temples and then on out and up to Heaven, from which it descended, with increased force, upon the crowd.

The crowd, as I said, was held only in part by Aimee's will. They had a will of their own, sometimes called "mob instinct," really a collective clairvoyance. The people of Mount Forest sensed something was going to happen, something out of the ordinary, and their purpose was not only to witness but enact the event.

For many people the twentieth century was a nightmare from which only an ecstatic religious experience could awaken them. The controversy over Darwin had further defined the painful conflict between the rational moderns and those who needed "the old time religion" as an anchor in the tempestuous new century. History shows that the charismatic and premillennial religions have the greatest appeal to the dispossessed. These include immigrants, slaves, victims of political oppression and drug addiction, disenfranchised women and agrarian people herded into industrial cities. Between 1890 and 1910 the United States population grew from 63 million to 92 million. More than half of the increase was owing to immigration. By 1920 the population had climbed to 105 million and the census showed for the first time that the farm population stood below fifty percent of the total.

So by 1915 a quarter of the population of the United States and Canada would fall into the category of the dispossessed— immigrants and farmers wandering the streets of town in pursuit of urban comforts and opportunities. In farm towns in Kentucky and Maryland, and in the factory neighborhoods of Chicago and Baltimore, Aimee's revival would catch fire like a box of dry tinder.

Mount Forest in 1915 was not so volatile. Yet, in the category of the dispossessed it had women, adolescents, and a number of farm folks emotionally starved by Victorian social structures and the cold formality of intellectual religion.

These people were ready for action.

And so Elizabeth Sharpe invited Aimee to come and see what she could do. After two nights of preaching to an empty hall, Aimee suggested they take to the streets and "sound an alarm," which led to her silent theatrics on the street corner.

Even with her eyes closed Aimee could feel the critical mass of the crowd when it grew to be fifty spectators gaping and hooting and jostling. When at last a man touched her arm to test the "cataleptic" theory of her immobility, the young woman opened her eyes and looked around her. The eyes were the color of newly turned earth.

"People," she shouted, leaping off the chair, "come and follow me, quick."

Hooking her arm through the back of the chair, she pushed through the crowd and started running back down Main Street. The people chased her, boys first, then men and women, past the grocery and the dressmaker's, past the bank and the print shop. They followed her right through the open door of the

Victory Mission. There was just enough room for all to be seated.

"Lock the door," she whispered to the usher. "Lock the door, and keep it locked till I get through."

––––––

From that day forth, Aimee recalls, she never had any trouble drawing a crowd.

That night she preached for forty minutes to an audience of fifty. The next night there were as many standing outside listening and trying to get a glimpse of her as could fit in the hall. So someone suggested she preach outside on the lawn behind the mission. The yard swept down to Sister Sharpe's porch, which Aimee arranged as a pulpit. The piano was trundled out on the grass. Farmers unhooked the lanterns from their wagons and tied them up in the trees all around. For a penitent form, Aimee used the steps of the porch.

They came from all over the countryside to hear the woman preacher. Families came in wagons and on foot, on horseback and bicycles and in buggies. Nightly Aimee preached outdoors under the stars to broad-shouldered farmers in denim overalls who answered the altar call. They came with their wives dressed in their Sunday best, weeping "to give their hearts to the Lord." By the end of the week the crowd had grown until she was preaching to more than five hundred.

To hear her tell it years later, with gentle humor and a sense of innocent triumph, Aimee's debut in Mount Forest was full of grace from first to last, as the good-hearted rustics gave in to the Lord. You would think she had presided, in calm and dignity, over the peaceful conversion of a country village that wanted nothing more.

What actually occurred, to draw such crowds to the little town, amounted to guerrilla warfare in the realm of the spirit. Aimee said later:

A woman preacher was a novelty. At the time when I began my ministry, women were well in the background of life in Canada and the United States . . . Orthodox ministers, many of whom

disapproved even of men evangelists such as Moody, Spurgeon,
Tunda and the rest chiefly because they used novel evangelistic
methods, disapproved all the more of a woman minister. Especially
was this true when my meetings departed from the funereal, sep-
ulchrelike ritual of appointed Sundays . . .

As an understatement, this ranks with the best epigrams of
Calvin Coolidge. A female preacher in 1915 was, to many people, a horror. To the Episcopalians of the time, Aimee's meetings appeared like orgies scripted by the Witch of Endor.

From the moment she arrived in Mount Forest, Saturday
evening, she rocked the sepulcher. She found Sister Elizabeth's
house full of young people waiting for Sister Aimee. They began
to pray, and sing hymns, and speak in tongues. Sister Elizabeth's
son, ten years old, fell lengthwise across the body of another
young man slain in the spirit, and began to speak in a language
he had never learned. Soon after this her younger boy, only
seven years old, received the Spirit, and began to chatter in a
language Aimee readily identified as Chinese.

Sometime that night they slept.

During the next few days Aimee held meetings in the Victory
Mission. They were sparsely attended, yet made an impression.
At one of these, Sister Elizabeth got up a head of steam in
offering her testimony. She began to sing in one breath and
testify loudly with the next. "The mighty Comforter came upon
me with power and set the joybells ringing." The joybells had
a stirring effect on the young man standing next to her. He
began to shout, "Glory to Jesus" in response to her "Hallelujah"; every time she yelled, he yelled a little louder. It was a
shouting match without anger, a spiritual duet that delighted
Sister Aimee. She dearly loved such commotion in the name of
Jesus. The young man began to vibrate and roll his eyes. When
he had turned up his voice as loud as it would go, he began to
shake and tremble. This shaking and trembling Sister Elizabeth
encouraged with her wide-eyed cries of hallelujah.

This frightened some people, who were used to quiet church
services. They ran out into the street, crying that the young
man named Jim had been hypnotized by the fanatic women.

In a few minutes the hall was full of infidels, including a photographer, printers and compositors, a dressmaker and a grocer; they all wanted to know what was going on in the Victory Mission. It did not look good for local trade. A physician dragged Jim off his chair, still trembling and shouting. He called for ice, which he wrapped in a cloth. Opening the young man's shirt, he applied the icy compress to his heart "to keep the fire from burning," but the fellow would not be calm or silent.

The boy's parents were sent for, and informed their son was dying. While Elizabeth Sharpe kept up her part of the opera, and Aimee sang and prayed, another doctor arrived. He pinned Jim's shoulders to the floor of the Victory Mission by kneeling on them. This stopped him from shaking, but seemed to make him cry out all the louder, "Glory, glory, glory," until Jim's father appeared on the scene, and collared and dragged his hysterical son home.

This was the first time in Sister Elizabeth's memory that the Holy Spirit had descended in the mission hall or in any public place in Mount Forest. Shortly thereafter Sister Aimee filled the mission with her "chair trick," and within a week the crowds were ruining the lawn of Sister Elizabeth's house. When at last Aimee took up a collection, it amounted to sixty-five dollars. This gave her an idea.

Hearing of a man in the next town who had a tent for sale, she boarded the train and went to see him.

He told her the tent had cost him five hundred dollars but she could have it for a hundred and fifty.

"I can pay no more than sixty-five," she said.

"Well, lady, I'll tell you what I'd do for you. Seein' as how you're a preacher, I'll let you have it for sixty-five on one condition."

The condition was that she buy the tent in the bag, without putting him through the trouble of unpacking it for inspection.

Back in Mount Forest she summoned the faithful to help her "get my canvas cathedral out of the bag," and they laid it out on the lawn. The tent was pathetic, full of rips and tears and eaten with mildew from one end to the other. The women went to work with needle and thread, and by evening they had got it up, with much difficulty. For this was the old push-pole type of canvas tent, which required not only great strength but dexterity to hoist the heavy poles into position. Making it taut in one place, driving in the tent stakes with a sledgehammer and securing the guy ropes, Aimee would find the tent sagging at the other end. With blistered hands, and perspiration-damp hair sticking to her cheeks, she would start on another end. Back and forth she went, until she had raised the flimsy sanctuary.

This was her first tent, the first of dozens she would pack and unpack from Ontario to Florida and from Providence to Los Angeles. In rain and snow and heavy winds, she would drive stakes until she developed a lumberjack's strength and the expertise of a circus roustabout, and until there was no tent on earth that would hold the crowds that followed her.

She got this tent up in time for the Sunday morning service. The women had decorated her canvas with religious mottoes and garlands of smilax. And Aimee admired it "as proudly as the Archbishop of Canterbury treading the aisles of his Cathedral."

The canvas, thirty by sixty feet, was filled to capacity when she mounted the pulpit. The tent flaps lifted in a stiffening wind. Looking out over the hundreds of people in the shelter of the tent she had worked so hard to raise, she was overjoyed.

Halfway into her sermon the canvas sighed, and then shrieked as it ripped from the pole directly over her head. The wind bore down on Aimee's end of the tent; the whole canvas slowly began to slide. The crowd lost interest in the sermon, their eyes fixed upon the billowing canvas about to collapse on the meeting.

Aimee believed that Satan had come to break up her service.

"In those early days of evangelistic enthusiasm everything was either the Lord or the Devil to me."

The memory quoted above is a serious religious reflection. It expresses a primitive dualism we do not associate with our thoughtful contemporaries. And this was the young woman who at fourteen had debated Darwinian evolution with an archbishop.

What was it about this dualistic world-view that appealed to her? The belief that the world is a battleground between the forces of light and darkness, between God and the Devil, is ancient and universally compelling. It springs from the very earth we inhabit, with its seasons and cycles, its rhythms of birth and death, growth and decay, love and conflict.

Perhaps no more need be said of Aimee's dualism than that she was a farmer's daughter with mud on her heels. She had seen cows and pigs in rut and horses shot for mercy and chickens running headless in the barnyard leaving circles of blood. Recently it was discovered that young Aimee was a witness at a murder trial, the rather grisly murder of a neighboring farmer by his crazed wife. This, too, must have been important in framing her moral universe. The extremes of harmony and violence might have presented themselves to her as the work of a God constantly tested by the treachery of Satan.

There is one more thing' to be said of Aimee's dualism and the battle between the Lord and the Devil. This is the theology of power, the rhetoric of crowd control, and it has been thus from the dawn of civilization. There may be wiser beliefs, but none so dynamic. A crowd is not moved by logic or subtlety. A crowd is not moved by noble ideals, purity of purpose, or by the everlasting truth. The crowd of humankind is moved by raw passion, which catches fire instantly upon the identification of a villain. The statesman or preacher who can describe to his audience a simple conflict between themselves and some enemy will have started the engine to drive a crowd where he pleases.

TRIUMPH

She was not about to have her first tent meeting broken up by anyone, not even the Prince of Darkness.

The wind howled, the canvas shrieked and ripped near the axle pole. Air sighed out through the rent above her head. The audience forgot Aimee and looked to heaven.

"Stop!" she shouted louder than the wind. Lifting her arm, she pointed toward the top of the tent. "Stop in the name of Jesus, I command *you* to stop right where you are, till this day's meetings are over."

She was commanding the Devil. Now if the wind had thumbed its nose at Aimee and blown the tent down on her worshipers, this would be a different story. In the stifling confusion no one would have remembered her furious command to Satan. But a roped tent seam caught on a nail in the center pole and held; the wind, as if it had someplace more important to go, passed on in silence.

The audience, stunned, was left in the natural quandary of down-to-earth eyewitnesses of a coincidence who are sorely tempted to call it a miracle. Easy enough for Aimee to call it "the Lord" and go on with her sermon. Someday she would preside over out-and-out miracles, and she knew this was not one of them. Yet she was a showman of the first order. If a crowd suspected she had influenced the very elements of nature, she would not intrude upon their beliefs by presuming to correct them.

At the rear of the tent was Sister Elizabeth's porch. Her parlor became the "tarrying room" where folks stayed after the service to seek the baptism of the Holy Spirit. During the main service Aimee had wonderful visions, and "the Lord gave us many songs through her while she was in the Spirit." Her voice was clear and strong, and she could improvise at the piano. Sister

Elizabeth spoke in rhapsodies of tongues, and Aimee interpreted. These things were so amazing and inspiring that more and more people flocked to Mount Forest from towns and cities all over Ontario. Every train delivered a fresh cargo of souls to be saved; carriages and motorcars lined the narrow streets and made traffic jams at corners, frightening the horses.

But the strange transformation of their town crier and bell ringer, Monkey Abe, was what finally drove the town fathers to take action against the revivalists. Monkey Abe was one of those characters so essential to the mental balance of small communities years ago—the scapegoat and laughingstock of Mount Forest.

He was a stumbling drunk with long arms and short legs and simian features that earned him his nickname. The mayor gave him a handbell and the charge to ring it upon the noon and dinner hour, and for public meetings. They gave him a few pennies to spend at the saloon. And folks would feed him table scraps they would leave in a bowl high on the porch, where dogs couldn't reach it. He was frequently bruised and cut, as men out of humor in the saloon used him as a punching bag, or as a football when he was sleeping. Everyone loved him more than they understood because he was always there where he was needed, drunk or sober, ringing the hour; he was always where he was supposed to be, to be blamed or punched, pitied or laughed at or used as a bad example for children who did not obey their parents and teachers.

Aimee, of course, realized at once this was a job for Jesus. Monkey Abe had taken on the sins of a whole people who had not the slightest idea of what they owed him. For years the bell ringer had endured three running sores upon his ankle, which may have been staphylococcus or worse. Untreated, they made him limp, which may have suited the public's crude sense of the picturesque. But the doctors of Mount Forest could think of nothing to do for the bell ringer except cut away the foot just above the ankle, and get him a good crutch.

Like a wounded animal with an instinct for the hand of sympathy, Monkey Abe limped to the Victory Mission. He had heard something about the healing power of God, and came

begging the women for "mission ointment." They told him
they had no mission ointment but the healing ointment of Calvary. All began to pray, laying hands on the poor drunk. They
called down the name of Jesus and the Holy Spirit to cast out
the demons that had been gnawing at Abe's ankle.

Meanwhile somebody doused a cloth with "oil." (It may have
been old-fashioned "bag-balm," the cure-all for milk cows,
laced with iodine or gentian violet.) They wrapped the leg and
ankle in the cloth all the while they trembled, and rubbed Monkey Abe, and chanted the name of Jesus. Then they sent him
on his way to the saloon, where he might ponder the day's
events in the peace of familiar surroundings.

According to Sister Elizabeth's account, Monkey Abe returned to the mission the next day, pointed to his bandage and
complained it felt as if little needles were pricking all through
his lower leg.

When they unwrapped the bandage, there was a chorus of
shouting and praise, because they saw "he was perfectly healed,
and all the blackness was gone—he walked without a limp."

This gave the town crier something to think about, and a
new cry as he went his rounds ringing the hour: "Hear ye! Hear
ye! I have given my heart to Christ! Come down to the revival
tonight and hear Sister McPherson preach the Christ who saved
even me . . ."

Everyone heard of Monkey Abe's healing. They would soon
learn about his conversion, which was so dramatic and vociferous, it threatened to undo Mount Forest's social structure,
which had always rested upon his place at the bottom of it.

Sister Elizabeth was in the kitchen about 10:30 on a Saturday
morning. Her hands were in flour, preparing to bake. Another
lady, in an apron and dustcap, was sweeping, when someone
came to tell them to hurry right away to the tent. Sister Elizabeth's husband Mr. Sharpe and the town crier had been ar-
ranging benches and chairs for the meeting when the Spirit fell
like a tower. Now they were flat out, the two men, one on one
side of the altar and one on the other. Sister Elizabeth took one
look at her husband and began to shout "Glory to God," and
the woman with the broom dropped it so she could wave her

arms in benediction. The men were twitching and babbling in the Spirit. Then came Sister Elizabeth's mother, and the preacher, and Sister Elizabeth's sister, and Aimee Semple McPherson; and as each person passed under the flap of the tent, he or she was knocked down by the power of the Spirit, and hit the dirt with shouts and chants and moaning, until there was a wonderful racket.

The photographer could not get his customers to hold their pose; nor would the dressmaker's customers hold still for their fitting. They kept running to the window to see who had been killed. The printers and compositors in the pressroom were so distracted, no work was getting done. All these people descended on the tent in the forenoon, bringing the police, who summoned the doctors and ministers whose charge it was to determine "the cause of all these people being mesmerized."

By the time the tent had filled with infidels, the "power" had lifted from everyone but the town crier. Evidently the poor drunk had suffered so many years lacking God's grace, he was not about to let go of it now that he had it by the tail. And he possessed a seven-league voice after years of crying the hour. He lay on the ground under the altar, and rolled, and jerked, and danced as well as he could without getting up, all the while praising Jesus in the rhythm he had always used to tell the time. And there wasn't a thing anybody could do to stop him. He had been theirs for years, and now he belonged to Jesus.

A crowd was a crowd, as far as Aimee was concerned. When the tent began to fill with people, she got in the pulpit and began preaching, taking as her text the prophet Joel (Acts 2:16–18). Joel held the precise answer to the question on everyone's lips: What in the name of God or the Devil was going on here in Mount Forest, Ontario? This is that which was spoken by the prophet Joel: "And it shall come to pass in the last days, saith God, I will pour out of my Spirit upon all flesh; and your sons and your daughters shall prophesy . . . and on my servants and on my handmaidens I will pour out in those days of my Spirit; and they shall prophesy."

Aimee preached, and drove her celebrants forward in their devotions, over the vocal opposition of hecklers and pharisees.

The riot continued until mid-afternoon, when a policeman handed Sister Elizabeth a summons. She was ordered by the court to appear before the magistrate that evening at 7:30 (the announced meeting time) and give cause why she should not be held for disturbing the peace of Mount Forest by "praising Jesus with a loud voice."

She was honored, she was overwhelmed. Nothing short of the Second Coming could have delighted her more. "Oh what glory filled my soul when I took that paper from the police constable for the sake of Jesus. The Lord was good to me; I danced around the constable in the Spirit. This brought Sister McPherson, who, when she saw me dancing, began to dance around him also. He went away remarking to others: 'We cannot do anything with these women.' "

This was true. The dam had broken and the flood was loose. Sister Sharpe would remark, in a rare personal reflection, "I hitherto had possessed a man-fearing spirit, but I praise the Lord for sending Sister McPherson into my life . . . she taught me how to praise the Lord and to get out of bondage to man . . ."

They could not do anything with these women. The Lord seemed to be with Sister Elizabeth Sharpe in the courtroom. She faced her accusers—mostly people from the Methodist church where she had been a worker for years before her conversion. Arguments in the courtroom focused upon the authority of the Pentecostal inspiration, upon whether it came from the Holy Spirit or the Devil. The tradesmen, for the most part, believed it was the Devil in Sisters McPherson and Sharpe that had disturbed the peace, and cut into profits, though the hotelkeepers had no complaints, nor did the Catholic expressman whose business had doubled. The Devil might have won the argument had it not been for the Reverend John Clark, the Methodist minister himself. Aimee was preaching to an uproarious crowd just outside the courtroom, invoking the verses of Joel, "*This is that* . . ." while the Reverend Clark convinced the magistrate that the Devil had no hand in the riots of Mount Forest, and indeed these were holy women and "this was of God."

Sometime in the midst of this drama, Aimee Semple Mc-

Pherson looked out over the heads of the crowd and saw her husband, Harold. He had come all the way from Providence to bring her home. Once he saw his wife, he thought better of it. She was radiant, more lovely than he had ever seen her. Before nightfall he had given in to the power of the Holy Spirit, he was speaking in tongues. By the time they left Mount Forest together, he was her fellow servant in Christ, though she would always be a few steps ahead of him.

2

HER RISE TO FAME

CORONA, NEW YORK, 1916

The Lord called Aimee back to Providence for the autumn of 1916 so that she might quietly prepare for a seven-year campaign. It would be an odyssey such as no woman had ever undertaken.

Flush with the excitement of her victory in Mount Forest, she aspired to get the whole of humankind under her tent. She would break up the household on Benefit Street her husband had lovingly made for her, sell off the furniture and pots and pans, and hit the sawdust trail.

Her daughter Roberta stayed in Salford, where she would live with Minnie for the next two years; her son Rolf lived with grandmother McPherson in Providence. Aimee says that during this first leg of her journey "the enemy" was still testing her, trying to draw her back, and it is clear she means her domestic responsibilities.

These are the years of her rise to fame. Her tent-show triumphs would bring the evangelist corporate power, and responsibility she did not seek or desire, when her religious dreams came to earth in a concrete temple in Los Angeles in 1923. But from 1916 until the Temple's dedication, Aimee's prodigious gifts flourished under optimal conditions. It is this period that chiefly interests historians of religion, medicine, and social psychology. For seven years she had maximum freedom to develop her potential as an evangelist and healer, and the results were astonishing if not miraculous.

By train and automobile the young preacher crisscrossed the United States, coast to coast, six times, and made the round-trip journey from New England to Florida twice. We believe Aimee was the first woman (with her mother and children) to cross America in an automobile without a man's help. Between 1917 and 1923 she preached in more than a hundred cities and towns, staying from one or two nights in towns to more than a month in cities like Philadelphia, Baltimore, and Denver. Later in life she would boast she had given more sermons than any preacher who ever lived. After the Temple was built, she preached twenty sermons or more a week. During the early period we are now considering she probably faced four thousand different audiences—from a handful of passersby on a street corner to twenty thousand in the Denver coliseum.

Like an athlete in the heat of competition or an artist absorbed in the act of painting or composing, from 1916 to 1923 Aimee Semple McPherson emptied herself entirely into her evangelism. She was what she did during those years, nothing more and nothing less. She was driven to the point of obsession, and thoroughly inspired.

Roberta Salter says that the first two years, before Minnie Kennedy joined Aimee in Florida, the young preacher traveled "on faith." (Aimee's daughter, Roberta, married Harry Salter in 1941.) She means, literally, that Aimee wandered up and down the Eastern seaboard on impulse, without a budget or a plan. It nearly drove Mack crazy, because she preferred God's help to her husband's. He begged her to let him sign up for day labor or go fishing for dinner when they were flat broke in some town in Georgia. No, she would say, God will provide. And He did—someone would come to the tent with a basket of food or a bag of clothes. The next day the tent would fill with the faithful, who would take up a collection, which would carry them through to . . . where? She followed the weather, and she went where she was invited. She listened for the Lord's instructions, and she watched the world and heavens for a sign. A newspaper would blow across the floor of the tent, showing the phrase "Long Branch" in a headline; the next day she would break camp and head for Long Branch, New Jersey.

While she was in Onset Bay, Massachusetts, she began to hear the word "corona" as she prayed. The word appeared before her eyes as if it had been written in bold type upon the air. Aimee had been praying for a typewriter, so she thought at first that the trademark Corona was appearing in answer to her prayer. But when she saw the postmark Corona, Long

Island in a pile of invitations, she hurriedly tore open the envelope.

The letter was hardly legible, the laborious handwriting of a semiliterate or someone whose age or health had made him unaccustomed to holding a pen.

> Dear Sister McPherson:
>
> For two years I have been lying on my face before God beseeching him to send a revival to Corona.
>
> He has now revealed to me that a mighty city-sweeping revival is to be sent through your ministry. Souls shall be converted in great numbers, saints receive the Pentecostal baptism of the Holy Ghost, and miracles of healing be wrought here at your hands.
>
> My home is open to you. Your room is all prepared. Come immediately. Expecting great things of the Lord.

The letter, as Aimee reprints it, is unsigned, to represent a thousand such letters the evangelist received during her career. The invitation, Aimee's response, and the events that followed in Corona establish a pattern she would follow up and down the Eastern seaboard for two years, until the crowds were so huge, she would have to submit to a touring schedule.

She did not recognize the name or the address. Until Aimee picked the letter out of a stack of correspondence, she did not know the place existed. Yet she packed up and headed for Long Island in November of 1916.

The street was in a colored neighborhood. Aimee Semple McPherson of Salford, Ontario had not seen half a dozen black faces in her life. Now they were staring wide-eyed from street corners and stoops and second-story windows at the pale young woman walking along through the streets with her suitcase in one hand and an open letter in the other.

At last she found the house and rapped on the door. It opened upon an enormous black woman who completely filled the doorway. The following quotes in dialect are from Aimee's own account.

"Is y'all Sistah McPherson been preachin in a big tent?"

Aimee admitted that she was. Whereupon the black woman opened wide her arms and crushed Aimee against her bosom.

Her job was done, for the most part, though she would provide lodging for the preacher, up the narrow staircase in an attic bedroom. A neighbor had helped write the letter. Aimee never did learn how the woman had found her.

Much to her dismay, Aimee discovered that her hostess had no further plans. As the woman spread blackberry jam on a slice of bread, Aimee asked in what church the campaign was to be held.

"Why bless yo' heart honey, ah don't know nuffin 'bout dat . . . Yo know more bout dem things than ah do!"

"But, Mammy, who is supporting and sponsoring the meeting?"

"Ah reckon I 'bout de only one yo'all can depend on right now; there be plenty mo' when de meetin's get started."

As Aimee ate her bread and jam, she looked at the woman in disbelief and weariness, and asked her once again if there were no preparations.

"Preparations! Preparations!" she burst out. "Deed dere is preparations, chile! Preparations aplenty. Didn't ah tell you I'se been a'prayin fo dis heah meeting for mor'n two years? Ah's got it all prayed through now."

She had it *all prayed through*. Aimee had entered a world where the borderline between thought and reality was obscure. Her faith had led her into a channel of life where faith could move mountains, and did. The black hostess of Corona was the first of many spiritual helpers whose prayers would move Aimee along the path that would lead eventually to California. As she prayed with the woman after the meal, she observed: "Here was one who communed with the Master as friend communed with friend. She looked like a radiant black angel."

———

The radiant black angel sent her guest into the streets of Corona to look for a meeting place, with the warm assurance that the Lord "has prepared a place awaitin somewhere."

It was not immediately evident. For several days Aimee walked the streets knocking on doors without finding an available hall, theater, store front, or vacant lodge room. A saloon keeper offered his back parlor, which she declined. At last she got an invitation from the pastor of the Swedish Methodist Episcopal Church to conduct some meetings there.

She preached the night she was invited, to a half-empty church, and announced she would be in the pulpit the next afternoon. She so moved them that the next afternoon the church was full; and that night it was overflowing to the streets. Local ministers warned people to stay away from these wild Pentecostals, though Aimee had been on her best behavior, preaching only in the mildest way in the beginning.

But as the crowd grew, she heated up. One week later, a gentleman who had been a Sunday school teacher for many years glided up the aisle during the altar call, his eyes fixed upon the comely preacher, transported by her invitation to be baptized in the Holy Spirit. His tongue loosened, and through his lips the Spirit gave utterance. A prominent society lady followed him, and several dozen members of the Swedish Methodist Episcopal Church gathered around the inspired pair, to bathe in their reflected glory.

Aimee noticed these folks were "stiff," fearful and self-conscious. Their ministers had cautioned them against the power of hypnotism. So Aimee was careful not to touch anyone or to speak directly to the seekers. She just knelt by her own chair near the pulpit and prayed in an incantatory manner for the Holy Spirit to descend on the church.

"Oh Lord, send the power. Lord, honor your Word just now."

Mrs. John Lake, a woman widely respected in the Christian community, rose from the altar, moved by what she had seen but outwardly composed as she walked down the aisle. As she took her seat beside Mr. Lake, she felt a strange weight in her head that caused her to rest upon his shoulder. Someone shouted that Mrs. Lake had fainted. But Aimee knew different, and kept up her prayer mantra from the front of the church: "Lord send the power. Baptize her just now." A crowd gathered around the unconscious woman and someone ran for a glass of water.

Meanwhile Mrs. Lake's lungs began to fill and heave, and the chin on her chest quivered and then lifted. A sound came through her lips that seemed to be coming from far off. The vowels took on consonants that formed phrases, and the phrases strung along the music of the vowels in strange sentences. On and on she spoke, and her face seemed to shine with an inner light.

"Oh isn't it wonderful, marvelous!" someone said. "How I wish I had the same experience!"

If the distinguished matron Mrs. John Lake could have this experience, then so might anyone. News spread through Corona, Long Island. A member of the Free Gospel Church went to his pastor, W. K. Bouton, to tell him of the amazing woman who was preaching in the little Swedish church. "You ought to hear her, she speaks in other tongues and it seems the Spirit of God is wonderfully using her." Pastor Bouton scowled. He warned the parishioner to avoid the meetings or become tangled in a bondage he would regret. A woman came to him with the same news, and he warned her likewise. Two more came a day later to tell how one of his flock had received the blessing of Spirit baptism and spoke in other tongues. Pastor Bouton lost patience. "If she does this kind of thing, she will have to leave our church, for she cannot come to our church with this nonsense."

Crowds in and around the Swedish church grew in size and enthusiasm as more and more seekers received the baptism. Members of Pastor Bouton's Free Gospel Church kept coming to him, saying he "must hear this woman."

At last, W. K. Bouton sat with his arms folded in the last pew of the Swedish church and listened to the rich tones of the young woman's voice. She had a way about her. "Sister Aimee is honest, and she sure knows her Bible," he told his wife when he went home. Mrs. Bouton eyed her husband narrowly. "Now you look out, or you will be ensnared in these 'latter-day' errors," she warned him.

But the Baptist minister found himself in Aimee's presence the next night, vastly interested. When the beautiful woman spoke of the churches' falling away, he found himself saying Amen almost without realizing it; likewise when she raised her lovely dark eyes and spoke of the Lord's coming, he said Amen;

and he said it when she cried of the tribulation that would fall upon the whole earth.

"Amen," said W. K. Bouton, and at times he was uncertain whether it was his own voice or the congregation's that had echoed through his larynx.

When he heard Sister Aimee preach on the text of Joel 1:4, that settled it. This was the famous "Lost and Restored" sermon Aimee first delivered *ex tempore* as a girl in London, England. When it was over, Pastor Bouton came forward and eagerly took her hand. "Sister," he said, "I wish to extend to you an invitation to come to my church and give the same message. You are crowded-out here. Our church is considerably larger . . ."

He had not consulted the trustees of the Baptist church. The first night she mounted the pulpit, the trustees and a number of other visiting ministers, clad in clerical robes, ranged behind her on the dais. The large church was packed from the pulpit to the door that opened upon the crowded street outside. The windows were open all around, and people stood outside on boxes, craning their necks to see. Aimee would recall that the dignified clergymen "sat like human interrogation marks at the very thought of a woman preaching the Gospel." She figured she had best deliver the sermon they had asked her to give, thank everyone, and sit down.

So she stood and preached in her sonorous voice the eloquent proof that down through the centuries the Church had lost the gifts of the Spirit, the powers of prophecy and tongues-speaking and divine healing; she spun out her inspired belief that God would restore these gifts before the Second Coming, that indeed he was restoring them even now, in Corona, Long Island in November of 1916.

Amid a chorus of Hallelujahs she sat down.

This is not what they had expected. Folks shifted in their seats. But Aimee's instinct was absolutely sound. She had been invited by the pastor to preach, and preach she did, to the delight and wonder of the crustiest old cleric in the jury behind her. She had not been invited to give an altar call, or incite a riot, which was a possibility whenever she turned loose "the power"

in a space this jammed with people. If they wanted the full treatment, an all-out Holy Spirit revival prayed for by the black sister who had invited Aimee to Corona, they could have it for the asking. But they had to ask. Aimee was not about to take the initiative in this Baptist church, or the responsibility.

The trustees and visiting ministers, in a state of surprise and disappointment that the show was over, put their heads together. They decided to invite the little woman preacher to return the next night. Further, they encouraged Sister Aimee "to say anything she felt led to," and this might include a summons to seek the baptism at the altar.

So the clerics could not blame Sister Aimee—and they might take some of the credit—for the wild outpouring of enthusiasm that rocked the Free Gospel Church the next night she preached. When Aimee sounded the call to be baptized, people leapt from their seats and jammed the aisles on the way to the chancel rail. They surrounded the rail and filled the chancel, jammed in behind the pulpit; they knelt down and prayed between the pews. One woman fell behind the organ, another on the far side of the church. Two brothers who had not spoken to each other in a year met in the center aisle. One, weeping, begged forgiveness and fell back into the other's arms as Sister Aimee prayed for the power of the Spirit. His brother lowered him to the floor, speaking in tongues. The crowd moved in waves toward centers of ecstasy as seekers fell to the floor.

The pastor knelt by the pulpit, praying with his hands over his face, peeking now and then through trembling fingers. He had long yearned for God's power to visit Corona. Now he wondered what God had wrought. His church had resisted the corruption of socials and suppers and worldly amusements. Now people might think it had surrendered to a bacchanalian orgy led by a woman who would have done credit to Ziegfeld's Follies.

Aimee thought she heard the Devil's voice whispering in her ear: "There never was anyone stretched out under the Power on that green carpet before. They will never ask you back here again." Yet she prayed for the Power to fall; harder and harder.

Toward midnight the meeting began to break up. Pastor

W. K. Bouton got up from where he had been kneeling, and huddled with the trustees of the Free Gospel Church. Then, approaching Aimee, he touched her on the arm and said, "Sister, the church is yours for as long as you want it, and when you want it."

Word had gone out all over town. The next night not only the church was filled but the vestry and the Sunday school rooms. Catholics as well as Protestants had come to weep and pray and cry out the Lord's name and seek the baptism of the Holy Spirit. There also came a number of curiosity seekers, scoffers, and hell-raisers, the sort of people who chase fire trucks and gather at traffic accidents.

"I feared," recalls Bouton, "we might be arrested."

———

W. K. Bouton had reversed his own prejudice, defied his wife, and taken a professional risk in opening his church to this young woman preacher and her followers. We might well ask what the pastor thought he was doing. We should consider his thoughts, because he was the first of thousands who would put himself in this position for Sister Aimee.

Aimee's power was a combination of will and faith, prayer and oratory. The thoughtful man or woman who believes deeply in something as remarkable as the Pentecostal charisms is actually rare. Those who have depth are often filled with doubt, while those who give themselves blindly to a creed may be easily swayed by rhetoric or emotion.

Everyone who saw her was curious; everyone who heard her voice was moved. Men fixed in the principles of mainline Protestantism began to doubt them. Men already full of doubt, who are always in the majority, found themselves swept up in the current of faith. Bouton recalls that after preaching successfully for twelve years, he began to realize something was lacking in his life. But he did not know what it was. He did not know it is natural to yearn for the miraculous. The pastor used to go about saying to his friends, "God is about to do some strange things in our midst, but what it is I do not know."

Yet the pastor did not dare dream of the baptism of the Holy

Spirit for himself. His teachers had told him never to look for "supernatural things," that the time for that was gone forever with the Apostles. Still, Bouton wanted the Holy Ghost to take him by the scruff of his neck and give him a good shake, and fill him up with the joyful music that flows forth in strange tongues.

Sister Aimee's arrival in Corona provided a window of opportunity. He wanted the Spirit to run riot through his church, he wanted the church packed and rocking not only with his own people but with everyone in Corona who had hands and voices to pray, everyone who would fit under the roof.

When everyone in the church seemed to have received the gift but the pastor himself, he began to realize how great was his bondage. The meetings would run on until two in the morning. On the night of November 26, Aimee knelt at the altar, praying a young woman through to the baptism, when out of the corner of her eyes she noticed Pastor Bouton kneeling at a distance. He was peering through his fingers, as if afraid to see the thing he most desired.

She beckoned him to come where he could really see and hear. The pastor came and knelt beside the young woman, whom he knew intimately from her work in his church. As Aimee prayed, the seeker's voice seemed to feed upon the vibrations until the women prayed as one. Rose color came to her cheeks and her eyes shone as the words of the prayer were suddenly translated beyond their understanding. The pastor watched the transformation of the baptism, and a wistful look passed over his face.

He got up and returned to his place beside the pulpit. Kneeling down and closing his eyes, he lifted his hands and began to pray. "Oh Lord, fill me." Over and over the pastor spoke this simple prayer.

Aimee got up and went behind him and knelt, and began to pray as simply as he: "Lord, fill him," but with a difference. As Aimee Semple McPherson prayed, she saw the living figure of Jesus Christ in a white shepherd's robe hovering before W. K. Bouton in midair in between the crossbeams and the chancel floor. Each time she called the Lord's name over the pastor's shoulder, a little more of the figure appeared to him too as he sought the Spirit, until in wonder and holy terror for a period of fifteen minutes he saw "no man save Jesus only," and the Lord poured out the Holy Ghost upon W. K. Bouton.

The pastor swayed from side to side. Then he fell backwards, rolled off the little step, and lay in a trance, only the whites of his eyes showing, just inside the chancel rail.

Mrs. Bouton, who had been in a distant pew watching the spectacle with some concern, bounded into the aisle and ran to the front, calling, "Will, Will, speak to me!" Aimee begged the woman not to disturb her husband.

"Oh but he's dying. He's dying," she wailed.

Aimee explained that this was the power of the Holy Spirit, that her unconscious husband was safe in Jesus's arms. If she would just be patient, she would see him receive the Holy Spirit.

"Oh, but I know he is dying! He had a vision once before and he almost died then!"

At the moment when Aimee thought she could no longer restrain the frightened woman from shaking her husband, when the crowd was leaning over the chancel rail and standing upon pews to get a peek at their stunned pastor, his eyes blinked. His lips moved, and he moaned. He began to speak in tongues, and in his own words, "It seemed as though heaven had opened and I had entered the City."

Aimee watched in triumph as W. K. Bouton then delivered, in English and in the voice of angels, "such a Christ-exalting message as one seldom hears in this old world."

———

Ministers warned their flocks against Aimee's "hypnotism." The hypnotist's skill lies in superimposing his will upon the will of his subject, to induce the trance and then maintain rapport with the person while sewing seeds of suggestion, seeds that will bear fruit when the trance is done.

That the incantation of prayer induces a trance, we cannot doubt. Mystics discovered this long before the time of Christ. Aimee Semple McPherson was only one of a long line of religious adepts who perfected the instrument of incantation in order to unlock their own spiritual potential and that of others.

How is the religious trance the same as the waking/sleeping state of clinical hypnosis, and how is it different?

Men and women "slain in the spirit" display vital signs resembling those of subjects under deep hypnosis: eyes roll back in the head, limbs grow slack, the pulse and breathing are markedly reduced. In this condition the "seeker" is suggestible, like the patient under hypnosis.

But here the similarity ends. The seeker is only narrowly suggestible, to the group's spiritual manifestations: tongue-speaking, automatisms. To call the religious trance just another form of hypnotism ignores its intention and content. Clinical hypnosis exposes the subconscious. What exactly does the religious trance expose? The subconscious? God? It is anybody's guess. Clinical hypnosis often has no agenda—it works to expose the subconscious to a variety of suggestions that the patient may not anticipate. In contrast the man or woman who seeks the baptism of the Spirit has a clear goal, religious enlightenment. The seeker is looking for God through the doorway of the trance.

If you believe in a God that is somehow involved in human affairs, it should not seem surprising that the Holy Spirit should enter Pastor Bouton through the doorway of his trance, hypnotic or not.

A MIRACULOUS HEALING

Aimee Semple McPherson's bible, bound in white calf, rests in the vaults of Angelus Temple in Los Angeles. The worn book falls open naturally to the thirteenth chapter of St. Paul's letter to the Hebrews. The open pages have turned pale gold from exposure to stage lights and the moisture of the woman's hands. Here is her favorite verse of Scripture: Jesus Christ is the same yesterday, today, and forever. She had it inscribed upon the proscenium arch, in her temple, when it opened in 1923.

Her knowledge of the Bible, from burning the midnight oil with Robert Semple, was exhaustive, encyclopedic. He taught her to mark and annotate the book, to read aggressively. Rolf McPherson remembers seeing bibles his parents had studied. The texts were so crisscrossed with notes and so battered, they fell apart. Her choice of Hebrews 13:8 was well informed.

Augustine had not singled it out; Martin Luther had not taken it up; neither John Calvin nor John Wesley nor William Booth had seized upon this line from Hebrews 13. But Sister Aimee grabbed hold of it and illuminated the sentence, and sang it out in 1916, making this the touchstone of her contemporary theology and healing ministry. This insight of St. Paul is a religious analogue of the general theory of relativity (completed circa 1916) and modernist definitions of time in the works of Henri Bergson and T. S. Eliot.

Properly understood, it permits time to collapse upon itself "in the body of Christ which is the world."

"Jesus Christ is the same yesterday, today, and forever."

She was preaching this text one night in Corona when a taxicab pulled up to the door of the Free Gospel Church. Two people got out of the cab quickly and came around to open the curb door for Louise Messnick. You could hardly tell whether Louise Messnick was a little girl or an old lady the way she was scrunched down in the car seat. She looked as if she had passed out with her chin on her chest. But she was wide awake in pain, looking up out of the corner of her eyes through the car window above her head.

Louise Messnick was a young woman in the advanced stages of rheumatoid arthritis. The disease begins with inflammation of the joints of hands, feet, and knees. Each joint is a complex capsule where the bone ends meet, a capsule lined with a soft membrane. Viscous synovial fluid lubricates the gliding surfaces of the bone ends and their cartilage. No one knows exactly why the joint becomes inflamed, why the flow of fluid suddenly increases, swelling the capsule and inflaming the surrounding tissues. Sometimes the cause is an injury or infection. But neither trauma nor bacteria can account for the overreaction of the membrane, whose fluid begins to granulate, attacking the cartilage it is supposed to protect.

Modern medicine considers rheumatoid arthritis a disease of the immune system, which is known to be susceptible to suggestion.

The young woman curled up in the back seat of the cab could not lift her head. The inflammation had impaired the neck muscles and the jaw, so she could hardly chew. The vertebrae of her neck were skewed with the swelling, and the ligaments of her back had begun to shorten, so she could not stand erect. For a long time she had not been able to lift her hands high enough to comb her hair. Her fingers were gnarled and twisted.

Louise, a Catholic, had heard about the controversial revival meetings going on in the Free Gospel Church. This Sister Aimee people were arguing about had brought to the town a spirit that worked wonders. This was just what Louise needed. Every time Louise thought of Sister Aimee, she felt a thrill of hope, a tingling in her blood and bones.

Now the crowd made way for the twisted young woman on crutches. On either side a friend supported her as she came through the door and started down the central aisle. Sister Aimee had just been declaring that Jesus Christ was the same yesterday, today, and forever, with the same power to heal the body and mind, and deliver the gifts of tongues and prophecy via the Holy Ghost, as He showed in ancient times.

The crippled Louise Messnick entered like a dramatic challenge to Aimee's sermon.

There must have been moments of silence after the crowd's sigh of pity, a long suspension of breath; for Aimee would not forget how one of the crutches squeaked each time it came down on the creaking floorboards. She thought that the poor woman would never get to the front. But with the help of many kind hands she at last arrived, and sat enraptured as Aimee preached her sermon.

Aimee tells us that before this night in Corona she had not

discovered the gift of healing. "Indeed very little had been said or done about this great doctrine at the time." Yet she had seen her own broken ankle healed in Findlay, Ohio in 1909, and she had witnessed the overnight healing of Monkey Abe's lesions in Mount Forest a year ago. Most important, perhaps, was her own resurrection from the physical and mental collapse in Hong Kong, where she lost Robert Semple, and the internal damage she had suffered in the Providence hospital.

As Aimee looked at Louise Messnick (whose eyes were downcast because she could not raise her head), she could tell the girl was weeping. The audience watched Aimee looking at the arthritic woman, as if to say: If Jesus is the same yesterday, today, and forever, what about Barnabas, and the lepers? What about Lazarus? If He is the same yesterday, today, and forever, why doesn't He do something about this crippled woman in our midst? Are you just going to stand there and preach?

"Oh Lord," Aimee cried out in her heart, "you are able to heal her." And she realized she was going to do something she had never done before. It might disappoint everyone terribly if her instinct failed her. "How I did wish that I could begin with someone who looked a bit more mendable . . ." she recalled. But it was too late for such considerations. She was already caught up in the process that had begun in Louise Messnick's body and in the body of the crowd days before.

She decided in that instant that she would pray for the crippled girl to be healed. But she would do it as inconspicuously as possible during the altar call; she would slip down to the front seat and pray quietly with her. In the back of Aimee's mind was the thought that if Louise was not completely healed there, the failure would be less noticeable.

But the young cripple had whispered to her friends to carry her up at the very beginning of the altar call. Aimee gasped as she saw the woman being carried to the front, all eyes upon her.

Since she could not kneel, they set her down in the central minister's chair.

Sister Aimee had called all these people together in the presence of the Holy Spirit, for an anointing, an infusion of the

divine presence. Young and old, rich and poor, man and
woman, became a single body. This was her gift as an orator,
her charisma, which came from a deep understanding founded
upon years of reflection and prayer. The crowd's body was a
healing body like that of Christ, the wounded healer. Now she
had a vivid image of Christ's body which she projected in their
midst so powerfully that those who could not literally see it
could still feel the Lord's presence. When she prayed in His
name, the prayer had a physical as well as psychic force. Every
man, woman, and child in the Free Gospel Church had been
transported by Aimee's gift into a cell of the healing body of
Christ.

In her mind was a blueprint of the human body in radiant
health. Now Aimee looked into the downcast eyes of Louise
Messnick and prayed for her healing. She laid hands upon the
woman's head. As she did this, she felt an energy surge like an
electric charge coming up from her heels right through her spine
and into her tingling fingertips. It seemed, as she closed her
eyes, that the charge came from Christ's image down through
the body of the rapt audience and then up through her legs.
This was pleasant and soothing, like warm water. It seemed to
have an immediate effect upon Louise Messnick's skin color, as
well as her temperature. The woman's cheeks flushed and her
heartbeat increased.

Aimee told her to lift up her hands and praise the Lord. Louise
Messnick looked at her hands, lifted them slowly. And as she
lifted her hands, some people in front gasped in wonder. The
hands unfolded from their clawlike deformity, and straightened
out. Like hands pulled from above by a puppeteer, limp at the
wrist, Louise Messnick's hands rose to the level of her chin.
The shoulders thawed as the hands then rose to her eyes, and
then to the top of her head. She could feel a mild vibration in
her limbs, a pleasant warmth like spring sunlight coming from
Sister Aimee's hands and dark eyes. "Praise the Lord," she
muttered, "this is the first time I have been able to lift my
hands . . ."

The hands went up until her arms were nearly straight above

her head. Her chin, which had been fastened to her sunken chest so long, it seemed to have grown there, began to move slightly to the side. Then it straightened again as her neck muscles relaxed. Aimee smoothed the hair back from the woman's brow, and the woman's chin lifted, and they looked into each other's eyes.

Louise Messnick gazed heavenward, her arms outstretched, and, as Aimee held her, she rose to her feet.

People cried out in praise and wonder. She tottered, and Aimee helped her get hold of the chancel rail. Her face and hands were streaming with sweat as she moved slowly along the rail, hand over hand.

And with every step she took, her limbs straightened; the fingers clutching the chancel rail unknotted.

Louise Messnick walked out of the church that night alone, without her crutches.

———

The healings present a monstrous obstacle to scientific historiography. If events transpired as newspapers, letters, and testimonials say they did, then Aimee Semple McPherson's healing ministry was miraculous. Since a miracle by definition is a thing which defies reality, there is no place in scholarly or scientific history for recurrent miracles.

It would be convenient if we could find some evidence that Sister Aimee's miraculous healings were faked for the benefit of publicity; but there is no such evidence. Alas, the documentation is overwhelming: very sick people came to Sister Aimee by the tens of thousands, blind, deaf, paralyzed. Many were healed, some temporarily, some forever. She would point to heaven, to Christ the Great Healer, and would take no credit for the results. She did not actively pursue a healing ministry, as did Oral Roberts; she did not relish it. And after seven years of being pursued and mobbed by the blind, the lame, the tumor-ridden, and the deaf, she virtually withdrew from it. The account we have of Louise Messnick's recovery from arthritis comes mostly from Aimee's recollections. But accounts of her healings are scattered humbly through her autobiographies. And they are modest when compared with the spectacular reports in the daily press.

We cannot ignore the mountain of press clippings, testimonials, and private correspondence bearing witness to the healings, but neither can we prove a single one of them. The burden of proof, where miracles are concerned, rests upon the believer, as the Catholic Church so wisely asseverates. And we have not a shred of evidence to support Aimee's narrative, apart from the letter she reprinted from the healed woman herself.

To us it seems amazing. To Rolf McPherson, Roberta Salter, and the reporters who traveled with Sister Aimee in 1920 it was a routine occurrence, like a christening.

The record is staggering but not absurd. The majority of healings do have documented equivalents in contemporary medical literature. They are mostly diseases of the immune system, or attributed to hysteria. Sister Aimee is not credited with raising anyone from the dead, correcting a harelip or cleft palate, or restoring a missing limb, digit, or internal organ. Her effects were never preposterous. The thing that was so wonderful about the healings was their number and their startling suddenness.

Between the hour Louise Messnick heard the name Aimee Semple McPherson and the moment she rose from the minister's chair with her chin up and her eyes raised to heaven, her body was very busy. The miracle the crowd witnessed did not happen all in a moment, though it surprised the crippled woman as much as anyone. The instant she stood up was the climax of a drama that had been going on in her mind and body, waking and sleeping, probably for days.

She had been depressed. She had been in despair, lost in inward-shrinking emotions. The idea of Sister Aimee filled her with expanding hope. A physician explains that emotions have a direct effect on the brain, the hypothalamus, which releases a chemical mediator to the anterior lobe of the pituitary gland, where the powerful hormone ACTH is stored, a long-chain polypeptide. The pathways of the neuropeptides, scientists have discovered, are so complex they defy chemical description, crying out for metaphor: the working of the neuropeptides and neurotransmitters in the body is an intelligent conversation. It is their ultimate responsibility to regulate the molecular architecture throughout the body.

In the case of Louise Messnick the neuropeptides had instructed her red corpuscles to reduce their rate of sedimentation. Thus the synovial membranes could begin to reabsorb the fluid that was attacking all her joints. The fluid that remained would regain its clear viscosity, so that again it could oil her rusted joints.

By the time her cab arrived at the door of the Free Gospel Church those joints were unlocking. The twisted shape of her body was now only a habit of shortened ligaments and tendons; she might have walked before Aimee ever laid a hand on her, if she had the courage to try. Aimee and the crowd, in their collective faith that she would get up and walk, were only telling Louise Messnick's brain what her body had already discovered: the physical cause of her infirmity was gone. Now their prayers and the electromagnetic power of Aimee's hands would give her the extra shot of adrenaline she needed to stretch and loosen her muscles, and pull herself out of the twisted shape which was her habit.

Could Louise Messnick have found hope elsewhere, a hope that would have produced these same results? Maybe. The point is, she did not. There was only one Sister Aimee, whose faith provoked no less dramatic changes in several thousand invalids. She had the gift. It was not so much a miraculous violation of natural laws as it was a miraculous affirmation of them.

Aimee did not understand what happened that night in Corona. She knew nothing about arthritis or the hypothalamus or neurotransmitters. She gave the credit to the Holy Spirit. All her life she would remember the healing of Louise Messnick as one of the greatest miracles she ever witnessed.

It is one thing to read about these phenomena, another to witness them, and almost impossible to imagine the strain of being an actor in such a drama. A woman comes to the altar to be healed. The evangelist lays hands upon her, and she gets better—or she doesn't. If one has a gift like Aimee's, it is largely the result of a deep emotional investment.

Aimee's gift was emotional and religious, but it would yield returns of another sort: cash flow. While she was in Corona, Aimee "felt the leading of the Lord" to preach in Florida during the winter months, though she had no idea how she would get there. She never discussed money with Pastor Bouton.

The night before she left, they placed a table by the altar, an open bible upon it. The pastor announced a special offering would be taken for Sister Aimee's services in the Free Gospel Church. The people who had witnessed so many baptisms in the Holy Spirit, conversions, and the miracle of healing, now crowded the aisles to reach the open bible. They would lay their dollars and coins upon it, until the book was buried under money enough to convey the evangelist to her next meeting in Florida. She would go with Mack and Rolf. Minnie Kennedy insisted that Roberta was too frail, and kept her in Canada.

After the travel expenses there was enough Corona money left over to buy a typewriter.

FAME

"The fields were waiting for the gospel," she wrote. But they were not simply waiting. Sister Aimee was entreated to preach in hundreds of cities, villages, and cattle crossings, from Jacksonville to Savannah, in the winter of 1916–1917; how strongly entreated, we can only guess. Her account makes it sound as if she and her husband and son landed in Jacksonville on a whim, without mortal sponsors.

But immediately someone loaned them land near the center of town. As they were erecting the tents, building seats, and installing the lights, a carload of Pentecostal workers were driving from Atlanta, Georgia, a thousand miles away, to join Sister Aimee. They must have started out when Aimee left Providence. Long before she arrived in the South, folks in Florida, and Georgia too, were eager to look upon the evangelist.

The world was at war in France. In a twenty-four-hour period 20,000 soldiers had died in the trenches. As the German U-boats grew more arrogant in their defiance of neutrality regulations, Americans debated their own neutrality. In the winter of 1916–1917, from the cloakrooms of Congress to the cotton fields, our involvement in the war seemed inevitable.

This was a new kind of war. It sent men across the sea to battle with invisible enemies, to live in holes in the ground and fight with remote and impersonal weapons: airplane bombers, land tanks, poison gas. The real reason for the war was surely not the "demon" Kaiser Wilhelm; it was a mystery to parents who sent their sons to be killed in it. To the working class, this war—which America trembled on the verge of entering as Aimee arrived in Jacksonville—seemed to be waged against an abstract enemy, the Devil. Many simple souls considered the war a punishment for mankind's wickedness.

Aimee was obsessed with the war, and with the poverty she saw in the South. On the eve of her debut in Jacksonville, just after the carload of recruits arrived hungry and dusty from Atlanta, she gave her last cent to a black beggar.

Everybody was hungry, and Aimee had spent all the money but a nickel on lumber, electric lights, and a piano. The nickel might have bought a loaf of bread. But then came this woman begging for money or food for herself and her children. Sister Aimee thought this might be a good time for her troops to fast, in preparation for the first meeting; then the offerings would come pouring in.

So she gave the beggar her last nickel.

The delegation from Atlanta was not pleased. Evidently they had already done their share of fasting, having spent their money on gasoline.

As the story goes, Aimee excused herself so she could pray

in private, a modest little prayer that the Lord might feed them tonight if He liked. If not, it was no great matter. Doubtless the hungry men and women expected—from the illustrious evangelist—a more impassioned plea.

But evidently it was sufficient. As she got up from praying, she heard a man's gruff voice on the street. He announced that a prepaid shipment of clothing and food had arrived from Corona: canned corn, peas, salmon, rolled oats, sugar, condensed milk, and a box of crackers.

Aimee seems to have done this more than once, tempting fate by giving away her last nickel, dime, or quarter. Her husband, during that winter in Florida, was driven to distraction. That she clearly preferred God's help to his hurt his pride. While they were on the road, he was more or less in charge. And when they were raising the tents and nailing the lumber to make grandstands, he was foreman, a man doing a man's work. But when the crowd arrived and Aimee began to preach, Harold McPherson faded into the background. Hardly anyone knew who he was.

Aimee Semple McPherson, on the other hand, was already becoming a cult celebrity whose name preceded and followed her in whispers.

Mack took snapshots of her in St. Petersburg, fishing on a wooden bridge. She is wearing a long dress with buttons from neck to hem and a lace collar. From under the broad brim of a black Quaker-style hat she smiles sweetly over her shoulder, a portly young woman without a care in the world. She looks well-fed and happy and chaste. In another picture she peers out of a bower of hibiscus blossoms. She looks like everybody's schoolmarm sister, with a sense of humor, or a jolly nurse in the obstetrics ward.

At this stage she had yet to draw upon her erotic energies as a source of power. She was feminine in her grace of movement and speech, but very maternal. Aimee would have to appeal first to women—and she could not win them if she looked like she might steal their husbands. She was louder and stronger than most men. As she appears in the photographs with that bull neck and those broad shoulders, sometimes she reminds us of Emma Goldman, the anarchist, except that Aimee was always pretty, and slightly vulnerable.

She made things happen wherever she went, things people remembered and talked about. In Jacksonville there was a munitions plant where a young man got his arm caught in a conveyor belt. The arm was broken in three places and dislocated at the wrist when the man came to Aimee at the revival meeting. In the presence of several workers from the munitions plant who knew the condition of the young man's arm, Aimee laid her hand upon the cast. She prayed. Before she had finished the prayer, the pain was gone and the man found he could move his fingers freely. Against everyone's advice he insisted they cut away the cast to see how Christ had healed him.

To everyone's astonishment the bone was whole.

In Tampa she raised enough money to buy an automobile, a 1912 Packard touring car. It became a rolling church. Aimee played a baby organ. She stood up and preached from the back seat for eight to ten meetings per day, and handed out tracts and handbills announcing the tent meetings. Men and women would step out of the crowd and kneel at the running board, confessing their sins and undergoing conversion.

At night Mack pitched a little tent for them to sleep in. Sometimes during the day they would turn back the front seat of the Packard and take a nap.

On her way to a meeting in Tampa, as she stood in the car shouting invitations through a megaphone one evening, her voice grew weary. A young Christian worker offered to take over the megaphone for a while so Aimee could save her voice for the meeting. The young man looked around. When he saw a fellow coming from a deserted side street, he shouted at him:

"Say brother! Do you know you are on your way to perdition?"

The errant sheep jumped as if he had been shot. Aimee grabbed the megaphone away from the fanatic, furious at him. "Why did you do that?"

The Christian worker recited the Fundamentalist party line of 1916: The stranger was on his way to Hell, was he not? Aimee was about to change all that.

"How do you know?" she demanded. "And even if he were," she continued, "one can do more with the bait of love than with the club of bombastic preaching." Anticipating the "creation theology" of Matthew Fox by sixty years, Aimee would stress grace above original sin; with the bait of love she would go "fishing for whales." Her preaching was anecdotal and affectionate, never threatening.

And the woman evangelist kept shocking her audiences by making things happen that defied natural probability.

She held a revival in Durant, Florida, twenty miles from Tampa, in a wooden tabernacle that held 1,500. The crowd dispersed at midday for lunch. While Aimee was preparing for the night meeting, a skeptical minister got up an "opposition meeting" on the other side of the fence that guarded the Pleasant Grove Camp where Aimee presided. She was adjusting a calcium carbide lamp. The opposition preacher was loudly defending the "cessation of charismas" theory, that all supernatural power had ceased with the writing of the last chapter of the Bible.

As the preacher was proclaiming that miracles were only for Bible days, the lamp exploded in Aimee's face. Flames enveloped her. A man standing next to her dropped to his knees. Others crept under the seats, terrified.

Aimee's first fear was that the wooden tabernacle would go up in flames. She managed to stay where she was until she turned off the tap and put out the fire. Her face was black, her eyebrows and eyelashes gone. She had been wearing a hat which was more or less fireproof, but the front part of her hair was singed away.

She plunged her face into a pan of water. Some ladies brought baking soda to make a salve for her red face, which was bubbling up in blisters. Aimee walked up and down under the trees while the crowd began to gather for the evening service. She could see car headlights coming up the road, and wagons unloading dozens of people at a time.

The time for the meeting came and went, but she was in too

much pain to go on. When she was ten minutes late, the preacher who had been holding the opposition meeting stood up. He announced to the crowd there would be no meeting that night. The lady who preached divine healing was ill; she had burned her face.

When she heard that, Aimee became so angry, she forgot her injury. Washing the baking soda from her face, she strode into the tent. She mounted the platform, her starched collar spattered with water, her hair singed, no eyelashes or eyebrows, a comic figure except for the lines of pain on her blistered face.

As she sang the first hymn, her lips were so stiff from the burn, she could hardly shape the notes. At the end of a verse she raised a hand and cried out: "I praise the Lord that he heals me and takes all the pain away!"

A shout went up from the crowd.

We understand now the mind's ability to trigger the production of opiates, endorphins, and enkephalins. More powerful than any drugs we can buy, these block pain by filling a certain receptor in the neuron and preventing other chemicals that carry the message of pain from entering. Strong emotions can thus override pain signals from the body, as in the case of the mother who saves her child from the burning house or the wounded soldier who fights on heedless of his bleeding.

So it is not so remarkable that Aimee's pain was instantly relieved.

What *is* remarkable is that, according to Aimee, her face, as she sang the hymn with her loving congregation, began to change color. It went from lobster red to a vivid pink in the matter of two or three stanzas. The blisters that had covered much of her face began to smooth and disappear. We know that blisters can be induced and dispersed rapidly in subjects under hypnosis. Olga Worrell is documented in 1962 and 1965 as having healed third-degree burns by the laying on of hands. Yet the effect upon that audience in 1916, as they watched the evangelist's face transformed from a mass of red welts to its smooth bloom of health, must have been earthshaking. It certainly turned the tide of the local controversy in favor of the acceptance of God's power to heal.

———

Aimee and her entourage arrived in St. Petersburg in February, during Mardi Gras. Bands were playing as people in masks and costumes danced in the streets. Standing on the corner watching, giving out handbills for her tent meeting, Aimee realized she would have a hard time luring these merrymakers into her tent to find salvation. Parades of silver-harnessed horses and automobile floats passed through the festooned streets and buntinged avenues.

The floats represented states of the Union and businesses.

The Lord told Aimee to join the parade. She was not sure she had heard Him right. "Christian friends," she reflected, "would be utterly scandalized . . . and yet, why not? Desperate conditions require desperate measures.

"My state was the state of Salvation! My business that of preaching the Gospel in a tent!"

She and Mack built a wooden frame tent onto the Packard. They stretched a sheet upon it; they covered the doors and hood and running board of the car with green palmetto and ferns and gray Spanish moss. The float looked like a hill with a tent on top: on one side of the tent Aimee painted JESUS IS COMING SOON and on the other side I AM GOING TO THE PENTECOSTAL CAMP MEETING. R.U.?

Aimee got under the tent with the baby organ and Mack drove into the parade line while the policeman's back was turned, because they did not have a parade permit. They fell in behind the float for the Chamber of Commerce, ahead of the baker and the telephone company.

When people saw the float, they began to laugh. They clapped when they heard the organ and tambourine chimes sound from under the floating tent on the motorized hill:

> Just as I am, without one plea
> But that Thy blood was shed for me.

"The very audacity of the thing which we had done," she recalls, "seemed to appeal to them."

That night, and every night Aimee preached in St. Petersburg, the Gospel tent was full. With its handwritten sign GET RIGHT WITH GOD and the logo of a halo transfixed by a sword, the tent crowded with worshipers must have amazed Aimee's parents when they came to visit that winter.

A snapshot of James Kennedy, age eighty, on his hands and knees playing horsie with little Rolf on his back, shows how close the family remained. Minnie, Aimee, and Mack look on in merriment. These women had abandoned James after Aimee's marriage a decade earlier; yet he was there for them, always. If God failed now and then to provide directly, He might work through the ready agency of Ma and Pa Kennedy. Roberta recalls how her grandmother used to read Aimee's letters aloud to her in the kitchen. "Sometimes the letters were gay and lighthearted and full of special little jokes and pictures for me; and other times, when she wrote mostly for Minnie about the troubles she had patching the tent when the hurricane tore it to ribbons, Minnie blew her nose loudly and sent me off to fetch her checkbook."

James, as ever, was amusing, and amused by his daughter's notoriety, her command of a crowd. Minnie saw something more, the promise of a dream come true, the vague outlines of a colossus. She wanted to be involved.

———

With the new typewriter Aimee began to write and edit a newsletter that would become *The Bridal Call*.

In the back seat of the Gospel Car with the machine in her lap, Aimee typed her sermons, poems dictated to her "in the spirit," and the journal of her evangelistic touring. She had to maintain contact with the faithful in cities she left behind, while sending news of her adventures ahead, to summon new audiences. In June of 1917 *The Bridal Call* was just four pages published from Savannah, Georgia. Soon she arranged with the Christian Workers' Union at Framington, Massachusetts to publish and mail a sixteen-page monthly, in a seven-by-ten-inch format, at a subscription price of twenty-five cents per year.

Printed under the masthead of *The Bridal Call* was a verse from the Song of Solomon: "Rise up, my love, my fair one, and come away." Thus, early in 1917, Aimee identified the gentle exhortation of her own feminine voice with the voice of the Church, a remade Church. It would give up the themes of damnation and sin and take on the tone of a celebration, a happy wedding.

The young preacher in her white dress with the lace-trimmed collar may have appeared to men in the audience like a country bride. To women she may have evoked memories of their weddings long ago. But Harold McPherson understood that as a bride of Christ his wife was irrevocably translated beyond the earthly pattern of conjugal life.

In Savannah she received the "call" to Long Branch, New Jersey, when a newspaper with the headline DON'T FAIL TO GO TO LONG BRANCH blew across the floor of the tent where she was praying and landed at her feet. From Savannah they took country roads up through the Carolinas, Kentucky, and Maryland, stopping at every town and crossroads to hand out tracts. Where there was good attendance they lingered; if there was little response, they moved on. From the back seat of the car Aimee preached to laborers in the cotton and tobacco fields. At night Mack would pull the car into a quiet field or forest near a stream; there they would pitch a tent and build a campfire. Aimee typed and prayed. She told Bible stories to her little son until she could not hold her eyes open.

At Long Branch they discovered that a band of seven Pentecostal workers had already prepared the ground. For years these people had been praying for a revival. While they raised the tents, Aimee rounded up a crowd by driving thirty miles a day with a bullhorn in her hand, shouting invitations, distributing handbills, and holding street meetings. At Long Branch she held baptism services by the ocean. There "the power of the Lord fell," and people leapt and shouted and danced in the waves while crowds sang and praised God from the shore. Young converts had visions: of the Savior hanging on a cross in midair, of Him descending from the clouds to carry away the faithful.

War had been declared in April, while the McPhersons were campaigning in Georgia. The growth of crowds and enthusiasm at the tent meetings that year must be seen in the context of the war. The war caused a fierce anxiety in the women whose sons, husbands, and brothers were arming for battle in France. If hundreds came to see Aimee in Long Branch, in Hyde Park, Boston (July 12–August 5) it was thousands. The enormous tent bulged with people. Thousands more fringed the edges of the canvas, some standing so far out into the road they could not possibly have heard a word of her sermon.

A policeman who lived nearby complained to his chief that he couldn't sleep for the racket of the tent meetings. The noise, said Aimee, was mostly caused by the Catholics of Boston who were doing their best to break up the Pentecostal services. The chief ignored her requests for police protection, and when the patrolman complained, he summoned Aimee, Mack, and the "brethren" to the station. They arrived in the Gospel Car, which they parked in front of the station door.

The chief told them to take a seat while they waited for the patrolman who had made the complaint. As the Chief paced up and down the room, he kept looking out at the Gospel Car, with its sign lettered in gold saying JESUS IS COMING SOON.

He read it softly, as if to himself. "Coming soon?" he said. "Well maybe so. I don't know."

Aimee looked hard at the Chief. "Are you prepared to meet Him if He should come?" she asked matter-of-factly.

No response.

"Do you know your sins are washed away, that you have passed from death unto life?"

"No, no, I cannot say that I do."

There was much more at stake here than local police protection: Aimee saw a soul in peril. The brethren invited the chief of police to give his heart to Jesus; but, stiff-necked, he refused, giving all sorts of reasons why he could not do it just yet. He kept going to the window and reading the gold letters on the Gospel Car, JESUS IS COMING SOON, repeating it in a wistful and bemused voice and then saying, "Well, well, maybe He is."

Meanwhile they waited for the patrolman, who never came

to make the formal charge against the Pentecostals for disturbing the peace. The chief stared at the car.

But he never gave his soul to Jesus. And he never provided the protection that Aimee begged for, to keep the Catholics from rioting outside the tents. That night the mob made more noise and mischief than ever.

And the next day the same uncooperative police chief was sitting at his desk. He thought he had indigestion; then he felt the enormous pressure of an invisible hand in the center of his chest. Within a few hours the police chief was dead of a massive heart attack.

This story spread quickly in the Catholic community. And though Boston never became a haven for Aimee's Pentecostal movement, she won the government's respect. The next night, and every night until August 5, when Aimee left the city, three uniformed officers of the law saw to it that her meetings were undisturbed.

Her power was eerie when it was not simply dazzling. And, as in the case of the police chief, her influence did not begin and end in the pulpit.

She was welcome in Huntington, Long Island, where her white tents nestled under locust trees, where twenty-six received the baptism of the Holy Spirit, and where she healed a girl with a withered leg. In Montwait, Massachusetts, thirty received the baptism, and many more were healed before the great camp meeting in Washburn, Maine that September. With each conversion she inspired and witnessed, with every healing that occurred under her hands, she grew more confident in her gifts and the energy of the Holy Spirit.

Over and over in her recollections of those meetings we encounter the phrase "The power fell so no one could preach," or "The Spirit took control in such a way that preaching was impossible." With small numbers the emotional outbursts and automatisms she inspired could be kept, just barely, under her control. But when a thousand or more people gave way to their emotions, the most she could do was guide them, through music, storytelling, and theater, to a spiritual end. Those early tent meetings were riotous scenes that spread the evangelist's reputation, favorably and unfavorably, statewide, wherever she camped. The meetings attracted every sort of thrillseeker, rabble-rouser, and pickpocket, who came to the Gospel tent as to a circus.

In Boston she took to playing the piano "in the Spirit," improvisations upon hymns to calm the converts who had gone out of control. During the two and a half weeks in Washburn, her preaching crossed the line between narrative and drama, when she directed a little play "in the Spirit" to present the story of the Wise and Foolish Virgins.

Ten women, dressed in white, represented the virgins. Aimee narrated as they acted out the scenes: going to meet the Bridegroom and falling asleep on His threshold; the wise virgins dancing for joy to find their lamps full of oil and burning; the foolish virgins knocking at a door, haggling over the price of oil, and refusing to pay it; the foolish virgins weeping and tearing their hair to discover that their frugal sisters, meanwhile, had been carried up to Heaven, while they, the fools, had not been willing to make the sacrifice required for salvation.

This was her first "illustrated sermon." It was the beginning of the theater that would pack the Angelus Temple in the 1920's, contributing to religious drama one of its most significant experiments since the passion plays at Oberammergau.

When Aimee tells us the little drama was "all worked out in the Spirit," she means that the play, like her preaching, piano playing, and dancing during this frantic period, was spontaneous, rooted in the necessity of the moment, inspired. In these years when Aimee was living "on faith," there was little distinction between thought, prayer, and action.

How revealing, that the first of her soon-to-be-famous illustrated sermons arises from that erotic text with its ten virgins and invisible bridegroom. Some know the value of oil and some do not; some waste on earth the fuel required for Heaven. When Aimee cut school the snowy day she decided to seek baptism, half-crazy with love for Robert Semple, this is exactly how she had expressed it: "You need oil in your vessel with your lamp."

Here was a woman with full knowledge of the symbolic resonance of the Wise and Foolish Virgins. Before she was done, Aimee would play both roles in the spotlight of public life.

THE GYPSY LIFE

In September of 1918, Aimee, Mack, and Rolf drove south in the Gospel Car. On one side of the Packard in six-inch-high letters were the words JESUS IS COMING SOON, and on the other side WHERE WILL YOU SPEND ETERNITY?

They drove through New York City in a changing caravan. Automobiles followed Aimee as she shouted through the megaphone her message of salvation, or they fell away to carry her message home. She drove down through Philadelphia, Maryland, Virginia, preaching and distributing thousands of Gospels of St. John and issues of *The Bridal Call*. Members of the caravan would stand in turn on the hood of Aimee's Packard. They would give their testimonies until a crowd gathered, and then Aimee would step forward and preach a sermon. If she did not love the gypsy life, she was in such a constant state of nervous excitement, she did not mind the rain, the hunger, or the uncertainty.

They traveled all day, down through the Carolinas and Georgia, and slept at night by the roadside. In these states Aimee was moved by the deep response of the black workers in the tobacco and cotton fields. They were so grateful for the chance to hear the word of God, because the town churches shut them out. She visited their homes, where she found herself at ease with the poor blacks, being near as poor as any of them.

Crowds welcomed the troupe upon their return to Jacksonville in October. Folks cheered them along the road from the Atlantic to the Gulf of Mexico as they preached and pamphleteered their way back to Pleasant Grove. There the Durant tabernacle with its fifteen hundred seats was filled to overflowing under the trees. The altar was more crowded than ever with people seeking salvation.

The only limit to Aimee's audience would be the size of the canvas to cover them.

But all was not well. She was happy and excited while she worked, eighteen hours a day. Yet sometimes at night when she could not sleep, in the Packard or under a damp tent, Aimee heard the voice of the Devil. He sounded like Harold Mc-Pherson. The Tempter described the comfortable homes of rich folks with warm beds. He would point scornfully to the canvas cot, or the smoky campfire, or to her little boy shivering in his sleep—telling Aimee that the price she was paying for her vocation was too great.

Of course she was prepared with the answer of the wise virgins, that no sacrifice is too great in the Lord's name. But she had a husband to contend with. And Mack, as hard as he had tried to match her enthusiasm, was wearing out.

As they left Tampa with the car loaded down with tracts, Aimee had left no room for the sleeping tent. Christmas was coming. And as they crossed the prairie near the Okeechobee, it rained as if it would never stop.

Rolf McPherson remembers waking to the sound of rain and the sight of his mother holding an umbrella over his head, asleep in the dark with one eye open. They slept in the car; they slept wrapped in a blanket by a smoking fire on the shore of the Okeechobee; they slept in a fisherman's shanty near Palm Beach; they slept in a railway depot to get out of the driving rain.

They drove past houses, looking in at families gathered around the Christmas trees or eating their dinners. They drove the car to a beach. There they built a palm-leaf shanty and hung their makeshift gifts, wrapped in newspaper, from a low tree branch.

Harold McPherson, by the Christmas of 1917, found their celebration all too pathetic. His wife, a born performer, lived for the crowd's adoration, bathed in the applause, calling it the Holy Spirit, and found this so rejuvenated and refreshed her that nothing, between camp meetings, mattered to her at all. For him, it was just another town, another show.

As they drove toward Miami, barnstorming, he stood in the front seat of the car as Aimee drove, and shouted through the megaphone until he was hoarse: "This war is a fulfillment of prophecy. Awake! O thou that sleepest, Jesus is near."

On January 4 he raised the tents in Miami. Crowds there were larger than ever. Aimee would preach one night in a rich white neighborhood, then strike camp; and Harold would raise the tents the next night on the far side of town for the black folks.

This defiance of racial barriers and social class is one of the most remarkable features of Sister Aimee's early ministry. She went wherever she was wanted, and the black community loved her. They had good reason. She would write, and publish, in 1919: "It was about impossible for me to pass one of them on the street without such floods of love welling up in my heart . . . I think they must have felt my love for them, for they flocked about me while distributing tracts in their neighborhoods." In 1919 this sort of effusion was unique. The establishment thought she was stark raving mad, holding revival meetings in colored town, stirring up "the niggers" to sing and testify in sessions even louder than her meetings in the white neighborhoods.

Her accounts of the "colored camp meetings" show that there she was in her element. She recalls the singing, the handclapping and dancing with great relish. The meetings spilled out of the tent, in long marches through the Miami streets; blacks in aprons and overalls, in straw hats and bandannas, teeth and eyes flashing. In their midst a small white woman in a white dress danced with a rhythmic sensuality that seemed not wholly spiritual.

It was glorious, and it was scandalous. Before Aimee left Miami for Key West, the white converts, out of sheer curiosity, were jostling the black folks for standing room when Aimee preached on the dark side of town.

In Key West the meetings arranged for the colored population became integrated instantly.

At the first meeting in the colored neighborhood a venerable old black man entered the tent, saw Aimee, and walked up to her. The gentleman spoke aloud for all to hear. This was the woman he had seen in a vision, her face and hair. Weeks ago he had seen her in this vision, leading him through a river, where a dove glided down and perched on his shoulder as she led him into the presence of God.

"It was impossible to keep the white people away. So for the first time in the Island [Key West] the white and colored attended the same place of worship and glorified the same Lord side by side."

———

But in this moment of her public triumph there was private heartache. Sometime during the campaign in Key West Harold began to complain about their gypsy life. They argued all night. He got up early next morning to go fishing for the noon meal. When he returned, the car and Aimee and the boy were gone, leaving nothing but the ashes of the campfire.

He returned to Providence.

From Key West Aimee wired Minnie, who was back in New York City doing her Salvation Army work and caring for Roberta. They took the coastal steamer to Miami, and arrived in Key West on March 10.

Roberta was now seven and a half years old. She had seen so little of Aimee since her fifth birthday, she refers to the meeting in Key West as the "discovery" of her mother, whose personality "burst upon my consciousness in all its glory like a comet flashing." Roberta sat with her grandmother on a rough plank bench under her mother's mildewed revival tent. She writes:

I gazed in breathless admiration at the copper-haired, white-clad angel on the platform above me. Mother's arms were outstretched as she blessed her humble congregation, her face aglow with some mystical inner light, her voice vibrating, joyously alive. Sometimes it boomed like a mighty surf, and sometimes it fell to the hushed whisper of a butterfly's wing-beat, but always it pulled me toward her with the force of an invisible magnet . . . Could this glorious creature really be my own, my very own mother? Was it true that

I was going to live with her forever? Whatever happened from now on, I knew beyond a doubt that my life would never, ever, be ordinary again.

Roberta did not understand or recollect the sermon. It was probably one of Aimee's war sermons. In these homilies Aimee seized upon an image in the headlines and milked it for all its religious potential. In the sermon "Liberty Bonds—Over There" she begins with a prosaic explanation of the need to purchase the government's war bonds upon the third issue of the Liberty Loan. And quickly she works up the metaphor:

B-U-Y	of me gold tried in the fire;
A	crown of righteousness, which the Lord shall give you at that day. Stand fast therefore in the
L-I-B-E-R-T-Y	wherefore Christ hath made you free. And above all things put on charity which is the
B-O-N-D	of perfectness.

Then she develops a rhythmic accounting of the Biblical allusions to the concept of liberty bonds: how Abraham made his liberty loan instead of saying, "No, Isaac is mine . . . I will keep my son"; how when Daniel loaned his all "unto his God and entered the lion's den, he received a Liberty bond, an interest-bearing certificate"; how Joseph and Job bought their Bonds, etc. Driving and funny, it sold bonds.

Most important, such sermons brought together the audience's concerns about the war and the salvation of their souls: "The battle to the death now going on in the worldly realm is analogous with that now going on in the spiritual realm." This sermon, and the "Peace Palace Parable," in which she satirizes the Peace Palace in the Hague and compares it to institutional Churches, and the sermon "Modern Warfare—Over the Top," in which she works out an elaborate conceit comparing the war in France with the War of the Spirit, anticipate the incantatory news-headline poems written by Allen Ginsburg and others in the 1960's, with an evangelistic twist. Her mind had become a kind of cosmic transmitter relating the tragedy of the faraway war to the immediate hardship of the poor laborers of the South.

Nowhere does she refer to the breakup with Harold McPherson, except to say that the Lord helped her "while left alone at Key West." The wind and rain had been terrible that winter. The effort of hammering extra stakes, tying the guy ropes, and staying up all night to keep the tents from blowing over drove Aimee to exhaustion.

"At present," she recorded, "I am very weak in body, and have to hang on to God for strength for each meeting."

Minnie Kennedy's arrival in Florida was more than a relief to her daughter. Aimee had created a crowd phenomenon that was growing beyond any amateur's ability to control. Anyone with rudimentary business sense could see that Aimee Semple McPherson, for all her unworldliness, was a hot property. Everywhere she went, she drew a crowd. Minnie Kennedy had been prepared for this all along. Not only would she take care of the two children and the lists of *Bridal Call* subscriptions and correspondence; she would take charge of booking Aimee's road show, quickly transforming a hobo's odyssey into a continental tour, out of the ragged tent and into the convention hall.

The last meeting of the winter campaign, in Orlando, was its crowning success. The 1,500-seat tent was filled to capacity for two weeks running. This surprised Aimee, who had been told the town was too "aristocratic" to warm to her message.

———

The photo album of that spring celebrates the reunion of the family, minus Harold McPherson. There are snapshots of Aimee hugging her mother, who appears forebearing rather than delighted by Aimee's spontaneity; pictures of Aimee on one knee, grinning as she hugs the children, whose delight is unmistakable.

Most revealing are the photographs of Rolf and his older sister

Roberta hugging each other joyfully, with clear affection. Rolf had been virtually an only child, in the gypsy life with his parents. He could have resented his father's departure and his older sister's intrusion. But he did not. With all Aimee's frenzy, with all her obsession with her work, she was able to hold her children's emotions in a comfortable balance.

Independently, Rolf McPherson and Roberta Salter have commented that these years of traveling with Aimee and Minnie were a wonderful time of adventure despite the physical hardships. It was fun, when it might have been frightening, because both felt secure in their mother's love. Minnie was stern and demanding; Aimee was a constant source of affection and comfort.

As they drove in the Gospel Car from West Palm Beach to the colored camp meeting at Miami, then all the way up the coast to Orlando, the women and children were often without food, warm clothing, or shelter. So Aimee wove about them the story of the Israelite children. In the wilderness, God was always with them in their travails; He would provide. Rolf recalls that many times when they were hungry, they would pray for food. Then someone would arrive with a basket of goodies, some kind "sister" who said she had heard a voice telling her to cook extra "for the evangelist and her children," just as had happened in the early days with Mack.

One of Rolf McPherson's earliest memories is a strange story about his shoes. Throughout the Florida odyssey he had gone for months barefoot. Sometimes other kids teased him. His mother told Rolf a shipment of clothes was coming from Providence, and there would be shoes for him along with new clothing.

At last the shipment caught up with them. They tore into the box eagerly. Aimee found Rolf's shoes and held them up, but her smile melted. She could tell the shoes were too small. Try as he would, the little boy could not get his feet into them.

"Mama," he asked his mother, "what did God do for the Israelite children when their feet grew?"

"Well, Rolf," she said, "I guess He stretched their shoes."

Roberta asked, "Mama, do you think God might stretch Rolf's shoes?"

"I suppose He might," said Aimee. "Anyway we'll pray about it."

It was evening. They all prayed that God might stretch Rolf's shoes to fit his feet. They meditated on the problem late into the night, having a measurable effect either upon Rolf's feet or the shoes themselves as they lay beneath the cot—because when he tried them on the next morning, they fit perfectly.

Only a few months later, at summer's end, it would be not shoe leather but the flesh of his feet that would be changed by a supernatural power.

In Philadelphia the barefoot Rolf McPherson, romping on the campgrounds, came down on the pointed tines of a steel rake. One of the points pierced the sole of his foot. The pain was dull and deep, the blood a dark color. Rolf cannot remember the attentions of a doctor; but he does remember his mother catching him up in her arms, carrying him to the small tent where they had set up housekeeping, and laying him down on the army cot. As she held the bleeding foot in her hand and gazed into his eyes, he felt a remarkable warmth in her hand and the pain seemed to drain into it. He went to sleep.

When he awoke, he was by himself. Far away he heard the roar of a crowd. It seemed to him that he had been deeply asleep for days. He remembered that he had stepped on a rake. There was brown dried blood on the sheets. He sat up and grabbed for the wounded foot, turning it up to look at the puncture hole. Not finding it, he figured he must have grabbed the wrong foot.

He turned up his other foot and found no sign of any wound there either.

————

Between Orlando and Philadelphia, where they drove to attend the Nationwide Camp Meeting, Aimee preached for ten days in Pulaski, Virginia. For a week she preached in Roanoke, at the Pentecostal Holiness churches. In Roanoke she argued with

church authorities against the teaching of sanctification as a
second definite work of grace.

"Sanctification" is a sticking point for Fundamentalist theology. It is supposed to be a second state of grace, after conversion, in which the Christian attains moral perfection. The
idea is that, beyond the conversion experience there is a further,
deeper plane of holiness in which one becomes complete and
whole—in effect, Christlike. The Shakers believed this. So did
some of the founders of the Holiness movement in the nine-
teenth century. Present believers in Christian perfection are the
Church of God in Tennessee, the Fire-Baptized Holiness
Church, and the Mountain Assembly of God.

It is a doctrine of such subtlety and persuasion that sanctification deserves more serious attention than we can give it here,
more perhaps than Aimee gave it. She was far more concerned
with its insidious rhetoric as sanctification influenced the simple
souls she wished to win to the Church. The idea of perfection
seemed undemocratic, snobbish, and narrow. It led to a division, in any community, between those who had achieved sanctification and those who had not. The notion led to stratification,
and the glorification of priests, and hundreds of regulations in
conduct codes. Those who claimed or pursued Christian perfection often turned their backs on the world, the onrush of
history, and modern technology. They became strange.

Aimee wanted her religion to fit everyone. She wanted no
part of an idea that might exclude people out of hand from the
experience of Christianity. She believed in the idea of perfection
as a Christian goal, but rejected this principle of sanctification,
which dangerously suggested it was attainable in this life.

So, like any skillful rhetorician, Aimee simplified the discussion. She reduced the argument until only her own voice could
be heard saying: "Whatever fancy name you give it, sin is sin
. . . God looks on the heart and as for holiness, why, without
holiness no man shall see the Lord. We must be saved, must
be sanctified, but 'tis all through the precious atoning blood of
Jesus Christ." This was simple, it was democratic, it was glorious. All sins, actual transgressions and "inbred" original sin,
would be wiped away in the very instant of conversion!

PHILADELPHIA, 1918

By the time she arrived in Philadelphia, a few days before July 21, 1918, Sister Aimee was thoroughly prepared for her debut on the national stage. Her oratorical skills she had fully developed on the stump. She had defined a populist theology that emphasized grace and salvation, and had begun to focus her powers as a healer.

Aimee had helped to plan this nationwide meeting on her way down through Philadelphia the previous autumn. At the same time she prayed for a new tent to accommodate vast crowds. She had placed a notice in her *Bridal Call* to raise the money, and collected fifteen hundred dollars. But no tent was available, because it was wartime: the government had commandeered all the large tent makers. Months of letter writing and hunting for a tent of the right specifications brought no results. She would have despaired, except that God kept telling her: "You shall have your tent."

Evidently the Lord had answered the prayers of another evangelist in Philadelphia, sending him the perfect tent: ten-ounce Army duck, double stitched, with strong rope, block and tackle, twenty-five hundred dollars' worth of tent. It lay tied up in bags, poles and stakes complete, in the attic of a building in downtown Philadelphia.

The tent remained brand-new in its bags because the evangelist had fallen ill. It seems that this divine had taken a strong stand against the Pentecostal outpouring of the Spirit; then he suffered a breakdown. Now he was living in a sanatorium for the mentally ill, and so had no use for the excellent tent the Lord had provided. Aimee got it for fifteen hundred dollars.

What transpired in Philadelphia, under the enormous white Gospel tent with its freshly painted poles and the green altar rail, may be seen as a turning point in Aimee's career. Yet it differed only in scale from the meetings in Orlando and Washburn.

These camp meetings, in the clear light of an American summer, had the festive atmosphere of a carnival. Rows of tents were erected around the tabernacle. A kitchen, store and outhouses were boarded in. City water was piped up, and overflow and dormitory tents were pitched. Families motored, *en caravan*, from twenty-five states to attend the Philadelphia meeting. They came on holiday, leaving their farms in the countryside or their factory jobs in the city. They sought an inspiration their parishes had failed to provide. In the wake of an industrial revolution they had yet to embrace, and a foreign war that deprived them of sons and husbands, the campers sought comfort. In photos they look joyful, hundreds of women in sunbonnets and full skirts milling about the packed tabernacle, fewer men in shirtsleeves and straw boaters. The gathering breathes an air of expectation: anything might happen, if they can only keep their faith.

In 1918 the field of white tents reminds us of the military camps in France, and the very different hopes in the faces of American soldiers. Some may have believed survival depended upon a mother's prayers in the cool shade of the revival tents across the sea.

Aimee understood these things. As a great performer she knew the needs and expectations of every audience. Her own sense of urgency she betrays in a sentence written for *The Bridal Call* but stricken from the article as reprinted in her autobiography. She describes "this great convocation, which may be the last before Jesus comes." Aimee's theology had become millennial.

The morning service opened with songs and praying in unison. With chins and hands raised and eyes closed, the thousands abandoned themselves to the Spirit. The beat of Aimee's tambourine as it flashed in arcs was irresistible.

When she had melded the crowd into a unit, she began to preach in a thundering voice. It seemed to roll up and out of the earth behind her, up through her diaphragm and then into every ear on the way to Heaven.

The lightnings flash as visible signs of the wrath
  and fury of Almighty God.
Listen! The thunders are rolling and resounding from
  Hill to Hill.

Below is a green pasture field, and in its enclosure
  a beautiful flock of white lambs.
Surely they shall know no fear or terror,
For there is One in their midst who holds in one hand
  his crook,
And in the other a cruse of oil.

The storm increases, the winds howl, the waves roll,
The lightning flashes, the enemy draws nearer,
  emboldened by the darkness.
Whither shall the sheep escape?

Stand still, little flock. The indignation of the Lord
Is being poured out upon the wicked,
  but He will pass over thee.
The storms are raging, but behold
  the heavens are rolling apart.
There cometh One whose appearance is all glorious,
His garments are as robes of light,
His face is filled with tenderest compassion,
His arms are out-stretched—

With her face upturned, radiating Heaven's light as she felt it,
her eyes half-closed in hypnotic suggestion, Aimee envisioned
the brilliant Shepherd. With arms outstretched in compassion,
she projected the mental picture of the Good Shepherd so that
the people, with eyes half-closed, could see Him too.

The lions roar, the serpents hiss, the wolves bare
  their fangs,
The enemy rages against the righteous,
But they shall know no terror,
For there is an invisible power betwixt them and their
  enemies.
Their leader is with them, even the Spirit
  to lead them. A lamb is on His bosom.
He speaks to the flock that they should wait and be
  patient a little longer.

Soon will the Shepherd come to gather the sheep of His
    pasture away from out of the dark and cloudy day
And take them to that fold where the sun never sets
And they will be with Him forever.

The voice was deep, incantatory, rising at the top of a verse
and falling at the end, creating its own antiphony of excitement
and satisfying resolution, music supporting the vision she shared
with them through half-closed eyes.

Now and then her dark eyes in mystical wonder would flash
wide, as if the vision had become too intense to dwell in the
half-dark of the trance in which she had found it.

Ah little flock, He cometh, *He cometh*.
Soon thou shalt hear His voice saying,
"Come home my sheep, come home."
To the world destruction cometh, but
to the flock the Shepherd cometh. Look up!

The sharp command was like a snap of the fingers, waking
everyone from their revery and making their focus upon the
reading of Psalm 91. This was followed by testimonies, and
manifestations of the Spirit.

Strong men have fallen off their chairs between the rows of seats
and in the aisles . . . hundreds have gotten through to God in
salvation and been filled with the Spirit, speaking with other
tongues.

The greatest desire of each worker has been that the Holy Spirit
might have right of way. There was a time when each of us used
to try to lead meetings, but we have long since gotten through
leading meetings, and now the reins are in His hands . . .

I have seen the Spirit of song fall upon the people, and they
would sing for hours; preaching and testimony was out of the
question. At other times the spirit of testimony would fall upon
the people; and witness after witness would spring to their feet . . .
again there would be a message in tongues and interpretations
would come from different parts of the tabernacle, also messages
in prophecy.

The peculiar antics of these holy rollers attracted the attention
of several neighborhood gangs, young men from Catholic families who resented the Pentecostal invasion. These men began
attending the meetings. Whenever a convert spoke in tongues,
or danced in the Spirit, the young hoodlums laughed uproari-
ously. They jeered, they aped the Pentecostals. At the altar
service they stood over the seekers, taunting and mocking so
that no one could pray in peace.

News of this disturbance traveled fast, swelling the crowd at
the Nationwide Camp Meeting that already was approaching
ten thousand.

The gang leaders, employees of two major factories in Philadelphia, hatched a plot to wipe the revival tents off the face of
the earth by the second Monday night of the revival. They
delivered threats. Aimee's pleas for police protection went unheeded because on the same day a race riot broke out in the
center of Philadelphia.

So that Monday night, the gangs turned out in force. They
carried clubs and blackjacks. Their leaders had police whistles
they used to disrupt prayers and deploy the hoodlums back and
forth, elbowing and clubbing their way through the passive
crowds of the faithful, who swayed back and forth like waves
of wheat in a strong wind.

One policeman finally showed up, but he could not control
the situation. Ten thousand people were driven back and forth
by squadrons of juvenile delinquents trying to disperse them.
Aimee, who could not make herself heard, decided to dismiss
the night meeting without even attempting an altar call. The
crowd ignored her, showing no inclination to leave, mumbling
or shouting as they milled around through the tent and all over
the campgrounds.

So Aimee gathered the revival leaders in a huddle. She announced there would be an "all-night" of prayer. "To settle
this matter once and for all," she would recall, "we began to
pray one after another for the salvation of the boys and men."

Sister Elizabeth Sisson rose up from Aimee's side and pro-
claimed for all to hear: "The people shall become our bread . . .
He that sitteth in the Heavens shall laugh."

After this, Aimee ordered the crowd to their knees to pray. People began to kneel, in widening circles. This left no one on his feet but the hoodlums, who looked wildly about them, as if they had been caught naked.

The faithful prayed in unison while the rowdies strode back and forth, threatening this one and that one on his knees to no avail.

"Now dear ones," said Aimee, "just let us be quiet and see what God has for us."

In the ensuing silence the Spirit worked variously upon the thousands gathered in the electric light under the broad tent. Many moved their lips in soundless prayer. Some trembled. Some swayed to and fro or waved their arms, and the hoodlums mocked them, pointing and guffawing.

Aimee had moved aside to a space at the far end of the rostrum. Damp with sweat, her white dress clung to her. Her wide eyes, flashing, sought out the center of concentric spheres. Raising one arm high, she touched the axis of the innermost sphere, lowered her eyelids, and spun gracefully beneath the pointing hand.

All eyes immediately fixed on her.

With both hands above her head, palms facing the crowd, she turned her head to one side, listening. Her body began rhythmically to sway, right and left, as the hands above her head held still. She moved beneath the hands, shoulders counter to hips. Somewhere there was music, a slow pronounced drumbeat nobody could hear at first but Aimee. She could recall it from a meeting in the black ghetto in Miami, or the colored camp meetings in Key West where the converts danced ragtime in the Spirit, to guitars and drums. Listening to the music within her, Aimee danced, as gracefully as she did everything in sight of a crowd, her eyes half-closed.

She danced for a long time, until the beat she was hearing under her heels on the hollow stage was audible to the several thousand people under the tent. They fell into a physical rhythm, snapping their fingers, swaying from side to side. Without missing a beat of this rhythm, Aimee moved over to the upright piano. With both hands she came down hard on a dissonant chord. It was sure and defiant. She hit another chord, and another, maintaining the beat, "weird heavenly chords," according to one correspondent, "that never man could produce in the natural, chords that struck to the very soul." Aimee nodded in syncopation to the rhythm.

She played and played in time to the beat. What sounded "weird" to the churchgoing provincials in 1918 was probably no more than the virile dissonances, E-flat blues progressions and diminished chords, which Aimee had brought from the Deep South, where they had so recently been discovered.

The hoodlums meanwhile had gone beyond hostility to fascination; now caught up in the music, they were being entertained. Religion may have divided the Catholic youths and the Pentecostal campers, but this music was something else. It brought them together, made them move and clap on the same downbeat. Sister Aimee began to sing "in the Spirit," an improvised song in perfect rhyme and meter, about the Lord's coming. Now she had them in the palm of her hand.

Aimee would shift, gradually, from the ambiguous content of music to a clear religious message. Rising from the piano, she lifted her voice to an eerie and earsplitting volume and began to speak in tongues. It was incomprehensible but compelling all the same, and the hoodlums cried out in curiosity, wanting to know what on earth the little woman was doing now. Was she still singing? Was she casting a curse upon them? Dark eyes wide and ablaze, she grabbed up a megaphone, which stood near the pulpit by a flower vase.

She took the flowers from the vase and filled the megaphone with them, proclaiming that this was the horn of plenty.

Next she strewed the flowers on the ground. She took up a glass pitcher from the pulpit. Without losing a step of the rhythm she had created in the dance, she watered the flowers on the ground. She sang that all the saints of heaven would be revived and watered with the Latter Rain which soon would fall upon them.

"Get ready," she cried. "Get ready for the soon oncoming King Jesus."

Still dancing, Aimee moved to the outstretched arms of a

woman caught up in the same subaudible music. In silence they danced together. Aimee backed the young woman against the pulpit and lovingly spread her arms to either side over her head like a crucifix. With slow circular movements Aimee mimed the driving of spikes, through first one hand and then the other, as the Christ figure swooned in the ecstasy of her pain.

She laid her down, as in the tomb.

She raised her up, as in the Resurrection, and the voice of thousands cried Hallelujah and Praise the Lord.

When this was done, she spoke again in tongues, in that low melodious voice. And the tongues gave way to simple sentences as she interpreted the scene that just transpired:

"Behold the Lord is calling. He is searching for a people for Himself. Who will be willing to go all the way? Such a one will reign with me . . ." Notice how she moved in and out of Christ's voice, speaking of Him at one moment, and for Him the next. The listeners were so far under a spell that many had begun to feel Christ's presence in their leader's flesh.

"Wilt thou, wilt thou follow me?"

She moved, as if on a carpet of air, out into the audience.

"Behold the way is long: the night is dark: the road is thorny: yet trust thou me. I will be with thee . . . Behold thy hands, thy hands that are busy with the cares of the world . . ." Her voice now rumbled like the bass notes of a barrel organ, with a tone of foreboding that sounded like menace to the young men.

They had cooled on the idea of wiping the tents off the face of Philadelphia after hearing her declare: "They must be nailed to the cross!"

"Art thou willing to have thy hands nailed to the cross? Thy busy feet that have walked for this world must be nailed to the cross. Thy heart that has beat for this world must be pierced for me."

The depth and power of the voice commanded reverence. How could it be coming from that little woman in the white dress soaked with sweat until her pink skin shone through it? The voice must have a deeper source, divine authority.

A prayer of consecration followed, and as Aimee finished the long prayer, dawn was breaking.

From that day on, the meetings went forward in peace.

The Nationwide Meeting in Philadelphia continued all summer. When it closed in September, 1918, Sister Aimee Semple McPherson had a national reputation as a Pentecostal evangelist and healer.

That summer so many letters flew out of Philadelphia, singing the woman evangelist's praises, that she received invitations from New York to Tulsa to come and speak the Gospel.

Faith was all very well, said Minnie Kennedy. But "faith without works" was dead. No more blind bookings. The letter-writing campaign she had begun in Florida was paying off in a series of scheduled dates. To Minnie, evangelism was organization, not just faith. Minnie's aim was to get Aimee in front of the greatest number of people with a minimum of effort. This included raising the tents. Now that Minnie handled the schedule, she responded to invitations with "We'll be happy to come if you can get us a lot rent-free, borrow a piano, and round up a corps of workers . . ."

Thus the two women toured New England in the autumn. A small cash surplus built up. In October Minnie booked Sister Aimee into the fashionable 700-seat Harlem Casino, at 100 West 116th Street in New York City, her first auditorium. Aimee filled it from the 6th of October until the 10th by preaching, speaking in tongues, singing, and playing the piano.

The New York meeting, planned originally for the tiny Mt. Olivet Assembly Hall, blossomed into a regional convention. On the last night more than a dozen Pentecostal assemblies from Brooklyn to West New Brighton testified, and gave special thanks for Sister Aimee's inspiration.

America needed the kind of comfort the woman evangelist was offering. The Germans were falling apart along the Hindenburg line, but the battle cost us dearly: 120,000 Americans killed and wounded. And as if in response to the catastrophe abroad the influenza epidemic in America hit its peak—two hundred deaths a day. In poor neighborhoods of cities like New York, where Aimee was preaching, there were not enough coffins to bury the dead. They lay unburied for days, and the smell of death was inescapable. Nearly one person in four got the flu; before the disease ran its course a few months later, half a million people would die of it, four times the number killed in the war.

In the midst of this suffering and despair Sister Aimee appeared like an angel of mercy, a cross between Florence Nightingale and Joan of Arc. Americans needed some explanation for all this suffering, some hope of deliverance. And they wanted healing.

The year before, preaching in a church somewhere in Rhode Island, she noticed her dresses were threadbare. With seven dollars in her pocket she went to a clothing store, where she could not find a dress for less than eighteen dollars.

"Oh Lord what shall I wear?" she wondered.

And a Voice came back saying, "You are a servant of all, are you not? Go upstairs to the servants' department and ask them to let you see the servants' dresses."

The maid's uniforms were white or black. Five dollars for two of them.

"I did not want to be a crow, I wanted to be the Lord's dove, so I asked to see the white," she recalls.

From that day until she became an obsession of the national press in the mid 1920's, Sister Aimee wore only those white maid's dresses to preach in, and a secondhand military cape. So she looked, in her portly and efficient kindness, exactly like a battlefield nurse.

As influenza threatened to decimate the cities, and Aimee's reputation as a healer grew, she soon found herself preaching over scenes of human suffering that resembled the field hospitals in France.

Because of the epidemic there were bans on public assembly in most places. Somehow Aimee escaped the bans. Churches closed up in cities just after she left, and opened for her just as she arrived.

She came to New Rochelle on October 13. During that week, she herself was stricken with the influenza, but she preached in spite of chills and fever. Roberta got it, and with the complications of double pneumonia the child lay near death. As she shivered in a furnished room without proper heat, Roberta wished aloud for a real home. She wanted a place to live where she could go to school like other girls.

One afternoon Aimee returned from a meeting, and a woman met her at the top of the stairs. She warned Aimee that Roberta was feverish. Aimee knelt to pray for the Lord to spare her daughter's life. And in the surreal inner clarity that sometimes comes with fever, Aimee heard the Voice, the same Voice that always chose its words so carefully and always spoke the truth. The Voice told Aimee that He would raise up her daughter, and He would do more than that. "I will give you a little home in Los Angeles, California." With the Voice came a vision: of Abraham laying Isaac upon the sacrificial altar and then being spared the agony of seeing him die; then a house bathed in golden light, a bungalow with a rose garden.

Los Angeles, California. The vision was so specific, remote, and strange, she believed it. As soon as Roberta's fever broke, Aimee told her what God had promised. She told Rolf as well, and the three of them joyfully detailed the home in sunny California, filling it with dream furniture and pets and flowers.

All the while, Aimee heard another voice, which was not the Lord's, whispering: "An awful thing for you to build these children's hopes up like this. What if you should be disappointed?"

"The thing is," says eighty-year-old Roberta Salter, smiling as her forehead furrows in wonder, "we didn't know how remarkable it was. When Mother told us something would happen, it was like money in the bank."

CALIFORNIA

Aimee Semple McPherson may well have been the first woman to drive a car from New York to California without a man to fix flat tires.

Long-distance travel by automobile in 1918 was a perilous adventure reserved, for the most part, for soldiers of fortune and test drivers with advanced training in auto mechanics. The problem was not so much the machine itself. Henry Ford mass-produced the reliable Model T in 1910; other manufacturers worked to improve on his standard. The problem was the roads. Before any cross-country highway system appeared, the roads were mostly carriage tracks. These became creeks in the rain, or dust corridors during the dry season.

The lack of service stations proved just as troublesome. Between cities you could drive for hours without finding a fuel pump, particularly if you weren't sure where you were going. And the tires were not much better than thick balloons. They would overheat and blow out every forty or fifty miles. Tires had to be hand-patched and inflated with a hand pump. Before the autumn of 1918, snapshots show Harold McPherson fixing flat tires. Thereafter we see Aimee with a wrench in her hand, grease-smeared, grinning into the camera.

Aimee loved the automobile. She spoke of her car as if it were a talking horse, a valiant coworker for the Lord. "A crowd has gathered about the faithful car which is holding its own street meeting and preaching all by itself . . ."

Before she headed west, Aimee sold the Packard for almost as much as she had paid for it, and bought a brand-new Oldsmobile touring car, a seven-seater. Minnie came up with the cash to pay the difference. Aimee had the signs repainted in six-inch gold letters: JESUS IS COMING SOON—GET READY on one side and WHERE WILL YOU SPEND ETERNITY? on the other.

On October 23, 1918 they loaded up the car with tracts and newsletters, blankets and suitcases, and headed out on the Lincoln Highway from New York to Philadelphia. From there they would pick up the National Road to Indianapolis, and the Big Four Highway to Kansas City.

Minnie sat in the back with Rolf and Roberta under a buffalo robe. Aimee drove. Beside her in the front seat rode the matronly Louise Baer, navigating with the Automobile Blue Book.

Sister Louise, a bespectacled middle-aged Christian, had appeared in answer to Aimee's prayers for a stenographer. She was the first of many sisters who would devote their lives to the cause. She took dictation as Aimee drove all day, and typed at night. Roberta grew so accustomed to the pecking of the typewriter that she couldn't sleep without it. Aimee had decided she ought to write a book, an autobiography to sell at her meetings. Never did she have so much leisure as while she was driving.

They traveled all day. When night fell, Aimee pulled off the road and folded out a cot that had been built into the running board along with brackets for tent poles. Folding the seat back in the Oldsmobile, the three women could sleep in the car while the children slept on the cot.

Covering eighty to a hundred and twenty miles a day, the car rolled through Gettysburg, Pittsburgh, and the coal-mining section of Claysville. There Aimee preached to the miners, whose electric lights shone on the caps above their coal-darkened faces.

The travelers had their first taste of danger on a mountain pass near Wheeling. They lost their way, and came to a turn barely wide enough for the wheels of one car to pass. Rocks hung overhead, and a sheer chasm hundreds of feet deep yawned below. "Angels seemed to hold the car to the road even though it was wet and slippery."

Roberta Salter recalls the journey as a magical adventure with her mother, who despite the danger found time to enjoy moments, the "beauty in little things." She would point to rainwater splashing and say to the children, "There are fairies dancing." Crossing the Blue Ridge, she explained how clouds made rain. "Oh, Mother," said Roberta, "let's get a cloud in a bottle." And Aimee pulled over, parked, and held a bottle up in the mist till drops showed in the glass.

Their Oldsmobile passed abandoned cars that would have to be hauled out of ruts by horses.

The family arrived in flu-stricken Indianapolis on October 30, just as the ban on public meetings was lifted; so Aimee could preach in the Pentecostal tabernacle. On November 1 they drove out through prairie farms and the wheat fields of Tuscola toward Springfield, Illinois. West of Illinois the roads sometimes deteriorated into cow paths, with fallen boulders or tree limbs Aimee had to haul away before the car could move on. Sometimes a road would end suddenly around a bend, defying the maps in the Automobile Blue Book. They would backtrack for hours, searching for an alternate route.

Aimee's strong shoulders and arms grew even more muscular from long days at the wheel. Roberta recalls that some nights her mother could not sleep because the steering wheel's vibration continued in her arms long after the engine had quit.

The script on the car, in gold letters, caused a stir everywhere they went. So did the phenomenon of these Pentecostal gypsies traveling without a male escort. As they crossed the Mississippi River into Hannibal, people gathered around the car, asking questions, thanking the women for their religious tracts and newsletters.

From Missouri to Oklahoma Aimee heard these words over and over again: "Well, this is just exactly what I have been thinking; that this war, and all of these plagues must be a sign of the coming of the Lord. Lady, give us some literature."

The small towns of Kansas welcomed them warmly as they passed through that pastoral birthplace of the Pentecostal movement. Over vast stretches of prairie, past oil rigs, they motored on toward Oklahoma. At noon on November 10 they drove into view of Tulsa, where Aimee had been invited to preach. Sighting the skyline, the women and children shouted and cheered, "For it seemed that must be the way it will be when a soul is nearing Heaven . . . no more stones, mud, deep ruts or ditches to be avoided, but smooth streets that are paved with gold."

For three weeks Aimee preached in Tulsa. The flu epidemic had closed the churches there until the week she arrived. She held services and prayed for the sick for hours at a time. She led street meetings and visited the homes of the dead and dying. At the close of the last meeting in Tulsa several hundred who had been baptized in the Spirit marched out of the tabernacle to put their hands upon the Gospel Car. They asked God to protect the car and its passengers.

Word of healings and conversions preceded Aimee to Oklahoma City, where she was invited to preach on the first of December. On the way they stopped for fuel in the little town of Stroud. Earnest folks ambushed them, shouting, "Praise the Lord." These Christians, coming from all over the countryside, had stood waiting in doorways and at street corners since early morning to invite Sister Aimee to a mission in Kendrick, ten miles away. People there were sick; they needed a revival. When Aimee told them she was due somewhere else that night, they would not listen. So she called Oklahoma City and told the workers there she would be a day late.

In Oklahoma City they urged her to extend her visit, to hold meetings among the Indians. But winter was coming. Snowstorms had been reported in the mountains, so she had to keep moving.

The roads leading to Santa Rosa were poor, the steep mountain passes and deep gulches hazardous in the mud and snow. Aimee drove miles and miles without any sign of life but a prairie dog. The car wheels cut deeper in mud, until mud flew over the Oldsmobile. Aimee got out and fastened on the skid chains. She cranked up and drove on, still nine miles from the safety of Santa Rosa, watching the car odometer as the tires spun in the mud.

Darkness fell. They crept forward in low gear, headlights shining. Sister Louise and Minnie Kennedy walked beside the car to reduce the weight.

An icy wind was sweeping over the prairie when the car ran so deep in the mud, it sank down to the fenders.

Neither Roberta nor Rolf McPherson recall a moment of fear in their mother's presence, even in such extremities. Evidently Aimee rarely felt fear, and her courage conveyed itself to everyone around her. Her first thought was to find a piece of lumber so she could jack the car up. But no one had seen so much as a tree for a hundred miles.

Leaving Minnie with the children, Aimee and Sister Louise set out across the prairie. A light in the distance led them to the adobe home of a Mexican farmer.

For several hours by lantern light the Mexican worked his team to haul the car out of the mire, to no avail. Minnie and Sister Louise returned with him to spend the night in his house, and Aimee stayed in the car with the children, all huddled together under blankets to keep from freezing. At daybreak the Mexicans returned with enough horses and planks to put the car back on the road.

"We had not gone more than a mile when we saw God's reason for holding us back; deep washouts and gulches had to be crossed, where only good light, and careful driving could have saved the car and its passengers."

From Santa Rosa, where they rested, they passed via Socorro across New Mexico. The women and children drove through the desert in caravan with three other automobiles, taking turns in the lead and in the rear, eating the desert dust. Giant cactuses towered over the car and coyotes howled in the distance. To mountaintops and on through mountain passes leading down the long grade they rode, coasting through the winding paths and opening vistas toward the gorgeous landscape of San Bernardino.

She felt like Balboa discovering an ocean. After the dry deserts and mud gulches and freezing passes, they found themselves in a sunny garden of orange and lemon trees.

Rialto, Upland; Glendora to Pasadena; and from Pasadena to Los Angeles, where a party of the faithful surprised them with a hearty welcome.

The car odometer, a string of zeros when they left New York City, now registered over 4,000 miles.

That transcontinental auto journey has a shadowy quality to

it, like the underworld passage of an epic quest. Despite Aimee's pluck and lightheartedness, the effort, undertaken for reasons obscure and mysterious, was larger than life.

The date of her arrival is uncertain. But we know she approached California just after the winter solstice, when the days are shortest. From late December of 1918 the sunlight of fame would shine with increasing brilliance upon Sister Aimee, until inevitably it would burn her.

She arrived in Los Angeles famous. This was clear from the number of Pentecostal Christians who welcomed her, and what they were prepared to do for the woman evangelist and her mother and children.

Black preacher William J. Seymour had established the Azusa Street Mission in 1906. There, on April 15, 1906 Jennie Evans Moore spoke in tongues at the close of the Easter service. Four days later, on the morning of the San Francisco earthquake, the *Los Angeles Times* reported "a weird babble of tongues" amid "wild scenes" in the mission. A crowd of blacks and whites created a long service where they sang a cappella, gave testimony, shouted, and preached in the Spirit.

The core membership of that pioneering mission never exceeded sixty. Yet its publicity attracted thousands who tried to enter the forty-by-sixty-foot building to see the spectacle of colored and white folks worshiping together. For three years the meetings increased in influence. Seymour incorporated his ministry as the Pacific Apostolic Faith Movement, and published a magazine called *Apostolic Faith*, whose circulation reached 50,000 subscribers. Visitors to Azusa Street included Charles Parham, William Durham, who brought the revival to Chicago, Cecil Polhill of England, "Mother" Elizabeth Wheaton, and Carrie Judd Montgomery, all important figures in the movement.

The curious behavior of the Pentecostal worshipers would have caused a stir if they had been black *or* white. But the fact that the Azusa Street Mission was interracial made its meetings a public scandal. The mix of blacks, whites, Hispanics, and other ethnic minorities in the melting pot of the Pentecostal fire is the stunning social achievement of the revival. The movement's chief chronicler in Los Angeles, Frank Bartleman, commented: "The color line has been washed away by the blood."

But by the time Aimee got to Los Angeles, late in 1918, the Azusa Street Revival was little more than a memory. "Doctrinal differences had gotten the eyes of many off the Lord," Bartleman explained. The sizable Pentecostal community was looking for leadership to inspire a new revival where the seeds had been sown ten years before.

From all they had heard, Sister Aimee was the woman for the job.

Two days after she arrived, she opened at the upstairs Victoria Hall, which seated 700. She preached on the text "Shout!: for the Lord hath given you the city." It was prophetic. Within days, mobs of people were not able to find room in the hall; chairs were ranged on the elevation covering the baptistry; and the pastor threw open his office suite of four rooms. The stairway and corridors overflowed into Spring Street, into First and Second avenues.

So Minnie searched for a larger meeting space, and found Temple Auditorium. Facing Pershing Park, this hall is now known as Philharmonic Auditorium. In 1919 it seated 3,500 and cost a hundred dollars to rent for three hours, a lot of money then. But Minnie knew that Aimee was worth the gamble, after the crowds she had seen on Spring Street.

Long before the meeting, the seats were full. People sat or stood wedged for hours between the rows. Ushers pushed their way up and down the aisles in an effort to enforce the fire regulations. Children sat on the floor in front of the altar, and on the platform itself. Men raised the windows and sat on windowsills. Aimee could hardly reach the pulpit without stepping on people. Many of them had come just to gape at her.

Her chief public relations organ was *The Bridal Call*. This she continued to dictate to Sister Louise in hours stolen from sleep, or between bites of dinner; but *The Bridal Call* was modest. What reached the ears of the multitude, and made them stand in line for hours to get a seat in Temple Auditorium were fabulous tales of a wonder woman who had brought dozens of the dead to life in Oklahoma during the influenza epidemic. She was known as a miracle worker who brought alcoholics, drug addicts, and fallen women weeping to the altar to find their salvation.

The people of Los Angeles could not do enough for her. Less than two weeks after Aimee's arrival, a woman at a packed meeting sprang to her feet testifying:

"The Lord shows me that I am to give a lot to Mrs. Mc-Pherson . . . I am not called to preach the Gospel, while she is, and by giving the land that the little ones may have a home and she may be free to come and go in the Lord's work, I will share in her reward."

She sat down. A man sprang to his feet, announcing, "I will dig the cellar."

All over the hall men and women got up and pledged: "I will do the lathing," "I will do the plastering," and so on, until rose bushes and a canary had been provided as well.

The lot lay across the street from a public school. On the day of dedication and earth-turning, the crowd formed a line. They marched, singing and praying, around the property, asking the Lord for the means to pay for the materials. Aimee wrote a column in *The Bridal Call* under the heading "The House That God Built," inviting contributions.

"You will be glad to know you had a little part in The House That God Built. Pray over it and address communications to the Editor, 125 South Spring Street, Los Angeles, California."

Aimee had promised Roberta a home as she recovered from influenza in October. The house with its gabled porches and brick chimney was a reality by April.

While the house was under construction, Aimee and her family loaded up the Oldsmobile with tracts. They headed for San Francisco.

In the strong sunlight of California Aimee's ministry began to change in ways she had not anticipated and hardly could control. The first hint of this comes from her recollection of the meetings in San Francisco in February of 1919, where she asserts, for the first time, this evangelistic priority:

"Throughout our meetings everywhere we have put the ministry for the soul first, then the ministry for the body; nevertheless miracles of healing have been wrought in almost every meeting."

It is the word *nevertheless* that haunts us, with its sense of inevitability and hint of panic.

Chronic invalids migrated to California upon their doctor's advice. Southern California has always attracted patients with "ideational" diseases like asthma and rheumatism, pathologies with a strong psychological component. When strangers meet in Southern California, they automatically inquire, "Where are you from?" and then, "How do you feel?" Illness and transiency have been the chief catalysts of cultism in the region.

Sister Aimee became famous for working wonders, transformations spiritual and physical. Naturally, the thousands of invalids who had flocked to California seeking a physical "cure" in that perfect climate would jostle to monopolize her attention. She understood the crowd's psychology and its fatal control over her meetings, yet she insisted upon a ministry for the soul first, then for the body. This was her preference.

But a crowd is more body than spirit. Her preference to heal the spirit went against the crowd's will. Christ had found the same problem with His ministry.

BALTIMORE, 1919

In her lengthy prose-poem in *The Bridal Call* of February, 1919, titled "The Temple," Aimee describes a mystical temple as revealed to Isaiah and seen by John on the Isle of Patmos

. . . of such vast proportions . . . there can be no end of the universe where God is, to which this great temple does not reach. Of such grandeur is it, this temple with God for its Architect, Christ for its High Priest, made up of living stones composed of blood-washed souls, its domes and arches of divine love and adoration, with saints and teachers for its pillars, and worshippers for its pavement, that it hath need of neither the sun nor the moon to shine on it, for the glory of God doth lighten it.

She might as well be describing the shape of her career.

This is the mystical temple of her dreams, the visionary space she has sketched, from coast to coast, in the shade of her revival tents. The bungalow under construction while she wrote "The Temple" is a chamber of it, and the great Angelus Temple dedicated in 1923 will be its earthly model.

Her power to build, in 1919 or 1921, was equal to her power to inspire an audience. This peaked during the years leading to the dedication of the Temple. The Great Revivals of 1920, 1921, and 1922, in Baltimore, Dayton, San Jose, Denver, and two dozen other cities, generated the income to pay for the Angelus Temple. It was the physical expression of a spiritual ideal she had described in the prose-poem, a temple "made up of living stones."

Sister Aimee had two faces:

From the time she began to write, the girl signed her letters "little Aimee." She seems to have treasured this demur self-image her whole life, this sense of herself as God's little girl, saucer-eyed, innocent, and vulnerable. Little Aimee is God's darling because she is small, and not too bright, and full of love for Him and all His creatures, and she is good, mostly. She needs taking care of.

This is the Aimee that is irresistible to old ladies, children, horses, dogs, frogs, and at least half the men in America. In her writings this voice is full of exclamation points and double adjectives. At times it seems on the brink of baby talk, though her innate good taste in diction keeps her within the bounds of nineteenth-century sentimentality, the world of Dickens and "Little Nell." This is not a pose—it is real. Anyone inclined to doubt Aimee's naivete has only to discover the disastrous choices she made later in her personal life and finances.

The other side of Aimee is the dark-eyed sibyl, the commanding prophetess with the booming contralto. This is Aimee
inspired, the queen who reigns at the revival meetings. It is also
the strong-armed woman who wields the sledgehammer driving tent stakes, and drags boulders and fallen timber out of the
path of her Oldsmobile in New Mexico.

This Aimee is the idol and muse of newsmen, bible salesmen,
restless clergy, church ladies yearning for the Second Coming,
and a growing corps of bespectacled, hard-featured assistants
beginning with Louise Baer.

On their motor trip to San Francisco in late February of 1919,
Ma Kennedy snapped dozens of photos of her handsome daughter: a romantic figure in a long dark dress, Rubenesque, her
hand on a chair back, gracefully balanced; round-faced Aimee
peering out of a crowd of lilies; Aimee charming a goose; Aimee
amongst the roses, a mysterious apparition in a cape and broad-
brimmed hat. She is posing, mugging, delighted to search for
new roles, pleased to make herself at home in them. Hers is
not the face of the photographer's model, beautiful beyond
change from all angles; it is the chameleon face of complex
character, ever changing. The camera loves her. She had driven
the car to L.A. just before Christmas, a buxom twenty-eight-
year-old wearing a wide-lapeled bomber jacket and a garrison
cap with silver wings pinned to the crown. That is what she
wore as she drove the car, most of her waking hours. When
time came to preach, she removed the cap and coat. Then she
looked like a nurse.

The thirty revivals Sister Aimee conducted from mid-1919
until mid-1922 had a mass appeal unequaled by any touring
phenomenon of theater or politics in American history. Neither
Houdini nor Teddy Roosevelt had such an audience, nor P. T.
Barnum. Lasting from one to four weeks, these meetings in-
variably overflowed the armories, opera houses, and convention
halls rented to hold them. Aimee's voice created an excitement
in the crowd bordering on hysteria.

The newspaper coverage of these meetings runs to several
hundred pages, just as Aimee's account of her odyssey begins
to trail off. This timing is fortunate, as the story becomes so

fantastic, nobody now would believe it, were it not for the voluminous newspaper record. No one, surely, would take Aimee's word for it.

She was too busy now, or too exhausted, to write as much after the first printing of *This Is That* in 1919. The second edition, appearing in 1921, as well as the third in 1923 would rely heavily upon newspaper reprints and photographs to bring the autobiography up to date.

The newspapers "discovered" Aimee in Baltimore, in December of 1919.

The reporter from *The Baltimore Sun* is received by Aimee and her mother as they sit, side by side, in the red plush parlor of the Belvedere Hotel on December 5. He finds a striking woman of twenty-nine, five feet six inches in height and weighing, "by her own confession," a hundred and fifty pounds, and with a wealth of vital brown hair, which she piles high on the top of her head. "Her complexion is good, her features generously sketched, slightly inclined to be heavy in repose, her large, hazel eyes capable of great fire."

He opens with the defensive question: "How did you arrive at the conclusion that Baltimore was on the downward path morally and needed a revival to save it?"

The eyes flash, the lips purse as she prepares her answer. The hands turn palms-up in gestures that draw the city into her monologue.

"As soon as I entered the city," she says, her brow furrowed, "I saw the need. Women were sitting in the dining room smoking with the men. I took up the newspapers and I saw card parties and dances advertised in connection with the churches. There was a coldness. Card parties, dances, theaters, all represent agencies of the devil to distract the attention of men and women away from spirituality . . ." The newsman scribbles. He has heard this sort of thing before, though coming from the lips of this vibrant young woman, the Fundamentalist party line acquires a peculiar force. Then comes the clincher:

"There is too much fire in the furnaces of the churches and not enough upstairs."

The newsman blinks.

"Did you hear those people at the Lyric sing yesterday afternoon?" The contralto voice rises in the question, expressing wonder and delight, maintaining its pitch into the middle of the next phrase. "They turned the corners on high, and oh, how they sang!"

Her automobile jargon leads to the information that the little lady has driven her car across the continent, and four times from Maine to Florida.

"She looks," notes the newsman, "as if she might be capable of taking the car apart and putting it together again. Indeed, there is little in her appearance to suggest the evangelist until her face lights up with the evangelistic fire."

Indeed. The uncorseted madonna with the abundant brown hair and "features generously sketched" could not possibly suggest any evangelist in recent memory—she is the wrong sex.

This thousand-word feature column runs right beside a story on Dr. Florence Meredith, the "girl health expert." The doctor's examination of 12,000 young women has assured her that high heels and corsets are not a cause of premature death. "They merely lower efficiency. The woman who wears them is merely less alive. She is 75 percent alive instead of 100 percent." The voluptuous heroine in the news column next door, the preposterous evangelist, would sooner be caught naked than in a corset. One hundred and fifty percent alive, Sister McPherson is the spirit and image of the "new woman," though her morals would warm the heart of old Cotton Mather.

She charms the newsman, telling the story of her life: how her mother consecrated her to the Lord at birth; her wild and misspent youth among theaters and Darwin and dancing with the Presbyterian minister; how she fell in love with the Irish preacher whose blue eyes and brown curls transformed her; how they were married under a bower of cedar and then sailed for China; how he died there and she returned home alive with her baby daughter . . .

When she has the reporter (and the imagined reader) eating out of her hand, hungry for the story's ending, particularly for the current details of her personal life, she shifts the course of the interview, teasingly.

She attacks the vanities of dress and jewelry. Women "go forth with their faces painted as does the Indian, and with a vanity bag to answer the place of the tomahawk."

The reporter asks if Aimee believes silk stockings are evil.

"It depends altogether," says the Rubenesque subject, crossing her powerful legs, "on how much of them is shown."

About the remarkable cures reported at her revivals, Aimee is evasive. "I do not claim to have the power to cure them," she explains, "but I or some other person at the meeting lays hands on them and they are cured by Christ through their own faith."

The interview is nearly over. He remarks that she is sometimes called "the female Billy Sunday," which does not amuse her. She dislikes Sunday's "slang."

Aimee says she expects singers and musicians and others who attended her meetings elsewhere to descend upon Baltimore in great numbers. Lastly, she remarks that she appears in the Port City with no financial guarantee.

What she does not tell the reporter is that James F. Fielder, representing Pentecostal groups in the city, has been promoting this event for months, distributing 24,000 circulars, mailing 10,000 postcards, and putting up a thousand cardboard signs from one end of Baltimore to another; that Minnie has booked the Lyric Theater for fifteen days at the astronomical cost of $3,100; that Brother Robinson, the greatest Gospel pianist in Pentecost, and his Slide Trombone Singers will be opening for Sister Aimee; that the assemblies of Brooklyn, New York and Philadelphia are sending contingents for whom Brother Fielder is briskly booking hotels and rooming houses. One would think, from reading the article, that the Great Baltimore Revival is a public accident, the work of a moment sparked by Little Aimee's casual visit.

By now it was big business. Minnie knew there was a lot more than religious pressure to fill the Lyric Theater, though her daughter might continue to ignore this.

The Baltimore Star, following the lead of *The Sun*, decided that something newsworthy was going on at the Lyric Theater. So they sent their lady journalist, E.F.Y., around to the Lyric on the evening of December 8. E.F.Y. arrived late.

"A lone newspaper woman straying into the Lyric at 10 o'clock in the evening heard only thunder."

The revival meeting, which had filled the great hall of the opera house with prayers and hymns and cries, was over. Someone pointed upstairs. At each step the journalist took, it seemed the din grew louder. She wondered if she had ever heard anything like this before, and images of intense moments from literature and personal experience flashed in front of her: the storming of the Bastille, Armistice Day, the Harvard-Princeton football game.

What she had stumbled upon, as the doors of the upper hall swung open on an uproar, was a tarrying meeting. A hundred people sat or knelt in a circle. Trembling hands reaching for the ceiling, mouths twitching, and eyes rolling, the supplicants cried out to Heaven for the forgiveness of their sins.

In the center sat Aimee Semple McPherson in her nurse's uniform, her arms spread as if to receive the prayers, her body tense. The exercise had been going on for some time. Strained white faces of the participants suggested that they had exhausted their mortal vitality and were now drawing upon some ethereal source. The lady journalist observed "bodily contortions that would have done justice to trained athletes." Next to Aimee knelt a musician who prayed when he was not strumming on a mandolin. E.F.Y. could not discern the words of their song, "but sing they did, with streaming eyes and violent motions."

After the music they resumed their prayers, which varied, according to their level of exhaustion, from a plaintive wail to the sharpest outbursts by those still capable of it.

E.F.Y.'s account for *The Star* is the first of many clippings Aimee reprinted in *The Bridal Call*. While she does not invent new text, a comparison of Aimee's reprint with the original newspaper shows that she deleted sentences and whole paragraphs. She does not edit in the interest of brevity. What she cuts from the news story are details she wishes to conceal from her followers. These are of signal interest.

Aimee censors, for instance, these paragraphs:

> Mrs. McPherson frequently interrupted the general trend of their prayers in an effort to bring the crowd into unison.
>
> "Now let's pray for the churches," she would cry, "and let us ask God to keep the ministers from treating us with indifference . . ."
>
> The procedure seems to have upon many of those present the effect of a narcotic. They saw nothing, heard nothing, and frequently their heads dropped wearily as prayers which had been undertaken with violent effort died away into unintelligible mumbling.
>
> The ceremony would, no doubt, have gone on until the supplicants dropped from sheer exhaustion, but word came that the management was preparing to close the Lyric. Mrs. McPherson rose to her feet, and her action seemed to be a signal for her followers to arouse themselves. That they did, with considerable nerve, their cries and shouts ringing sharply upon the air.

With her red pencil, the editor of *The Bridal Call* excises those descriptions from the record. This is not the way Aimee wishes to be seen, barely in control of a mob drunk on religion. It is an ironic turn she takes, at the end of 1919. The power that made her famous by word of mouth, the power to drive a crowd out of its senses toward religious ecstasy, must be tempered to play in the national spotlight. The primitive tarrying meeting, with its barbaric yawps and wild automatisms, rolling and babbling and twitching, may have drawn mobs to the tent show in Georgia. But Aimee had arrived in Baltimore, Mencken country, the Lyric Theater. Under the narrow-eyed review of E.F.Y. of *The Star* and her kind, the Spirit's grosser manifestations might appear too bizarre for the general public.

In Baltimore the evangelist would stun her followers by announcing that the Devil had entered the writhing body of an ecstatic worshiper. This was the beginning of her "quenching of manifestations."

The crowd lingered. Women and children kissed each other.

Men embraced. They one-stepped, two-stepped, goose-step-ped, shouting Hallelujah and congratulating one another on their salvation.

"See," yelled an old man, pointing to a well-dressed middle-aged citizen. "The gift of tongues has come to him."

The man so moved stood surrounded by worshipers, his eyes closed. His lips framed words with a fluency and speed which astonished the journalist. She could not understand what the man was saying, but someone told her it was an obsolete Eastern language.

"Praise the Lord, brother, praise the Lord," sobbed another gentleman, also very respectable-looking, much to the surprise of E.F.Y. She had thought such transports foreign to the better class of Baltimoreans. She watched amazed as he clasped another man in his arms and the two rocked and reeled from one end of the floor to the other.

"Did you get victory tonight, sister?" a gray-haired woman was heard to ask another.

"I sure did," was the response. "Why, I was drunk as a loon the entire time."

Sister Aimee had noticed the lady journalist and made eye contact. Now she drew her to one side.

"Aren't they the loveliest crowd?" sighed the evangelist, in a voice hoarse from overwork. It was not precisely the way E.F.Y. would describe them. But she did find Mrs. McPherson lovely, fresh-looking despite the "torturous experiences of the evening," with clear eyes, a highly-colored complexion, and soft light brown hair. She observed that the evangelist was plainly an emotional rather than an intellectual type, and yet her personality was decidedly pleasing.

"You want to hear about my work? Fine," said Aimee, as if it had been goat herding or stonemasonry. "I'll get them all out of here and then we can talk."

Beaming, she shook hands with each person on the way out the door, whispering, "Praise the Lord, brother," or, "Thanks be to God, sister." And when she had sent the last lingering sister on her way with a pat on the shoulder, Aimee turned her full attention upon the journalist, who was struck by the silence in the theater lobby, like the quiet after a battle.

"Now then," Aimee sighed, fixing E.F.Y. with her bright eyes, "I just feel as if I could talk to you the rest of the night."

The journalist had thought she might be tired.

"Tired? Indeed, I'm not," she said sweetly. "The Lord's doing all of this, and you are going to see what crowds He will send me before the campaign is over."

The smiling evangelist, in her high-buttoned shoes, stood solidly planted, like a tree trunk from her ample hips to the floor; it was a mineral solidity, in contrast to a birdlike mobility of her facial expressions, the quick eyes and full lips. The dazzling smile would dissolve instantly as her brow furrowed in response to a question about the specific purpose of the revival.

"To prepare for the second coming of the Lord."

Now her voice took on weight, despite fatigue. The journalist scribbled in her notebook, reluctant to make eye contact.

"We have Biblical references which prove to us beyond all doubt that Jesus Himself will come here soon again. The exact day and hour we cannot predict, but we know that it will be sometime soon."

The journalist had heard such words before, but never spoken with such authority. Before jumping to conclusions, E.F.Y. would ask Aimee if she interpreted the prophecy literally.

"Entirely so," said the evangelist, her eyes darkening.

"Jesus, Himself, is to come in a cloud. He will bring all his saints with Him; the graves will open, and those who are prepared will be carried up from the earth to have their part in the wedding in the clouds."

The evangelist's eyes were lambent with the vision, which suddenly was as real in the theater lobby as a Renaissance fresco come alive. And the voice . . . the voice was like nothing the journalist had ever heard, rising in wonder and then falling in the resolution of the prophecy. A chill descended upon the journalist scribbling in her notebook. She realized that this passionate woman was either horribly right, or stark raving mad.

"To many His advent will sound merely as the rumbling of

thunder. That is the way it was in former times, you will remember. A few heard the Lord's voice, but the majority heard
only the sound of thunder or the distant rumbling of an
earthquake."

Perhaps, if pressed, Aimee might back off from the absurdity
of her position.

"Can you tell us," demanded the newswoman, "exactly how
someone who *is* prepared for this aerial expedition might be
removed from her mundane surroundings?"

Aimee's wide brow wrinkled for an instant as she considered
her next move. It was always, *always* to maximize the dramatic
potential of the moment.

"It will be like this," said Aimee. And with a wave of the
hand she transformed the lobby into a business office.

"A little stenographer who is prepared to receive the Lord
will be working in an office." She held an imaginary pad and
pencil, taking dictation.

The stenographer was little Aimee.

"Suddenly, somebody will look up and discover that she is
not there."

She leapt sideways, leaving an emptiness.

The actress faced right and then left, assuming the roles of
inquiring office workers. " 'She must have gone home,' one
will say. 'But I was talking to her not a minute ago,' " said a
deep voice.

The journalist was fascinated by the evangelist's gift for
mimicry.

"Then," continued Sister Aimee, returning to the role of
narrator, her body quivering with the tension, "they will look
everywhere for that girl, but they will never find her." She
grew wistful. "Perhaps at some time during that day those men
had heard a sound of thunder; but the little stenographer had
heard the voice of the Lord, had answered, and had been caught
up to take her part in the wedding in the clouds."

As she finished, the actress seemed on the verge of taking a
bow.

Aimee Semple McPherson was beaming, rejoicing in the
triumph of the stenographer she had just invented and now

seemed to believe in as completely as she believed in the doomsday prophecy. E.F.Y. bent over her notebook, a one-woman
audience. She did not know whether Aimee was pulling her leg
or truly believed all of what she said. Aimee had succeeded in
distracting E.F.Y. from her intention to reduce the doomsday
prophecy to an absurdity, by *adding* to the absurdity, making
an imaginary stenographer vanish before their eyes.

"These are the last times," Aimee declared in a sepulchral
monotone. "Much that we have prophesied has come true, and
still other predictions will be verified as time goes on."

Aimee told how she had prophesied the Great War when the
world laughed at her and called her crazy.

"The book of Revelation is now being fulfilled, literally Armageddon has been fought." She seemed to look through and
beyond the journalist as her voice deepened, assuming an incantatory rhythm: "The next great event will be the second
coming of the Lord; after that there will be seven years of
suffering more horrible than anything which can be imagined.
The war was merely the foreshadowing of it. During these seven
years there will be a terrible famine for the word of God. People
will suffer anguish because they cannot find God, but all those
who know Him will have been taken away from the earth."

Her pronunciation of *God*, with the wide vowel and over-
stressed consonants, sounded like the beat of a kettledrum. It
was the voice of incontestable, terrifying authority. E.F.Y.
asked if the prophetess could explain some of the present social
disorders in the light of Revelation.

"That is the Red Dragon," Aimee boomed, "and you will
find it spoken of in both Testaments. The labor movement is
prophesied at length in the Bible and the 'mark of the beast' we
know to be the union seal. The time is coming when none will
be able to buy or sell save those who are stamped with the mark
of the beast."

The interview was nearly over. Near dawn the journalist must
have doubted how much more of this she could stand, while
the subject seemed to grow more animated and bright-eyed by
the hour.

"The Jews will be the ruling nation of the earth in years to come," Aimee stated, "because at the second coming of the Lord they will receive Him. After that, their years of exile and of suffering will have ended and they will establish at Jerusalem a kingdom more wonderful than any the world has ever known . . ."

Finally the newswoman asked Aimee about the healings, which had caused such a stir in other cities. The response was subdued. At last a note of weariness crept in.

"The saving of souls is the most important part of my ministry," she said, "but disease can be cured by the Lord now just as it was in the time of Jesus." She sounded like a schoolteacher repeating a simple lesson for absentminded students: "I have seen blind men have their sight restored, and I have seen the lame leap up and walk without crutches . . ."

The journalist had seen nothing of the kind. But, then, she had never met a character like Aimee Semple McPherson either. Walking into the cold night air of Maryland Avenue under the stars, she was forming a phrase that would appear in her story: "The obviously genuine belief which she holds that she is acting under divine guidance impresses one favorably . . ."

She would continue to cover the healing sessions as a responsible skeptic, on guard against her emotions, hoping against hope a miracle might occur before her eyes.

————

Mrs. Sarah Matthews lived at 41 East Montgomery Street. From her front door she could walk two blocks west, on the arm of a neighbor, and climb the steps to the battery of Federal Hill.

From the north and east slopes of the hill was a spectacular view of the harbor, and beyond—the masts and sails of the merchant vessels, the tall buildings and gleaming copper flashings and church spires of downtown Baltimore. Sarah had known the view for most of her life.

But during the last few years her field of vision had shrunk to where she could see only a narrow corridor right in front of her, and then a narrower tunnel off to one side, so that she had to tilt her head queerly to make headway even in broad daylight.

And then that scant opening flooded with mist, so that Sarah Matthews could see nothing from the height of Federal Hill but light itself, like sunshine through a blizzard.

Her memory of the buildings may at times have seemed as clear as her vision might be should she recover it. She could not abandon the hope that her vision would return, by degrees or all at once, like a glass tube blown free of smoke.

Sarah Matthews' cataracts had troubled her for thirteen years before Sister Aimee came to Baltimore. She had sought cures from "medical specialists." As a Fundamentalist she was familiar with John 9:1–13, where the disciples ask Jesus about the blind man: "Master, who did sin, this man, or his parents, that he was born blind?" Jesus answers: "Neither hath this man sinned, nor his parents; but that the works of God should be made manifest in him." Then Jesus spits on the ground, makes clay of the spittle, and smears the man's eyes with the clay. When the man returns from washing away the clay in the pool of Siloam, he can see as well as anyone. More clearly than most, in truth, because he understands that Christ, "the light of the world," is the cause of his vision. His neighbors and the Pharisees are blind to this; they immediately begin to question the man's identity, hilariously. In an important sense he is *not* the man he was, the blind man, now that God's works have been made manifest in him. He has become a source of light.

Sarah Matthews knew this parable from the inside out. As a woman of faith, she would accept the first opportunity to re-enact it.

Modern medicine tells us that real cataracts are irreversible, resulting from a change in the chemical structure of the lens protein. Cataracts are now surgically removed—we find slender evidence of "remission" in the medical literature. Yet Sarah Matthews, walking the wintry terraces of Federal Hill, got wind of the miraculous possibility in the rumors of Sister Aimee Semple McPherson. Maybe from the day she heard that the healer would come to Baltimore in Advent, she began to remember how to see, and glimpsed figures through her perpetual fog.

On the afternoon of December 11, Sarah Matthews was driven to the Lyric Theater to attend Sister Aimee's healing service. The auditorium was crowded with spectators, the faithful and the skeptical. They had come to see what comfort the lady evangelist might bring to scores of the afflicted. These were stumping up the aisles on crutches or being wheeled or carried toward the altar. Twenty-five clergymen of various denominations had come, as well as "a number of eminent physicians," who were probably hoping nobody would recognize them.

Aimee, in her nurse's uniform, stood on the platform. The hall was full. She heard the testimony of men and women who had been healed. She read a psalm and delivered a deep-throated speech about God's wonderful works. She made time collapse upon itself, present time and the ancient days of Christ in Galilee and Jerusalem. She spoke caressingly of Our Lord's promises to those who seek him in their hearts, and how the power of healing is the same in Jesus Christ "yesterday, today, and forever." To the blind woman, who no longer knew the seasons or the hours of the day in visible terms, this held a special meaning.

When Sister Aimee called for those who sought to be healed, Sarah Matthews moved toward her voice with such a certain step that when she arrived at the altar rail, Aimee had to inquire what ailed her.

Sarah explained she had a cataract over each eye. For many years she had sought a cure from the eye specialists.

The evangelist led Sarah to the platform, and walked up and down with her, praying, for several minutes. It grew quiet in the opera house, as if the enormous crowd somehow had been subsumed in the roles of the healer and the invalid. Facing Sarah, the evangelist placed her fingers gently upon the older woman's eyelids. Sarah felt a peculiar warmth. Her heart was pounding. Aimee, with her eyes closed, declared she believed "God had returned her sight." And in a burst of light beneath her eyelids under Aimee's fingers, Sarah Matthews realized even before opening her eyes that they would see. And she did not stop proclaiming her joy until it was drowned in the cries of "Praise the Lord" as she walked unaided from the platform.

E.F.Y. recorded the event, the first of several healings she describes in prose touched with wonder.

> There were many there who were afflicted with tumors, cancers, tuberculosis, and other incurable diseases. Their confidence in the evangelist was pathetic, and Mrs. McPherson's sympathetic, considerate fashion of handling each one, both before and after the "laying on of hands" procedure, was quite noticeable. Tiny babies were carried to the platform by their mothers; old people bowed with the infirmities of age were taken there on the arms of friends or relations; children, boys and girls were among the great crowd . . .
>
> Mrs. McPherson, supported by a coterie of four . . . gathered about a subject . . . Hands were laid upon the head of the invalid and upon the part of the body said to be afflicted. One of the four, a young man with a conspicuous gold tooth and marvelous lung capacity, seemed to have the office of intercessor, for as each sick person was brought up he loudly petitioned the Lord for immediate healing.
>
> First the hands of the subject were extended upward; next there were loud cries of "Praise the Lord," accompanied by further intercession of the young man with the gold tooth; then a few steps were taken forward; after that a skip and jump; finally a swift bouncing exercise which varied between a Maypole dance and a series of jumps.
>
> The recovery of every patient was accompanied by some genuine old-time camp meeting song, with a swing and a rhythm to it. Needless to say the musical schedule was the inspiration for many terpsichorean inventions. At intervals, when his services seemed to have been dispensed with by Mrs. McPherson and the "elders," the young man with the gold tooth walked to the platform and did unmentionable things to the piano.

A deaf woman regained her hearing, and another blind woman recovered her sight. E.F.Y. was most moved by the recovery of an arthritic old man: "A man who limped painfully and stooped as though under a great weight of suffering was seen to straighten up wonderfully, walked with ease, and finally even responded to the evangelist's suggestion that he take a little step." It is a pity no physicians are quoted.

Modern ophthalmologists would insist that if Sarah Matthews was blind before entering the Lyric Theater, and left there with a clear view of the avenue, then she never had cataracts. Her blindness resulted from a blockage of light that lay deeper, somewhere between the woman's stunned optic nerve and her damaged psyche, a place that might only be touched by a religious stimulus. Aimee's voice and fingers provided that. This seems marvelous, if not a miracle equal to the remission of cataracts or the growth of a third eye. Like the blind man in John's parable, Sarah Matthews became a different woman in that moment with the healer in Christ, and her restored vision was the mere outward symbol of the change.

Though Aimee had not come to Baltimore to promote a healing ministry, the response to her healings was so passionate and clamorous, she was persuaded to include prayers for the sick at every service. On Friday evening, December 12, after Aimee prayed over him, a local minister who had been stone deaf was startled by the sound of spoken language for the first time in twenty years. That same evening, the reporter from *The Baltimore Star* observes breathlessly, "a little boy who removed the brace from his foot at the altar is said to have recovered almost completely from a deformity which dated from infancy; and a woman whose entire side was paralyzed and who walked at the meeting last night is said to be 'still walking.'"

What did the evangelist think of these developments?

She wrote: "I was never so frightened in all my life. Taking one look at the throng of sick people, I ran downstairs, buried my face in a chair in a corner and began to weep." She said that she wept because too much was expected of her. She might take comfort it was God and not herself that did the healing. But could the mob, which daily increased its volume and expectations, be made to understand this?

Aimee had reason to be frightened. She was losing her command of the revival she had led since 1916. Once the newspapers made her healings a matter of public record, the public focused upon that to the exclusion of all else. A physical healing worked upon the popular imagination like an addictive drug. Crowds would expect her to repeat the performance of human dramas she did not understand, and over which she had no control. If her prayers made a blind woman see, Aimee could give the glory to God; if she failed, then the audience might call her a fraud.

Paradoxically, Aimee's power had attracted an audience that now could dictate the direction of her meetings.

It is precisely at this point in her career that she pours water on the fire. Toward Christmas the heavy publicity of Aimee's healing services had begun to test the Lyric Theater's capacity. Crowd control had become a constant concern. At the Sunday afternoon meeting on December 21, 1919, Sister Aimee suddenly had "a strange but overwhelming presentiment that the devil was going to lift up his head . . . as the Lord was winning too mighty a victory, and would sweep many hearts with His power unless the devil put a stop to it."

In the middle of the auditorium a woman got up. Her face was rosy with excitement. Waving her arms about her head, she pushed her way to the aisle and started toward the altar, knocking off ladies' hats with her wild arms as she cried, "Praise the Lord." Her voice was strained and unnatural, as if it came from some mechanical source outside her.

Aimee nudged the elder next to her on the dais, and whispered:

"Go! Go quickly brother, get that woman in her seat; this is not of the Lord."

At first he refused. In the early days of the Pentecostal revival there were strict prohibitions against the "quenching of manifestations." But moved by Aimee's urgency, he got up. While the evangelist roused the crowd to a chorus to cover the incident, he guided the flailing zealot back to her seat.

In a moment she was in the aisle again, moving from row to row and grimacing. She waved her arms, knocking off hats and eyeglasses, shrieking, "Praise God," and shaking her fist in people's faces.

Aimee could not leave the platform to restrain the woman—such a thing on the evangelist's part would be so shocking a transgression of Pentecostal custom, it might ruin the meeting.

So she persuaded one of the choristers to get the woman out of the auditorium and into a smaller meeting room. There Aimee later observed her.

> There the enemy showed his true colors and purpose. The woman proved to be a maniac who had been in an asylum. Her delusion seemed to cause her to believe herself a preacher. She paced the floor, crying disconnected sentences, raving and preaching to the chairs . . . Yet this was the kind of woman many of the saints would have allowed to promenade the platform—fearing lest they quench the Spirit.

This account, published soon after the Baltimore meeting, is Aimee's defense of an action for which she was severely criticized. The turn-of-the-century revival had labored to achieve such "manifestations" as Sister Aimee was now appearing to "quench." She was in a peculiar position, as the first evangelist to bring the emotionalism of the full Gospel revival from intimate church meetings into the public arena. There the fire they had prayed for in storefronts somehow had to be kept in bounds.

"Looking backward," she wrote, "I can see that this meeting marked a turning point not only in my own ministry but in the history of the outpouring of Pentecostal power."

She was leading her religion into the mainstream. The theater of healings attracted an interdenominational crowd, who might be frightened away by the more extreme forms of Pentecostal expression—so Aimee held them in check. While she alienated a few "saints," she charmed Methodists, Episcopalians, rabbis, and others.

After that last service on December 21, the ministers of the United Brethren Churches gave Aimee $200. This was to pay the train fare back to Baltimore after her Christmas holiday in California, if she would conduct a revival in the denominational churches.

———

Aimee returned to Baltimore in the second week of January, 1920, intending to concentrate on the more cerebral aspects of her ministry. The popular press, which sensationalized her healing services at the Lyric Theater, did not follow her into the Salem United Brethren Church, or the Franklin Street Church, where her campaign opened on January 18.

According to the reports of the United Brethren, Aimee preached to overflow crowds of thousands despite the streets being covered with ice; there were three thousand conversions, and "about one hundred and fifty Christians were wonderfully filled with the Spirit" (i.e. they spoke in tongues). Many of these were ministers from Baltimore, Washington, and Westminster.

The same report says that "hundreds were healed of their afflictions." But for the time being neither Aimee nor the public seem as fascinated by the healings as by the conversions, the spiritual transformation that Aimee's preaching evoked in the dead of winter.

In mid-February she hurried to Winnipeg, Manitoba, where she had been invited to preach in the old Wesley Church. Finding it half full, she went the rounds of the dance halls, cafés, and bawdyhouses, "recruiting for an army—the army of the King of Kings." An escort of plainclothes police and Canadian journalists assured that the evangelist would be welcome and safe in the dance halls and stews on a Saturday night. The Sunday *Winnipeg Tribune* described Sister McPherson's audacious barnstorming:

> On each occasion when she asked for a show of hands of those who would come to her meetings at the church, she was greeted with enthusiastic response . . .
> Throngs immediately besieged the church, until the galleries creaked and groaned; aisles and passageways, doors, stairways and basement were jammed. Multitudes swarmed about the church and street, and were augmented momentarily by loaded streetcars which emptied themselves at the door.

Canada had not caught up with Aimee's reputation as a healer. On her native soil, the evangelist was able to escape the hysterical expectations that had attended her in Baltimore.

3

THE HEALING TOUCH

WASHINGTON, D. C., 1920

At midday on April 8, 1920 Aimee Semple McPherson hiked up the skirts of her maid's uniform and climbed through the back window of the McKendree Methodist Episcopal Church. She shouldered her way through the mob that burdened the creaking platform and looked out over the auditorium.

There were two thousand people upstairs and downstairs and as many surrounding the church. They had been gathering since dawn. Littering the center aisle, where they had been wheeled and carried in a ragged tide that washed up on the altar rail, were five hundred of the sick, maimed, deformed, blind, and paralytic. They gaped at Aimee, waved wanly their hands, their crutches, whispering her name, heads lolling, tongues loose, eyes rolling. The heat and the stench were oppressive.

The revival at McKendree Methodist Episcopal Church had begun on March 21 quietly, "for the conversion of sinners and a deeper work of grace among believers," according to the report of one religious monthly, the *Gospel Mission Tidings*. Another reporter, from a Methodist newspaper, remarked that "The driving method sometimes used by evangelists is entirely absent in her procedure, but the presence and charm of the Holy Spirit are manifest in her words and actions."

Sister Aimee did not need to shout. By now the mere whisper of her name opened the minds of strangers to unforeseen spiritual possibilities. People came from all over the city. Invalids journeyed from hundreds of miles away. Throughout the revival the McKendree church was packed from the sanctuary to the schoolroom. That was why Aimee and the pastor, Charles A. Shreve, had to climb through a back window to reach the platform. An effective healing service, well publicized, would make future meetings impossible in this space. Indeed from the day the healing services were announced, at the end of March, the church could not seat half the people who wanted to enter.

There were to be only two healing services, one this afternoon, and another at the last meeting before Aimee's return to California, April 11. Deferring the healings to the end of the revival had been a carefully considered tactic.

As a Pentecostal evangelist she could not deny her gift to the lame and afflicted; but as a performer she was keenly aware of the risks it involved. The larger public buzzed in anticipation of the healing service. Failure might spoil the revival. Better to keep them waiting until the last meetings, so a successful healing service might provide a dramatic climax to the campaign—or so failure might be gracefully covered by an exit.

Little Russell Blassie, ten years old, had arrived with his mother. As he came up the aisle, his torso surged and his neck bent back with the strain of keeping his legs untangled. Paralyzed in infancy, the boy had learned to drag himself along but with difficulty. With each step the crooked knee of one leg would strike the other knee. Nicholas Berezoski, twelve years old, another victim of infantile paralysis, had come on crutches, dragging his stunted legs in a brace that seemed scarcely to hold him together. The son of Russian immigrants, Nicholas was well known in the community for his courage and good humor. Russell and Nicholas sat among the deaf and blind, and several patients twitching with St. Vitus's dance.

The reporter for *The Washington Times* moved through the crowd taking names and addresses: Miss Emily Kruger, thirty years old, of 414 Tenth Street, Southwest, crippled from birth; Henry Zebulon, 1002 M Street, Northwest, bad eyes; Mrs. Fannie Wallace of 1913 Vermont Avenue, her left side paralyzed for fifteen years. The Baltimore journalists' dispatches had been emotional and sometimes impressionistic. Here in the capital, the editor of the city desk would insist upon a strict standard of verification. *The Times* must not become accessory to a hoax.

Sister Aimee looked at the tide of suffering humanity at her feet; she breathed deeply. It was worse than she expected. But she had the gift, the "charism," and had to use it. She had been broken and healed. She had a clear vision of the divine blueprint of perfect health, of a mystical transformation from Christ's wounds, and she could catalyze the crowd's energy; this was her gift and her burden.

Briefly Pastor Shreve explained that God helps all who place their faith in Him. Then he yielded the stage to Aimee Semple McPherson.

In a cheerful contralto she started singing, "The Great Physician now is here, the sympathizing Jesus." Aimee gazed above their heads and then directly into their eyes, as if the twisted and painful bodies did not exist. Joining her in singing, they became a single voice as the gentle hymn ended.

"I cannot perform miracles," she said, matter-of-factly and without sadness. "I can only help you to get faith in the Lord. It is He who heals. As Jesus healed the multitudes while He was on earth, so He can and will heal those who place their faith in Him."

She read from Luke and John, the beautiful stories of Jesus and the blind man at the pool of Siloam; of the cripple told to take up his bed and walk; of the hemorrhaging woman who touched the edge of His cloak and was healed. From these stories Aimee passed on to modern cases, men and women she had seen cured by their faith. Her voice was soft and musical and supremely confident, assuring the crippled and sick that they too could be cured if they had faith. The crowd murmured approval. Russell, in his mother's arms, felt encouraged by the sound of the voice, and felt an unaccustomed strength in his mother's embrace as she gazed from his twisted legs to the evangelist.

Miss Emily Kruger imagined herself walking without aid.

A deaf woman, who in twelve years had grown adept at reading lips, wondered if the evangelist's visible rhythms might break through her silence into audible music.

Aimee introduced Mrs. W. W. Jackson of Baltimore. Mrs. Jackson had been thrown from a streetcar on February 3, 1919, injuring her spine. It became infected with the tubercle bacillus. X-rays revealed that her vertebrae were badly damaged by the tubercular lesions and deteriorating rapidly; the doctors had no idea how to treat her. They placed the woman in a cast from her armpits to her knees, and she lay on her back for sixteen weeks without improvement.

Her case is the first of Sister Aimee's that has medical documentation. Mrs. Jackson's physician, the distinguished Dr. S. R. Wantz of Baltimore, would testify:

> So far as medical skill can determine, Mrs. Jackson's pelvic bones in the rear of the junction of the spinal column were diseased as proven by x-ray pictures and physical examinations.

He informed his patient of what he had seen at the healing services in the Lyric Theater. Because she could not walk, and Mrs. McPherson could not go to her, Mrs. Jackson's son took a handkerchief to one of the healing services, to be prayed over and anointed with oil. Then the handkerchief was pushed up under her cast to rest upon the diseased spine. And Mrs. Jackson prayed to God that she might be healed.

"In several days I was so much improved that the cast was removed, then I began to walk and now I am as healthy as ever."

By three o'clock the preaching and testimonies were done. Aimee left the pulpit, stepping down in front of the altar. She called for all sinners to come and be saved. Dozens of men and women without infirmities pressed toward the altar rail. There they knelt, and Aimee and the church elders prayed over each one.

Then she called for the sick. "Give up your worldly pleasures and give your heart to Jesus. Come!"

Five hundred people wanted to go at once. There was confusion. Ushers arranged that thirty would gather at the altar at a time.

Aimee in her white dress, flanked by four elders in black suits, moved from right to left along the altar rail. In her left pocket she held a round chrismatory flask of sacred oil, which she used in obedience to James 5:14: "Is any sick among you? let him call for the elders of the church; and let them pray over him, anointing him with oil in the name of the Lord: and the prayer of faith shall save the sick . . ." The composition and the source of the sacred oil remain mysterious, though some say it was olive oil particularly spiced. No one recalls where she obtained it, nor observes that she ever ran out of it after anointing hundreds of people in services like this one, when she prayed long into the evening.

She lubricated her hands with the spiced oil, making them shiny and warm. The heat that so many recall at Aimee's touch was partly the effect of the oil on the capillaries in the evangelist's palms and fingers. They seemed to glow. If the chrismatory oil on her hands assumed the healer's powerful alchemy of spirit and flesh, which became transferable, Aimee did not need to explain it. The transaction was plain in the vibration of the woman's hands.

She perspired heavily. Roberta Salter recalls that her mother came off the platform so drenched that merely touching her gown would cause water to spring from it. During the healing service she was, as Rolf McPherson has observed, "under the influence of an anointing that came upon her." She became a medium between God and flesh, evidenced by the oil on her palms and the salt water that bathed her as she worked.

Kneeling among the scores of others at the altar was Emily Kruger, thirty years old, an invalid since birth. She had never been able to take more than a few steps unaided. Pouring oil from the flask on her palms, Aimee touched Emily's legs, raised her skirts to apply the oil to her knees and thighs. She held Emily's hands above her head, and gazed intensely into the invalid's amazed eyes as she said: *Reach up and touch the hem of His garment.* She called everyone to unite in praying to God to heal this woman.

A babble of voices, then suddenly a hush swept the church, as if a passing angel had brushed away their voices with its wings. Aimee spoke gently and firmly, like a mother assigning a household chore to a child.

"In the name of the Lord Jesus Christ, you shall walk. Rise, and you shall be healed."

In the deathly silence, the *Times* reporter observed that Miss Kruger cast a swift glance about. She seemed dazed, but took one step. Then two. Three. Four. Then on and on, to the end of the aisle.

"It's wonderful," she murmured, "I have never done this before, I could only walk a few steps without help. God has cured me! Let me try again!"

She turned and continued walking as the wide-eyed witnesses made way for her—up the aisle once, back down again, and on and on, as if this were some dream she must walk out of, into the reality of permanent health, pacing until unassisted she had measured the aisle six times. Then, overcome, she took a seat.

"The crowd in the church," writes the journalist, "looked on bewildered . . . more than five hundred men, women, and children waited their turn. Some were kneeling and praying while others attentively watched the scene at the altar."

Sister Aimee knelt before a woman who had entered the church deaf; she rubbed the woman's ears with her oiled hands while whispering prayers into one ear, then the other. Louder and louder Aimee spoke, until the woman flinched, startled by a holy thought so insistent, she thought she heard it. She did hear it. Then she heard Mrs. McPherson asking her to face the others, to tell them that she could hear their prayers, even their whispered amazement and disbelief, could hear clearly for the first time in twelve years.

At this point in his dispatch the journalist begs us to trust his perceptions, which are giving him cause for concern. Common sense tells him, as it will tell a hundred future reporters, that a hoax on such a grand scale is inconceivable; a hoax would indeed be more miraculous than the healings that are occurring more rapidly than he can record them. "*These persons the* Times *reporter saw and talked to. The reporter watched the entire service*," he says piteously.

His account abounds with names and addresses: H. G. Busch, 619 Second Street, Northwest; Mamie Breckenridge, 1600 First Street, Northwest; Henry Zebulon, who entered the church blind, and when Aimee touched him, he rose to describe the Bible scenes in the stained glass windows; Russell Blassie, ten years old, of 218 Twelfth Place, Northeast.

The boy, small for his years, had been carried by his mother to the altar. There he knelt, calmed by the brown eyes and friendly smile of the pretty evangelist in the white dress. She took his face in her warm hands, as if she were about to kiss him. The crowd and the commotion seemed to recede, so that Russell wondered how she could have been the center and source of it. Her hands were warm. She rubbed the twisted flesh of his knees and thighs. They hummed strangely as she took his wrists and held his hands high over his head. Three men in black suits mumbled around him while Aimee held his wrists. Suddenly he felt pulled up from his knees, by a draft, toward the ceiling. He stood on straight legs, not legs that he could remember, and took firm steps toward his mother.

"My God! Look at my son! He walks . . ." The woman's lower lip trembled; she began crying; she picked her child up and held him in her arms, kissing him.

When she put him down, the boy started out into the aisle. He hesitated at first, then walked faster, and gradually began to run.

The evangelist was drinking a tumbler of water.

"Look, mama, look," he cried out, "see how I can run! Oh, mama, see! You're crying . . . but look, mama, I can run and it doesn't hurt me either."

Aimee moved down the altar rail as the ranks of invalids advanced with heightened expectations, thirty at a time. Nicholas Berezoski, polio victim, was healed, and the women formed a human wall around the boy, a dressing room where he could remove his brace forever. Anna Wiggins, eight years paralyzed, lay down her crutches and walked. So did Fannie Wallace and Catherine Jones . . .

It was seven in the evening before the last invalid had been anointed and prayed for.

If the evangelist went to bed that night relieved that she had done her duty in Washington as God's paramedic, she was in for a rude awakening. Though there were no more healing services scheduled, they became inevitable, command performances. On Sunday, April 11, the day before Aimee's return to California, the journalists arrived at daybreak for the 11:00 revival. *The Washington Times* reports:

Automobiles filled the streets nearby and it was necessary to call
policemen to direct the traffic in the neighborhood. Cripples came,
carried in arms or in rolling chairs, the sick came leaning on the
arms of friends and relatives. By 9 o'clock there were close to 2,000
people in front of the church.

At 12:30 the regular services were concluded. Crowded with sick
and crippled, the church presented a pitiful picture. So touched was
Mrs. McPherson with the requests of the afflicted that a healing
service be held that she asked the sick and crippled to remain and
be prayed for.

By the time she returned to the parsonage fourteen hours
later, it was estimated that "in Washington Mrs. McPherson
has personally prayed over more than 1,000 crippled and sick.
She has preached to more than 50,000 people." And before she
rose the next morning, there were several hundred people waiting outside with handkerchiefs for the healer to anoint with her
precious oil.

THE RISING TIDE

Seventy years later, the Church Aimee founded in Los Angeles
is one of the fastest growing denominations in the world, with
17,000 churches in sixty countries, under the direction of Rolf
McPherson, Aimee's son.

On his office wall hangs a panoramic enlargement of a well-
known photograph: his mother conducting a healing service in
Balboa Park, San Diego. Artfully hand-tinted, the photo shows
Aimee in the foreground helping a woman out of her wheelchair. To the evangelist's left a dozen elders, aides, and physicians stand in a choral triangle against the backdrop of a
classical colonnade and distant cypresses. The white stage cuts

a diagonal across the dark crowd. The multitude in hats and bonnets blurs into infinity at the horizon, endless.

The composition is as dramatic as Thomas Eakins's heroic paintings of the surgical "Grosse" clinic at Johns Hopkins, or Raphael's life-size illustrations of the Book of Acts. The miracle registers not so much at the center of the composition, where the pathetic woman in her wool cap is rising from her chair. It radiates outward in the faces of the witnesses. They draw back in sundry postures of defensive amazement, brows furrowed, shoulders hunched, as if they have been affronted and now may be attacked. Only the healer herself gently smiles, and the woman discovering that she is no longer bound to the wheelchair.

Obviously those witnesses on the platform seventy years ago, well-dressed and dignified aides and officials, were just as incredulous as we are. Rolf McPherson, a surviving witness, is patient, sympathetic, and good-humored.

"It was a phenomenon peculiar to the times," he offers. With the gentle precision of an engineer turned preacher, he continues: "Medical science lacked the techniques of today, so more patients naturally were open to the possibilities of faith healing. They had more faith in God because they had less faith in science. You see, it was a matter of faith. No, I cannot imagine this sort of thing happening ever again."

On such a scale. Dr. McPherson, a leader in the mainstream of Pentecostalism for fifty years, is aware of recent evangelists with notable healing ministries: Katherine Kuhlman and Oral Roberts, to name two who have captured the public's imagination. Religious healing continues to be documented in religious, medical, and popular literature. But no one has ever been credited by secular witnesses with anywhere near the number of healings attributed to Sister Aimee from 1919 to 1922.

The newspaper accounts are overwhelming. The coverage of the Denver Revival, or the one in San Jose, would make a sizable book in itself. The crowds, the ritual service, the astonishment, the press reports are the same in Washington, St. Louis, Philadelphia, Dayton, and Alton. The photograph in Dr. McPherson's office, with its crowd of supplicants blurring into infinity at the horizon, is an accurate picture of what Sister Aimee faced in those years. There was really no end to it, the tide of human suffering, of pathetic hope, once that line formed in Baltimore. The service would go on until the oil burned out.

———

Aimee spent the last of April, 1920, with her children in Los Angeles.

Minnie booked the 3,000-seat Memorial Hall in Dayton, Ohio for Aimee's next revival. They arrived on May 3 to find the hall roaring with an ecumenical crowd of ministers, workers, and curiosity seekers from twenty states. Pastor Shires of Covington, Virginia wrote: "Sister McPherson's great meeting in Washington filled me with a hunger to know more . . . after the meeting at Dayton began, I grew more and more restless every day, until I found relief by boarding a train for Dayton." Thousands like him hungered to know more. These flocked to Memorial Hall. So did hundreds of the blind, deaf, paralytic, tubercular, who had received news clippings from relatives, friends, or friends of friends, in Baltimore, Washington, Tulsa, testifying to the lady preacher's powers.

She delayed the healing prayers until the second week, after twenty thousand had heard her voice and five hundred had been converted. The first healing service, on May 13, attracted reporters from three Dayton newspapers. These corroborate that the crowd of four thousand in Memorial Hall witnessed the instant healings of Grace Fultz, crippled from birth, and Mrs. Mary Overholzer, blind from cataracts. Frank Kesslor, afflicted with locomotor ataxia for eleven years, walked from the stage unaided, his little son by his side carrying the discarded crutches.

The reporters interviewed the neighbors of Mrs. John F. Fraga, crippled from childhood, and recorded how the neighborhood rejoiced as Mrs. Fraga strode home after the healing service. She walked down Park Street to embrace her husband. He scarcely knew her. She came in the door without a limp, and made supper. She walked up and down the house, stopping only to view herself in the mirror.

"Oh, I am afraid it is all a dream," she told a reporter.

More than five hundred invalids, some on crutches, some leaning on canes, some in wheelchairs and on stretchers, crowded about the platform. The reporter from *The Dayton Journal* observes:

> One by one the healer prayed over them with clock-like precision . . . So many were appearing for aid that each necessarily received brief attention and only the machine-like and orderly manner in which group after group went forward enabled the evangelist to prescribe for the many she did before the services closed.

The newspapers give dozens of names and addresses of invalids cured, mostly of paralysis and deafness, but also of heart trouble, tuberculosis, and cataracts. The reporters, swamped, were unable to record most of the healings, but also knew that the city desk would devote only so many inches of copy to freaks and prodigies. The evangelist, too, had more than she could handle. Sometime that evening she halted the service, with hundreds still to be prayed for. She announced that a similar service would be held the next Thursday afternoon and retired to her hotel.

Between the night of May 20 and the opening of her next revival in Alberta, Canada on May 30, Sister Aimee found time to write an eight-thousand-word description of that meeting, which she called "One Day at Memorial Hall, Dayton, Ohio." Her notes suggest how it felt to move at the center of those events before the spectacle grew so enormous that it defied rational comprehension.

The following reconstruction is based on Aimee's account.

At midday the limousine bearing Aimee from her hotel snarled in traffic two blocks from Memorial Hall. Turning the corner, the driver found the streets full of people hurrying in the same direction, very quietly, as if listening for instructions.

The limousine stood in a line of streetcars, automobiles, ambulances, and hearses. These were unloading paralytics in wheelchairs, sick men and women on cots and stretchers, children in arms and octogenarians on their grandchildren's backs, unloading them all onto the steps of the white-columned portico of Memorial Hall. As policemen held up the traffic, groups on crutches crossed the streets. Two men carried shoulder-high a woman seated in a rocking chair. Many wore white bandages on their arms, legs, heads.

"Oh God," Aimee whispered, looking through the windshield, then settling back in her seat, biting her thumbnail. "Is the whole world sick? Are they *all* coming to Memorial Hall?"

The police and the fire department had been called out to cope with the crowd. With their help the limousine reached the building, which had already been locked, hours before the service, because no more people could fit inside. Aimee heard a strong man pleading for a helpless woman: "Please. You must let her in. I know she will be all right if I can just get her in the door . . ."

The driver pressed on to a side entrance. Instantly the car was surrounded, the windows all darkened with arms and hands outstretched.

"Oh lady! Pray for me. Oh! lay your hands on this man and pray just for a moment."

"We have brought this child forty miles, surely you can let us in." A man held a boy up to the window.

Six policemen made a line from the stage door to the running board of the limousine. They were perspiring heavily. Several of the big men seemed on the verge of tears as they held back the people reaching under and over their arms in hopes of touching the healer as she passed.

The door opened wide enough for Aimee to enter, and she was pulled through. The door slammed but could not stifle the moan that went up from a hundred souls realizing at last that they were shut out.

Entering the stairwell, Aimee glimpsed the basement through an archway; it was full of people—crippled, dying, in wheelchairs, being comforted by relatives. Police officers and church workers passed among them, taking names and notes on index cards. By a hasty triage they were trying to identify the worst cases. If the hundreds of invalids upstairs were prayed for in time, some of these could be carried above to the altar. Guards stood by the basement windows, where faces pressed to the glass. "We had to lock them, Sister," said a guard apologetically. "People were passing the sick through the windows."

Aimee felt dazed. There was a dreamlike hush in this atmosphere of patient agony. She almost wished someone would cry out.

In the ladies' cloakroom, to the right of the stage, forty women choristers knelt in prayer before entering the seats reserved for the choir. On the other side of the stage, forty men bowed in silence. Laying aside her cape, the evangelist knelt for a moment to collect and center herself in the field of her devotion. Then she tiptoed to the stage entrance to see that all was ready.

Minnie Kennedy directed the ushers, nineteen women who wore wide sashes of crimson ribbon. Among the seven hundred seats roped off for the sick, these sisters of mercy moved, cheering and comforting the sufferers.

In the gallery and the auditorium there was hardly a square foot of standing room. Wheelchairs, rockers, cots, and stretchers jammed the altar space. The fire department yielded its regulations to the police, who at the moment feared riot worse than fire.

Yet there was surprisingly little confusion. Each patient had filled out a card showing his name, faith, and disease; each card was numbered, "so the stronger could not press past the weak, the deformed, and the mothers with little children." A blackboard on the stage would post the numbers.

Center stage, someone propped open the lid of the grand piano. A tall man at the keyboard softly played:

> Sweet hour of prayer, sweet hour of prayer
> That calls me from a world of care . . .

The choir filed in on either side of the stage and knelt.

Aimee slipped into her seat. The dark-suited pastors of the Methodist, United Brethren, Baptist, and Christian Missionary Alliance sat in their reserved places in the front row.

The air of the auditorium was dense with longing, faith on the very edge of desperation. Aware that she more than anyone had produced this atmosphere, Aimee was momentarily terrified of her responsibility; she knelt as the others knelt, but prayed with a silent intensity no one could emulate: *Thou omnipotent King of Heaven and earth, Thou Sun who dispels all darkness, Thou Lion of Judah who breaks every chain, Thou Son of the living God, if ever we loved Thee, needed Thee, trusted Thee it is now. O rise up! Rise up dear Son of Righteousness, with healing in Thy wings* . . . Looking up into the dome of the great hall, she saw daylight streaming through the clerestory windows as a brigade of angels come to lend strength.

The pastor kneeling beside her glanced at her Hellenic profile, the strong chin trembling. He was distracted, then alarmed by the inner violence of her silent meditation. Her heartbeat, visible at a vein in her throat, was so pronounced, he thought he could hear it. The choir rose to their feet. He stood up with the others along the row while Aimee finished her struggle, relaxed suddenly, becalmed, nodding almost imperceptibly, as if an invisible hand had come to rest upon her head.

She got up to lead the singing. Everyone sang, from the pale boy wrapped in blankets and propped by pillows on the cot down front to the women in the highest seats in the gallery. Aimee felt God's presence like a bright cloud settling; the effect was to melt the barriers of flesh and identity that normally serve to defend and distinguish us.

Men and women wept at the sight of so much suffering, or for joy in the hope of recovery, or for both reasons. Aimee saw their tears as a symbol of the melting that must bring them together so that the healing could begin.

She prayed aloud, as four thousand people bowed their heads. The same voice that had prayed within her silently before, disturbing the harmony of her features, now thundered upon the sounding board of the crowded hall. *O Thou Lamb of God, whose ear is ever open to our cry* . . . The voice descended along the vowels of the first phrase, as if to capture the Deity's attention by the bass vibrations of the ground of being. Then it rose in trumpet tones of hope, *whose ear is ever open* . . . *As the moon and stars withdraw their shining before the sun at noonday, let earthly cares pale and disappear before the glory of Thy power* . . . Aimee raised her fine head, spread her arms. *Stretch out Thine arms, our father, enfold this suffering multitude unto Thy breast* . . . Commanding and then soothing, she crossed her hands upon the bosom of her white dress. *Draw us up close, oh close, Thou son of God* . . . And with that graceful gesture, head tilted, eyes half closed, the evangelist gathered the affections of four thousand individuals to a single source.

The prayer done, she opened the meeting to testimony. One by one the witnesses rose. From the stage, the gallery, the floor, they shared their healing stories. A man was paralyzed from the waist down—he now walked; a woman had a tumor under her arm that surgery failed to remove—she waved her arms in the air to show the tumor had melted away.

A young man leapt to the stage.

"Many of you know me, Gibbons is my name. I am employed in the Ideal Cafeteria, in this city. For eleven years I had a cataract on this eye, shutting out the light. I came to these meetings, gave my heart to God, and was prayed for and believed the Lord could remove the cataract. Look at me now! I can read fine print and see perfectly with what was my poor eye."

And when a dozen had testified, the people leaned forward in their seats, impatient with stories, ready for live action. Now Aimee must take the stage, dark-eyed with her vision, she must deliver the message. No time for a sermon, only rhythmic speech, the higher mathematics for the astounding physics that is to come. There may not have been five people in the building who understood the meaning behind her language, but it did not matter. They would drink her words like a potion that goes straight to thought's source; on some level everyone would draw what he needed from this stream of speech.

He was wounded for our transgressions. The chastisement of our peace was upon Him and with His stripes we are healed. Jesus came to destroy the works of the Devil. On Calvary's Cross He bore not only our sin, but that dire result of sin, sickness. The chief business in the ministry of Our Lord was forgiving sin and healing the sick. The two were not divided; but went hand in hand. They should walk side by side, and know no division today. Christ is the great physician for body, soul and spirit. It is He *who forgiveth our iniquities, and healeth all our diseases.* When the multitude pressed upon the Lord in those years long ago He had compassion . . . None were in such darkness but He could bring them light . . .

The crowd, with its Sunday school education, saw the barefoot shepherd on Galilee's shores, gentle-eyed as Aimee, molding broken limbs as if they were clay, brushing away pain as if it were dust.

Aimee saw nothing of the kind. Gazing into the depth of all those eyes, she saw God's blueprint of a human form with heart and lungs and limbs all perfect, the idea of the body. She was summoning this even as she evoked in the crowd's mind the Bible-school image of Jesus, the Lamb of God. Her own vision of the human form, at first vague, waxed ever more vivid and radiant as the crowd moved closer to becoming a single mind.

It was her job to bring them together, using the only instrument she had ever used to heal, the image set forth in the Gospels: the figure of the suffering Christ. *Put first things first. To take Him as your physician, accept Him as your Savior first. The fountain lies open, the precious blood is still efficacious to cleanse from sin.*

She must make them understand that they can become one body in Christ and that He, the Living Word, can live in them. He would raise them up for His glory. Their eyes and faith must be fixed upon Jesus. They must come like the woman of old, saying, "If I may but touch his garment, I shall be whole." They must remember that although Aimee prays for them and lays her hands upon them, it is Christ who heals and He alone.

And now, dear heart, remember that Jesus sees you. He is looking right down into your heart.

Be honest with God.

Be honest with me.

Be honest with yourself.

She was preparing them for the altar call. Hundreds in the auditorium thrilled for the first time at the evangelist's uncanny power to evoke the holy presence. The effect was hallucinatory. *If you are now unsaved, come quickly to Jesus. Rise from your seats —make your way down these aisles, kneel at His feet in heart contrition.*

In a matter of minutes two hundred men and women had come, dazed and weeping, to the altar, many of them fixed upon a mental image of the Lord more vital and radiant than anything they had ever seen. (Several journalists wrote that Aimee so convinced them of Christ's presence at various meetings, they craned their necks and strained their eyes in expectation of seeing Him.)

Meanwhile the singing choir consolidated on the right, clearing half the stage. The crowd was spiritually whole, invigorated by the tingling blood of fresh converts, ready for the ministry for individual bodies to begin. A worker arranged seven chairs on the open stage, the chairbacks turned obliquely away from the audience. He placed a small table in front of the chairs. On it was a silver urn of anointing oil.

Seven at a time the invalids filled these chairs.

Aimee anointed one, asking, *Brother, do you believe and step out upon His promise now?* She laid hands upon him, conducting the crowd's faith like a lightning rod, and he felt a charge run through him. He who had been carried to the chair walked away from it, weeping.

Aimee scribbled on a pad for a deaf woman: "Sister, do you believe that Christ can open these deaf ears, right now?" Silence in the hall honored the forty years of silence in which the woman had suffered. The woman nodded, and Aimee's eyes flashed fire, for she knew that true deafness is spiritual and earthly sound cannot touch it. The evangelist sensed the Evil One's presence in the shape of a black demon stopping the woman's ears. Aimee shouted in a furious voice that would have deafened the poor woman were she not already deaf, a voice that the locked-out crowd could hear in the streets: *In the name of Jesus Christ, thou deaf spirit, I command you to come out of her! O ear, be opened, and hear the word of the Lord!*

Thousands heard that voice blast through the silence, thousands in such unanimity of faith in the healing power of Christ's

blood, they represented to Aimee's mind a perfect Ear. The
Holy Spirit coursed through the crowd.

"Sister, rise," called the evangelist. "In Jesus' name, can you
hear me now?" It was like a distant voice at the mouth of a
cave, calling to her within.

"Yes! Oh, yes—thank God!"

No sooner was her seat vacant than a young woman suffering
from curvature of the spine struggled to the platform, on her
mother's arm. She looked back shyly at her mother, as Aimee
drew the dress from her shoulders and worked chrismatory oil
along her backbone toward the base of the spine. All the while
the evangelist was praying softly, the girl had the sensation of
being pulled, like a marionette, by a string from above threading
the pearls of vertebrae.

The evangelist took her under the arms from behind, lifting
her out of the chair. And then, as if her mind had suddenly
turned to more important matters, Aimee asked:

"Now my dear, where is this curvature in your spine?"

"Right here," she answered, pointing.

The whole scene had not taken more than two minutes, but
already Aimee looked impatient.

"Where is it now?" Aimee asked again, as if the two of them
had lost a key or an earring. "Put your hand back and see if
you can locate it."

The mother approached, to point out the cursed defect so
that the evangelist could get on with her wonderful work in
healing it. Mother and daughter, in obvious confusion, searched
with trembling hands from the neck to the base of the spine,
searched for the curvature that always crooked her back in exactly the same hateful place.

They could not find it.

It was gone.

That afternoon and evening, Sister Aimee anointed and
prayed over more than six hundred afflicted people. She did not
stop to rest or take food. Pastor Shires observes that she worked
over the endless stream of sufferers "before she was finally
literally taken away by compulsion . . . her helpers pulled her

away from the crowd that was thronging her, and her own mother pleaded with her to rest . . .''

She would rest a little on the train to Alberta, Canada, where she preached for the first half of June.

————

From Lethbridge down through the Canadian Rockies she traveled to Alton, Illinois, where a crowd greeted her at the depot and the White Hussar City Band played "Revive Us Again."

Aimee and Minnie were surrounded. Ladies of the welcoming committee pressed bouquets of roses into their arms. They were paraded down Main Street in Pastor Kortkamp's car, followed by a marching band, a truck filled with Sunday-school children, attorney Wilson in his white suit and straw boater, and an entourage of assorted merchants, lawyers, and bankers concerned with the city's spiritual health. All wore white and sported red carnations.

Pastor A. W. Kortkamp of the First Methodist Church had long ago petitioned the famous evangelist for a revival. As demands upon Aimee's time increased, the pastor and his elders continued to fast and pray she would work Alton into her schedule, awaiting "a cloud the size of a man's hand" in the form of a favorable sign. When Aimee agreed, Alton was ready. A "big top" seating two thousand had been pitched on the grounds of the high school. Meetings would also be held in the First Methodist Church.

Reporters came to the huge prayer meetings, and struggled to find words to describe the sound. "Did you ever hear three or four thousand people pray at once?" writes one. "Not in unison, but every individual praying, using his or her own words. She asked them to pray, forgetting themselves and everybody else . . . The fervor could be understood though the words were not . . . It caused one to think of Niagara, a deep roll of thunder. The spirit mounted upward as if to the top of a mountain." They described the baptismal service on the Mississippi, the multitude on the shore, on rooftops, watching the baptized rise from the blue water, the boats drawn around, the

white-robed children singing. The reporters came to the healing
services, as the crowd swelled to six thousand, filling Seminary
Square in downtown Alton and spilling over into Sixth Street,
where people looked on from automobiles parked bumper to
bumper. Reporters described the healings and interviewed
hundreds of invalids before and after the evangelist laid hands
on them.

> Such a mass of twisted, suffering, misshapen humanity as was
> assembled yesterday afternoon when Mrs. Aimee Semple Mc-
> Pherson appeared to conduct her healing service, had never been
> seen by any of those present—except, of course, Mrs. McPherson,
> who sees such gatherings often but never gets used to them. In
> some cases it was evident that the evangelist was expected to put
> brains in heads where none had been; to put use into limbs that had
> never been used in all their being; to straighten out horribly de-
> formed backs; to loosen up joints that were permanently fixed and
> immovable.
> The sight of it brought tears to the eyes of Mrs. McPherson.

The Alton newspapers followed Aimee's every move from
June 23 until her departure on July 12. Jews and Gentiles, Catholics and Protestants came from all over the Midwest to feel
the healer's touch. She had given in to the desperate clamor for
healing services, and in Alton appears to have conducted them
daily. A new theme emerges in the news dispatches: "Her physical endurance is equally remarkable with any feat of healing
that has yet been accomplished."

The witnesses, growing accustomed to blind men regaining
their sight, tumors vanishing, and cripples taking their first steps
under their own power, become more and more fascinated with
the little woman in the white dress who stands at the center of
the commotion. They refer repeatedly to this *light* that radiates
from her cheeks and forehead, whether or not she is smiling,
as she stands for five, six, seven hours at a time, praying. A
ten-year-old boy was carried to the platform, holding his shoe
in his hand. A victim of infantile paralysis, the boy had so much
faith, he had brought his shoe with him to wear home on the
foot that the brace covered. *How can she hold her arms above her*

head again and yet again in that appeal to Heaven—are they mortal arms, or wings? How does her voice maintain such resonance after the strain of so many impassioned pleas? These questions haunt the reporters as they watch her bless the boy holding his shoe.

Mrs. McPherson is filled with an energy that seems to be almost tireless, almost inexhaustible. Yet, she labors hard, she concentrates so much of her great energy in the work, she does become tired. Several times toward the close she would appeal to others to help her by offering prayer, because she was so tired. But she would quickly leap into the work again and go ahead.

When it was all over she was asked as she was being led away to her automobile, whether she was physically worn out. Instantly the tired, sad look on her face disappeared . . . "I'm all right. I'll be all right and strong for the meeting tonight."

She had undergone an ordeal that would wear out almost anyone, but . . . it seemed she had instantly recuperated.

One writer, covering a later service in the mid-July heat, was struck by the change in the audience since the first healing ceremony. The galleries of the First Methodist Church were loaded and the aisles blocked—yet there was a reverent hush instead of hubbub and outcries. People had begun to accept the healings as God's will but they were increasingly curious about Sister McPherson: "All undismayed they fanned themselves, wrapt in attention on the young woman who in deep perspiration was wholly taken up with her weird-looking task."

The *Times* reporter went on to say that she "put every particle of her strength into the effort to heal, every atom of her being. Her face literally beamed and it was plain to the uninitiated that she was wearing herself out."

At the last healing service under the big top in Alton (population 25,000), the horde of ten thousand who desired merely to see what they had heard about was so dangerous, it became necessary for the police to stretch a fence around the tent. And then the swarms of spectators, in their eagerness to witness the service, kept threatening to surge over the fence.

———

Exhausted, Sister Aimee retreated to Los Angeles during August and much of September 1920. On the train she kept wondering "Why, Lord, did you give us a home in far-off Los Angeles?"

Little is known about this interval except that it must have been voluntary, a concession to her health. There was no shortage of invitations for Aimee to preach.

She reappeared in Piedmont, West Virginia, on September 26, complaining about the fumes from the paper mill and about the racket of seventeen locomotive engines parked next door to the clapboard mountain tabernacle where she was preaching. For the first time she expressed concern about her voice, that incomparable instrument:

> I preached under great handicap, having to cough and choke from the coal dust, acid fumes and warm smoke which poured through the building from the great engines . . . whenever I was not screaming my sermon loud enough, an usher at the rear was to lift his hand so that I could raise my voice still more to be heard above the railway engines.
>
> At the last meeting, while shouting my loudest, my throat felt as though filled with splinters, and a sudden pain pierced my right lung as though I had been shot with a bullet.

She had time to recover before October 24, when she opened in Philadelphia. Since her first success there in August of 1918, Aimee had wished to return. But she was at loggerheads with the Pentecostal authorities of Philadelphia in her bid for a mainstream audience. In response to several mission invitations, she said that God had informed her that the next time she preached in the City of Brotherly Love, it would be in a large denominational church.

Hancock Hall, with its great horseshoe-shaped gallery under a high ceiling studded with light bulbs, with its fifteen hundred seats, was not nearly large enough.

Aimee and her mother failed to grasp the change in public perception during the first half of 1920; they still considered the revival in each city as a separate and therefore governable event. After the hysteria in Dayton and the crush in Alton, the evangelist had withdrawn. During that retreat she planned to regain some control over her revival by holding meetings without promotion or fanfare. But in Piedmont scores of people, unable to find seats inside, had climbed the lower roofs of the tabernacle. They had lain on their stomachs so they could look down through the high windows, where the people within saw upside-down faces pressed to the glass, and screamed in terror that the roof would cave in. Desperate to witness the miracle of healing, dark-faced miners and their pale children had pulled the siding off the building as Aimee preached in her white dress.

She did not advertise the meeting in Philadelphia, but it made no difference. Everyone knew someone who had heard what had happened in Baltimore or Dayton or Piedmont. They knew when Aimee was on her way to Philadelphia. In the last years before radio and newsreels, it is notable that Aimee's following, from city to city, was foremost a word-of-mouth phenomenon. Her presence was anticipated even by people who had no intention of going to hear her.

Curiosity got the best of them. In Philadelphia the crowd's heterogeneity fascinated Aimee. They began gathering under the stone steeple of Hancock Hall hours before the service: Russian and Italian women with black shawls pinned on their heads and holding sick children to their breasts; aristocratic-looking women dressed in silks and velvet, with jewels on their fingers. "The rich and poor stand on one level here in these hours of waiting . . . they are driven by the same desperate need; they are seeking help from the same Source."

She held prayer meetings for five days before the first healing service on October 30. If she hoped for greater calm in which to save souls in Philadelphia, she was disappointed. The horde in the street would part only for the clanging trolleys to pass through, one after another, unloading at the doors.

Aimee would recall with horror how the eighteen policemen and dozen ushers were required to open the front door, counterbalancing with their ranked shoulders the thousands of pounds of pressure the crowd exerted from outside. Aimee stood wide-eyed behind the phalanx of strong men. She watched them strain to open the door slowly to keep the roaring sea of humanity from tumbling in upon itself. She watched as the light cracked the door at the top and two ladies, dazed and faint from their ordeal, fell forward headlong and had to be yanked inside to keep from being trampled by the mob as the doors swung wide.

No wonder she became phobic about doors, warning her children never to stand in a doorway. Her own temple, when she designed it, would have doors galore, more than a dozen wide ones in the front of the building alone. Nobody would ever have to worry about getting in or out of Aimee's temple.

Frederick Norcross of *The Public Ledger* writes: "On Thursday night she had a 'healing service,' exhibiting such marvelous powers in bringing relief to the crippled, the deaf, the dumb, and the blind, that a congregation which filled every seat and every inch of standing room in the church was literally amazed by what was seen and heard." A reporter of *The Inquirer* corroborates: "Persons seeking aid for physical and mental ills received it in a manner so startling and dramatic that those who went to scoff, stayed to pray . . ."

The Bulletin describes a scene at the altar, where an old blind man knelt next to a lady with an ear trumpet, and next to them a child twitched in its mother's arms with St. Vitus's dance. *The Inquirer* takes more interest in the crippled children:

> Mothers who had learned of the healing mission and had firm faith in its efficacy bore to the church babies and children hopelessly crippled since birth. They carried these helpless youngsters in their arms, and their grief and emotion were pitiable.

What the papers describe resembles the Alton healings in all but scope. The hall's limited capacity seems to have discouraged the statewide mobilization that kept Aimee praying for six hours at a stretch in the Illinois schoolyard under the big top. There is no sign of faintness or fatigue. She is

> a picture of healthy young womanhood . . . the starched white collar framing her face and a luxuriant head of hair, immaculately simple, wearing no ornaments but a plain little breastpin and the simple gold band that encircles the third finger of her left hand.

Yet beneath that brilliant, healthy surface Aimee grows increasingly melancholy, trapped, desperate. In the report she makes in *The Bridal Call*, written on the train to Montreal after Philadelphia, she recalls the crowd's hungry faces, their cries of distress. She remembers the balcony audience overflowing down the steps, the aisles roped, five hundred filling the chancel, standing in vestibules, sitting on altar cushions on the floor. Seventeen hundred people were jammed into a space made to hold one thousand, while the ushers filled the basement Sunday-school rooms with invalids. Remembering this, and thinking of the population that awaits her down the railroad line, she turns to her reader: "If you were once caught in a crowd like this," she says in desperation approaching panic, "if you then went to the doors and saw the crowd outside was still larger than the crowd inside, and they pressed you" . . . and the reader shudders at the thought of the heat, the breath of disease, iodine, boric acid, the concentration of agony and yearning . . . "wouldn't you just realize how Jesus had to get into a boat and push away from land, in order to preach to the people?"

Far greater crowds awaited her in the West.

CALIFORNIA, 1921

At fifty years of age Minnie Kennedy's face, large-featured, handsome, is a clear variation on a genetic theme—she is a coarser grained, more Celtic version of her daughter. Her figure was still youthful when her forehead was deeply lined. "Good peasant stock," says Roberta Salter; the peasant blood is more obvious in Minnie. Aimee's seems to have settled into her lower legs so she could stand on them around the clock, praying.

Minnie Kennedy's full-lipped smile, when it condescends to the camera, is Aimee's without the long teeth, humorous but more temperate. The eyes are what distinguish mother from daughter. While Aimee's wide gaze is usually lifted toward Heaven, Minnie's vigilant eyes, fiercely intelligent, are watching the side door. Much of Aimee's charm comes from her air of vulnerability; no such vulnerability affects Minnie's level gaze. She was, in her granddaughter's words, a tough customer, grilling every agent and hustler who approached her famous daughter.

Much has been made of the fact that Ma Kennedy ran the show during these years of Aimee's rise to fame. What remains to be clarified is the older woman's motives. From first to last, they were to protect Aimee from her own impetuousness, then to preserve her from the springtraps of the world of commerce. There Aimee remained incurably naive. She had the temperament of a Gypsy artist, totally in command on the stage and heedless everywhere else; she was inattentive to business details, which bored her. If Minnie had not come to her rescue in Florida in 1918, Aimee might have lived and died as a tent-show queen, consumed by the fanatics and deadbeats that were beginning to follow her.

Minnie lived in her daughter's interest, the daughter she had consecrated at birth to God's service. The movies have portrayed the mother as ambitious; Bette Davis plays Minnie as a stage-door mother who worked her gifted daughter for dollars and glory. This makes high drama but poor biography. The truth is more fascinating. The truth is that mother and daughter, during these years of furious activity, had no one but each other to comfort and confide in. They were more like sisters than friends, more like intimate friends than like mother and daughter.

Aimee was dominant, and in most matters she had the last word. Yet she accepted most of her mother's practical arrangements, because it was too much trouble to argue.

To call Minnie Kennedy ambitious denies the fundamental condition of their life together in 1920; it assumes a master plan. But Minnie did not know if the crowd would ignore them in the next town or eat them alive. They had no long-range strategy. Mother and daughter were swept up in a windstorm of public sentiment they could neither understand nor control.

Minnie would go to the hall hours before Aimee, to work with the invalids, interviewing them, comforting them, filling out their healing cards. She was stern and tireless. She stood alongside Aimee on the platform and often led the singing. She held the cruse of oil as her daughter laid vibrant hands upon the cripples. Minnie understood perhaps better than anyone how her daughter had come by her unique gifts, but she was just as astonished by the miraculous results.

She was concerned most of all with her daughter's health, physical and emotional, for without health Aimee's success would be meaningless. Moving from city to city, booking auditoriums and hotels, Minnie's position was basically defensive.

As Aimee's energy flagged, the women decided that the time had come to build a church of their own. It was time for not only a monument but a fortress. Aimee always insisted that the project was divinely inspired and directed, but it also answered a practical human need. She tells how she was called, again and again, "to build a house unto the Lord in Los Angeles." She wrote, in the 1930's, "when this burden first came from heaven, I tried to shake it off, supposing that the idea might be of self." And: "Who ever heard of a woman without earthly backing . . . undertaking the raising of funds and the erection of such a building?" Actually it had already happened on a smaller scale, with the two-story bungalow on Orange Grove Drive. And since the completion of "the house that God built," a growing stack of letters from potential backers urged Aimee to build a revival tabernacle in Los Angeles.

Weary of riding the rails, the two women retreated to Los Angeles in late July of 1921. They began looking for a plot of land.

Turning the corner of Figueroa and Third streets, at the wheel of the Oldsmobile, Aimee felt herself drawn toward Echo Park and a section of the city she had never seen before.

Palm trees, eucalyptus, and willows surrounded a magnificent blue lake. Swans rippled through the reflections of the trees in calm water. Aimee told her mother, sitting beside her, that this was heaven on earth and the ideal spot for a house of the Lord:

the trees, grass, benches, the sparkling fountain. Aimee remembered scenes in the heart of Dayton and Philadelphia, where people stood in the blinding sun or freezing rain for hours awaiting a service. Here in Echo Park they could relax on benches under the trees.

Facing the entrance of the park, they found a plot.

Aimee and Minnie looked at each other. *This is the place*, they agreed. "Never for a moment, in the months that followed, did we doubt that this was the location."

An elderly realtor informed the women they had picked the only piece of property around the park that was *not* for sale. An old woman owned it; she was rich, had a world of property and would not part with a patch of it. Other people, in fact, had offered a pretty penny for this very piece of property, and the old woman had turned them down flat.

"Praise the Lord," said Aimee.

"What?"

"The Lord has been keeping this property for us," she explained.

Thanking the gentleman, Aimee and Minnie left him shaking his head in bewilderment. When they returned later to show the property to a friend, they found a freshly painted sign saying FOR SALE, SNAP UP THIS CORNER, with the owner's name and address. With a lead pencil Aimee sketched her vision of the temple upon the sign board. In the back of her mind was the memory of straining to make herself heard in rented auditoriums, while she drew the platform, the choir, the balcony . . .

She drew it exactly in the shape of a megaphone. And it resembled Albert Hall in London, where she had given her first sermon.

They did not come to terms with the old woman until their return in December. As the price was fair, we may assume that Minnie needed four more months to raise the money, in Piedmont, Montreal, and Philadelphia.

During Aimee's rise to fame, the newspapers never mention money changing hands—no collection plates or love offerings, no donation of funds in gratitude for healing. All that comes later. In 1920 Aimee appears far removed from the jingle of coins in the collection plate. Someone passed the hat, surely, or the evangelist could not have fed her children in the bungalow on Orange Grove Drive, where a housekeeper cared for them. But beyond travel expenses (which were considerable) Minnie did not demand an up-front guarantee for her daughter's appearances or wrangle over the collection plate. And Aimee did not make emotional appeals before the offerings. They took what tithe the sponsors gave them, believing that "the Lord would provide" them with all they needed.

In January of 1921, after three years on the road evangelizing to several hundred thousand people, Aimee and her frugal mother had saved $5,000. Jerry Falwell or Billy Graham, reviewing the ledger, might shake their heads in disbelief, wondering what became of the money. And some of this sum must have been Minnie Kennedy's nest egg from her Salvation Army work. Although $5,000 may have been worth ten times more in 1920 than today, it is still paltry, considering Aimee's accomplishment. If Minnie had been the hustler some say she was, they could have closed on the land deal for Echo Park and built the temple with cash on hand.

But this was their only capital. And they spent it on the lot in Echo Park, all of it. In the January 1921 *Bridal Call* a headline announces: "Echo Park Revival Tabernacle to be Erected in Los Angeles." The original idea was to build a tabernacle of wood that would seat 2,500; the change from tabernacle to stone temple, seating 5,000, had to do with the rapid growth of Aimee's audiences early in 1921.

"The crowds you are drawing to your meetings almost scare us," wrote the contractor Brook Hawkins. He was probably thinking of the San Diego revival, which began January 9 in Dreamland Boxing Arena. In mid-February it climaxed in Balboa Park with the healing service immortalized in that famous photograph on Rolf McPherson's wall.

These epic healing services, only a hundred and fifty miles from her home town, made Aimee's reputation in California, and paid for the temple's ground excavation.

The campaign was "undenominational." This means that many Christian denominations had a hand in it. The sponsors chose the largest venue available: Dreamland Boxing Arena had 3,000 seats.

Aimee might joke about preaching in the boxing ring, but she was prepared to use it. The night before she was scheduled to open, the arena was howling with fight fans and a full card of bouts. Between matches Aimee climbed gingerly through the ropes, a vision from another world right down to her white high-button shoes planted on the bloodstained canvas of the ring.

Manager Keran shouted to the assembly through the cigar smoke: "Ladies and gentlemen, in this corner . . ." He was so nervous introducing a woman to this crowd, he was shaking —and even forgot to remove his hat.

Under the shaded glare of the overhead light Aimee struggled to see faces through the smoke. They could hardly believe what they were seeing: this round-cheeked, bosomy cherub with hair piled on her head, eyes flashing, smile reaching out to the raucous crowd. And when the woman in white began to talk in her trombone voice, delivering a river of words about Jesus and love and His precious blood as she eyed the real blood on the canvas, what they really wanted to do was laugh. But something about Aimee kept them from laughing. This was a crowd that respected power and sensed immediately who in the ring had it and who didn't. Nobody laughed until she began to laugh at herself, putting up her dukes against an imaginary pugilist and shadow-boxing, calling out to them to come, come one and all, to Dreamland Arena tomorrow night. Because tomorrow night Aimee Semple McPherson was going to knock out the *Devil!*

Then, as she continued to speak, they began to clap and cheer at every pause. They nearly lost control when she asked them to bring along "the worst sinner to be found in San Diego." This was too rich. They began to guffaw and point at each other, crying, "That's him over there, Sister," and, "No!—that's him over yonder!" But seeing her smile melt into displeasure, they got quiet, schoolboys fearing the paddle. And then they cheered and applauded again when she issued her last invitation to "be there tomorrow night," stepped through the ropes, and headed up the aisle out into the night.

San Diego, events would prove, was spoiling for a revival. Aimee's intrusion upon the precinct most likely to resist her, invading it to charm or at least surprise the fight crowd, was ingenious. By the next morning the whole town was talking about it.

Fight fans who took her up on her invitation the next night scarcely recognized the boxing ring. The canvas had been scrubbed snow-white. Aimee had ordered a truckload of palm and pepper-tree branches to weave along the ropes, with calla lilies, carnations, and orange blossoms. A grand piano stood in one corner. The great ring lamp with its shade advertising restaurants and jewelry shops had been replaced with "a new one advertising Jesus."

She made jokes and wry comments about Dreamland Arena ("Whenever it is possible we prefer to pray at the chancel rail, or at the altar; but they don't seem to build them in boxing arenas, and we had to do the next best thing and use the platform"), but the crowds there, the conversions, and the wonders of the healing services were from the beginning equal to everything she had experienced in the east. The multitudes who had migrated to Southern California seeking health heard of Aimee; in two weeks these created an assemblage in San Diego that neither Dreamland Arena nor any building in the West could accommodate.

Two weeks into the campaign, the crowd discovered the home where the healer had been staying. Then there was not a quiet moment left, day or night. Telephones rang and doorbells rang, and mothers pressed right into Aimee's bedroom with sick children to be prayed for. She moved to a hotel, and bound the clerk and the bellhops to silence.

With a few minutes to eat between services, she sat down to a meal of steak and potatoes in the hotel café. In the midst of saying grace, she was interrupted by a middle-aged woman who looked at her suspiciously.

"Excuse me, but isn't this Sister McPherson?"

"Yes, dear."

Relieved, the woman called: "Papa, come over here and sit down; we can talk to Sister as she eats."

An old man with a bandage on his neck shuffled over.

"Now, Sister, Papa here has a cancer on his neck." She pointed to the old man. "Beneath that soft handkerchief. It is so painful—and raw," she said, groping for words, "just like that steak."

Aimee shuddered, pushed her plate away. "It would have been impossible," she recalls, "to touch another bite." Noticing Aimee's pallor and discomfort, the woman excused herself. She departed, leading Papa, whose fate Aimee does not record.

By that time she had prayed over hundreds of invalids in Dreamland Arena and seen many recover.

Aimee writes: "As soon as one was healed, she ran and told nine others, and brought them too, even telegraphing and rushing the sick in on trains." Soon the population of the port city swelled with invalids unable to find hotel rooms, invalids camped out in automobiles gridlocked around Dreamland Arena. Efforts to keep the crowd moving by issuing tickets to newcomers helped but did not solve the real problem: each day Aimee preached, the horde outside the arena increased. For every hundred people who went away, five hundred arrived. Approaching the end of their engagement at Dreamland Arena, Aimee observed "though we stayed and prayed until exhausted, we had only touched the fringe or the outskirts of that great multitude clamoring for prayer."

So Minnie Kennedy moved Aimee's revival to Balboa Park. "Jesus didn't attempt to pray for the 5,000 in a building like this: He went out into the fields . . ." Surely the women had no illusions about being able to *heal* any more people in Balboa Park than in Dreamland Arena, since Aimee only had two hands. But at least no witness would be excluded. And the collective energy of all those people praying at once would be wonderful indeed. Not to mention the offerings: Minnie had her eye on the collection plate, and couldn't very well watch it through the walls of Dreamland Arena.

They put the question to the audience, inside and outside the boxing arena, and the answer was a deafening "Aye." The chaplain of the U. S. Marine Corps in San Diego approached the Park commissioner, who called an emergency meeting of the Board. They approved, for Aimee's use, the magnificent organ pavilion in Balboa Park, with its seating for many thousands, acres of standing room, and a broad platform with its unique outdoor pipe organ.

Under the circumstances a reporter might be surprised to see Aimee, days later, in a leather jacket and aviator goggles, standing in the cockpit of an airplane. At noon on January 28 she preached a sermon from the plane, at the municipal pier, before flying over the city to shower the downtown area with 15,000 handbills announcing her revival meeting in Balboa Park.

Was this stunt necessary? Whose idea was it? Minnie's? Or aviator Hennessey's, whose Hennessey Flying Squad shared the publicity in the first news of Aimee ever to hit *The L.A. Times?*

Having gained momentum in San Diego, the evangelist would take no chances on losing it—particularly given Balboa Park's wide open spaces and her financial commitment to the new Echo Park Tabernacle. She had become, as of January 28, 1921, not merely a servant of God but an enterprise in urgent need of capital. She had to fill the Park.

Aimee got what she wanted: a revival meeting that stretched to the horizon. At dawn they began arriving, in cars, ambulances, and special streetcars from the railroad station, a caravan. The cripples came in handcarts, children's wagons, wheelbarrows, and baby buggies; they came in dogcarts, were borne on the clasped hands of fathers and brothers, or brought pickaback to be laid on the grass within the broad perimeter of date palms and Grecian columns.

A detachment of U. S. marines had been deployed to help the police force handle the traffic and the crowd. At 9:30 A.M. the evangelist, driving over the bridge which spans the canyon, driving under the great arch built as the gateway to a World's Fair, bogged down in a sea of pedestrians. At the exit road to the organ pavilion the police turned away all vehicles except ambulances and others bringing invalids. Here a marine leapt on each running board of Aimee's car as a squadron of police led her slowly through the human crush, the horn blaring continuously.

Beyond the stage the organ pipes cast their long shadows upon a crowd spread out fanwise as far as the eye could see: bodies in braces and casts, emaciated, almost skeletal faces, women bloated with dropsy, hundreds in wheelchairs, on stretchers. Against the blue sky, on distant buildings, on the colonnade cornices stood photographers cranking newsreels, reporters with binoculars and panoramic cameras, who had climbed to get a bird's-eye view of the throng. It was remarkably quiet, unreal, like a memory rather than a flesh-and-blood event.

The police estimate of the crowd was 30,000.

Sister Aimee did not keep them waiting. Kneeling at one side of the platform, she prayed, finding the center of her faith: *Look down from the open heavens of blue this morning upon us all*, she prayed. And: *How we have learned to love them!* What she had learned was a passion that is beyond love, a compassion for men and women based upon knowledge of disease and sin, the reality of Christ and the transience of the flesh.

When she got up to face the crowd, they were all singing. A young naval engineer, lately healed of tuberculosis, James R. Flood, gave his testimony. Aimee spoke briefly, deep-throated, dark-eyed under the brilliant sky. She spoke on the "double cure" of the soul and body, challenging the known laws of physics, weaving a further spell upon this throng already spellbound.

Then the endless cortege of sufferers began to flow over the platform, and she laid hands on them one by one. Doctors Ferris, Belding, and Wilt assisted. Among the first cured was the lame woman immortalized in that photograph in Rolf McPherson's office. She had been paralyzed from the waist down since childhood. When her toes touched the wooden floor of the stage and her stiff knees straightened, the crowd thundered its joy to see her walk. And those waiting in the long line thrilled in expectation.

As the sun climbed and the shadow of the pipe organ shortened, Aimee prayed. Ears long deaf began to hear the organ. Old men threw away their crutches. A woman held out her infected arm, blackened with abscesses. As Aimee rubbed it with oil and prayed, the skin tingled, faded, and in a rush of blood regained its natural pink color. A man came to her with eyes shining and at his throat a goiter the size of a grapefruit. With infinite tenderness she cupped her oiled hand upon the goiter; and, as if someone had pricked it, the sphere began to shrink. The goiter shrank, in what may have seemed a short time for those who witnessed the flesh change in fascination and terror. It shrank and finally melted away, and the man's collar was left loose and hanging.

She prayed until the sun lay on the western horizon and three hundred and eighty sufferers had turned in their healing cards to Minnie Kennedy. But there were hundreds more, beginning to grow uneasy, wondering if the healer would ever get to them. Aimee's feet ached and burned. Her voice was worn to a whisper, and dark specks swam before her eyes while the nurses, ushers, and marines conducted the orderly rows of invalids to the platform. Wanting to reach more in a shorter time, she decided to go down among them and pray from seat to seat. But in a matter of minutes she found herself, hands high, gasping for air, beaten back to the platform steps, despite the efforts of the police and marines. Mothers with their babies were getting crushed by the more hearty invalids. So Aimee was pulled back onto the stage, where she kept praying—swaying with dizziness, holding the baluster—until the sun disappeared.

Panicked that she might slip away from them, the crowd broke past all barriers to reach her. A cordon of police was required to deliver the evangelist, fainting with fatigue and dehydration, away from the victory of Balboa Park.

She returned to Los Angeles with $5,000, as much money as Minnie had been able to squirrel away in the three years previous.

A snapshot of the groundbreaking in February of 1921 shows a crowd in a semicircle around Aimee, who is wearing a cloche hat and black shift, grinning, wielding her shovel with bravado. Brook Hawkins told her that $5,000 might pay to dig the *hole* for the foundation. She told him to crank up his steam shovels. "By the time you dig the hole, I expect to have money for the foundation."

And so it went. There are two things in the life of Aimee Semple McPherson that seem more mythic the more we know about them: her healing ministry, and the building of Angelus Temple in two years. As the climax of the healing ministry provided the dollars to build Angelus Temple, Aimee's career assumes a logical shape usually reserved for works of art: the Temple rose as an enduring symbol of transient miracles.

While the steam shovels dug the hole for the foundation, Aimee and her mother were on the train to St. Louis. The evangelist had been booked for three weeks beginning April 19 in the 3,000-seat Masonic auditorium, Moolah Temple. They discovered, with amusement that concealed their dismay, that the befuddled sponsors (a church with sixty-seven members) had done no advance work. Minnie would never let this happen again—the stakes were now too high.

St. Louis was probably their last campaign launched solely by word of mouth. On the afternoon of April 19 Moolah Temple was half full; that night the attendance was not much better. In 1921, St. Louis was the sixth largest city in the United States, with three-quarters of a million people. Minnie Kennedy shook her head in exasperation at the empty seats.

By April 24 the auditorium was full, afternoon and evening, with people who had "just heard about it." On April 25 a headline in *The Globe-Democrat* blares: MAN BARKS AS WOMEN AND GIRLS MOURN AND SHRIEK AT REVIVAL. This was not the sort of clipping that would find its way into the Church scrapbook, but it did the job.

After that the sergeant of police assigned regular details,

changed twice a day, to keep people from being trampled or
crushed against the temple, where thousands were unable to
gain admission. People shut out the day before would begin
gathering at the doors at five in the morning. By nine o'clock
the streets would begin to fill; at 12:15 the police would open
the doors, and in five minutes the house would be packed. Police
estimated that on several occasions 4,000 or 5,000 were turned
away. Learning of the physician's son who, deaf and mute since
the age of two, was healed at twenty-five; hearing of the blind
girl who said that the white veil melted instantly from her eyes;
compelled by rumor upon rumor, people would stand outside
the temple through an entire service. They would cling to a
brick corner or ledge, in the hope that just touching the building
in which God worked so powerfully must be a blessing.

Two weeks of this hysteria galvanized the religious community of St. Louis. Methodist, Baptist, and Presbyterian
worked side by side with Pentecostal, Lutheran, and Nazarene.
All had something to gain. The revival never pretended to be
an end in itself—nor was it intended to produce a cult following
for Sister Aimee. In St. Louis careful records of the converts
were kept, so they might be guided to membership in a denominational church after Aimee left town.

The YMCA was committed from the first, and their Gideon
Band showed up. A delegation of choristers came over from
Alton to help with the singing. At the end of two weeks, when
the party had outgrown Moolah Temple, an ad hoc committee
of ministers raised $1,500 to rent the 12,000-seat St. Louis Col-
iseum (with standing room for 4,000 more) for the last week
of Aimee's campaign.

This cavernous building, with its ovals of galleries trimmed
with red-white-and-blue bunting, took up an entire city block.
Like Madison Square Garden, this was typical of the turn-of-
the-century coliseums used primarily for political conventions
and world-class prize fights. In the dim light of the clerestory
Aimee could scarcely see from the podium to the topmost seat
under the roof.

Any promoter can tell you how difficult it is to fill a hall that
size today, for only one night, with or without an admission

charge. Only pop stars can do it, and a few political personalities;
and they require elaborate advance publicity. Before rock 'n'
roll, only an act like Mary Garden, the soprano, or Harry Houdini would book the St. Louis Coliseum for several nights—
and neither star would have risked this without several weeks
of advance drumming.

Upon thirty-six hours' notice Aimee transferred her meeting
to the coliseum. The next day it was full, and for the rest of
the week Aimee preached three times daily to overflow crowds
of 16,000, so that the police were again called to keep people
from being crushed against the doors.

In those days before loudspeakers, the great halls had a
wooden sounding board that tilted forward above the podium.
Aimee would recall "the consciousness of having to stand immediately under the great sounding board" and her voice

> which seemed almost to burst my lungs as I attempted to make
> myself heard to the uttermost parts of that great building . . .
> thousands and thousands and thousands of people, row after row
> in the auditorium, boxes and galleries, encircling the entire
> building—the hundred and fifty foot platform filled with ministers
> . . . an elevated choir . . . the immense altar calls wherein hundreds
> rose from all parts of the building . . . filling the platform, the altar
> space and the aisles . . .

Saturday, before the closing, was designated as a "wheel chair
and stretcher meeting" for the sick. From daybreak Minnie and
the ushers toiled to unbolt the opera chairs from the floor and
remove them from the auditorium. The space was then roped
off for the rows of stretchers that began to be hauled in from
the waiting ambulances: broken backs, broken necks in casts,
men and women eaten with cancer, feeble with consumption,
many drawn "in queer contortions."

At this point in telling her story, Aimee admits what must
seem obvious: "These things blend and mingle and whirl round
and round in my mind with the clapping and shouting of the
throng till I cannot seem to sort them all out . . . endless rows
of sick and crippled . . ." how several goiters went down instantly before the gaze of the multitude, and the tumor on a

woman's spine "melted like a snow ball before a hot flame."

The janitor left alone at midnight to clear the stage might lean on his broom, musing. Or, making a pile of cast-off crutches, braces, trusses, casts, ear trumpets, he might pick up one of these and study it, with more composure than Aimee Semple McPherson. An old janitor rolling away an abandoned wheelchair might bring to the situation a clearer apprehension of the wonder of it all.

THE GREAT CAMPAIGNS

The money had become a job for Wells Fargo. Thousands of dollars came down the aisles in a single service, more than enough money to get a man killed in 1921. When after a night service Aimee had hardly the energy left over to drag herself off to bed, she was lucky to have her hawk-eyed mother there to mind the till.

Aimee's gratitude to Minnie was deep, affecting. She watched her mother retire sometimes at three in the morning only to rise at five. From daybreak until midnight Minnie never left the coliseum. Under a bare bulb in the locked office she counted the money. If she didn't carry a revolver in 1921, her faith in God defies comprehension. She never sat down to a meal, but ate sandwiches at odd moments when she was not busy registering invalids, greeting delegations from out of town, or directing ushers and medical volunteers. Minnie's work with the sick was, in its way, as remarkable as Aimee's. With toughness and compassion she screened everyone she could. She excluded cranks, fakes, and invalids whose faith was unequal to the occasion, though few were turned away for lack of faith. Most important, Minnie spent long hours on her knees with the invalids in meditation, to prepare them for their healing.

Seventeen thousand dollars in cash returned with Aimee to Los Angeles in May of 1921. This was enough for Brook Hawkins's construction crew to make a good start on the temple walls.

And this is how it would go for the next fourteen months, as Aimee campaigned in coliseums and outdoors in eleven cities, and Minnie did the advance work, counseled the sick, and counted money to build Angelus Temple. A complete chronicle of this period, while marvelous, would contain a hundred pages of repetition. We can convey its scope by focusing on three well-documented campaigns, San Jose in August of 1921 and the Denver campaigns of June 1921 and July 1922. San Jose we value because it exhibits the faith healer at the height of her powers, in a situation beautifully controlled—it yields the most perfect picture of the fine-tuned healing service that would later electrify Dallas, Rochester, San Francisco, and Wichita. By contrast the Denver revivals were anything *but* controlled. They were explosive, as that entire city was swept up in religious hysteria. In Denver we see the beginning of the end of the revolution Aimee started in 1916, as at last she finds her cause espoused even by the government.

Before her trip to St. Louis, Aimee had spent the week of March 20, 1921 in San Jose. She preached twice a day and held three services for invalids. As remarkable as were the number of conversions during altar calls, the numerous reports of people being "slain in the Spirit" in their homes were even more amazing. Folks who had nothing to do with the Baptist church where the meetings were going on suddenly found themselves swept off their feet, in their own kitchens or parlors, twitching involuntarily and speaking in unknown tongues. San Jose, it seems, was ripe for a major revival, and during that week in March the Spirit gained momentum at every service.

On March 27 Aimee was officially ordained by the First Baptist Church of San Jose. The larger Baptist Association never ratified this ordination, so a lengthy controversy ensued over whether Mrs. McPherson was Pentecostal or Baptist. Whatever she was, they loved her in San Jose.

Six months later, in August, the city was prepared for "a great tabernacle campaign." For those who wonder about the permanence of the healings, San Jose provides evidence that they "held up" (at least in this instance) for six months. The healing service feeds upon testimonials; these would ring hollow in a community that had been disappointed. Faith healers historically have been nomads because their cures, hypnotically induced, fail the test of time. The snake-oil salesman does not get invited back. Aimee was exceptional in that many triumphs of her healing ministry were "return engagements." San Jose, Denver, Oakland, and San Francisco were all places where the faith in her power had a firm basis in local testimony. In San Jose, Dr. William Towner sent letters of inquiry to those healed at the August meetings. The replies, published in February of 1922, show the majority of correspondents were still healthy.

Aimee drove the Oldsmobile to San Jose, taking the highway between the sea and the mountains. Then she motored inland through the Santa Clara valley. As they rolled along, she admired the acres of peaches, prunes, and walnut trees, the apricots and figs "now hanging in luscious, ripened glory." She was thirty, in good health, and well rested after a month in Los Angeles overseeing the Temple's construction. She was traveling with her secretary Emma Schaeffer, an assistant secretary, a housekeeper, her mother, and her children. Roberta would soon be eleven, and Rolf was seven.

The children loved to go along. Every time Aimee left them, she would explain that once again she had to go out and save souls: whereupon the children would sigh and groan, *Haven't you saved all those souls yet, Mama? You mean there's still some out there you haven't saved?* Now she took them whenever school was out, and sometimes sent for them in the middle of a campaign.

Harold McPherson had sued for divorce in Rhode Island, charging desertion shortly after Aimee arrived in California in 1919. On legal advice she filed countersuit on the same grounds. The newspapers were intrigued that the evangelist of a sect that condemned divorce was seeking divorce. They followed the story. And as interest in Aimee's personal life grew into an obsession during the twenties, reporters frequently quoted testimony in the McPherson case. McPherson said that his wife was of a roving, restless disposition, that during one quarrel she threatened to kill both of them. His mother, Annie Mc-Pherson, testified that her son's wife was "a difficult woman to live with." A boarder from Annie McPherson's rooming house testified that "Mrs. McPherson was more interested in her evangelistic career than anything else . . . She had a fiery temper and made life unendurable for her husband. She could throw herself into a fit at any time."

The husband was awarded the divorce about the time Aimee was driving to San Jose in 1921. Mack was also awarded custody of Rolf McPherson on weekends, Rolf who was 3,000 miles away. Mack declined, explaining, "I would rather give up the pleasure of seeing my own son than put up with even the slightest connection with my former wife." A surprisingly bitter remark, considering Roberta Salter's conviction that he remained incurably in love with Aimee.

(A biographer who went to the Providence courthouse to see the divorce file in the 1970's learned that it had mysteriously vanished, from an archive otherwise in good preservation.)

———

So Aimee was independent not only physically and spiritually but also in the eyes of the law in 1921 as she sped toward the climactic scenes of her career. She had to caution herself to slow down to the limit of 35 miles per hour as she approached San Jose's city limits. She had a habit of speeding.

As she neared San Jose, she saw the enormous white tent pitched in her honor by Barnum and Bailey, and fifty smaller tents aglow with lights, on the exposition grounds at South First Street and Almaden. A journalist describes it as resembling an Arabian city, with water fountains, dressing rooms, a restaurant, "and every convenience that can be given the sick to permit them to stay throughout the campaign." An area had been subdivided into streets, marked off by stakes and numbered, for five hundred cars bringing invalids—each space large enough for a car and a tent beside it. These had been arriving for days and from as far off as Montana.

At last Aimee had purchased some nice clothing to wear when

she was not in uniform. The reporter who spies her entrance on the exposition grounds finds her clad in a fresh pongee suit, white shoes, and a large black hat.

The thin raw silk of the beige pongee reveals a powerful, voluptuous body; a neck as wide as her jaw-line; the muscular trunk of a world-class contralto, a great diva, which she in fact is. Constitutionally nervous, she seems to have put on weight during this demanding season, in order to provide ballast for her emotions and a greater reserve of caloric energy. After eight hours of continuous chanting and praying for the sick, hours on her feet without food or drink other than water, Aimee will sit down to a meal at midnight and eat like a field hand or long-distance swimmer. One cannot imagine her working or eating like this ten years later, when she will have lost a third of her body weight and look altogether different.

The journalists all remark on her brown eyes—large eyes, wide-set and meltingly soft, doe eyes: in the pulpit they project every expression from deep sympathy to darkest fury. Certain photographs of Aimee inflamed with the inspiration of a prophetess remind us of Judith Anderson as the demonic Medea. Offstage, playing "little Aimee," the brown eyes can widen to full circles of innocence in the presence of aggressive reporters. They can also sparkle with humor, glint with irony.

Aimee confronted her own image on the huge poster at the entrance to the grounds. It was startling. There she was in white, grinning, an open Bible on her left arm, her right raised over her head like the starter of a footrace. A streetcar passed, bearing the same poster. Huge letters at the top blared AIMEE SEMPLE MCPHERSON IS HERE. "True enough," mused the evangelist, reading on through the dates to September 7, 2:30 and 7:30 every day, reading on to the next block of oversized boldface: DO YOU BELIEVE IN MIRACLES? Well, she did and she didn't. The next line on the poster irritated her. "Thousands," it said, "will see miracles of healing wrought by God through this famous evangelist and healer."

It was overkill. And it might be promising more than God would deliver. Palms turned up, shaking them at her image in mock admiration, she exclaimed so her entourage could hear:

"What a *unique* form of advertising! Never heard of *that* before . . ." and walked away shaking her head.

The reporter, notebook in hand, was at her heels.

"Is there anything you would like to tell the public previous to your revival meetings, Mrs. McPherson?"

"I'd like them to *know*," said the evangelist, turning to him, "my meetings are ninety-nine percent *soul*-saving and *one* percent healing." He wrote this down. As he was not satisfied, Aimee continued, in a deep tuneful voice that was strangely like someone talking to herself, but a voice, the reporter noted, that would easily fill the four-pole big top: "God heals that they may go out to save others. He does not heal that the sick may take up worldliness and travel in sin again. The central thought they must have when they come to me is first and last and all the time—save their souls."

True to her word, Aimee would not lay hands upon the sick until the revival was well under way. With the support of a two-hundred-voice choir and an orchestra of horns and violins, she bent her energies, as so often before, upon conversion. She worked at "melting" the crowd into a unit, and persuading them of the transience of matter and the collapsibility of time. In the shade of the big top she spoke of the Great I Was and the Great I Am. "Everyone has spoken of the power that the Lord *used* to have, how He healed the sick, the blind, and made the lame to walk . . ." Each time she paused for breath, cries of "Hallelujah" and "Praise the Lord" burst from the front row to the far corners of the crowd of thousands.

Aimee held up the open Bible.

But listen here, in my Bible I find *the works that I do shall ye do also*, meaning those who preach the Gospel. And further, *these signs shall follow them that believe* and we who are here today are going to believe as we never believed before . . .

God's omnipotent presence has never ceased to be. Ministers preach to empty churches while the crowds rush to theatres and everywhere else because the "I was" is given them in place of "I am." I base the success of my revival meetings upon the preaching of "I am."

This was the same formula as "Jesus Christ is the same yesterday, today and forever," rescuing the Christian moment from
history and making it inhabitable for the crowd gathered under
the big top in 1921.

Meanwhile the newspapers called her "divine healer" in headlines; they followed her constantly, anticipating the dramatic
moment she would lay hands on some invalid. "The number
of invalids and hopeful sick who gather at every meeting," says
The Mercury Herald (August 9), "has increased until the front
row beside the altar resembles a great convalescing ward. In
wheel chairs, on stretchers and crutches, others hobbling and
almost unable to walk, they rise to their feet at every prayer
. . ." The reporter observes that "Mrs. McPherson brought
loud exclamations of grief from men and women laboring under
a terrific tension."

Her voice thundered, "Your chains will be shattered, your
fetters crushed, your troubles healed"—then softened as she
pled with them—"if you only *believe*—for where the spirit of
the Lord is, there is liberty." The last word rang like a bell.

The *Herald* reports that there were 150 conversions on Monday, the eighth: "Prostrated with the depth of their emotions,
many burst into tears and threw themselves full length before
the altar." The next night the reporter describes a scene continually on the brink of hysteria—

> Cheers, sobs and exclamations of those touched beyond control
> pierce the quiet of the tent in the midst of the speaker's sermon.
> Occasionally an emotional person will become slightly hysterical
> . . . and in order to calm her the choir softly breaks into a hymn
> for a few moments.

Aimee was speaking on Matthew 4:19, *Follow me, and I will
make you fishers of men*, inviting the faithful to bring loved ones
into the church. And she took the opportunity to condemn the
method of Billy Sunday, the teetotaler who yelled at sinners
and threatened them with damnation and hellfire. "Let us lead
them by kindness and sympathy," Aimee advised, and the re-

porter was struck by the contrast: "Mrs. McPherson in a clear, sweet voice talks to her congregation as a mother to her brood of children."

The crowd grew toward 10,000 in anticipation of the first service for divine healing on August 10. But the newspapers announced that only seventy-five persons had received cards that would admit them to the altar to be prayed for, because it would not be possible "to devote entire attention to more than 75 cases in one evening." Of course Aimee had prayed for more on many an evening. But she and Minnie had learned from their mistakes. Better to promise *less* than you can deliver rather than risk exhaustion and the dissolution of the gift. So they told the newspapers that seventy-five was the limit, and that "those who do not receive individual treatment tonight will be given an opportunity on Saturday night."

One would think that under such circumstances the public pressure to produce wonders would be intolerable. After all, this was not a play or a magic show. It was a spectacle whose risks compared, emotionally, to a bullfight or a duel with pistols—except that the participants here entered already wounded, with nothing to lose but their hopes and their faith in Mrs. McPherson. Eventually this *would* become intolerable to her. What is fascinating about San Jose in August of 1921 is that the "divine healer" is caught square in the spotlight. For years she had operated in the twilight as a mysterious public persona, relying upon the spontaneity and surprise of her road show. Now a life-size poster advertised her powers, and the newspapers built her up. As her children sat behind her on the platform, Aimee went about her queer business with the inspired expertise that one might expect of a tragic actress or a trapeze artist.

Now she understood the healing process as well as she ever would. In fact she probably understood it as well as anyone ever has.

The press, of course, was not interested in Aimee's profundity on the subject. Their questions were simple, and she answered them simply.

Hadn't the days of divine healing passed with the Apostles?

She replied: "No gift that Jesus ever gave was temporary."

Would the healings be permanent?

She told them that she did not know. "It all depends upon the lives they lead from the moment they descend this altar. God does not cure your twisted bones that you may dance better . . . the way to be healed and to stay healed is to give your lives to Jesus." Of course she could cite testimonies of hundreds who had remained healed for years.

Is healing instantaneous?

On this subject she was eloquent. The work of preparation was all-important. People who came rushing into the meetings saying they that had heard "there is a miracle woman here who can heal them at once," that they wanted to be "treated" promptly so they could catch the next train, were quickly set straight.

> They are bidden to settle themselves down and take part in the meetings just as though they were going to the Mayo clinic and were preparing for it for days, obeying each order—so they are bidden to prepare their house before coming into the presence of Jesus, the Great Physician.
>
> There is no miracle woman here at all, only a simple little body whom the Lord has called from a milk-pail on a farm, bidding her tell the good news of a Saviour who lives and loves and answers prayers.

She used the metaphor of the light bulb, likening the spiritual health of the candidate for healing to a clean connection: The wires must be strung and the links properly made back to the powerhouse before the light bulb can shine in your home. And she loved the metaphor of the railroad: Every rail must be fastened and the last spike driven before the train can go through; it takes a great deal longer to lay the track than for the express to pass.

Would she lay hands on a Catholic, on a Jew?

"I will pray for any Catholic bringing a letter from a priest saying it is his will for the subject to receive our prayers. [None would.] I will pray for any Jew," Aimee declares, "who will accept Jesus as his Messiah." No irony intended here, no anti-

Semitism. Jews were welcome to watch. It was a practical choice. The divine healing service was chancy enough even when the subject was prepared for Christ's intervention in a manner Aimee understood. Without faith in Christ the intermediary, the Jew couldn't get on the railroad—Minnie would not spend a healing card on him when there were a thousand Christians standing in line.

Why were some healed, while others were not?

When she was younger, Aimee was certain this had to do with the degree of active faith—later she admitted she did not know. Aimee distinguished between active and passive faith, explaining that passive faith ("If it is His will to heal me, I am willing") brings no results.

"Do not let yourselves mistake hope for faith," she declared. Active faith engages the whole will of the invalid, submerges him in the pursuit of spiritual harmony to the point where "the healing of your body will be but a secondary thought."

Finally, avid for a clue to the mystery of her power, they asked: Who shall be chosen to pray for the sick?

And she distinguished between the "prayer of faith" and the "gift of healing." Anyone can pray for the sick, and should. James advises us to call upon the Church elders who are filled with faith and the power of the Holy Spirit. Any earnest Christian should be able to pray the prayer of faith, which is simply, "O Lord Thy Word is true to everyone that believeth."

But the gift of healing, coming as a special unction from God, at special times, in special cases, usually according to the tide of faith, *commands* the blind eyes to be opened ". . . as though the power and authority of God through the Holy Spirit had descended upon and enveloped one, for the time being, even as the mantle of Elijah fell upon and clothed Elisha."

She understood the rare gift was hers. But she could no more explain why *she* had it than she could account for the far-reaching resonance of her voice. She could not say why *she* had been called instead of some other milkmaid.

But she walked into the tent knowing that men and women were going to be healed; she knew this would happen, as Pavlova knew when she leapt that the air would hold her aloft a second longer than any other dancer.

Over the heads of thousands packed into the tent in San Jose, moths swarmed around the strings of electric lights.

Roberta and Rolf took particular interest in the three sisters led to the platform by their father, the Reverend Preston of Cupertino. Children no older than they, dressed in their Sunday best. Their faces were gay with the quick mobility of the features of the deaf—all three of the Preston girls were born deaf, and came deaf to San Jose. They were particularly excited now, because their father and the revival workers had convinced them that very soon they would be able to hear.

The change in the three sisters could have begun days earlier, in the eardrum and the tiny bones of their middle ears. The eldest, beaming with hope, now stepped toward the healer in the starched nurse's uniform. Aimee might be heard humming, weirdly. She took the child by the shoulders and turned away from the crowd, shielding her from them as she looked into her wide eyes.

With oil Aimee began to rub the child's forehead, rubbed until the curls flattened against the skull, shining. She rubbed the whole head, the pink ears, all the while commanding the spirit of deafness to quit the dwelling of this innocent head. It was startling to the spectators, incredibly brazen. At last she held her thumbs over the ear openings and her fingers firm on the jaw under the earlobes. She hummed and felt the charge surge through her legs with an erotic force her heartbeat accelerated then conducted through her arms and hands to the child's temporal bones.

For a few seconds the girl felt a vibration in her skull that was like riding on a tractor, and then the rushing fury of water. Now, as the lady in white stepped away, the girl did not know she was hearing voices, but she was so happy she grinned from ear to ear. Aimee was gulping water, giving directions. A bearded man put his hand over one of the child's ears while he held a shining pocketwatch up to the other. It was not until that moment that the girl understood and nodded yes, yes, the

silence has come to an end. And in less than fifteen minutes her
sisters were served likewise. The reporter from the San Jose
Mercury bit his pencil and then scribbled, "The little girls nodded
their heads when asked if they could hear, not knowing one
word of English to respond."

———

One girl healed of congenital deafness might be explained away
as a hysterical cure of hysterical symptoms. If the child were
anonymous, it might be a hoax. Three girls healed of congenital
deafness, daughters of a minister, present a spectacle so preposterous, Sister Aimee would have been laughed off the face
of California if there had been any evidence of foul play.

But it was all dead serious, as were the other healings that
occurred that August 10:

> Arthur Frisbee, a well-known San Jose man, who for the past eleven
> months has been an invalid, making his way through the streets on
> crutches . . . when his turn in the long line came and he was told
> to walk, his frail body straightened, and throwing the crutches to
> the floor he ran up and down the platform while the multitude
> cheered. (*The Mercury Herald*, August 11)

Eight-year-old Estel Davis of Gridley, California heard through
ears her father testified had been closed almost since birth.
L. M. Nichols, deaf for sixteen years, heard Aimee's voice. And
dozens of the paralyzed and lame left their crutches behind on
the platform as hours passed, and toward midnight the tent
contained nearly ten thousand people watching the healing.

Soon a carpenter would hammer up a twenty-foot rafter between poles high over the altar as a "plank of memories." There
the healed celebrants would hang their crutches, canes, and iron-
and-leather braces before they walked off the platform.

Coverage of the San Jose revival began by special dispatch to
The San Francisco Chronicle on August 11; an article and a large
photograph of the evangelist touching the afflicted appeared
August 12. Within the week, Aimee's heart-stopping healing
services had stirred up a fiery controversy in *The Mercury Her-*

ald's letters column. Professor G. H. Culliver and other theologians attacked divine healing as "magic, mesmerism, and damnable doctrine" and "crimes committed in the name of religion," implying there must be chicanery involved. Ultimately this would be settled by the medical community.

But as of August 17 reporters like Louise Weick of *The San Francisco Chronicle* approached the spectacle with polite skepticism. In addition to the healing services on Mondays, Wednesdays, and Saturdays, a special service for children was scheduled for Friday the 19th. Assuming that trickery would be easiest to detect at the children's service, Weick chose to cover this for her major feature story in the *Chronicle*. Like E.F.Y. of *The Baltimore Sun*, she was in for a surprise.

Pressing through the crowded village of tents and parked automobiles, Louise Weick thought the scene resembled a circus or county fair. She was surprised how difficult it was to obtain entrance to the big top on Friday afternoon, though the guards had roped off the crowd surging about the entrances. They would permit only children to pass, and their parents, and reporters.

What met her eyes?

She did not know there were so many sick children in California. The panoramic photo is like a dappled ribbon spanning the *Chronicle* centerfold, a sea of children's faces. They had come from Montana, Nevada, Idaho, and Colorado, as well as California.

On the long platform facing these thousands was a choir of children, beautifully dressed in summer suits and frocks. They held flowers in their hands. The boys and girls sang enthusiastically, and between hymns all were remarkably well behaved, though no one appeared to be directing them.

In front of the choir, from one end of the stage to the other, and piled in mounds around it, were baskets of flowers and fruits, hampers of candy, and toys of all kinds. The citizens of San Jose had donated hundreds of dollars' worth of toys and dolls to be distributed after the service that afternoon.

The contrast between the brilliant chorus of children high on the stage and the crowd that faced them below was wrenching.

Hundreds leaned on crutches, lay flat on their backs in wheel
beds. Some shifted about with distorted or jerky movements,
their limbs encased in steel and leather. There were sober, serious faces, prematurely lined, and faces that bespoke the distance from life that sometimes comes with deafness. Blind
children held the hands of brothers and sisters. Here and there
the reporter spied the alarming features of mongolism, the
sloped forehead, unfocused eyes. And hundreds of children old
enough to walk lay helpless in their parents' laps and arms.

Suddenly the crowd was swept with "an electric alertness.
Even the tiniest child stiffened with attentiveness."

Aimee had entered the tent from the back of the stage.

> She was a robust young woman of 30 or so, having about her
> that efficient, wholesome, clean look of the trained nurse . . . one
> of those capable, cool-fingered women one sees at hospitals tending
> the sick. She wore the starched white muslin dress and blue serge
> cape we saw much of during the war. Her abundant brown hair
> was becomingly coiled about a well-shaped head.

Roberta and Rolf followed Aimee to the platform, and Minnie
Kennedy brought up the rear. The reporter was surprised to
hear Roberta address as Grandma the "youngish, sweet-faced
woman who did not seem 40," and observed the striking re-
semblance among the three generations.

"Let's all sing something nice and cheerful," said Aimee,
beaming, gesturing to the choir. "Let's sing 'My Hope Is Built
On Nothing Less.' " The evangelist began humming as she
nodded to the pianist and orchestra, and clapped with the
rhythm.

Under the manic brilliance of that smile Weick sensed the
depth of anguish in the healer. The children could not. When
the singing was done, Aimee began to clown. She made them
giggle and then laugh aloud at stories she told about her childhood, when she was good and when she was bad. She told
them the story of the stolen cookies, the pantry avalanche, and
the frogs that escaped from the bucket under her bed. Head
thrown back, teeth flashing, she laughed at herself and slapped

her leg. She made everyone laugh, until there were tears in her eyes, then sobered and warned them gently about the dangers of disobedience, how unrepentant children grow up with hearts of stone.

Taking up in her palm a field stone, she called out in a booming voice: *A new heart also will I give you, and a new spirit will I put within you: and I will take away the stony heart out of your flesh, and I will give you a heart of flesh.* The text seemed beyond the children, so she must have been crying it out for herself, with eyes wet and shining. Yet the reporter noted with amazement that

> no mysticism or talk of symbolism confused the children. The vast audience, a typical aggregation (apart from their infirmities) such as one could see at the movies or circus, followed the talk with a degree of attentiveness that was a curious manifestation of mass psychology.

When she was sure they were ready, Aimee asked them if they *really* believed what she had been telling them about deliverance from sorrow and sickness. In a tone of voice that was like *Cross your heart and hope to die?* Aimee persisted, *Do you really believe in the Divine Promise?* And when all the heads were nodding, she asked for a show of hands—and up went all the little hands, thousands of them.

"Then began a procession toward the platform that continued all the afternoon."

Like many another journalist, Weick was loath to admit that her stock-in-trade, language, failed her, but she *had* to admit it: "The written word can convey but the merest phantom of the dramatic scene that followed." Like so many reporters who witnessed these scenes, she was forced by the laws of reason into a defensive attitude. Yet she wrote so eloquently, we will quote from her at length.

> What followed beneath that tent on San Jose field will probably sound like the veriest hocus-pocus to many. But nevertheless it did happen. It happened not in the misty, nebulous long ago, to white-robed men and women in a time we cannot quite visualize as ever

having had reality, but to children and men and women who had
street addresses and telephone numbers, who came in automobiles
and not on camel-back by caravan, as it was said they did long ago.
The blind saw again; the deaf heard. Cripples left their crutches and
hung them on the rafter.

Lucille Rhodes had been blind for nine years, since infancy.
She lived with her mother and father at 1511 Thirty-third Street,
Oakland. They had brought the child to San Jose days earlier,
and the family had been following Minnie's instructions, earnestly praying and fasting the day before. Now the child, clutching at a small bouquet, was led to the altar by her mother, both
of them looking brave and confused.

"Jesus said, Forbid them not, for of such is the kingdom of
God," called Aimee with upraised hands as the child stepped
through the darkness toward her. The girl anticipated light in
the ring of the evangelist's voice, full of hope. First Aimee would
call upon the thousands to bow their heads and close their eyes
to join this child in her shadows and pray at once for her sight
to be restored. Over the babble of a thousand prayers Lucille
Rhodes heard the evangelist's clear, spacious voice as she recited
from Job and the Psalms.

Aimee was pouring oil from the cruse into her palms. The
healer's hands were so large, she could cover Lucille's whole
face with one of them, a broad, square palm with long tapering
fingers. There is only one photograph (taken by Cameracraft,
Los Angeles in 1935) that really shows the palms. It reveals a
strong "heart line," a deep but shorter "head line," and a deeply-
jointed, long thumb that would give Aimee's hand a preternatural span. The hump of the thumb, the "mount of Venus,"
was round and plump, the "life line" short.

Shining with oil, the evangelist's hands went out to the bowed
head of Lucille Rhodes. Thousands of voices prayed for the
light to enter. Aimee's left hand held the back of the girl's head
while the right thumb and forefinger rubbed oil into the notches
above her eyes. The healer knew the blind child was supersen-
sitive to the tactile vibration—the blind know things by touch
we cannot know by sight. The charge in the healer's hands

might wake the optic nerve if the child's blindness was a disease of the cranial nerves, the nerves behind the eyeballs. The prayer of thousands was entering Aimee's palms, the "mount of Venus" at the base of the thumb, which she gently rested upon one eyeball at a time. Aimee stepped away.

One side of Lucille's face became contorted, then the other. She squinted in pain. Like someone who has been shut up in a dark cellar for days and suddenly let out into the noonday sun, she covered her eyes to protect them. Then she let go finger by finger as her field of vision returned in rapid bounds from the periphery to the center.

Lucille's mother held her.

"Can you see, child?" a gentleman asked.

"Yes," she replied. "I can see my Mama."

All of this happened in minutes, and the line moved ahead.

The reporter from the *Chronicle* would recall one of many infantile paralysis cases: "the daughter of Mr. and Mrs. John Sinz, a beautiful child slightly under three years of age." John Sinz, a tall, athletic-looking man, about thirty, carried the child to the altar. Stricken at age one, she had no use of her legs. "They dangled helplessly, no articulation whatever in the joints."

Aimee began speaking softly to this girl as if she were her own: "Do you believe Jesus can heal you and make your legs so you can stand and run and jump like the other children can?"

She stroked the child's head rhythmically and addressed the father without looking at him, in a tone that seemed more like a challenge. "Do you believe?" John Sinz was struggling to speak without sobbing while thousands of people stared at him. The reporter noted "the greatest exertion of will" as the man spoke the words the healer needed in order to continue. Healing a child of three in her father's arms was tantamount to healing the father.

"Yes, I do believe," he replied.

Then Aimee began to pray. She invoked the promises of healing in the Psalms, in James, and other scriptures. Minnie prayed with her, and so did the elders on the platform, not in unison but in low voices. Aimee's large hands moved from the infant's thighs to the arch of the feet and back again as she prayed, and the reporter observed that the baby smiled and was completely at ease.

The healer's eyes now seemed lost in her head, from a distance looking like two large crow-black circles, caves of concentration while the prayer dissolved into a chant: "Have faith in God and nothing shall be impossible unto you. Thou hast said *ask in my name and that will I do*." She prayed and prayed, until her lips moved but no sound came out. Then she opened her eyes wide.

"Now, set her down on the floor," Aimee commanded. She never took her eyes off the child to look at the father. He just stood there holding the baby, dumbfounded.

"*I* think she can stand," said Aimee politely, as if she were contributing to a larger discussion. And then, when John Sinz appeared to be frozen by disbelief or terror, she said more forcefully: "*You* say she never walked at all. See if she can't."

Slowly the man bent down. Gently he laid his daughter on the floor. Smiling, as if a cloud of anxiety had been lifted from his face, the man stepped back. The audience was silent and expectant. The little girl, also smiling, put her weight on one arm, pivoted in a half-circle, and stood up shakily. On her feet she tottered, took a step, and regained her balance. She was beaming as the audience burst into applause.

"Hold her hand now," said the evangelist, "because the child must learn to walk."

The father now was weeping openly. Louise Weick writes:

> He led the child down the length of the platform, then down the incline, at the bottom of which the young mother waited.
>
> Taking hold of the child's other hand, the parents walked down the long aisle, as unmindful of the crowd as if they had been alone in their own home leading their baby as its first steps were taken.

During the next week the offices of *The Mercury Herald* were flooded with letters attacking or defending Sister Aimee's methods. In bold type within a heavy black border the editor published his apology that he could not print more than a selection.

For the most part the critics attending the meetings had no quarrel with the results but objected, rather, to the doctrine: these professors insisted that faith-healing had no place in the modern world, that it put Christianity at the mercy of super-stition.

Then there were skeptics like L. J. De Souza, who went to the meetings armed with a notebook. Mr. De Souza fluttered and hovered over invalids when they came off the platform, directing his attention especially to those who were *not* im-proved, and recording their heartbreak and bitterness. Mr. De Souza complained that at one meeting he actually felt unwel-come; the invalids and the ushers made him feel awkward as he was interrogating some weeping paralytic. Shunned, he con-cluded that the revivalists had something to hide. This guardian of the truth wrote a letter to the editor which called for "a thorough investigation of the so-called healings," and other correspondents agreed that was a good idea.

Physicians from San Francisco had been following the story and the controversy in the newspapers for several days. Quietly, without the knowledge of anyone involved in the revival, the American Medical Association of San Francisco sent represen-tatives to the tent meetings during the week of August 22. The doctors submitted their report at the end of the week and sent a copy to Dr. W. K. Towner in San Jose, who read it aloud under the big top.

The report from the AMA of San Francisco stated that the work of Aimee Semple McPherson met with their approval in every way, that the healing was "genuine, beneficial and won-derful." A reporter nevertheless remarks, on August 30: "So great has become the controversy over the divine healing meet-ings . . . that as the believers descend the steps from the altar, they are seized by critics under the guise of scientific investi-gations and cross-examined as to the genuineness of the cure."

The crowds grew. As the end of the scheduled revival ap-proached, more than a thousand healing cards were left out-standing. On September 4, Aimee announced to a crowd of 12,000 that she would not stop until every one had been reached. Already she was near exhaustion. She had been preaching four times a day, with tarrying meetings in early morning and late at night, and baptismal services at noon before the huge tent meetings. Now she was beginning to turn to the elders in the midst of the healing services, asking them to take up the burden of laying hands upon the sick, since she could not continue.

Because of the Labor Day holiday, the campaign was extended. On September 5, 1921, Aimee began at dawn her last healing service in San Jose. Reporters detected a note of despair in her voice as she preached to the crowd of 20,000. Sixteen ministers of various denominations assisted with the healing by praying over separate lines of the afflicted. But of course everyone wanted Sister Aimee. Panic approached riot when somebody started distributing counterfeit cards bearing the wrong numbers, throwing the line into confusion. One woman, informed her card was fake, was ordered to give up her place. "Frantic for fear that she would not be healed, she clung to the railing and refused to move."

Aimee prayed for the sick from dawn to midnight, then lay in bed with her eyes open. She had begun a lifelong struggle with insomnia.

———

The services we have described represent less than two percent of all the healing services that Sister Aimee conducted. After San Jose she launched nine major campaigns before preaching in Denver in July of 1922. In Fresno (January 1921) reporter Robert Middleton attended the initial healing service and wrote: "I thought it would fall flat. I visioned the necessity of working the people up into a state of religious fervor, self-hypnosis, an easy path for a temporary cure." But Middleton was shocked by what occurred. "I hardly survived this service . . . the thing that couldn't be done was being done and with a calmness and a surety that was startling." There were dozens of healings at that service, and hundreds more at other healing services which the reporter covered.

At the end of three and a half weeks in Fresno, Middleton estimates that 325,000 persons (half from out-of-state) heard

Aimee speak at sixty meetings. Untold thousands were converted and more than 2,500 crippled, sick, and infirm sufferers prayed over. "In the face of these wonderful results, many say miracles, the greatest of the miracles was the recuperative power of the evangelist: her ability to work 14 to 18 hours per day . . ."

It was not much different in other cities.

And then Aimee discovered the radio—a way to reach even more people with less effort. The Oakland Rockridge radio station invited her to be the first woman to preach a sermon over "the wireless telephone." She found the station full of buzzing and flickering machinery and electrical wiring strung high and low. In addition to the radio operator there was a studio audience, and a newspaper cameraman. "After putting them all out except the operator, I felt more at ease," she recalls, "that is, as much at ease as it is possible for one to feel facing that great horn and having only its dark, mysterious-looking depths for a visible audience."

As she began to speak, the room with all its electrical apparatus seemed to fade away. She found herself talking into the horn with surprising ease, thinking of the thousands listening in their homes. This signaled a new beginning. As the automobile and megaphone had served Aimee in the first half of her career, so the radio would serve her in the second half. She would soon become the foremost pioneer of religious broadcasting.

But first she had to finish building the Temple. That project had grown from the modest sketch of a wooden tabernacle to plans for a concrete-and-steel auditorium with two balconies and an unsupported dome a hundred and ten feet above the floor.

Critics asked why she was building such a grand structure, when Jesus would be coming soon.

"I want to build so solidly as if Jesus were not coming for a hundred years, though we are ready for His coming any day." She said it smiling, and thus she embraced the contradiction. Her sermons on the Second Coming made listeners shriek in

terror, made grown men and women faint. Yet she could build
in stone enthusiastically, ironically, against the chance that her
prophecy was wrong.

A nickel-and-dime account of how Angelus Temple was fi-
nanced would be fascinating. But the records are lost. So we
must piece together the puzzle from far-flung evidence. Robert
Middleton gives us a window on the business arrangements in
Fresno, which by 1922 had become a standard policy. The collections of the first two weeks paid all the revival expenses.
This included the cost of the two thousand bibles Aimee gave
away and the five hundred dollars cash she donated to the poor.
Collections from the third and last week went to build the Echo
Park tabernacle. In April of 1922 Aimee said the average donation at a meeting was two cents. This seems impossibly little.
But when we begin to review the attendance figures of Middleton and others, as against the capital raised for the Temple,
the two-cent average seems only slightly underestimated. Minnie probably left Fresno with less than $5,000 for the Temple,
which cost nearly a million dollars. (Estimates vary. In the mid-
twenties Dun & Bradstreet valued it at $1,250,000.)

Aimee found novel ways to raise money, gimmicks that
personally engaged the donors. She sold little bags of cement,
five dollars apiece. She sold miniature redwood chairs, which
represented shares in the building's cost, at twenty-five dollars apiece ("chair-holders" punning on "share-holders.") The
chair-holders were financing not only a seat in the Temple but
the floor beneath and the roof above. Aimee raised a hundred
thousand dollars from the sale of four thousand dollhouse chairs.

But, above all, the coins from the collection plates at the great
municipal campaigns—the humble people putting in their two-
cents' worth—bankrolled Angelus Temple. And the greatest of
these campaigns was Denver. There the evangelist is supposed
to have raised $70,000.

The contrast between the San Jose campaign in August and
Denver ten months later illustrates a critical transition. San Jose
shows Aimee's revival at the peak of perfection, well under her
control. In Denver the campaign loses its boundary and becomes
something different—a public uprising beyond anyone's con-

trol. In Denver she healed the wife of the mayor, who decreed five minutes of prayer at noon for the entire city, and later a twenty-four-hour fast. In Denver the governor and his wife, the judge of the Superior Court, congressmen, and generals wept along with hard-boiled reporters at meetings of 20,000 and more. In Denver she healed the Gypsy chief and his dying mother, and converted the American Gypsies, who would have made her Queen. In Denver she was kidnapped by the Ku Klux Klan, who wanted her to preach at a secret meeting.

In the midst of this turmoil Aimee was able to function, preaching and laying hands upon the sick as she had done in San Jose. And the documentation of healings is even more plentiful. But it is obvious that she had broken the boundary that lay between a revival with an intensely personal center and a chorus-and-mob scene out of Cecil B. De Mille. The political historian would tell us she had crossed the sacred line that separates Church from State in America. Anyone reviewing the clippings will see that the Denver revival cannot be excelled, equaled, or even continued beyond its anniversary encore. And, because of its nationwide reverberations, Aimee would never regain control of her religious career. Henceforth she must adjust to being the artistic director of a glorious pageant.

The Great Revival of Denver came in two stages a year apart. The second tour confirms the lasting impact of the first. On the first tour Aimee preached to half a million people in three weeks. There were more than 12,000 conversions, on one occasion more than a thousand at a single altar call. Most were men. Twenty-thousand healing cards were requested at two services—no one knows how many invalids altogether requested healing, but reporters estimated that Aimee laid hands on and prayed for 3,000.

The Denver municipal auditorium was built in two parts, a theater at one end and a convention hall at the other, separated by a stage and asbestos wall. A corps of workmen tore down the stage and the wall, making one seating space for 15,000 people. It was still too small. Hundreds knelt outside on the steps and sidewalks night and day, praying to get in. People climbed into the attic and scrambled over a network of electric wires to find a hiding place. At night they crawled beneath the gallery seats, taking food with them; they hid there until the morning meeting. Women barricaded themselves in the ladies' rest rooms, determined to stay all night in the basement so as not to be shut out of the coliseum in the morning.

During the first visit Aimee prayed for the mayor's wife, the king of the Gypsies, and the king's mother.

Mrs. Dewey C. Bailey, the mayor's wife, was a serious, bespectacled matron in her fifties. Dark hair pulled back, wearing a simple strand of pearls and a flowered print dress, she limped with dignity on the arm of her husband. She went with him to the auditorium, where he saluted the evangelist on the platform, and she listened while he addressed the throng.

"Mrs. McPherson has done things that two thousand years ago would have been called miracles."

Mrs. Bailey was in pain. Three years earlier she had broken the arch of her foot; arthritis seized it, and she had been lame ever since.

Seated on the platform, she watched in growing wonder as the line of a hundred invalids began its solemn movement toward the healer. She leaned forward in her chair with stupefaction as Aimee went about her business. The crowd prayed along, or cheered reverently, or gasped.

Mayor and Mrs. Bailey recognized the attorney Horace Benson, injured years before in a horrible accident in the Kittridge building, when the elevator in which he was riding slipped its cables. When Horace was found on the floor of the elevator car, he was surprised to see everyone's lips moving but no sound coming out. He never recovered his nerves, or his hearing.

Now as he moved forward in the line, Horace Benson prayed. As his turn came, Mrs. Bailey watched him bow his head beneath the healer's clasped hands; as she raised him up and spoke to him, his eyes shone and he nodded.

"Congratulations, Horace," said the mayor as Benson, smiling, walked past him, turning when he heard his name.

"Thanks, Mayor," came the answer.

Aimee closed the meeting when she felt the stage sway beneath her. Mrs. Bailey begged Aimee to do what she could for the pain in her foot, so Aimee knelt and held it tenderly in her warm hand. There was no immediate effect, but by the Wednesday morning following the Saturday meeting, Mrs. Bailey's foot was healed completely. Although this was not the most remarkable of the cures reported in Denver, the healing of so prominent a citizen lent a sort of official authority to the campaign.

Even more influential, in the long run, was the healing of the Gypsy king and his mother. Dewy Mark, chief of the Mark tribe of Gypsies, suffered from respiratory disease until Sister Aimee laid hands on him in Denver. His mother was healed of a "fibroid tumor," which melted away, the tribe declared, within fifteen minutes after the healing service.

Gypsies live today in a subculture where madonna statuettes and crucifixes coexist with pagan star charts and crystal balls. The infusion of Christian symbolism was largely the result of Sister Aimee's Pentecostal influence: the American Gypsies were virtually pagans before she got to them in the 1920's. But she spoke their language, so to speak; they saw her as a Gypsy, one of their kind.

Aimee had no idea what she had accomplished in healing Dewy Mark and his mother. The Gypsy king devoted the next year of his life to Sister Aimee and her capital fund drive. By letter and telegram he spread the good news of the healing, urging all Gypsies to follow Sister Aimee and her wonderful Lord Jesus.

They came in caravans from all over the country. Their campfires could be seen surrounding the revival tents, or in vacant lots near the coliseums where Aimee preached. They followed her on tour through the Midwest that autumn and winter, to Canton and Rochester. Hundreds of Gypsies filled the front rows of the Rochester Convention Hall, poor Gypsies in rags and bandannas, rich Gypsies in deep-hued silks and Persian shawls, flashing bracelets and gold-hoop earrings. Some wore jewels upon their fingers, but the dark-skinned women all wore necklaces of gold coins.

"Where is she? When is lady coming? Tell her touch me please, mister . . . Tell her Gypsy king send us, we got gold."

"Please mister, you tell lady she heal my baby . . ."

Gypsies crowded around Aimee when she appeared, showering her with flowers and gifts, kissing her hands and feet. In Rochester she had to set aside an entire service for the Gypsies, to heal them and teach them how to pray. They called her Holy Lady and wept with enthusiasm as they came to the altar for conversion.

They followed her to Wichita, where on the night of May 29, 1922, a crowd of thousands witnessed the evangelist hold up her hand and stop the rain. The Gypsies studied trickery and knew sorcery, so perhaps their admiration ran even deeper than that of the others who stood in the downpour in Wilson Park. The Arkansas City ministers were struggling to make themselves heard above the storm when Aimee sprang forward, inspired, and called out:

"O Lord, stay this rain and this storm. You can just hold it in the hollow of thy hand," she advised, demonstrating with her own hand. Then, humbly, "We don't *mind* going home in the rain, dear Lord; but if it is thy will to stay it and if the land hath need of it, let it fall *after* the message has been delivered."

As if someone had turned off a faucet, the rain stopped. The clouds rolled away, and the stars shone above the cheering crowd.

The Gypsies watched this, and nodded at each other in understanding of the woman's power. Hundreds of the Mark tribe and the Mitchell tribe were converted in Wichita. They held a banquet for Aimee in Riverside Park, loaded her arms with bouquets of roses, and spread baskets of flowers all around. Gypsy women planted little American flags in loaves of twisted bread. The men dropped to their knees while Aimee blessed their food. The Mitchell tribe sewed her a Gypsy costume and headdress to wear at the Gypsy services.

Gypsies cling to an ancient and foreign system of values. They prize gold and loyalty, in an ancient manner we find hard to understand. Gypsy Chief Mark was a man of influence. He stood in debt to Sister Aimee for his life, and for his mother's life, and for the healing of many of his tribe. The only way the Gypsies knew to repay the Holy Lady was in gold. And they

Childhood   Aimee, 1915

Robert and Aimee Semple, Chicago, 1910

Aimee and her children, 1917

Going to Florida, on St. Mary's River, Georgia, 1917

Palm Beach, 1918 (the family from left to right: Roberta Semple, Minnie Kennedy, Rolf McPherson, Aimee, Harold McPherson)

Aimee with the Gospel Car, 1918

Balboa Park, San Diego, 1921

LEFT: Aimee and Minnie in the parsonage of Angelus Temple, circa 1924

BELOW: Boston Gardens, 1933

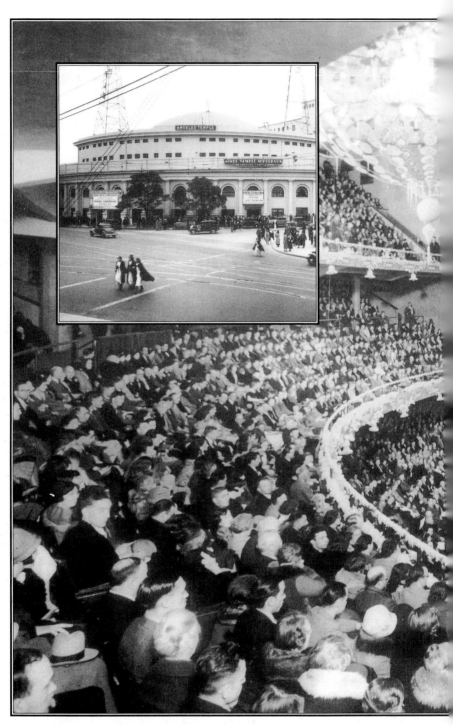

INSET: Angelus Temple, 1935

BOTH PAGES: Inside the Temple, Sunday

Chehalis, Washington, 1941

Aimee, 1944

Selling Victory Bonds in Pershing Square, L.A., 1942

paid gladly, stripping the gold coins from their necks and collecting them in heavy bags for the Holy Lady and her Temple. There was more gold where that came from.

The precious "Calvary" window of stained glass in Angelus Temple, the velour stage curtain, and the carved wooden legend on the proscenium were signed gifts of the Gypsies. How much more of the million-dollar temple was financed with Gypsy gold and jewels is a secret that lies buried with Minnie Kennedy.

THE FIRST ABDUCTION

On June 17, 1922, after the night meeting, Aimee was preparing to leave the auditorium. Frances Wayne of *The Denver Post* was standing at the stage entrance when she saw Aimee hurry down the hall in answer to a summons from an automobile outside.

"Someone wants prayers," she said to the reporter. "Come along and let us see what can be done."

Aimee stepped into the limousine and Frances Wayne got in after her. Aimee was seized by the wrists, pulled down into the seat, and Frances behind her. The door slammed.

On the jump seats were two figures in white robes and high-pointed hoods with narrow slits for eyes. Aimee could not see outside the windows through the silk curtains. Frances Wayne later said she believed they were driven over the Colfax viaduct, "then by a circuitous route back into the heart of the city, where the limousine stopped at the shadowed entrance of a high building."

The women were blindfolded before being led to an elevator which carried them into an assembly hall. They heard the men recite their credo: For one God, one country, one flag, for the supremacy of the white race, for chivalry toward women . . .

Her blindfold removed, Aimee found herself at one end of a rectangle formed by rank upon rank of white-robed, hooded Klansmen. The breathing of hundreds through the masks made a sound like wind.

"Number 8346 is now approaching," called a man seated at a desk.

Another spook stepped forward. Bowing low before the guest, he assured her of the Klan's respect for her services, which had brought a blessing to the city of Denver.

"We reverence your Godly mission and in token of our regard ask you to accept these flowers, white roses, indicative of the purity of your character and ideals."

As if trying to wake from a nightmare, Aimee shook her head. The reporter stood by to record Aimee's horror and courage, and the irony of the moment.

Smiling, Aimee accepted the flowers. She asked for her captor's permission to respond.

It was granted.

"I was glad," she began, with an excess of sweetness belied by the anger in her eyes, "to hear someone declare that the Klan is dedicated to the defense of the weak. Today in juvenile court I listened to the stories of young girls betrayed by men who should have been their protectors . . ."

In silence except for the sound of their breathing, the men listened as their guest delivered a brief and devastating sermon upon the text of Matthew 27: the story of Barabbas, the man who thought he never would be found out.

"Coming here in the car tonight, I thanked God that I was not a transgressor and had no need to be afraid. How many of you," she asked, her dark eyes seeming to penetrate the hooded faces into their souls, "are living lives that would stand the full light of day?"

And there was no sound but the wind of their breathing.

"So long as you stand for righteousness, and as defenders of the defenseless, I shall pray for you and ask you to pray for me. And so good night."

The interview was over. Three raps on the table brought two men from the far side of the room. These uttered a benediction, including the chilling promise that wherever the evangelist traveled, for the rest of her days, she would be surrounded by an invisible company that stood ready to defend her and the Gospel she preached.

Lights lowered, they prayed in the light of a flaming cross. Aimee and Frances Wayne were blindfolded again, led away to the car, and taken home.

Aimee heard and saw no more of the Ku Klux Klan until the 24th of July, shortly before she left Denver. She answered a knock at the door of her room at the Brown Palace hotel to find two hooded men. One held out a bag of money "which," he muttered, "we humbly present to your two little children, who we understand are in the city today." And the men turned on their heels and were gone.

Roberta Salter recalls the hooded men and the bag of money. There are other bizarre memories of that night.

Wanting to prepare her daughter for an event that might frighten if it did not delight her, Aimee warned Roberta: "Something may happen tonight while we are on the platform, a little surprise I think the people have ready for us . . ."

So as Roberta sat ramrod-straight on the stage, suddenly she saw them floating, one or two like dark snowflakes drifting down from the spotlights, and then a blizzard of red rose petals, which continued for nearly half a minute until the stage was blood-red.

———

Sailing to Australia in August of 1922, the evangelist might have wondered how her fame could fill a coliseum on the other side of the world. Her reputation had grown so quickly in five years.

The long sea voyage with Minnie and the children was supposed to provide Aimee with a much-needed vacation. Roberta recalls her mother trying to sit still in a deck chair, under her broad-brimmed hat—amazed at voyagers happily lounging about the ship doing nothing, and at women who changed their dresses five times a day.

"What shall we do with the days?" Aimee wrote. "Relax, sit

still with folded hands? We have lived at too high a speed and tension to do that . . ."

She sat with her typewriter on her knees, writing poems and letters. She designed the stained-glass windows, the interior, and the lobby of Angelus Temple on a lapboard, while the ship rocked on the sea. As the ship neared Sydney, the construction elevators were carrying the Temple nearer the sky with astonishing speed. No doubt Brook Hawkins was glad to have the evangelist halfway around the world, out of his hair while he completed the major work of the construction.

Sydney, Melbourne, and Adelaide welcomed Aimee, and she packed their largest exhibition halls for weeks at a time.

That she filled these halls despite her resolution not to pray for the sick shows the power of her oratory, years before the loudspeaker was invented. The buildings were damp and unheated. In Melbourne she complained of chills and fever, and an ulcerated throat, but she preached anyway.

Her decision not to pray for the afflicted is formally recorded in her report to *The Bridal Call*. "The Lord gave us a very decided *check in spirit*, that we should not take up this phase of the work in any public or special way, partly because healing had been unduly exploited prior to our arrival, as a means of advertising." Still the collection plates rang with coins, enough to pay for the crystal doors and the lobby of the new Temple.

4

THE TEMPLE

NEW YEAR'S, 1923

At 2:30 in the afternoon Aimee Semple McPherson mounted an elevated platform just outside the central doors of Angelus Temple. Facing a crowd of more than 5,000, she opened her bible and read from the book of Kings, of the building of Solomon's temple, and the Lord's glory that filled it. After a song and a prayer, the evangelist was lowered to the pavement by two elders. Someone handed her a trowel to lay the corner plaques. She wept into the mortar. Two marble tablets were unveiled and set in place upon the center columns. One bore the name of the Church and its founder. The other tablet read: DEDICATED TO THE CAUSE OF INTER-DENOMINATIONAL AND WORLDWIDE EVANGELISM.

The tablet was to remind us that Angelus Temple was *not* a church in the parochial sense, any more than an evangelist is a parish priest. The Church of the Foursquare Gospel was conceived as a learning center for evangelism, whose chief object is the conversion experience. Insofar as it *became* a parish church, marrying and burying folks, the Temple veered from its founder's original intent. Sister Aimee wanted people who found salvation at her meetings either to become evangelists themselves or return to their parishes renewed with the power of the Holy Spirit.

The problem was that people became so attached to the pastor's vision, they never wanted to leave. They thought the Temple was magnificent. Fifty miles away the pilgrims could see a lighted cross rotating on top of the dome. In daylight the great dome sparkled from the crushed seashells mixed into the cement. Inside, the interior curve had been painted pale blue with wisps of clouds to resemble a bright sky. Five thousand three hundred seats in the auditorium and two balconies faced the stage, where the baptismal pool's backdrop represented the banks of the Jordan river.

Carved upon the proscenium were the words JESUS CHRIST, THE SAME YESTERDAY, TODAY AND FOREVER. At the top of the walls art-nouveau angels had been painted standing wing-to-wing, representing a vision she had had in 1917. The balcony facades bore a frieze of tilting bells.

It is curious that Aimee was more famous in Denver, St. Louis and Melbourne than she was in Los Angeles until that New Year's Day, 1923, when Angelus Temple was dedicated. In Los Angeles Aimee had kept a low profile while funds for the Temple poured in from the East and Midwest. Her invisibility at home may not have been calculated, but it was politically wise. No denomination in the city could have built such a church from the gifts of local constituents. Ministers looked at the construction in wonder and envy, driving by in their cars.

All this changed at the turn of the year. Ministers came from all over the country, spirit-filled Methodists, United Brethren, Baptists, and others who had worked with Sister Aimee, to share the pulpit with her at the dedication. The event received full coverage in *The New York Times*. Thousands of Aimee's fans, including five hundred Gypsies, made the pilgrimage to Echo Park. At sunrise they began gathering outside the Temple doors. By midmorning the traffic was so heavy that the anxious police began turning cars away from Echo Park, and they struggled to keep people off the streetcar tracks so the trolleys might pass.

While thousands were admiring Angelus Temple in Echo Park, hundreds of thousands saw a miniature of it glide past them in Pasadena. It was the day of the Tournament of Roses. Aimee had directed the creation of a float for the parade, a Temple replica made with roses and carnations. The float had a tiny organ playing hymns inside, and was surrounded by singing choir girls. Set on the flat bed of the largest truck they could find, the Angelus Temple float announced the dedication of the Church of the Foursquare Gospel. It received the parade's Grand Marshal Award.

Aimee's anonymity in Los Angeles was over.

What a long way she had come since the days when she battled to pitch her tent against the wind.

"The Gospel tent?" she recalled. "Its sloping poles are now pillars, its sagging roof a mighty dome. The openings that showed the evening stars have now become arched windows, and through them streams the Light of His blessing, even as it did then."

Like most blessings, it was mixed.

Building the Temple was an incomparable achievement. But the task that now faced her was even more difficult.

A stationary revival is almost a contradiction in terms. They had loved Aimee in San Jose, but after three weeks there her healings caused bitter controversy. Now a comparable "campaign" in Los Angeles had its opening on New Year's Day, 1923 and no date to close. How was she to keep it going?

Knowing she was happy only when she was working, Aimee put everyone to work. There was a sisterhood, with sewing circles that stitched layettes for poor mothers. A brotherhood found jobs for men released from prison. Her commissary, which would evolve into the greatest welfare agency in L.A. during the Depression, provided food, clothing, and rent money for the needy, regardless of race or religion. Nurseries cared for children too young for the Sunday school.

Most important of the volunteer activities was the prayer tower. This was the spiritual nerve center of Angelus Temple. From the day the Temple opened, a corps of volunteers prayed around the clock in two-hour shifts, surrounded by telephones. They prayed for God's Church, for the welfare of the nation; they prayed for themselves and their pastor and anyone who called in need. The Temple switchboard had a team of ministers who gave advice to parents, husbands and wives, alcoholics and drug addicts. They talked despairing wives out of suicide and drunken husbands out of homicide. Aimee referred to the prayer tower as the "dynamo of power" that kept Angelus Temple functioning.

Seventy years later, it is still radiating spiritual energy. You

may call and ask them the time (theirs was the first telephone
time service), or you may ask them to pray for you. They will
cheerfully oblige.

———

Hollywood had a powerful influence on the character of budding Los Angeles. The cinema's vividness would eventually
alter our sense of reality and fantasy, and blur the line between.
But in Los Angeles the impact was immediate. Moviemakers
in pursuit of art invaded the lives of their city's real inhabitants.

Mack Sennett arrived in Los Angeles on a train with actors
Ford Sterling and Mabel Normand. The Shriners' convention
was in town, its fabulous potentates dressed in their capes and
tasseled fezzes. Sennett took one look at the parade forming and
yelled orders to his crew. They had not even unloaded their
baggage.

"We got us a spectacle, kids," he whooped. "Look at that
crowd scene—all free!"

In a matter of minutes one of Sennett's troupe had run to a
store and returned with a baby doll. Lovely Mabel Normand
wrapped a shawl around her, grabbed the doll, and, cradling it
in the crook of her arm, ran after the file of marching Shriners.

Sennett's cameraman cranked away, unnoticed.

Normand ran alongside the Shriners, holding the doll for all
to see, and gesturing pathetically in an effort to get the baby's
father to stand forth and identify himself.

The Shriners' reaction was perfect: they shrank from Mabel
in horror. All but one.

This gentleman, either half blind or very tender-hearted, finally stepped out of the ranks to help the lady in distress.

"Move in, Ford," barked Sennett.

Ford Sterling, wrapped in a bulky overcoat, ran up and
squared off at the fezzed Shriner. He waved his arms dramatically. The Shriner prepared to defend himself.

Meanwhile the police had seen the commotion. Several officers in their helmets and brass-buttoned uniforms surrounded
Sterling. He searched for words that would provoke them
enough to give chase without killing him. Then he broke

through the crowd and ran in a wide circle, past the camera, as the police gave chase, billy clubs in the air.

A few more shots in their new studio near Glendale, and Mack Sennett would have his first Keystone Comedy.

This sort of thing was a common occurrence around Angelus Temple. The particular scene just described has a poignant side, for if art invaded life, it also imitated it. The boom town had a problem the newspapers dubbed "the girl problem," which Sister Aimee would soon take on as a personal crusade. There were, by common estimate, 50,000 young women in the city who were virtually homeless, with and without illegitimate babies. They arrived on every train in flight from the judgmental provinces, looking for a new start in free-wheeling L.A. among the oil barons and real estate tycoons and movie moguls. Arrested for vagrancy, any woman could claim she was a movie extra.

The whole sprawling city was a potential movie set, since one never knew when life might be absorbed by art; and once the Angelenos saw themselves on the silver screen, they would in some degree regard life as a cinematic spectacle. Aimee was not immune to this. In the 1930's she would take steps to produce her own movie, *Clay in the Potter's Hand*, based on the story of her life.

During the roaring twenties, journalists descended upon Hollywood like the proverbial locusts. By the decade's end four hundred correspondents from all over the world (including the Vatican) were covering the movie colony's escapades. When they ran out of juicy material on the Mary Pickfords and Rudolph Valentinos, they lit upon obscure but photogenic young players and gossiped about their love lives, making them famous.

On a dull day one of these journalists might wander into the crowd at Angelus Temple, to take note of the pretty evangelist who made men swoon.

The scandalmongers' effect on journalism in the 1920's is well known. They created a kind of "inflation" of news interest in personalities, lowering standards of privacy. It began with Hollywood. But reporters who covered Hollywood also covered

City Hall, the racetrack, and Angelus Temple. Fast-breaking
political news that went out on the wire from Hearst's *Examiner*
vied with reports on Paulette Goddard's eyelashes, Chaplin's
latest escapade. Everyone in the public eye, everyone whose
business depended upon publicity, was affected.

This was the environment Aimee made her home in 1923.
She would live and die across from Hollywood, in the twilight
between fantasy and reality, in a love-hate relationship with the
press.

––––––––

Sister Aimee brought to Los Angeles her own brand of fantasy,
just as powerful in its way as the moviemaker's fiction. She
would prove herself no less inventive than Zukor and Lasky,
and as energetic as Goldwyn and Fox—and these giants of the
cinema admired her. Angelus Temple had perfect acoustics. In
moments of envy certain producers in her audience hoped she
might fail so they could take over the Temple and turn it into
a theater.

But Aimee had already done that. Her years on the tent-show
circuit had taught her that a religious service is sacred drama,
a species of nonfictional theater, pure and simple. The problem
with denominational churches, said Aimee, was that they had
given in to their profane competitors—vaudeville, movies, and
"legitimate theater"—and thereby had lost the attention of their
congregations, who took their excitement wherever they could
find it.

At first the climax of her services had been the altar call or,
in smaller spaces, the baptism of the Holy Spirit. Then, from
1919 to 1922, her meetings culminated in prayers for the sick.
But as of 1923 Aimee had so reduced her healing ministry, it
could not attract the crowds she needed to sustain her.

The Temple was indeed a mixed blessing, a costly haven.
She no longer had to leave her children and spend months on
the road; but now she had to make sure that the crowds would
come to *her*. She no longer had to strain her voice in drafty
coliseums; but the 5,000-seat auditorium with its perfect acoustics cost a fortune to maintain. She was under pressure to create

a religious theater that would guarantee an audience—and she could not repeat herself in her own pulpit.

As we have seen, she was a natural actress whose improvisatory power had quelled a Philadelphia riot in 1919. Now she would use the American revival meeting's dramatic structure to create a fluid form of religious theater that resembled, in all but content, a musical comedy.

On Easter in March of 1923 the temple organ, with its lofty pipes under the painted Savior's outstretched arms, was unveiled and dedicated. A fourteen-piece orchestra with a golden harp accompanied the organ's debut. Soon a choir of a hundred and a brass band of thirty-six—and numerous additional choral groups, trios, and quartets—would fill the sanctuary with their music. Aimee hired the talented Gladwyn Nichols away from the Salvation Army to be her musical director. The music was a mix of old hymns done in the traditional a cappella style and popular tunes with jazz arrangements. Sometimes Aimee would write religious lyrics for a current tune.

From Hollywood she could get costumes, props, and scenery to flesh out her message. After music, prayers, more music, and the offering, the audience would settle down for Aimee's sermon.

As she came to the story of Moses crossing the Desert of Zin, the organ played a dirge. The purple stage curtain opened on old Moses in his long Max Factor beard, in a blazing noonday spotlight. Toiling across the stage, he paused every few steps to lean upon his staff and wipe his brow. He raised his hands to Heaven, beseeching God's mercy upon his people. They were dying of thirst. Slowly the overhead lights focused on a gray rock upstage, and Sister Aimee read from Numbers 20:8 and 9.

"Take the rod, and speak ye unto the rock, and it shall give forth his water . . ." Watching the old man strike the rock with his staff, she cried out in horror, knowing the story's end—that this would cost Moses his entry into the Promised Land.

"Moses Crossing the Desert" was the first illustrated sermon played in the Temple. Aimee gave twenty-two other sermons a week, but it was the illustrated sermons that magnified her fame. They were so entertaining, it was nearly impossible to get within a block of Angelus Temple on Sunday nights, the crowds were so vast. For a decade the city had to schedule extra trolleys and detail special police to move traffic through Echo Park before and after services.

The tone of these little plays varied. By and large they were broadly humorous, poking fun at themselves, Satan, and human folly. The staging was professional, often superb; but in the 1920's the skits were shamelessly rough-hewn, full of missed cues and pratfalls. Aimee took every opportunity to use the actors' mistakes, and her own, as a good joke on herself to be shared with the audience.

Animals always got a laugh—they are natural comedians—and the former farm girl worked well with them. She made friends with Joe Flores, whose nearby stable supplied livestock for the horse operas. When time came for a sermon on the good shepherd and the hundredth lamb that went astray, Aimee telephoned Flores.

"Joe," she chirped in the little girl's voice she used on the telephone, "can you get me a lamb by the weekend?"

"Sure, Sister. As good as done."

The idea was that Aimee, in her shepherdess costume, would be surrounded by her painted flock, wailing in mock melodrama over the lost lamb. Suddenly the lamb would appear, wandering onstage from the wings, bleating forlornly. The shepherdess would shoulder the lost lamb and bear it around the stage in triumph.

Friday came. As Aimee had not heard from Joe Flores, she called him again to ask about the lamb. He told her he had not forgotten, and hung up. But Flores must have got very busy with something else, because Saturday came and went, and on Sunday morning Aimee called him in a panic.

"Joe, where's the lamb, Joe?"

Flores apologized all over himself: he was busy supplying a herd of cattle for a western. "What's the cue, Sister?" he asked. "I swear to God I'll deliver the lamb on cue."

So Aimee gave him the cue line. It was something like "Oh where, where can he be?" An indication of her faith—in the stablekeeper or her own improvisational genius—is that she went on with it. Dressed in her shepherdess costume, in front of more than 5,000 people, she preached toward the climax, which was to be the entrance of an animal she had never met. Aimee was probably prepared to pluck a child out of the audience, or a young man, and turn *him* into the lost lamb, down on his hands and knees making sheep sounds. That would do. Or maybe she would make comedy of the blown entrance, having an elaborate drumroll, fanfare, and spotlight upon— nothing, the absence of the delinquent hundredth lamb.

But Joe Flores was as good as his word. Aimee, dressed like Little Bo Peep, raised her big eyes to Heaven in mock despair over the hundredth lamb, crying out, "Oh where, where can he be?" The stage curtain ballooned ominously on the right as the animal blundered the wrong way before being turned toward the pulpit, bleating in the mature deep-throated tones not of a little lost lamb but of a disgruntled full-grown sheep.

She had forgotten to tell Flores she wanted a *portable* lamb.

Now it was too late. The animal eyed the shepherdess suspiciously as she approached, in a half-crouch, whooping and cheering and clapping her hands at the sight of her lost lamb. And the audience cheered, and then gasped at the thought she might try to pick it up. She did pick it up. Staggering hilariously back and forth, Sister Aimee regained her balance on those powerful legs, intoning from Scripture: "Even so it is not the will of your Father which is in heaven, that one of these . . . *little* ones . . ." She grunted, and the crowd laughed at the irony. ". . . should perish."

This made a wonderful show. So did the camel's entrance when Aimee preached upon the text: "It is easier for a camel to go through the eye of a needle, than for a rich man to enter into the kingdom of God."

The Eye of the Needle was a narrow gate to the walled city of Jerusalem. A camel could not squeeze through that gate until its burdens had been unloaded. Somehow Aimee staged the illusion of an enormous needle, tipped at such an angle that its eye might make a convincing passageway through which to lead the blinking camel, the smallest that the Barnes Zoo could supply. The camel was laden with bundles labeled Worldly Pleasure, Love of Riches, Selfishness, and Indifference to the Poor. Aimee made a comic business of trying to lead the camel through the passage with the burdens on, then removing them one by one to see if the beast could slip through, until all had been removed and the camel passed. We would find this hard to believe if Roberta Salter had not salvaged, from a crate of petty-cash receipts, one that amused her: From Barnes Zoo—$20.00, One Camel for the Eye of the Needle, May 12, 1925. And another invoice: Trucking—$12.70.

Roberta recalls the stage set for her mother's sermon on the Garden of Eden: papier-mâché flowers and trees from end to end of the stage, in bold colors like a child's drawing. Aimee surveyed the designer's work, arms folded, foot tapping. "It needs . . . something," she thought out loud. "It needs something *alive* in it." And as Aimee overpronounced *alive*, her face lit up.

"The circus is in town," she exclaimed, snapping her fingers. "I'll get a macaw."

Why she thought the circus would be a reliable source of macaws we shall leave to the historians of the big top. In any case, this was the kind of impetuous decision that opened the door to the unexpected, the wellspring of comic improvisation. She got a macaw from the circus.

The gorgeous green bird with the long tail sat chained to his perch near the pulpit in silent dignity until the orchestra struck up its first tune. Then the macaw expressed his opinion, in words that revealed his unchristian education among circus roustabouts, barkers, and fire eaters.

"Oh, go to Hell," cried the macaw.

There was dead silence in the auditorium as the congregation wondered if they could believe their ears. The bird did not long keep them in suspense.

"Oh go to Hell," he repeated, a little louder than before. It was his only speech, evidently, but he knew it well.

Sister Aimee, hardly able to conceal her amusement, feigned horror. No one had ever dared to speak thus in her sanctuary, and now, here, in the Garden of Eden . . .

Whatever the evangelist had planned for the evening, the hymns, the testimonies, the sermon, it would all now have to revolve around this running gag—Little Aimee versus the pagan macaw. If ever the show lagged and she needed a laugh, she would turn to the macaw and ask his opinion, and then gape, wide-eyed, as the bird delivered his inevitable judgment. She preached to him. She tried to convert him. She interpreted his sullen silences as acquiescence or as the deafness of the unrepentant. At last, in the play itself, she condemned the profane macaw, saying his voice was the voice of Satan that caused Adam and Eve to be banished from Paradise. But for his part in the little drama he would be granted absolution, a little perch in bird heaven.

The rich details of the early sermons are mostly lost, the pre-1930 skits and tableaus that built the Temple's membership. What has come down to us are their more spectacular effects, which legend has exaggerated. Aimee did *not* come thundering down the center aisle or the rampart of Angelus Temple on a motorcycle, as millions of people imagined she did. She was dressed in the uniform of a motorcycle cop, and she burst into the Temple from the lobby, cranking a hand siren. When she had got everyone's attention, she raised a white-gloved hand and shouted:

"Stop! You've been arrested for speeding."

That had been a rough week. The evangelist was so preoccupied with the administration of the commissary, the sisterhood, the Sunday school, the prayer tower, etc., that she could not find time to think about her Sunday sermon. She was suffering from a rare case of writer's block, when she took Roberta for a drive in the Oldsmobile. With her mind on the unwritten sermon, she heard the sound of a siren and over her shoulder saw a traffic policeman. The evangelist had been caught speeding.

The speeding ticket seemed a small price to pay for this lesson and the sermon it inspired. The sermon, in verse, was a long list of situations in which busy men and women might find themselves. You are preparing the house for a garden party, rushing here and there to shops for the perfect place set-

tings . . . You are five days from the meeting of the board of
the electric company to propose the adoption of your new in-
vention . . . Suddenly your daughter becomes weak in the knees,
faints with fever, and in the morning her legs are stiff, she cannot
walk . . .

It was terrifying the way Aimee built, brick by brick, in her
trumpeting voice, a glorious structure of worldly achievement,
then wrecked it suddenly in a whisper of reference to human
frailty—sickness, shame, despair. When the auditorium was
silent she cranked the horrible hand siren.

"Stop!" came the refrain. "You've been arrested for speeding."

God was the celestial traffic cop.

The sermon became so famous that a picture postcard of
Aimee was printed, showing the evangelist leaning on a motorcycle with her hand up in the gesture of arrest. The postcard's
effect is comic, and the motorcycle in the picture must have
contributed to the legend that Aimee drove the vehicle through
the church doors.

One night while Aimee was preaching on the theme that
Salvation was available to anyone who would "step out in faith"
and trust in the Lord, her sermon was interrupted by the screaming of a fire engine. Then the audience heard another scream,
and another outside the building, the sirens overlapping their
shrill rounds of alarm. The fear of fire in a crowded theater can
turn so rapidly to panic, it is fortunate the firemen did not delay
their entrance. With axes and ladders they burst through the
temple doors.

They rushed toward the pulpit with a gigantic rescue net.

Spotlights hit a platform high above the stage, where a frail
gentleman stood. He was in an obvious state of panic and in-
decision. Aimee explained to the congregation that the poor
man trembling thirty feet above them like a treed kitten was a
sinner. The audience exhaled an audible sigh of relief that this
was all part of the show; and a wonderful show it was, too, as
Aimee coaxed the sinner to step out.

That first step is a long one.

The firemen made a circle of strong arms around the net.

Aimee stood by, calling to the sinner that God would save him, would save him from the flames of Hell if he would but step out, step out in faith and fly, "Fly into His safety net of refuge." This the man finally did, abandoning his timid posture, to execute the perfect swan dive of a trained acrobat.

This kind of shenanigans, and the jazz tunes, and the sprinkling of rose petals in the baptismal water, got Sister Aimee in trouble eventually with the Los Angeles Ministerial Association. She had joined shortly after the Temple opened, about the same time she joined the Chamber of Commerce. As an evangelist Aimee was welcomed; as a parish minister she was an unbearable intrusion. Rose petals had no business in the holy water of the baptism, said the ministers. But their real, unspoken, quarrel with the rector of Angelus Temple was that she was raiding their church memberships. Since they couldn't come right out and say this, the preachers, in print and from the pulpit, denounced her "religious spectacles" as scandalous, exploiting the Gospel to attract attention to herself.

"Show me a better way to persuade willing people to come to church and I'll be happy to try your method. But please, please don't ask me to preach to empty seats," she said.

"Let's not waste our time quarreling over methods. God has use for all of us," she said. And:

"Remember the recipe in the old adage, for rabbit stew? It began, *First catch your rabbit.*"

AT HOME IN LOS ANGELES, 1924

"No tourist who came to California in the twenties," says Roberta Salter, "felt his trip a success unless he could boast of hearing one of Aimee's sermons."

In the late 1920's her notoriety itself was a magnet—the mix-

ture of achievement and scandal that had made her the most
famous woman in America, more famous even than the actresses who came to sit at her feet and study her movements:
Mary Pickford, Jean Harlow, Clara Bow. Roberta recalls: "Ambitious, social-climbing Hollywood hostesses, eager to provide
their dinner guests with a new thrill, paid any price asked"—
to scalpers who could guarantee good tickets for the Sunday
night services.

But in the early years of the decade Sister Aimee was not yet
a celebrity. She was well known, certainly, in religious circles,
an emerging public figure. But people flocked to Angelus Temple for the sheer emotional intensity of the services, a blend of
staged drama, music, and improvisational acting. Visitors never
knew what to expect. Aimee was known for making theater of
any human or animal eccentricity—a slip of the tongue, a foul-
mouthed macaw, an obstinate sheep.

One night, before the offering, a poor woman stumbled up
the aisle, her eyes shining. Hands outstretched, she announced
in a musical voice that she was the blessed Mother of Christ,
the Virgin Mary. Hearing this, the white-garbed evangelist
stepped down from the pulpit and met the woman's gaze. Aimee
needed to make sure the woman was truly insane and not merely
a heckler. Satisfied, she held out her arms to the pathetic woman.
She embraced her warmly, saying, "Oh Mary, how blessed are
we all, to have you here among us! Now come, come with me.
As the mother of God you shall have the chair of honor above
us all."

The madwoman beamed. She was overjoyed as Aimee led
her up the steps to the stage and seated her in the carved minister's chair with such sincere respect, you would have thought
the madwoman was indeed the Mother of God. From the seat
of honor she watched in peaceful silence until the service was
over.

Roberta and Rolf, now thirteen and eleven, often sat on the
stage while Aimee preached. One Sunday night before the sermon began, they heard the sound of footsteps marching through
the lobby. The doors burst open, several at once, and white-
hooded figures entered, the white robes of Klansmen. A thou-

sand of them filled four aisles of the Temple; a thousand people in the front rows silently gave up their seats to make way for the surprise visitors. The Klansmen sat in ominous silence, their arms folded across their chests, their breath whistling under the pointed hoods, as they waited for Aimee's sermon to begin.

Aimee turned to Roberta.

"Now you children go on home and study," she whispered. "You don't need to stay for the sermon tonight. Go home and do your schoolwork."

Roberta dutifully led her brother out the back door to the parsonage, where she left him with his books. But then she hurried back to the Temple and found a seat high in the last row of the top balcony.

The verses of a hymn were dying away as the sermon was about to begin. Aimee rose from her carved chair and slowly approached the pulpit, her open bible with the typed sermon balanced easily on her large hand.

Looking out at the congregation, she snapped the bible shut and laid it upon the lectern.

She spoke softly.

I have decided not to preach the sermon that has been announced all week. Unexpectedly, the Lord has placed a new message in my heart tonight.

But before I begin that sermon, I want to tell you a little story.

One day, in a city that shall be nameless, an aged Negro farmer came to see the sights. It was a warm, sunny Sunday, and he roamed the streets until he stood in the shadow of a beautiful church, far grander than any he had ever seen in his little country town.

The old Negro farmer stood gazing at the church spires pointing heavenward. And his heart filled with rapture as he listened to the sweet-voiced choir pouring out the praises of God.

"Oh I must go into *this* wonderful church," he told himself, "and worship my Master."

The actress rendered the cadence of the black man's voice so perfectly, the audience craned their necks to see if he stood behind her.

So very quietly he opened the door, and very quietly he sat down—in the *back* row.

Sister Aimee's eyes blazed as her audience took in the contrast between the humble farmer in the story and the bold intruders who now occupied all the front rows of this sanctuary.
She continued.

He sat, looking up in reverent wonder at the high ceiling and the stained glass windows, and the gold and silver ornaments on the altar. And he was about to find his place in the hymn book on the seat beside him.

All of a sudden an usher, in a frock coat, grabbed the old farmer by his elbow and jerked him to his feet. When the usher had led him outside, he said: "You can't come in here. There is a nice little Negro church on down the road about a mile."

"But I only wanted to worship the Lord," the old man said.

"Well," said the usher, "don't try to do it here. You'll have to go to your own church . . . Now get along." And with that the usher turned on his heel and went back inside.

Now the old Negro was weary. He sat down on the stone steps of that magnificent church, and for a moment he was so hurt by what had happened to him, he began to weep. "All I wanted was to worship my Master."

Just then he felt the gentle warmth of someone's hand on his shoulder. He heard the sound of a kind but careworn voice.

"Don't feel sad, my brother," said the voice. It came from a fellow traveler who looked neither young nor old, but his clothes and boots showed the wear of many days and nights on the road.

"No, don't feel sad. I too have been trying to get into that church, for many, many years . . ."

As the stranger stroked his silky beard, his sad eyes twinkled merrily. And the old Negro farmer was suddenly thrilled and then comforted. For he knew down deep in his heart that he was looking into the compassionate face of Jesus Christ, the Master Himself.

She paused for a long beat to let the parable sink in.

The Klansmen had come to Angelus Temple to show Aimee the support they had promised her years earlier in Denver. They had come to worship in the Temple which their dollars (in clandestine donations) had helped to build. The hooded terrorists had not come to this public place in order to be terrorized and humiliated.

Aimee's voice rang out over the auditorium:

> You men who pride yourselves on patriotism, you men who have pledged yourselves to make America free for white Christianity, listen to me! Ask yourselves how is it possible to pretend to worship one of the greatest Jews who ever lived, Jesus Christ, and then to despise all living Jews?
>
> I say unto you as our Master said, *Judge not, that ye be not judged!*

This was the text of her sermon. But first she paused for a long time and looked into the eye slits of the hoods with a furious intensity that made the men rise, first one by one and then dozens at a time, until there was a virtual rout of the white-robed spooks up the aisles and out the doors, into the night from where they had come.

That is quite a story in itself, but it is not quite the end. Roberta recalls that as Aimee preached her impromptu sermon on the brotherhood of man, one by one and two by two "pale-faced men drifted back into the church and seated themselves quietly to listen . . ."

And next morning the park attendants found hundreds of white robes and hooded masks wadded up and abandoned in shrubs and bushes across the street and all around the lake in Echo Park.

————

Protestant, Catholic, Buddhist, or Jew, any citizen of Los Angeles in 1923 had to admit that in a city of characters—movie queens, oil tycoons, gurus, and swamis—the pastor of Angelus Temple was the most intriguing character of them all.

Aimee had begun recording "canned sermonettes" which the radio producers were happy to broadcast on their new stations in light of her growing popularity. Her radio voice was as captivating as the woman in person. The architect of this popular triumph was Kenneth Gladstone Ormiston, a handsome, sharp-featured gentleman in his early thirties. The bespectacled engineer walked with a stately limp (he is supposed to have had a wooden leg) and talked with a kindly humor undampened by the religious seriousness of his prospective employers. Impressed, Minnie and Aimee were willing to overlook his agnosticism.

Minnie was not sure she could afford him, or his tailor, as she admired the young man's three-piece suit and carefully knotted silk tie. She lured him from the *Los Angeles Times* radio station with the hefty salary of $3,000 per year, on the understanding that the engineer would build a state-of-the-art broadcasting station and recording studio on the third floor of Angelus Temple.

So in February of 1924, Radio KFSG (Kall Four Square Gospel) took to the airwaves with the hymn "Give the Winds a Mighty Voice, Jesus Saves." Aimee's was the first religious broadcasting station; her commercial license to operate it was the first license granted to any woman by the FCC. There were more than 200,000 receiving sets within a hundred miles. Aimee immediately launched a daily sunrise broadcast called "The Sunshine Hour."

Her personality translated powerfully into radio space. In a few months she was preaching daily to hundreds of thousands, a congregation unprecedented in Christendom. Her expressive contralto, humorous, earthy, inspiring, became the most recognizable voice in the West.

She called her religion the Foursquare Gospel, after a vision she had in Oakland in 1922. Aimee was preaching on the prophet Ezekiel's vision of Man, Lion, Ox and Eagle, when suddenly she began to shake with emotion. She saw in the mysterious symbols "a complete Gospel for body, for soul, for spirit and eternity." In the face of the Man she saw the Man of Sorrows, the Savior of the world; in the Lion she beheld the "lion of the tribe of Judah," Christ as Giver of the Holy Spirit; in the Ox she perceived the Great Burden-Bearer, Jesus the Healer; and in the Eagle she beheld the Coming King of Kings.

Those four cornerstones—Regeneration, Baptism in the Spirit, Divine Healing, and the Second Coming—upheld an evangelistic association called the Elim Foursquare Gospel Alliance, which George Jeffrys founded in Ireland in 1915. He and his brother Stephen were England's greatest evangelists after Wesley and Whitefield, and Aimee had worked with Jeffrys. The Elim Foursquare Gospel influenced the American Assemblies of God, which embraced the same four principles before Aimee had her vision in Oakland in 1922.

The religion she was preaching now was mainstream fundamentalism, newly mainstream, strangely fashionable. From the time she was ordained by the Baptists in San Jose on March 27, 1922, her Pentecostal orientation had become a matter of controversy. Her written defense defines Pentecostalism as

> to be Spirit-filled . . . the grandest, proudest tribute of sobriety and piety one can possess. The Holy Spirit is not marked by wildness, hysteria, screaming, or unseemly manifestation, but by deep, sober exaltation of the gentle Christ of Galilee, an earnest passion for souls, a biblical and scriptural Holy Ghost, boldness and wisdom . . .

Clearly she has adopted the passionate tradition of John Wesley and the nineteenth-century Holiness Movement, in opposition to "cold, backslidden worldly formality." Yet she draws the line at "unseemly manifestation" (offensive behavior), the indulgence of emotions by one part of the congregation in a way that offends the rest.

To make her point, she would refer to her automobile, saying to a raging fanatic:

> "Brother, do you see that automobile over there?"
> "Yes."
> "It is able to run 70 miles per hour. Because I feel the power in that motor, have I any right to open the car up, and tear down Main Street yonder with its thousands of pedestrians, careless of life, or of the effect of my actions upon others merely because I have the power and capability of showing it off before others?"

Her rise to fame was inseparable from the growth of Pentecostalism. But now she found it more politic to avoid the term, though the practices of tongue-speaking, divine healing, and baptism in the Spirit remained a significant part of life at Angelus Temple. These "manifestations" continued in the intimacy of the "500" room, an auditorium next to the main sanctuary, where emotional outbursts would not disturb the devotions of the general public.

For the most part Sister Aimee avoided the designation "Pentecostal."

————

Alma Whitaker, star reporter for *The Los Angeles Times*, lived on a hill overlooking the glittering dome of the Temple. From her living room window she could watch the people gather, sometimes by the thousands, the streetcars unloading, the policemen directing traffic. On Sundays, from morning to evening, the crowd filled the Temple four times.

One balmy Tuesday evening in March, Alma Whitaker strolled down the hill to attend what she hoped would be a sparsely attended prayer meeting, so she could observe the preacher in a quiet, informal situation. She found the streets lined with automobiles blocks before she arrived at the Temple. Hurrying through the crystal doors, she took one of the last empty seats.

She was impressed with the evangelist's voice, her naturalness, and the quiet drama of her Bible reading. When Aimee read the Twenty-third Psalm, "The Lord Is My Shepherd," you *saw* the Shepherd, as if He were hovering in the air over Aimee's shoulder. You felt His affection, which was not something cloyingly sweet; it was big, hearty, and full of comfort. You would walk along with Him in good humor, through green pastures as vivid as any memory of your youth. You would drink deeply from the still waters as she read those lines from the psalm. In the quiet that followed her reading, the audience would arise, and go forth refreshed, as from a good dream.

As the journalist climbed the hill later that night, she was more curious than ever about Aimee Semple McPherson.

Alma Whitaker was a prominent "career woman" in Los Angeles. Like Sister Aimee, she was one of a handful of professional women in the city who did not owe their fame to the film industry's vanities. The writer felt drawn to the evangelist. Perhaps she understood Aimee well enough, from a distance, not to ask the busy preacher for an interview, though they were neighbors. The journalist lived just up the hill, but did not write about Sister Aimee—until she could no longer avoid it.

Like many journalists, Whitaker made a sideline of public speaking. She lectured at women's clubs, colleges, garden parties, and church luncheons. It meant supplemental income as well as reader support for her column in *The Times*.

During the past several months, no matter what she announced as a lecture topic, the audience's questions were the same.

"Please tell us about Aimee Semple McPherson." Nobody was really interested in hearing her talk about anything else.

So in the third week of March, 1924 she telephoned the Church of the Foursquare Gospel to ask for an interview. If she had been sick, or dying, or seeking the baptism of the Holy Spirit, it would have been easier. But as a working journalist, Whitaker had to deal with Sister Aimee's publicist, now a full-time staff member at $50 per week. This PR man, at first hired to attract and shape publicity, now spent as much of his energy protecting his famous client from reporters as he spent promoting the enterprises of Angelus Temple.

Evidently Aimee was not interested in personal publicity at the end of March. She was overwhelmed with calls from the sick, and with a breakneck schedule of prayer meetings, radio sermons, Bible classes, and "organizational meetings" of a dozen groups that were functioning in Angelus Temple's busy halls. Whitaker was put off, and ignored, and then told to be patient.

At last, on March 21, the reporter decided to take matters into her own hands. Hearing that the evangelist never retired before 2:00 A.M., Whitaker walked down the hill late on a Friday evening. She marched up the stairs to the rooms where Aimee and her mother had temporarily set up housekeeping.

She found herself in a line of people waiting to have a word with Mrs. McPherson, as if she had been a monarch or other head of state. Dressed in a riding habit, the great woman sat in an armchair, her head tilted thoughtfully as she rested her chin on her fist.

The journalist observed that despite her vast responsibility the woman looked much younger than her thirty-three years: weary, but alert. The room was sparsely furnished with a bed and a worktable covered with books and papers. To each petitioner as he or she approached, Aimee gave her full attention, responding to questions with a word or two that sometimes made the petitioner laugh. With another she would pray quietly, holding his hands in hers. Several men in suits approached with papers to sign, one with a page of sheet music, one with questions she waved away, unprepared to answer.

Alma Whitaker waited until almost everyone had left before introducing herself. She really needed no introduction. Aimee, an avid newspaper reader, had heard of the writer, and smiled warmly as she shook her hand. Knowing this was only a temporary slackening of the receiving line, she asked an assistant to mind the door for a while so they could talk without being disturbed.

The reporter's purpose was obvious. She had seen Aimee in the pulpit, at prayer meetings, and in her dramatic roles as diva of the illustrated sermons. Whitaker understood the basic organization of the Echo Park Evangelistic Association and Sister Aimee's increasing power as a public figure in Los Angeles. Now the journalist had come to get an impression—a glimpse would be better than nothing—of the woman *behind* the image, the character underlying the preacher, actress, and healer. Perhaps, if the conversation went just right, she might find a keyhole view into her private life, which would somehow humanize the heroine that had attracted such a huge following.

Of course nothing would please the readers more than to have some notion of what this lovely divorcee did with her time between 2:00 and 7:00 A.M., when she emerged daily from her rooms to broadcast "The Sunshine Hour."

Aimee had dark circles under her eyes from lack of sleep, but her complexion was brilliant. The journalist saw that the evangelist's youthful appearance was partly owing to her weight. An abundance of flesh filled out the lines in her forehead and around her mouth. The cherub's head was set proudly upon a bull neck. The wide smile Whitaker had seen projected over the length of an auditorium was, in private, a startlingly affectionate thing, meant for her alone. The journalist immediately felt as if the two of them were the only women in Los Angeles.

She complimented Aimee on her chestnut hair, thick and shiny, coiled upon her head in the old-fashioned way. And Aimee, blushing, said that it was very long indeed. Uncoiled, it would reach below her waist.

"Do you think bobbed hair is wicked?" asked Whitaker.

"No, not wicked," replied Aimee with a maternal smile. "Just undignified and unsuitable." Her opinion had an influence: the young women crusaders dispatched daily from Angelus Temple to preach in factories, hospitals, and business offices had taken to wearing hairnets to hide their bobbed hair, counting the days until it would grow back as long and thick as Aimee's.

"What sort of a little girl were you?" asked Whitaker. "Did you run to boys, dolls, books, animals, or athletics?"

"Well, I was brought up on Bible stories just as some children are reared on fairy stories." She laughed. "I did not like dolls and I don't remember being much concerned with boys. But I loved animals and can ride most any sort of horse, to this day. I ride sometimes now. And I can swim like a fish," she added, smiling proudly.

"Are those riding breeches, or skirts?"

"Skirts," said the evangelist, spreading her knees and grabbing a handful of fabric. Aimee liked to ride sidesaddle, and now went into a rhapsody about the new design of sidesaddle she had been using at Joe Flores's stable just down the road.

"They are coming in again," she grinned. "And in *that*," she added, "I am really in *advance* of the styles . . ."

"Were you a flapper?" the journalist probed. Aimee looked as if she would burst out laughing. "What sort of a very young lady were you?"

"I don't think I was exactly a flapper," she said softly, and then looked away from her interviewer as she recollected: "But when I entered high school, which I did with honors, I was enamored of the world. I loved to dance and go to theaters and all that." She waved her hand dreamily at "all that," and the journalist detected a certain longing in the woman's voice.

"And now you believe those things are wicked . . ."

"Oh not exactly *wicked*," Aimee responded.

"What do you tell your followers?"

"We don't lay down hard-and-fast rules on the subject. All the same," she said, smiling wearily, "I don't feel one can best serve the Lord without forgoing these worldly pleasures . . ."

"And smoking?" continued the interviewer.

"Oh I don't like it for either men *or* women."

The journalist went on to the subject of Aimee's marriages and found her obligingly talkative about her first husband, Robert Semple. About her marriage to Harold McPherson the evangelist would only say that he was still living but took no part in her work. He was a businessman "in the automobile trade," and they had a small son, now sleeping in the bedroom beyond.

All this was related in a somewhat mechanical voice which discouraged further inquiry into Aimee's current love life.

"Tactfully," Alma Whitaker would write, "she drew my attention to the little band of ardent praying devotees in a nearby room."

> "This room is called the Prayer Tower. Ever since the Temple was built 455 days ago, there has been no cessation of prayer. Every week, day and night, 340 people volunteer for this service in two-hour shifts, the women taking the day shifts and the men the night . . . We get requests from all over the country for special prayers —mountains of daily letters; prayers for the sick, prayers for the unhappy, prayers for wandering sons and daughters and husbands, prayers for agonized souls."

Animated and expansive in describing the Prayer Tower's mission, Sister Aimee was maddeningly evasive when the conversation returned to herself. Whitaker, who had interviewed dozens of celebrities, found Aimee's shyness to be more than the natural defense of privacy. There was something peculiar about it, as if the woman was avoiding something she herself did not wish to discover.

"When I was asking about Mrs. McPherson's childhood,"

the journalist would recall, "she laughingly said she was afraid she had *never really grown up yet*. And the longer I talked with her, the more I realized how engagingly young and childlike she really is."

Mentioning a recent attack upon Aimee by a fellow minister, the newswoman tried to get her to give an opinion of him, or of other preachers in town. "But she just tossed an attractive, childlike little pout at me and wiggled her shoulders. I quite expected her to grin and say *I'm not going to tell*. But instead she just said: *They are all trying to do the work of the Lord, and most of them are good men, you know*."

It was nearing eleven o'clock at night, but the late interview had not gone without interruption. The phone rang continually. And Aimee was called to the door every few minutes as the line of people waiting outside grew restless.

In response to more questions about her past, the young woman leapt to her desk and reached for a copy of the new edition of *This Is That*, her autobiography. Beaming, she presented her book to the journalist, by way of putting a timely end to their conversation.

"She bubbled with enthusiasm," recalls Whitaker, "in much the same way that my small boy does, when he brings forth his nursery rhyme book."

With thanks, the reporter took her leave. Aimee hugged her. To the reporter's amazement, in the same motion she embraced a colored woman, a Gospel singer who had just arrived. Aimee hugged them as if they were all three sisters.

Departing, Whitaker noted that the evangelist looked tired, and rather wistful, at eleven o'clock, facing a line of people still waiting to ask questions or seek solace.

Book in hand, climbing the hill above the lights of Echo Park, on her way home Alma Whitaker felt exhilarated by her encounter with the great woman—and very frustrated. She had set out to discover the real Aimee, the woman behind the image that inspired thousands; but what she found was hardly a woman, though Aimee's personality had a kind of nervous charm and undeniable warmth. Whitaker might have been more pleased had she known that the little she had seen was more,

far more, than any journalist would ever capture of the "real"
Sister Aimee, whose fascination was inseparable from an
enigma.

> She has a little way of wrinkling up her brow like a child per-
> plexed when you ask her to define wickedness. And she dances,
> and claps her hands, like a happy little girl in the pulpit, and she
> starts the singing with all the carefree exuberance of a joyous child.

The growth of Aimee's following in 1924 was so explosive, the
Temple activities and accounts so various, that the Echo Park
Evangelistic Association would have challenged the management skills of any seasoned corporation officer. The comings
and goings of exuberant audiences, students, and Temple workers resembled the bustling operation of a city university.

On a typical Sunday there were classes in progress in every
space of the Temple from early morning on: in the main auditorium, the balconies, the lecture halls. The young men's
Bible class filled the "120 Room"; while for children there were
the Rose Bud Class, the Dainty Dots, the Lamp Lighters, the
Soldiers of the Cross, the Cradle Roll, and many other classes.
There were fifteen hundred registered members of the Sunday
school.

Most of the Temple workers were volunteers, but these required as much supervision as the several dozen on the payroll.

The music department consisted of two orchestras, three
bands, three choirs, six quartets, and two dozen soloists. There
were a training school for radio announcers and a night school
for day laborers who could not attend day classes at the L.I.F.E.
Bible College, whose permanent quarters were under construction next to the Temple. The College had opened for classes in
February of 1923 and was formally incorporated under the state
laws on September 24, 1924. By the time its five-story building
was completed, in January of 1926, the College's enrollment
was nearly a thousand, with dozens of teachers.

The payroll ran between two and three thousand dollars a

week, about thirty percent of the collection proceeds. (By 1930, it was seven thousand dollars a week.)

The management, accounting, and banking were growing complex. Minnie took over the business and ran it like any talented and devoted tyro. Alma Whitaker observes that "somewhat as Mrs. Charlotte Pickford has fostered and protected the career of Mary (and spared her much of the business and mundane exactions of that career), so has Mrs. Kennedy served her almost equally famous evangelist daughter." Hard-headed and practical, the farm wife turned executive officer rode herd on the Temple's corps of workers, made and broke contracts, and determined salaries. With little of Aimee's personal charm but a streak of cynical humor, Minnie made sure that this Temple, its eyes on Heaven, had its feet firmly on the ground. Nobody got a free lunch or a free ride. And there was no middle management. As Aimee's right arm, Minnie had the last word in all *practical* matters pertaining to the operation of Angelus Temple and its subsidiaries. (Soon there would be a hundred branch churches.)

Boom-town Los Angeles was full of drifters, misfits, and others Minnie referred to collectively as "nuts" with a dismissive wave of her hand. At first the Temple was a magnet for them. Homeless girls and the girl chasers who pursued them —Aimee welcomed both with open arms. So it was Minnie's job to weed out, to purge the Temple of unsavory elements, defining the congregation's character. Bums got the bum's rush.

Minnie was tight-fisted and tough. When the Temple staff begged for a switchboard so they could make outgoing calls, she had pay phones installed in the lobby and told the department heads to use their own nickels.

Eight months after the Temple opened, Aimee received a three-page "complaint" against the autocratic rule of Minnie Kennedy. Signed "The Committee," this document presented the grievances of several workers. They accused Minnie of commercializing the Temple and then refusing to make its accounts public. The complainants had thought they were joining a church, only to discover that no church organization existed.

Mother Kennedy held all property in her own name. No board
of trustees supervised the Temple's activities. Donors who believed they had contributory rights to space from a chair "up
through the dome of Heaven" discovered they had no pro-
prietary rights whatever. If Minnie wanted to expel a member,
she would simply tear up his membership card. And there was
no higher court of appeal.

The complainants called upon Aimee to dismiss her mother.
Acknowledging Minnie's "splendid handling of financial affairs
thus far of the Temple," they suggested that Minnie receive
$25,000 in cash to bow out gracefully. If she didn't leave, the
letter threatened, and if the Temple didn't change its ways, the
district attorney would be called in: "Facts and witnesses are
being gathered for the preparation of the action to be filed,"
which would cause "much notorious publicity and a great
hindrance to our work."

Absorbed in the Temple's artistic and spiritual life, Aimee
had to trust her mother. The organization was based on this
sound partnership, and democracy was secondary. Confident
of Aimee's support, Minnie learned who the anonymous "committee" were. With a flourish she tore up all their membership
cards (kept on file) and showed them the door. She was not a
diplomat; she was ringmaster of a circus that without the whip
might dissolve into chaos.

The dangers facing these two women in 1923—women running a cash operation which grossed thousands of dollars per
week and had a membership in the tens of thousands swirling
around all that money—are terrifying to imagine. Minnie Kennedy was under a daily pressure familiar to managers of casinos
and racetracks; she dealt with it instinctively, ruthlessly, though
her inherent kindliness has been well established. The paradox
of any church's success is that a church, however well meaning,
is only human, and money and power will corrupt it as they
will corrupt anything human, except in rare instances. The
Church of the Foursquare Gospel had a strong moral center in
the partnership of Aimee Semple McPherson and Minnie Kennedy. But it rapidly challenged their control, as the complaint
of August, 1923 shows. The issue was power and money.

Though Minnie quickly put down this early revolt, it would recur again and again, in dozens of forms, before her daughter's death twenty years later.

Aimee was too busy to be aware of all the challenges to Minnie's control. Alma Whitaker, describing "a fairly average day" for the evangelist, refers to three church services, a theology class, two weddings, and a funeral, with a few conferences and advisory councils thrown in. "Of course, she ought to be a nervous wreck," says Whitaker (prophetically), "but instead she seems to thrive on it." William Jennings Bryan, visiting Angelus Temple during this period, warned Aimee that if she was not more careful, her obsessive work schedule would ruin her health.

Temple workers, Foursquare Gospel crusaders, bands and choirs stood on parade review outside the five-story concrete building for the gala opening of the L.I.F.E. Bible School on December 7, 1925. The women, dressed in white uniforms and capes like their leader's, saluted her proudly as she smiled and saluted back. The congregation's military bearing owed something to its evangelistic parent, the Salvation Army. But there was more to it than that. There was a crucial need for discipline. Sister Aimee had the strange power to inspire emulation—thousands of women wanted to look, think, and talk like her. With a congregation growing by hundreds every week, the need for order was so urgent that she and Minnie naturally adopted the military model. Whenever there was an occasion—a visit from William Jennings Bryan (September 30, 1923), a performance of the great Gospel baritone Homer Rodeheaver—marches and parades would celebrate it.

For Aimee's frequent comings and goings at the train station, the stationmaster learned to clear all tracks but one. The clamorous welcomes and sendoffs, with thousands of spectators and brass bands, made regular headlines for twenty years. Some parties, worthy of a president, were the largest public gatherings in the city's history—startling when one considers the film industry's aggressive public relations. Mary Pickford received less attention.

Sister Aimee's power to mobilize this growing army was

immediately evident to politicians. City officials now had to pay more attention to the firemen and the police when they came calling for raises, because Aimee had become their advocate at City Hall. When the firemen got their pay raise, they made Aimee an honorary battalion chief. She preached the next Sunday in the brass-buttoned uniform they had given her, wearing a fireman's waterspout helmet and urging higher salaries for the police.

Before dawn on June 29, 1925 the telephone rang in the foyer of the parsonage. It was a church member who had moved to Santa Barbara, a hundred miles up the coast.

"Sister McPherson," she stuttered, scarcely able to control her voice. "You've got to help us. We've just been struck by an earthquake. Whole buildings have fallen."

Aimee heard a crash over the phone.

"Oh, the house is shaking again. My dishes fell out of the cupboard. I have to get out of here. Sister! Please do something—"

Another crash, and the line went dead.

Aimee hung up, then called *The L.A. Times*. An editor confirmed the news. The earthquake had devastated Santa Barbara and left the population wandering the rubble, dazed and homeless.

"Excuse me," he said. "I can't talk. I have an extra to get out."

Aimee hurried out the back door of the parsonage and ran through the garden to the church. She bounded upstairs to the radio station, burst into the studio, and seized the microphone from a Gospel singer who was in the middle of a hymn. She began:

> Listen, everybody, this is Sister McPherson speaking. There's been a terrible earthquake in Santa Barbara. Homes have been destroyed. Thousands will be sleeping on the beaches and in the parks tonight.
>
> Ladies, stop what you are doing, now. Open up your closet doors and see what you can spare. People will need sweaters, coats and blankets before the sun goes down. Right now, pack up whatever you can spare and bring it to Angelus Temple.

Men, if you have any kind of truck, fill it with gas. Check the tires and batteries, make sure there is water in the radiator, and bring your truck to the Temple. Be prepared to drive emergency supplies to Santa Barbara.

Ladies, about the food. Send only food that doesn't need to be cooked. If you send eggs, hard-boil them first. And if you have nothing to give, give yourself—come on over and help sort clothing and pack boxes . . .

That was how the convoy of trucks loaded with supplies was heading north to Santa Barbara before the *Times* newspaper extra hit the streets.

Roberta Star Semple, fourteen years old, was in the middle of this commotion, helping to load the trucks. When the second convoy was ready to roll, she was on it, insisting she go along to bring back to her mother a full report from the scene of the disaster.

Roberta found the Santa Barbara business district in ruins. Seismologists said the earth had moved sixteen inches. A swimmer, far from shore, suddenly found himself high and dry upon the heaving sand. Walls trembled and fell—some fell in, and some out.

Guests in one hotel awoke to find their rooms full of light. The exterior wall had fallen away, leaving them safe in bed but exposed to the world like figures in a dollhouse.

Later that day the Red Cross called a meeting to discuss the appropriation of funds to aid the victims of the disaster in Santa Barbara. By that time Sister Aimee's second convoy was distributing blankets and food amidst the ruins.

The parsonage where Aimee lived with her mother and children is on the corner between the Temple and the portico of the Bible College, overlooking Echo Park. Pie-shaped like the Temple, the two-story Spanish house with its high arched windows, balcony, and balustrades on the roof looks much larger than it is, as one views it from outside the iron gate, through the palms and cypresses.

Inside, the marble foyer is bathed in light from a window on the winding staircase. In that window a family coat of arms shines in stained glass. Aimee designed it. In the upper right quadrant is an open book, the Bible; on the left, a harp, the symbol of Irish Robert Semple; in the lower left quadrant a sheaf of wheat represents the fields of souls to be harvested; in the lower right is a lion rampant, the Lion of Judah. Above the coat of arms is the Latin phrase RES NON VERBA: Deeds, Not Words.

On the other side of the foyer a back door leads to a little garden between the parsonage and the Temple. The walled garden and the alley beyond the wall soon came to be called "newspaper alley," because it was infested, night and day, with reporters. A path leads past the fountain pool, with its Rebecca-at-the-well statue, to a door that opens upon the second balcony of the main auditorium. Along this path the evangelist made her way to the pulpit twenty-one times a week, stopping inside the door to "center" herself, then sweeping grandly down the ramp along the east wall, to the stage below, amid thunderous applause.

Roberta Salter says that the one time of day she could be assured of being alone with her mother, or alone with her mother and brother, was the hour Aimee spent dressing before her sermon. Aimee loved to have the children with her in this private time. There was something soothing and regenerative about that ritual in her bedroom. It was a calm in the center of the hurricane their lives had become.

Roberta, looking over her mother's shoulder into the mirror, would have the endless questions of an adolescent about her mother's toilet and wardrobe. These had become interesting. And Aimee had begun to vary her appearance, departing now and then from the habitual nurse's uniform and cape. She wore costumes as the illustrated sermons required. One evening she would be a milkmaid; another, a princess out of a fairy tale. Now that she could afford nice clothing, she delighted in the latest fashions, lingerie, and scents. Her salary, well publicized, was twenty-five dollars a week, but the Temple maintained charge accounts for the evangelist at several fine shops in the city. It is no wonder that the veteran of a thousand noisome healing services would take particular delight in finding for herself the perfect scent.

"What is the perfume, Mother?" asked Roberta, filling her head with the fragrance as her mother dabbed it behind her ears.

"*Quelque Fleur*," replied Aimee. The perfume, by Houbigant of Paris, was fashionable and expensive in the 1920's. She would never be without it. And that rich essence, mingled with the sweat that poured from her during a sermon, was part of the atmosphere in which she moved and breathed—*quelque fleur*, the subtle sweetness of some mysterious flower.

There were four bedrooms off the balcony in the small house, but there were so many visitors that Aimee often shared her room with Minnie. Rolf had his own room, and Roberta had a room to herself for a while. But then in 1924 she began having "roommates." These were girls her own age who had got into trouble. They would come from all over the country to tell Sister Aimee of their misfortune, and Roberta claims that her mother could spot them in any crowd.

She would take the girl to the parsonage for a conversation Roberta heard so many times, it became a formal yet passionate ritual: "How far along are you? Shall we call your mother? Come, we'll call your mother and tell her where you are. She must be very worried."

And Sister Aimee, in her nurse's uniform, would dial the number and try to hand the girl the receiver, unsuccessfully.

"Mrs. ——? This is Aimee McPherson calling from Los Angeles. Yes, Aimee *Semple* McPherson. Your daughter is here with me, in my home. She's fine. Oh?"

And when she failed to convince the daughter to go home, or the mother to take the daughter back, she would say: "Well, then she'll be staying here with us for a while."

So Roberta would have a roommate for several months. And when the child was born, Aimee would make a second call to the home of the unwed mother, saying, "Mrs. ——? I have some *wonderful* news! Your daughter has just given birth to a healthy eight-pound boy!" Or girl. This usually brought about the desired reconciliation. The unwed mother returned home, with or without the child. And Roberta would have the room to herself, until another runaway appeared with the age-old problem.

Downstairs in the parsonage was a drawing room whose high windows looked out on the street. Behind the drawing room, with its stylish art deco furniture and angular lighting fixtures, were the kitchen and the dining room, where the family ate together whenever they could. Dinner prayers focused upon the missionaries who wrote Aimee letters from around the world. The family prayed for the missionaries' health, and Aimee told the children to spare the table sugar so they might send more to the hungry missionaries.

Dinner was interrupted, time and time again, by a knock at the door: a visit from the stork. The stork usually arrived at dinnertime, thinking to find the family at home and awake but slow to answer the door. There is no record of the number of infants delivered to the parsonage porch in baskets, handbags, and potato sacks. But the greeting and placement of such babies became part of life's routine at the parsonage. Everyone in the city knew that a baby delivered to this address would be well cared for.

Apart from the dinner prayers, the children recall, the famous preacher went light on religion when she spent time with them. At home, or on their frequent outings to the beach, or when they rode horses at Tom Mix's stable just down the road, Aimee felt that family time had a sacred quality in itself. She loved to ride the horse called Radiant, who would rear up dramatically at her bidding. The horses at Tom Mix's stable had strange habits from working in the movies. The horse saddled for young Rolf had a fake limp from the westerns where he was supposed to look as if he had been shot. Another horse had cultivated a "horse laugh" that was eerily human. Aimee and the children joked about their stagestruck steeds.

Aimee took the children to swing in the park, or they would go to the beach. She loved to swim even more than she loved to ride. This exercise, several times a week, was essential to her health, a tonic for the nervous system of a high-strung woman. At night, when there were no prayer meetings, Aimee would read to the children. *Tom Swift, The Wizard of Oz,* and *Snow*

White and the Seven Dwarfs were Rolf's favorites. These Aimee eventually chose as themes for illustrated sermons.

Thus the children recall times at the parsonage from 1923 until 1924. It was a frail privacy Aimee defended in the midst of the frenetic revival. After the opening of the Temple, her family time became much more limited. She was up at dawn preparing for the radio broadcast, and went to bed at night with her typewriter, in the wee hours, scripting sermons.

But soon the reporters began arriving, unannounced and at odd hours—first just a few, and then in great numbers. Then it was life in a fishbowl. In the last months of 1924 Aimee began to assert her right to privacy by checking into the Ambassador Hotel once or twice a week. She said the racket of the carpenters building the Bible College next door disturbed her. She could not sleep or write. But she also obviously needed to withdraw from the hubbub of the Temple and parsonage. Tongues began to wag, though her hotel stays were public knowledge, under press surveillance. So she "always requested Room 330 because it was at the end of a corridor and directly across the hall from a room occupied by one of the [female] Temple members."

About this time, Rolf McPherson was sent to board at the ranch of Mr. and Mrs. James Pleasants, old friends of Aimee's and Temple followers, who lived near Winters, California. Rolf recalls the decision without bitterness, though it must have been painful for him to leave his mother. After all, his father was three thousand miles away, and he and his mother were very close. Rolf remembers only that the newsmen had made life difficult, so difficult that the family could not all continue in that house.

It was a welcome relief for the boy. The city children had begun to tease him and then torment him about his mother, the lady preacher. He had to walk the long way around to school, avoiding the older boys who threatened to beat him up. One day they caught him and gave him a split lip and bloody nose before his big sister came around the corner and scared the ruffians away. The country children did not share the biases of the big city; they accepted Rolf as one of them.

Perhaps Rolf's mother felt that the parsonage, an environment dominated by women, was no place for a ten-year-old boy to become a man. On the ranch he would have his own horse, and establish an identity free of the smothering manners and day-and-night Temple activities. This he accomplished, beyond a doubt, and it is fair to say his years on the ranch were rich and formative.

"Bossy the cow gave a bucket of milk every day with an inch-thick layer of cream. I grew six inches," he recalls, smiling.

SCANDAL

Aimee's "honeymoon" with the Los Angeles newspapers lasted a long time. Until October of 1925, when her Santa Ana church revolted, they had almost nothing but good to say about her. When they had said everything good they could think of —when Sister Aimee had become a household word, her radio voice the most recognizable in the West—then the honeymoon ended. After the difficulty in Santa Ana, whatever she said or did was news, a headline that sold papers, particularly if it divided public opinion.

No one who remembers Aimee Semple McPherson and no one who has written about her says that she had a close friend. People loved her, and it is said that she had boundless compassion and love for humankind. She had many supporters. The coterie of women devoted to her—Harriet Jordan, Louise Baer, Emma Shaffer, Mae Waldron, and others—was charged with a keen jealousy which Nancy Barr Mavity observes was palpably sexual, though unconscious. But Aimee could not afford to show favoritism, and so she could never become intimate with any of them. She is the perfect illustration of the social

principle that power isolates a person from normal human relations. In the case of an unmarried woman of Aimee's stature,
the isolation was nearly complete, except for Minnie, Roberta,
and Rolf.

She had no close friend, but she had famous and wonderful
enemies. Foremost among them was Robert "Fighting Bob"
Shuler, head of the Church Federation of Los Angeles, of which
Aimee was the most prominent ex-member. Fighting Bob is
remembered chiefly because he put a curse on the State of California for failing to elect him governor. One or more earth-
quakes are supposed to have resulted from Shuler's curse, if not
all the state's later political misfortunes and embarrassments.

These two ministers, Shuler and McPherson, were as different
as fire and water. Aimee built her career by replacing the "Gospel of Fear, Hellfire, and Damnation" with the "Gospel of Reconciliation and Love." She disposed of the dirges and threats
of hell, and filled her Temple with music, flowers, golden trumpets, angels, and an unmistakable sexual energy.

"Who cares about old hell, friends?" she would sing out.
"Why, we *all* know what hell is. We've heard about it all our
lives. A terrible place, where nobody wants to go. I think the
less we hear about hell the better, don't you? Let's forget about
hell. Lift up your hearts. What *we* are interested in, yes, Lord,
is *heaven*, and how to get *there*!"

And with her head held high she would roll her wide-set eyes
slightly back in her head, under the blinking lashes, so the whites
flashed, in an expression that mingled heavenly and earthly
pleasure, that was somehow both sensuous and spiritual.

In the history of fundamentalism this was unheard of. Robert
Shuler was of the old school, a stereotype *The American Mercury*
described in 1924:

> The evangelist is roaring for red meat . . . fear and rage . . . fear
> of hell and wrath against the wicked. His technique consists simply
> of vilifying in the most unbridled language whatever group in the
> community fails to meet with his transient approval. Being human,
> he cannot approve, of course, that which he does not understand,
> and he can approve only with difficulty that which he envies.

He hated her. "Nine out of ten of her people," he cried, "are converts from Protestant Churches. Instead of her real estate being worth $300,000, it is worth nearer $1,000,000!" Fighting Bob's first attack on his rival was published in late 1924. The book, *McPhersonism*, is mostly a diatribe against Aimee's unorthodox manner in the pulpit, which he denounced as a disgrace to serious Christians everywhere. Most members of the Church Federation agreed with him. Several years later, when Shuler had the sort of ammunition he preferred—rumors of a moral lapse—his passion against Aimee would spawn an even bigger and more poisonous book. He drew mob strength from attacks on Catholics, Jews, and Negroes. But his greatest notoriety in the 1920's and 1930's he owed to his tireless denunciation of Angelus Temple and its leader.

While Robert Shuler led the municipal opposition, the imperial expansion of Aimee's Church caused internal strife. In 1924 the Church established several branches in the suburbs. Minnie Kennedy had put up money from "extension funds" for the building of a Foursquare church in Santa Ana, tens of thousands of dollars. When the church exceeded the budget, a dispute arose over its control. There was a misunderstanding: Minnie thought it was her church; the leaders of the new Santa Ana congregation, Mr. and Mrs. F. W. Garlock, thought it was *their* church. They engaged a "flapper evangelist," Bessie Mae Randell, cast in Sister Aimee's image, whose rousing performances built the membership to a thousand. They repaid the seed money to Minnie Kennedy, and then expected her to turn the title over to them.

Minnie, of course, would not surrender the title. It was a Foursquare church, built with Foursquare cash; so the deed should remain at the parent church, the Santa Ana branch being used for the benefit of the local Foursquare congregation. When the board of the Santa Ana church protested, threatening legal action, Minnie "excommunicated" the dissidents. She transferred their flapper evangelist to the Los Angeles Harbor branch. Then, on Sunday, she showed up at the church in a pickup truck, suspended the twenty-one Sunday-school classes, with her crew removed fifty folding chairs and the silver Communion set, and drove back to Echo Park.

All this took place in 1925. Meanwhile Aimee prayed, preached her illustrated sermons, conducted services on the radio, wrote and edited *The Bridal Call Foursquare* publications, and oversaw the curriculum for the Bible College. *The Bridal Call* had evolved into a slick magazine. In the September 1925 issue, Aimee describes the recent use of Radio KFSG to organize simultaneous tent meetings all over southern California, with two-way radio hookups from eight cities:

> When one was told to lift their hands, all lifted their hands. When one congregation was asked to wave their handkerchiefs, they all waved together; all listened to the same sermon, and the leaves of the Bible turned and rustled simultaneously in the various cities.

Hundreds of thousands of people believed that Aimee's broadcasts represented God's entrance into their homes and hearts. Hundreds claimed to be healed when at Aimee's encouragement they placed their hands upon the radio speaker horn as it vibrated with her voice.

The revolt of the Santa Ana branch was in fact a recurrence of the old schism between Minnie's supporters and enemies, the latter longing to decentralize the power of the Echo Park Evangelistic Association, now worth millions of dollars. (Aimee and Minnie signed grant deeds late in 1925, recorded in 1926, transferring their property to the newly incorporated, nonprofit Echo Park Evangelistic Association. Some thought this was just another name for the former partners. But in fact the transfer of assets to a nonprofit organization is one-way only and does not thereafter inure to the benefit of the individuals.)

Aimee, for the most part, held herself above the fray. She was insulated by her obsession with preaching and staging illustrated sermons, and by her naive denial of the difficulties Minnie handled, day in and day out: money, personnel, public relations, and church politics.

———

One of Minnie's greatest problems at the turn of 1925 was the gossip about Aimee's conversations with her radio operator.

Radio KFSG had gone on the air in February of 1924. Since then, Aimee had been working head to head with the radio operator, Kenneth Ormiston, to produce the "Sunshine Hour" as well as broadcast her spectacular Sunday services. The creation of decent sound values was difficult in those pioneering days of radio. The evangelist and the engineer worked long hours together, developing the mutual respect and humor that any such collaboration requires.

Ormiston was the first person Aimee saw every morning. And, according to Minnie Kennedy, "it was her habit to stop in at Ormiston's office after a service" to get his notes on the production. Thus he was also the last person she saw at night. Those who tell us that the famous woman never had a close friend are forgetting her colleague Ormiston—because that relationship, or whatever one chooses to call it, became a *cause de scandale*.

By 1925 Sister Aimee had become a religious idol to several hundred thousand people. Within the working family of the Temple she was adored, was the focus of petty jealousies among those who jostled for her attention, and the object of impossible expectations. Acceptable behavior for Aimee did not include the easy, relaxed tones of conversational intimacy, unless she was onstage, under the watchful eyes of 5,500 worshipers. Viewing the early newsreels, one can see the pressure upon her, in scenes where she has prepared a girlish, sentimental mask for the public. But the eyes give her away, furious, ironic eyes—it is all an act for the benefit of those who would find her spontaneity altogether terrifying. Candid footage reveals another woman entirely, poised, commanding, impulsive.

Queens have no "friends," nor do divine evangelists. Friendship would have diminished her in the eyes of many admirers, reduced her to the level of those who needed to regard her as somehow immortal, beyond human needs. So, what was this tone they were hearing in her conversations with Kenneth Ormiston, the radio operator?

The broadcasting studio was on the Temple's upper floor. Aimee kept in touch with Ormiston during the services by means of a telephone intercom beside her pulpit chair. She would pick up the phone during a choral number or solo and check how the voices were coming over the microphone.

These sound checks developed into comic exchanges between evangelist and radio engineer. Ormiston was not very religious. His view of the Temple proceedings made Aimee laugh in spite of herself. She would get the giggles, then have to struggle to get back into character. And she never seemed to realize that this behavior separated her from the other performers on the platform.

The Angelus Temple acoustics were so good that the casual dialogue between Sister Aimee and the radio operator could be heard, unknown to her, in the second balcony. And the tone of her voice, as she spoke to Ormiston, was unlike the tone she used anywhere else. Theirs was the sort of conversation you might expect to hear between brother and sister, between close friends.

The gossip started immediately. When it reached Minnie Kennedy, she confronted Aimee with it. Minnie warned her daughter that she was in a vulnerable position. As an unmarried preacher before the public "she should be more circumspect than any other woman." Even though Ormiston was a married man with a small son, Aimee's familiar manner with the engineer might be misconstrued by anyone inclined to suspect an intrigue.

Evidently Aimee told her mother to mind her own business. She went on working with Ormiston, went on talking to him on her radio intercom and in his office, which caused no end of gossip. Yet who can blame the thirty-five-year-old woman for continuing a working association so essential to the Temple's functioning? Aimee knew Mrs. Ormiston, and dined with the Ormistons at their home and in public. But this did not stop the gossip. Minnie began to put personal pressure on Aimee and managerial weight on Ormiston.

The year 1925 was stressful. In the summer the revolt of the Santa Ana branch made headlines.

All was not peace and love among the flocks of Aimee Semple
McPherson, pastor of Angelus Temple, yesterday, for a portion
of one of her flocks revolted and issued numerous charges against
her in a suit filed in Orange County courts. (*The L.A. Times*,
August 30, 1925)

The charges included refusal to account for contributions, removal of church property, unfairness, high-handedness. This
was Aimee's first dose of negative publicity, and it dragged on
into November, when the complainants finally gave up.

The daily round of preaching, writing, broadcasting, and
attending meetings had already begun to exhaust the evangelist's
nervous energy. The demoralizing public criticism now began
to wear her down. She complained, to Minnie and to others,
that she was tired. Newsmen covering the Santa Ana lawsuit
found her unavailable for comment. A church official explained:

> Sister McPherson always leaves the city after Friday evening ser-
> vices for her week-end rest. Nobody knows where she goes and
> it is impossible to get in communication with her because she
> seldom goes to the same place twice. Anyway, there's nothing to
> it. (August 30, 1925)

The choir chaplain, Rudolf Dunbar, had been watching Aimee's progress from close range. A wealthy insurance executive
with offices in Chicago as well as Los Angeles, Dunbar was a
gentleman whose judgment was highly valued in the Temple
community. Noticing Aimee's tenseness, the fidgeting of her
hands, her loss of weight and short attention span, he told her
that she should take a rest from her responsibilities. She was
risking a nervous breakdown. When the evangelist, rolling her
eyes, protested that she could not be spared, Dunbar suggested
that Paul Rader, the Chicago evangelist, might be persuaded to
fill in for her while she went on vacation. Dunbar volunteered
to get Rader's consent, and then personally guaranteed his salary
and expenses.

Aimee finally agreed to take a vacation. She announced that
she would go to the Holy Land in January of the coming year.
Fifteen-year-old Roberta would be her mother's traveling com-

panion. They would sail first to Ireland, to visit Roberta's paternal grandparents in Magherafelt; then on to London en route to Jerusalem.

On January 11, 1926 a crowd of several thousand gathered at the Southern Pacific railroad station to wish Aimee and Roberta bon voyage. The band played. Paul Rader led a prayer from the platform of the observation car while Aimee stood with her head bowed. She wore a finely tailored blue suit and held a bouquet of American Beauty roses. She waved, smiled brilliantly, and called out blessings to the crowd as her train pulled away.

Kenneth Ormiston had left his job at the Temple in December of 1925. Gossip placed an unbearable strain on his marriage. While Aimee was abroad, Mrs. Ormiston visited Minnie and told her she was going to sue for divorce, naming Aimee as corespondent. Ruth Ormiston soon gave up that plan; but she did in fact leave her husband, taking their child to live with her parents in Australia after reporting Ormiston missing on January 22, 1926.

Hundreds of journalists, Robert Shuler, and two courts of law spent five years and half a million dollars trying to prove that the evangelist and her radio operator had been lovers. The courts' magnificent failure might be seen as comic if it had not ruined Kenneth Ormiston's life and defamed the evangelist in her prime. Somewhere in the heap of evidence dismissed by the jurors is a check for $1,500 paid to Ormiston on March 15, 1926 from an agent alleged to be Aimee's. Maybe she had sent him money. But as far as anyone knows Kenneth Ormiston's resignation from KFSG that December was the pathetic ending of Aimee's last experiment in friendship.

———

The journey provided a change of scene, a kaleidoscope of scenes, but no one would consider it restful. Dropping Roberta off with her Semple grandparents in Ireland, Aimee proceeded to London, where the press besieged her, flashbulbs popping around her as she visited Westminster Abbey and Big Ben. Journalists noted a "coiffeur that might have been done in Bond

Street, pale yellow silk jumper, black silk gown, short skirts, and flesh-colored silk stockings." On vacation, Aimee had shucked her nurse's uniform. To the many invitations to preach in England she replied, "I am resting, not preaching."

She flew to Paris. On her way to the Riviera, whence she would sail to the Holy Land, she heard the voice of God saying, "My child, I want you to return to London and preach." So from Nice she telephoned the secretary of the Elim churches in London, that she was coming to preach for four days.

She began by preaching in a tabernacle and conducting overflow meetings. Then the church ministers rented a public hall that seated 8,000. A newspaper hailed her as "the greatest woman preacher in the world," and another reported that she "shocked the orthodox." "One of the merriest religious revivals the world has ever known," said *The London Daily News*. The ministers, of course, wanted Aimee to give up her trip and stay in London to conduct a full-scale campaign. She was tempted. She finally did agree to preach in Royal Albert Hall on her way home.

Roberta joined her mother in London. The two crossed the Channel together and took a train down to Marseilles, where they boarded a ship bound for Port Said. They crossed the Suez Canal in a ferry. Since childhood Aimee "had been building up of the fabric of which dreams are made a lovely Holy Land. I had seen it as it was in Jesus's day in my mind's eye. Would it be changed and different?"

Roberta and Aimee traveled to Nazareth, Jericho, Hebron, Joppa, and Galilee. Then they went to Cairo to see the pyramids. From Egypt they embarked for Italy, where they visited Venice, Rome, Naples, and Pompeii, before returning to London so Aimee could fulfill her promise to preach in Royal Albert Hall. Nearly twenty years earlier she had preached her first sermon there, extempore—now she would make history as the first woman ever to lead a religious service in that legendary theater. The 12,000-seat auditorium was packed from arena to dome as she spoke, at the closing meeting on Easter Monday, on the Second Coming.

From London Aimee went to Belfast, where she preached in the coliseum before returning to Los Angeles.

Arriving at the train station April 24, Aimee and Roberta were welcomed by the acting mayor, Boyle Workman, Judge Carlos Hardy, and a crowd of 12,000. Porters carried trunks of souvenirs Aimee had collected, as well as a suitcase of costumes she would use in her illustrated sermons. Flushed with excitement, the traveler shared the story of her adventures with an eager radio audience.

"I am weary, weary. I think only Christ could have been as tired as I," she confided to her colleagues.

Photographs of the evangelist from the spring of 1926 are disturbing, notably the two publicity photos for the illustrated sermon "Slavery Days." This sermon played on the theme of bondage to and emancipation from sin, from Exodus to the Civil War. Aimee is dressed in the full hoop skirt, crinolines, and lace bodice of the antebellum South. She poses against a painted backdrop of cabins, cotton fields, and a plantation mansion. Under a satin bonnet her long hair is loose, falling on both shoulders and to her waist, framing a gaunt face with deep lines around the mouth and hollow eyes.

These two pictures could serve for the masks of comedy and tragedy. In one she is seated, pensive, resting her head upon her hand, sad, as if she bore the slaver's guilt as well as the slave's burden; in the other photo she is showing off her wide skirts in a curtsy, grinning as the light hits her forehead above the wild eyes, and the triangular smile is manic, on the verge of hysteria. This is a woman desperately in need of a long rest, not seventeen European and Middle Eastern cities in ten weeks.

Slavery days, indeed.

She returned to the routine of writing, directing, and preaching she had left in January. Minnie was surprised to hear her ask for money—Aimee had always been content with her allowance of twenty-five dollars a week, since the Temple held charge accounts for her all over the city. Now she received the collec-

tion taken on the first Sunday of every month, hundreds of dollars, no questions asked. Minnie could not imagine what her
daughter would do with all that money. It remains a mystery.

Aimee went to the beach more often, particularly Ocean Park,
always in the company of her secretary Emma Schaffer. She
liked to work on her sermons in the shade of the beach umbrella,
between long swims far out beyond the surf.

On May 18, 1926, Sister Aimee gathered up her swimming
suit, bible, and the notes of a sermon on "Darkness and Light"
which would never be delivered.

Shortly after twelve noon she told her mother she was going
to the beach, inviting her to come along. Minnie had some
accounting work to do, so she declined. Aimee ordered her car,
an expensive Kissel, smiled at the garage attendant, and drove
away with spinster Emma Schaffer sitting beside her.

At the Ocean View Hotel Aimee changed into her pea-
green bathing suit. She and Emma ate waffles at the snack bar
before strolling down to the beach tent. The two women
made a humorous contrast: the long-haired evangelist, broad-
shouldered, broad-beamed, though leaner than ever now in her
green bathing suit and beach cape as she walked with the athletic
stride of a tennis professional; and gaunt Emma Schaffer in her
white Temple uniform and high-buttoned shoes, plain pious
Emma, squinting in the sunlight through her rimless spectacles,
walking stiff-legged in Aimee's shadow toward the broad and
gentle motion of the surf.

Aimee sat in the shade of the tent and doodled. She made
notes. Looking out at the sea, she thought of her students grad-
uating and sailing away. Watching the wavelets sparkle and
break softly on the beach, she imagined her students in cock-
leshells atop those tiny crests, sailing until they reached every
country and island in the world, to preach the Gospel.

> Between every one of those little crests there was a little hollow,
> and in the little hollow a shadow. It had been that way since the
> beginning; the glint of the sun, gleaming light on the tops, and
> shadow, darkness, in the troughs.
>
> Ah, light and darkness all over the earth, everywhere.

She drew a picture of the sun, with radial rays. She wrote a few lines of her sermon. Then she waded into the surf, dived, and swam far out, so far that the other swimmers she left behind looked like black dots between her and Emma, who stood trying to keep her mistress in sight. Aimee swam out until she was almost even with the end of the pier that jutted out into the sea. Then she came in, twisting her hair to dry it.

She had been preparing a list of lantern slides for a talk on the Holy Land she was to present that night. When she finished the list of pictures and of the songs and singers she wanted for the presentation, she asked Emma Schaffer to telephone the orders to someone at the Temple who would make everything ready.

As Emma walked up the beach toward the drugstore telephone, Aimee left the tent for another swim.

Emma later recalled that when she returned with a glass of orange juice, Aimee waved to her from far out in the water. She asked Emma to bring the orange juice to her, out there, in the ocean. Emma did not get the joke—and later thought that perhaps it was not really her mistress who had waved and called.

Whoever it was was soon out of sight, lost in the waves. Emma was used to Aimee's swimming toward the horizon, out of sight, so a long time passed before she grew concerned. She did not sleep or read. She watched the sea.

Emma trudged up and down the beach, squinting, wringing her thin hands. She watched as one swimmer then another emerged, dripping, from the surf. It was more than an hour before she called the lifeguard.

The manager of the Ocean View Hotel, Frank Langon, broke the news to Minnie Kennedy by telephone.

"I believe you know," he said, "that Sister McPherson came down with Miss Schaffer this afternoon to take a swim. It is now nearly five o'clock and we have not been able to find her."

"She is drowned," said Minnie Kennedy. And she felt certain of it.

———

Fishermen dragged for the body. Airplanes searched the sea
between Santa Monica and Venice, while thousands of people
patrolled the beach. Search parties in glass-bottomed boats from
Catalina Island peered into the ocean depths. Ed Harrison,
twenty-six, one of several deep-sea divers who went looking
for Aimee, died of exposure. Many of Aimee's disciples had to
be restrained from casting themselves into the sea; one woman,
determined to join the evangelist in death, succeeded.

Such a deep and universal expression of grief had not been
seen since the assassination of Lincoln. It would not be seen
again until the death of FDR. News extras hit the stands the
night of May 18. The next day, the entire congregation of
Angelus Temple and the Foursquare Gospel branch churches,
converged on Ocean Park, ten thousand strong. They sang
hymns, prayed, wept, and embraced one another. At night they
built bonfires, beat drums, and danced "in the Spirit" under the
full moon.

For thirty-two days they kept their vigil. A popular vision,
captured in penny postcards and newspaper illustrations,
showed Aimee hovering between the waves and clouds like
Christ in church lithographs. She was either coming or going.
Ambiguous, the image captured the two prevailing sentiments
of the public: Either the Lord had assumed her bodily into
Heaven for eternity, or she would return as mysteriously as she
had vanished. When a concessionaire exhibited a plaster figure
of Aimee blessing the crowd, it caused them to riot, to direct
their frustration and fury upon this crass mercenary and upon
anyone who tried to defend the fleeing souvenir-salesmen and
hot-dog and soda-pop vendors. Frank Langon had to call the
riot squad to restore order and protect his hotel.

Hopes and rumors that she was alive abounded. Letters, telegrams, and phone calls arrived from all over the country, saying
that Sister Aimee was here, was there, alive, dead. Some said
Sister Aimee had died in an underwater struggle with a sea
monster, who ate her. There was widespread speculation that
her disappearance was a publicity stunt.

Dr. Gustave Haas, who had treated Aimee in 1924, published
an article in *The L.A. Times* suggesting that the evangelist was

deranged, wandering the hills in a state of nervous exhaustion. It was all but forgotten.

District Attorney Keyes was informed that Aimee had been kidnapped by two men who were holding her for $25,000 ransom. Minnie, more desperate than hopeful, posted a $25,000 reward for the return of the Temple's leader, dead or alive.

Roberta hid in the basement of the parsonage as reporters charged into her home, into her mother's bedroom, rummaging through drawers and closets "looking for clues." Reporters found Rolf on the ranch. On the way to Los Angeles, the train conductor hid the boy in his private compartment while the newsmen searched car by car. Rolf later was filmed with his grandmother strewing rose petals on the waves at Ocean Park, on June 3.

A ransom letter from a different party arrived at Angelus Temple by special delivery June 19, demanding $500,000 and signed "The Avengers." The long letter was so preposterous that Minnie tossed it aside into the flood of crank correspondence.

That was on the eve of the twelve-hour memorial service at Angelus Temple on June 20. Minnie had to take over the pulpit. She addressed the 6,000 mourners in the auditorium and 14,000 more via loudspeakers set up in the streets. The pastor's empty chair was banked with flowers; her portrait hung above.

Sad and perplexed, Minnie faced the crowd. Groping for words, she explained that Sister Aimee's body had not been recovered because God held it so precious that He had taken it whole into Heaven, as He had taken the holy body of Elijah. The work she had started must be carried on. She had raised $100,000 for the college building; more was needed to finish the construction. The collection, in cash and subscriptions, totaled $30,000.

Meanwhile there were so many Aimee sightings—in Oatman, Arizona, Culver City, California, New York, El Paso, and Denver—that the coroner refused to issue a death certificate. On a single day she was reported to have been seen in sixteen places, coast to coast.

Three days after her memorial service, Aimee Semple McPherson walked in from the desert at Agua Prieta, Mexico.

KIDNAPPED

Minnie Kennedy appeared at Aimee's bedside a step ahead of the reporters. Her daughter, in a hospital nightgown, hair strewn on the pillow, whispered for a while to her mother, who then opened the door to the family and the press.

From the hospital bed in Douglas, Arizona, the haggard evangelist announced to the world that she had been kidnapped. On the afternoon of May 18 she was wading in the surf, watching the lifeguards drill in the distance down the beach, when she heard someone call her name.

She turned and saw a man and a woman.

The woman sobbed. "Our baby is dying, Sister. The doctor has given it up. We've come all the way from Altadena to have you pray for the child. Please come to our car."

This sort of thing happened so frequently that Aimee never thought twice about it. The woman had a dark coat draped over her arm, which she offered as a wrap for the swimmer. Then they led Aimee to a parked car whose rear door stood open.

The engine was running. There was another man at the wheel. The woman hurried to the door before Aimee, seating herself in the shadows and cradling a blanketed bundle.

"Just step in," said the man behind Aimee. Then he shoved her.

Somebody held the back of her head while the woman forced a compress to Aimee's face. Aimee smelled chloroform.

The back door slammed and the car took off.

When Aimee awoke, she was wearing a white nightgown, lying in a bed not her own, in a strange room with flowery wallpaper. She sat up, sick to her stomach. The woman held a basin for her, and Aimee vomited.

"Where am I?"

The woman ignored her, hollering, "All right, Steve, come in."

Steve was about forty years old, five feet ten inches tall, and two hundred pounds. He wore a brown suit and a fedora. A younger man followed him, a taller man, bony, hollow-chested, his face with the blue shadow of beard closely shaven. He had a gold tooth.

"You're being held for ransom," said Steve. And when he talked, he drew his heavy brows together. "We're going to get that damned Temple."

Aimee tried to rise. "I must get back!" she pleaded.

Her kidnappers cackled and exchanged glances—Steve in his fedora, Mexicali Rose (she had black bobbed hair and large breasts), and the blue-chinned man known as "Jake."

They held her there for a long time. They pumped her for details about her past, to prove to Minnie they really had her. When Aimee stopped answering and said she wouldn't help them raise the money, Steve growled, "Oh, you won't, won't you?" and grabbed her wrist. "*We'll* see about *that* . . ." And he shoved his lit cigar down hard against her fingers.

Mexicali Rose cut off a lock of Aimee's hair.

Steve said, "If the hair won't convince her people, we can send a finger next . . ."

No one suggested that Aimee write a letter to Minnie.

One night they woke the evangelist, blindfolded her, and led her to the car.

"We're taking you for a short time somewhere where nobody can find you."

They drove for a night and a day, then led Aimee blindfolded into a two-room shack in the desert.

A few days later the men drove away. Rose announced she was going into town for supplies.

"I'll be right back," said Rose, "but I am going to have to tie you." She bound Aimee's hands and feet with something like bed ticking. Aimee heard the second car drive away.

She prayed. Then she rolled off the bed and across the floor toward an open five-gallon syrup can. The top had been cut off roughly, leaving a jagged edge. She backed into the tin can and started working to cut the bonds from her wrists.

In her hurry to get away before Rose returned, Aimee climbed out the window. She never tried the door, and never looked at the shack once she got outside.

She walked across the desert for seventeen hours before she saw the lights of Agua Prieta, and collapsed just inside the gate of Ramon Gonzales's house, where he soon found her. Gonzales took her to the hospital in nearby Douglas.

How the newspaper reporters loved this story. Within twenty-four hours there were hundreds of them in Douglas, Arizona. They spent $5,000 in telephone calls. Western Union put eight extra telegraph operators on duty, around the clock, and the reporters quickly turned out 95,000 words of copy in conveying the story to the world. *The Los Angeles Times* and *The San Francisco Examiner* each had an airplane racing to bring back the first photos of Aimee in her nightgown.

They scribbled, wired, and ballyhooed the thrilling narrative all over the nation, ringing changes upon it as if the tale had been a gift to them from Heaven. Here was a story that needed no help—there was not a journalist alive who could improve on it, though some tried.

They loved the story as if it were their own, and noised it abroad, though they did not believe it. There was a different story they wanted to believe, that sounded more plausible whether or not it was true. Since May 26, rumors had been rife that the missing evangelist had been seen with Kenneth Ormiston. (*The Sacramento Union* published an article to that effect on May 28.) People suspected a love affair. Though this scenario did not have the melodramatic piquancy of the kidnapping story, it certainly had the universal appeal of sex, obsession, and high scandal.

So while a few police searched for Aimee's abductors, several hundred reporters began looking for evidence that Aimee had not been kidnapped at all—that she had been comfortably lounging in a hotel room with Ormiston, or somebody.

———

Minnie Kennedy, Roberta Semple, and Rolf McPherson arrived in Douglas June 24, in the company of Joseph Ryan, the deputy district attorney, and Herman Cline, the chief of detectives.

Aimee did not look as if she had been through the ordeal she described. Cline learned that when she appeared out of the desert, her shoes were not scuffed or worn. There were grass stains on the insteps. She was not convincingly dehydrated or sunburned. Her dress showed no sign of perspiration. She was wearing a watch Minnie had given her, which she had not taken with her to the beach. She did have a scar on her hand, which she said came from the lighted cigar.

Efforts to find the shack Aimee described in her deposition were thorough, covering a forty-six-square-mile triangle between Douglas and Niggerhead Mountain. There was no adobe shack (with a wooden floor) south of Agua Prieta. The rest of the inconsistencies of the kidnapping story became a laughingstock, the subject of newspaper cartoons, comedy routines, and broadside ballads. Raymond Cox, Foursquare minister and author of *The Verdict Is In*, has this to say in his well-documented defense of the kidnapping story:

> No claim of Aimee Semple McPherson concerning her disappearance is independently impossible. The unlikelihood of such an incongruous concatenation of events being fit together is, in and of itself, a demonstration of the truthfulness of her story. Had she been faking, she would have invented a far more believable yarn.

Dr. Cox has a point. But it does not apply to the genius of storytelling, only to amateurs. Truth is very often stranger than fiction, as was proved in the conflict between Aimee's kidnapping story and the District Attorney's conjecture of her tryst with Kenneth Ormiston.

The idea that the unmarried, pretty, thirty-five-year-old

woman would fall in love and run off for a few weeks with a forbidden paramour made more sense than the kidnapping yarn—to people who did not know Aimee. And the possibility delighted her enemies. In addition to the Federation of Churches, Robert Shuler, and a number of ex-Foursquare workers Minnie had fired, Aimee's enemies now included the Chamber of Commerce and certain lords of the underworld. Los Angeles, then as now, had a sturdy network of gangsters in control of drug traffic, prostitution, alcohol, and loansharking. Aimee's conversion of several prostitutes and drug addicts led these unfortunates to tell their stories on Radio KFSG. This exposed various middle-management hoodlums, who in 1924 began threatening Aimee.

(*The Times* reported an elaborate plot by Marion Ray to kidnap the evangelist on September 3, 1925. It was foiled by the district attorney. The Church and Aimee's family believe to this day that the Mob kidnapped her.)

But it was not the Mob that mobilized the public and pressured the district attorney to find a connection between Aimee and Kenneth Ormiston. It was the Los Angeles Chamber of Commerce and the national press. Hitherto the press had treated Aimee with uncommon courtesy. Now they set upon her like wolves.

No movie star in Hollywood shone with the brilliance of Aimee Semple McPherson. She was a symbol of the city that had ambitions to become the "Athens of the West" and host the 1932 Olympics. But now Sister Aimee was a civic embarrassment, a spectacular vulgarity.

Returning to the City of Angels on June 26, Aimee was greeted by 50,000 people. A pilot engine, swarming with gun-packing guards from cab to cowcatcher, ran ahead of Aimee's train in case the kidnappers should make another grab for her. An airplane buzzed her coach, showering it with flowers. The Los Angeles police assigned a special squad to protect her upon her arrival. The entire fire department turned out in their parade uniforms. The sheriff's department and the City Council, Acting Mayor Boyle Workman, and Superior Judge Carlos Hardy stood in a sea of roses waiting to greet the heroine officially.

As the band played, the beloved evangelist at last was carried from the train on a wicker throne woven with red roses.

"Many Presidents," remarked essayist Morrow Mayo, "have visited Los Angeles, but no other man or woman was ever given such an ovation in the history of this city."

It was more than the Chamber of Commerce could bear. The new aesthetes and boosters of Los Angeles felt that the nation-wide gossip about this bible-thumping femme fatale was making their city a laughingstock. They pressured District Attorney Asa Keyes "to determine if any other elements entered into the disappearance"—elements other than Steve, Jake, and Mexicali Rose. The press was only too happy to offer its services in the interest of truth, and proceeded to hunt for a connection between Aimee's absence and the whereabouts of Kenneth Ormiston. His wife had reported him missing months before.

Now it is well known that Ormiston had his hands full of domestic problems that had little to do with his former employer. There was at least one mistress that was not Aimee, and probably two he had been struggling to keep concealed from each other. The press and the general public mostly ignored these baroque complications. But the lawyers were painfully aware that Ormiston might at any moment produce "the mystery woman," whenever he decided that nothing less would serve to clear Sister Aimee's name.

The Los Angeles Church Federation, led by Fighting Bob Shuler, generated public support for the prosecution by publishing, above the preachers' signatures, a demand that Aimee answer a list of intimate questions.

> Either a crime of the most terrible nature has been committed against Mrs. Aimee Semple McPherson, or else a fraud and a hoax that is a shame to Christianity has been attempted.

On July 1, she answered a long list of questions *The L.A. Times* had prepared concerning the illogic in her kidnapping story. She answered cleverly, raising the controversy to the level of religious war.

Mrs. McPherson, you have said you were ill, in a state of nervous
and physical collapse to a degree that kept you in bed . . . Making
all possible allowance for the exaltation due to the opportunity to
escape, your doubters say that one in such a condition of illness
could not have traveled a mile in the sun over the desert without
total collapse.

To this she responded:

You get in the same position, and pray to the same God and have
the same courage that I have, and you would do likewise. My life
and work are built along lines never duplicated by either man or
woman. Many have said that a woman could not have built Angelus
Temple and do these other seemingly impossible things—but I did.
Before judging that I would have collapsed, look at the things which
I have accomplished and at the courage back of it.

And in the pulpit she reminded the congregation that Daniel
had been kidnapped, and St. Stephen, and Shadrach, Meshach,
and Abednego. "Those three Hebrew children came out of the
fiery furnace, even hotter than the Sonora sun, without their
garments being singed!" Peter was kidnapped, and returned
with his strange tale. Jesus in effect was kidnapped, and found
himself in Pilate's court. She would soon compare Pilate's jurors
to the Los Angeles grand jury.

Meanwhile the district attorney was rounding up witnesses.
Keyes had little difficulty getting the grand jury's permission to
conduct a preliminary hearing. On July 6, Aimee and her
mother were subpoenaed. The purpose of the hearing, bear in
mind, was to investigate the kidnapping and indict the villains
who had abducted Aimee.

Sister Aimee now faced the most crucial decision of her career.
Aware of the doubts about her kidnapping story and the rumors
of a tryst with Ormiston, the evangelist had a choice. She could
cooperate with the grand jury, or she could withdraw into the
dignified silence guaranteed by the Fifth Amendment. Submitting her story to the interrogation of prosecutors provided the
chance of complete public vindication, but it also ran the risk
of embarrassment or, worse, criminal exposure. Silence would

heighten people's suspicions in the short run—but with no courtroom drama to increase newspaper circulation, the journalists would quickly turn away and find a more profitable scandal.

The newspapers made this perfectly clear when Aimee returned to Los Angeles. An editorial in *The Los Angeles Record* said:

> Let's forget it while we are still good neighbors and good friends. Let's leave the mystery of the whereabouts of Aimee Semple McPherson from May 18 to June 23 for time or Providence to reveal. At the worst, Mrs. McPherson is accused by rumor of a moral lapse, and of lying about it afterwards like a gentleman.

She could choose to forgive her kidnappers and ignore the subpoena. Minnie begged her to do this, begged her not to testify. Her lawyer, Roland Woolley, pleaded with her not to repeat her kidnapping story under oath before the grand jury. It was unnecessary to face the double-edged questions of the district attorney, unnecessary and extremely dangerous.

Aimee listened to her mother and her attorney, then turned around and did the opposite of what they advised. On the radio, in the newspapers, and from the pulpit she declared: "My story is true!" She challenged the district attorney to go out and round up the suspects, Steve, Jake, and Mexicali Rose; she taunted Asa Keyes and Joseph Ryan, his deputy, about their ineffectiveness.

And she agreed to testify before the grand jury. Of course Minnie would have to go along and make the best of it—*she* had nothing to hide.

Full of faith that God was on her side in this religious war, Aimee did not realize that she was walking into a meat grinder cranked in turns by the press, Fighting Bob Shuler, and the Los Angeles Chamber of Commerce. She had chosen a fatal course of action—heroic, hubristic, and self-destructive.

———

Aimee Semple McPherson arrived at the courthouse on July 8 in a light show of flashbulbs, to testify before the grand jury. She marched to the jury room down a hundred-foot pathway formed by a double line of Foursquare Crusaders dressed as she was, in white uniforms and Navy capes, all holding bibles and singing.

Minnie would follow her to the stand on July 13.

Grand juries customarily allow a great deal of freedom to prosecutors seeking an indictment. They are not governed by the rules of evidence and relevance that operate during a trial. Nevertheless, Asa Keyes's conduct during this hearing stunned his colleagues.

Aimee appeared as the injured party. But she had not been settled in her chair five minutes before the D.A. put her into the position of a defendant. Everyone in the courtroom was far more interested in the evangelist and her past than in the kidnapping.

"Mrs. McPherson, it has been stated to me on several occasions that, to use the expression we used to use, you were run out of Denver at one time. Is there anything to that?"

The evangelist, dumbfounded, looked from the prosecutor to the curious faces of the jury. At this point she must have realized, in a cold sweat, that she was in over her head.

Run out of Denver. Why, the citizens of Denver had all but crowned her queen. Now what could she do but deny she had been run out of Denver?

"Oh, no," she said, almost apologetically, sweetly, like someone correcting a venerable old person. "The mayor was on the platform . . . I might refer you to the mayor and to the business firms there and to Judge Ben Lindsey . . . And when I left, they gathered washbuckets of roses, and poured them in the room until I was ankle-deep in roses."

The jury showed no expression. The prosecutor continued, clearing his throat.

"Well then. Mrs. McPherson. It has been stated to me that you were once run out of a town, in northern California . . . forgive me. I have forgotten whether it was Oakland," and he waved his hand vaguely, "or some other place."

Aimee denied that she had been run out of Oakland.

"Then was it Fresno?" Keyes snapped at her.

All she could do was deny she had been run out of Oakland and Fresno, and offer to submit newspaper clippings proving her welcome in those cities.

Next the district attorney read from the press reports that Aimee was planning a world speaking tour.

He paused, looking from the jury to the evangelist.

"One of the reasons that you might have for pulling a stunt like this is for the purpose of getting worldwide advertising or publicity for the sake of helping you in your work."

And so it went. Minnie Kennedy, taking the stand on July 13, was well armed. She told the jury that when Aimee disappeared, she believed her daughter had been drowned, and nothing shook this belief until she heard Aimee's voice on the phone. (No commentator has ever seriously doubted this.) She assured Keyes that there was no mortgage on the Temple, and no insurance policy on Aimee's life. As far as her own relations with Aimee were concerned, Minnie said they were splendid, adding the wry and often quoted remark: "I boss her around considerably and try to keep her from getting into trouble."

This got a good laugh from everyone but Aimee. The two of them were in serious trouble. On July 20, the grand jury decided that evidence was lacking upon which anyone could be indicted for kidnapping. And on July 22, the newspapers began telling of a "love nest" in Carmel. Joseph Ryan and Chief of Detectives Herman Cline had turned up four witnesses who identified Aimee as the "Mrs. McIntyre" who had occupied a cottage with Kenneth Ormiston in May. They had found books with passages quoted in Aimee's sermons; they had discovered a grocery receipt with handwriting alleged to be in the evangelist's loopy style.

———

The schedule of services at the Temple and classes at the Bible College and Sunday school continued unabated.

The public furor only increased the devotion of Aimee's followers, who drew closer together in their need to defend the embattled pastor.

On the evening of July 26, Aimee held her "Devil's Convention." At the climax of her illustrated sermon a swarm of devils with horns, tails, and goatees leapt from a fiery, smoking pit in the stage, brandishing pitchforks. These devils the evangelist presented to the audience as kidnappers, district attorneys, certain ministers, and politicians. The audience laughed, and hissed and booed each one. And when the crowd's fury reached a bloodthirsty pitch, a flock of winged angels came swooping down on either side. As thousands cheered and applauded, the angels chased the devils back to Hell.

"Thank you. God bless you!" cried Sister Aimee. "If you believe my story," she whooped, "shout Hallelujah."

And five thousand people shouted Hallelujah.

"Now I am like David with Goliath's scalp on his belt!"

They believed her, and they would always believe her. But the larger public did not. On August 3, the grand jury reconvened to consider the evidence from Carmel, and the possibility of indicting Aimee for perjury or obstruction of justice. But by now even the jury had grown somewhat disgusted by the lawyers' behavior. During a recess, one of the jurors took exhibit A, the incriminating grocery receipt, in order to examine it in the light of the women's lavatory. Somehow the exhibit got flushed down the toilet, and with it the strongest support of Keyes's indictment was lost somewhere in the bowels of the Los Angeles sewer system.

That should have been the end of it. But a woman named Lorainne Wiseman, who had appeared as a witness in Aimee's defense, testifying that her sister had been the woman with Ormiston, was arrested on bad-check charges. Thinking the Temple might help her, Mrs. Wiseman asked Minnie for bail money September 10. When Minnie refused, Wiseman became very angry. She told Keyes that Aimee and Minnie had hired her, back in August, to perpetrate a hoax—to lie and tell the grand jury that her sister was the Mrs. X seen with Ormiston at the cottage in Carmel.

So on September 16 the district attorney issued warrants

against Mrs. McPherson, Mrs. Kennedy, Mrs. Wiseman, and Mr. Ormiston. The charges: corruption of public morals, obstruction of justice, and conspiracy to manufacture evidence.

The next day Minnie was arrested. Police took her from the parsonage to the Hall of Justice. There, surrounded by staring newsmen, detectives, and what she later called "courthouse loafers," she was arraigned. Dignified, furious, wearing her dark cloche hat and a black suit with a scalloped collar over a pale blouse, she sat in silence until she was released on bail.

Aimee was so sick, she could not appear. She stayed at the parsonage.

The worst was still to come.

Though it had taken only one week for the grand jury to dismiss the kidnapping charge, it would take six weeks to consider the criminal charges against Aimee and her mother.

The hearing opened in the courtroom of Judge Samuel R. Blake on September 27, 1926. The press and the public saw it for what it was—a feast of scandal. The city had constructed grandstands in Division 2 of the Los Angeles municipal court to accommodate the gaping crowds. They arrived at dawn with their breakfasts and lunches in paper bags. Scalpers bought reporters' passes and sold them for twenty-five dollars a day.

For six weeks the spectators listened to Joseph Ryan call Aimee a fake, a hypocrite, a liar in the courtroom; and the newspapers echoed the prosecutor in headlines two inches high. She was called a tart, a conspirator, a homewrecker. She watched as a parade of house detectives and chambermaids who thought they had seen her in the Ambassador Hotel with Ormiston pointed their fingers at her. She listened as a flock of others identified her as the Mrs. McIntyre of the Carmel love nest.

Attempts to establish a link between Ormiston and the evangelist between May 18 and June 23 were, under cross-examination, as strained, elaborate, and ultimately as ridiculous as Aimee's defense of the kidnapping story had been. But the crowd loved the show. There were letters and coded telegrams alleged to have passed between the lovers, and between Ormiston and Minnie, which did not hold up under forensic analysis. There were colorful witnesses who thought they had seen the "lovers" together, in Carmel and San Luis Obispo, though they had never seen them separately, before or since. And where had all these people been back in May, when any one of them might have picked up the telephone and collected the $25,000 reward by producing Aimee then?

By day she watched the slow progress of what she began to call her crucifixion. By night, from the pulpit and on the radio, she worked for the "Fight the Devil Fund" to raise money for her defense, the cost of which was approaching a hundred thousand dollars. She preached illustrated sermons like "March of the Martyrs" and "The Greatest Liar in Los Angeles." She fought back, writing a widely published newspaper serial copyrighted by the Editors' Feature Service. It was called "Saint Or Sinner?—Did I Go from Pulpit to Paramour?"

> It isn't me that my detractors hurt—they do not realize that they are striking at God in their attempt to pull down His temple . . . Already the wraths of Heaven are descending upon those who have accused me . . . It is not I, but they, the detractors of His servant, who will soon be in the Hades of torment . . . I am being crucified by the very bats of hell who have gone the limit in perfidy—brutal, conscienceless, hardly human . . .

A few pictures from this long nightmare capture the defendant's poise: stylish Aimee in her cloche hat, seated, surrounded by reporters asking her for the hundredth time if she had *really* been kidnapped. It begins to look like a choral scene from a musical comedy—wisecracking Aimee, swinging her crossed leg, repeating her answer in a voice that heralded Mae West:

That's my story, boys, and I'm sticking to it.

As they chased her, the reporters admired her style, loved her irony, her invincible good humor. From time to time she looked over a shoulder at them, as if to say *This is nothing more than a show. I have my part to play in it and you have yours. There need be no hard feelings.* The parsonage was open to the press day and night; the same journalists who ate from her pantry and drank her coffee in the morning wrote the worst lines about her at night.

Her insomnia was worse than ever. She would recall:

My couch was a rack of anguish. As long as I was able to bear the physical inactivity I would lie still, trying to take some much needed rest, wide sleepless eyes staring up into the blackness . . . Then I would get up and walk the long upstairs corridor, up and down, to and fro in ceaseless pacing . . .

A few images define the nature of the courtroom drama: Aimee removing her hat and raising her large hands to the mass of chestnut hair piled up in a shining hive on top of her head. All eyes were on her. Some witness's identification of Aimee as the lady she saw in Carmel hinged upon her certainty that the lady's long hair was not her own but a fake getup of auburn switches.

"Look," said the evangelist, "my hair is truly mine; I'll show you." As if the hair had been a symbol of woman's virtue itself.

She plunged her hands into the hair and in seconds she had freed it to fall luxuriantly, magnificently her own, down over her shoulders, nearly to her waist. The effect was almost as stunning as it would have been if she had taken off her clothes.

Such images, and a famous speech, capture the defendant's emotion during this largest legal proceeding of its kind in the history of California courts. The 3,500 pages of transcript include this statement the evangelist was permitted to make in her own defense:

I have tried to confine myself just to the questions, but I have had it on my heart all day that I would like to speak a word. I didn't know whether I would have the privilege to speak again, and I want to say that I realize that this story may sound strange to many of you, may be difficult for some of you to believe. It is difficult for me, sometimes, to believe; sometimes it seems that it must be just a dream. I would to God that it was; that I could wake up and pinch myself and know that it was not true. I realize that, and whether that was a part of the plan of it all, I want to say in my own behalf—I want to say if character counts a little and if a person's past life counts a little, then I want you to look back. Our family has a family of ministers on both sides. My mother gave me to God before I was born. My earliest training has been in Bible and religious work. As a little child I lined the chairs up and preached to them as early as five years of age, and gave my testimony. I was converted at 17, married an evangelist, preached the gospel in my

humble way at home and then sailed for China, never expecting to
come back to this land, but willing to give my life for Jesus. They
buried my precious husband there. I came back with my little baby
in my arms, born a month after her father died. I took up the Lord's
work again as soon as I was able to go on. I have had no great
denominations back of me, but have been inspired only by my love
for God and my love of the work, and of this precious Word, but
I began very humbly.

Now, until this crushing thing that none of us can explain why
even God would permit, although we cannot question like that—
it would be wrong to do that—before that came I was on the
pinnacle of success as far as my work for God was concerned, but
I have not always been there. I began preaching to farmers, ranchers,
under the trees to farmers in their blue overalls sitting on the grass
and using the piazza as a mourner's bench. From there, with the
$60 that came in the collection, I bought a little tent, a poor little
tent very full of holes, and from that I saved my money and bought
a bigger one, and that has been the history.

I have never put my money in oil wells or ranches or even clothes
or luxuries. My great thought has been always—and this can be
absolutely proven—for the service of the Lord and my dear people.
I am not saying this in any unkindness, but I would rather never
have been born than to have caused this blow to God's Word and
to his work. I had rather I had never been born or have seen the
light of day than that the name of Jesus Christ, whose name I love,
should be crucified and people would say, "There is Sister; she has
been preaching, and if her story is wrong"—that is the sad part to
me, not only my children should go through life and people say,
"See what her mother did," but the blow to my work is the greatest
thing.

The turn in my career came at the International Camp given at
Philadelphia. I could bring to you, I believe, hundreds of thousands
of letters and telegrams over the route from friends in different
cities, and during all those years no one has ever said that they saw
me out with a man, nor never has my name been linked in any
way with anyone like that. I don't believe that I have told lies or
cheated or done anything that people could put their finger on.

I traveled for two years with a tent. I drove my own stakes,
patched the tent and tied the guy ropes almost like a man. And
then came the time when we began to get bigger buildings and
theatres and buildings costing sometimes as much as $100 a day in
buildings where I have preached to as many as 16,000 in a day.

Then came the building of Angelus Temple. I came here to a
neighborhood that had no special buildings in it, got a piece of land

and hired horses and scrapers and bossed the men myself and went out to build the foundation myself with a little capital. I told people my dream to preach the gospel as God had given it to me, and they came to me to help me, not here, but from other cities through the "Bridal Call," my magazine. I have been here for years. I have visited the jails. We have workers in the penitentiary. We have appeared at almost every bedside we could reach in the county hospital, and at the county farm we journey each week to gather the old folks and preach for them. We preach at the shops and factories to men at noon. We have never turned anyone away but give free food and clothes. And my life, I feel, has been lived in a broad spotlight.

Naturally, I have preached a gospel which made some enmity. I have gone unmercifully after the dope ring, gambling, liquor, tobacco, dancing, and made the statement that I would rather see my children dead than in a public dance hall. I have perhaps laid myself open to enmity in those lines about evils in the schools, et cetera, but in everything, I have tried to live as a lady and as a Christian, and I just want one more thought—it is so kind of you to grant me this opportunity. It does mean so much. I will feel happier for having said it. The thought is that one should doubt my story. Perhaps you are skeptical; I don't blame anyone, because it does sound absurd, but it did happen, ladies and gentlemen.

Suppose one should doubt it; a trained investigator, it would seem to me, would need but look for a month, so would I get by? As one said who was here at this moment, they couldn't think of any other reason than that I might be insane. I would not work with one hand for seventeen years, and just as I saw my dearest dreams coming true, sweep it over, and not only that, but attempt to heal little babies in Christ who were too weak to stand.

Motive? If I were sick—someone said, "Maybe she went away to rest"—but it was not that; I had just passed an examination for life insurance a while ago and they said I passed 100 percent.

Amnesia? It could not be that. I am willing to have my mind examined or any test that could be put on that.

And as for falling in love, I am in love with the work I do.

There might be a baser motive. I almost blush to mention it in the jury room, but some might think of it. They say the waters of the mind are like the waters of the sea, that cast up strange things, and that I might be in trouble of some sort, and had to go away and come back. I would like to say, although I apologize for having to mention such a thing, that I had a thorough examination upon coming home, although that was not necessary, as the history of my case for twelve years back would show that such a thing would be absolutely out of the question.

On November 3, Judge Blake bound over Aimee Semple McPherson and her mother Minnie Kennedy for trial in Superior Court. The charge was "criminal conspiracy to commit acts injurious to public morals and to prevent and obstruct justice," which threatened "the peace and dignity of the People of the State of California." The women were held for trial on three counts that carried a maximum prison sentence of forty-two years.

Aimee's trial touched off backstage intrigues that resulted in two mysterious deaths, a San Quentin sentence for Asa Keyes, and the impeachment of Judge Carlos Hardy. The untimely deaths of Aimee's attorney Russell A. McKinley (found in a car overturned in a ditch, August 25) and a "go-between," Dr. A. M. Waters (suicide, September 15), suggest Mob involvement.

It is said that William Randolph Hearst greatly admired Sister Aimee and wanted to help her. Just before the trial date, Hearst's *Examiner* reported that Keyes had decided to drop the charges —before this idea had occurred to the district attorney. Keyes denied the report, but suddenly learned that he had a big problem. His chief witness for the prosecution, the "whirligig of lying" Lorainne Wiseman, changed her story once again on December 29. After further consideration, Mrs. Wiseman decided that Aimee did *not* hire her in August to perpetrate a hoax.

So the government had no case.

On January 10, 1927, Keyes asked the court to dismiss the criminal charges against Aimee and Minnie, because he could no longer vouch for his chief witness.

Aimee was free.

"Let her be judged," said Keyes, "in the only court of her jurisdiction—the court of public opinion."

The court of public opinion, viewed from the eminence of 1993, was not kind. But it has not been so cruel as Division 2 of the Los Angeles municipal court, which held the evangelist up for ridicule and ignominy for half the year of 1926.

The public had as little faith in the kidnapping story as the grand jury. This hurt Aimee. Fighting Bob Shuler, and anyone else it pleased, could call her a liar in public. A lot of people did that, until it grew tiresome, and then they stopped.

Most of Aimee's followers believed that she had been kidnapped; she told them so, over and over. Some of her more critical followers felt constrained to accept the kidnapping story as poetry rather than fact. Of course Sister had been kidnapped—kidnapped at birth by the Salvation Army, kidnapped by Robert Semple and the Pentecostal movement, kidnapped by roaring mobs of the lame, blind, and deaf, who held her hostage for her healing power, kidnapped by destiny and held for ransom in the Temple she had built for the glory of Christ, until at last she had no life she might call her own. Then somebody or other kidnapped her at Ocean Park. She was drugged, and the drug damaged her liver.

That Aimee herself believed in the kidnapping, as poetry or as history, we are in no position to question. It had become a tenet of faith, with all its eccentricities and inconsistencies. Everyone who has studied the case, from its shocking beginning to its pathetic end, has remarked on this significant fact: Aimee's kidnapping story, with its goofy characters Rose, Steve, and Jake, and its melodramatic plot, *is the only story that did not change.* The prosecutors, detectives, and reporters had a million changing stories, and they all tried to get Aimee to change hers. They urged her to retract it or at least admit that she might not have remembered parts of the tale correctly. They challenged her, laughed at her, bullied her. They hammered to break her down. But then she would delve a little deeper and come up with some solution, ingenious or wacky, to resolve the contradictions and make the story come out right. "That's my story," she would say, smiling brightly, driving them a little nearer madness, "and I'm sticking to it." Any lesser woman caught in a lie (said many observers) would have fallen apart under the kind of exami-

nation she faced, hour after hour, day after day, with her head
held high. She could not possibly have defended the kidnapping
story so courageously if it had not become an article of faith.

Sister Aimee roused everyone's passions. For the first time
now she sparked the interest of the "intellectual" press—*The
Nation, The New Republic, The New Statesman,* even *The American Mercury's* editor, H. L. Mencken. The sage of Baltimore
admired her courage and intelligence, and took her part against
"the Babbitts" of L.A. who he believed were persecuting her.
She had made good on her prophecy "to split the country wide
open," dividing public opinion so clearly, her contemporaries
felt obliged to believe the kidnapping story *or* believe Aimee
had been frolicking in sin with Ormiston. To believe the one
thing was to disbelieve the other.

But in truth the majority who enjoyed the two stories believed
neither of them. Many of Aimee's supporters doubted her kidnapping tale. They loved her anyway. Hardly anyone in America following the details of the testimony could believe the
snarled evidence that suggested Aimee was the woman hiding
with Ormiston in Carmel. But they liked to think of the pretty
evangelist having a lover, rolling in adulterous sheets; they liked
to muse, and fume, and dream on it.

One more word on this subject. The idea that we must either
accept the kidnapping story in every detail or reject it entirely
is absurd. The lawyers preparing the case understood this. If
the evangelist was kidnapped and drugged on May 18 (as no
one has ever been able to disprove) and held prisoner, then it
was certainly a traumatic experience, a harrowing of Hell. And
victims of trauma are not always reliable narrators of their horror. Aimee's story might well be her psyche's defense against
a reality that was worse.

VINDICATION

She must have known the case would be dismissed.

On New Year's Eve, Keyes pledged the trial would go on; on New Year's Day, 1927, Aimee announced from the pulpit her plans for a nationwide "vindication tour." This stunned Minnie. She thought it was a foolish idea, drawing media attention to a subject that ought to be allowed to die.

The events of 1926 had damaged Aimee and Minnie in different ways. Aimee was hurt, angry, and profoundly disillusioned. The extent to which she was disillusioned with herself and the choices she had made, no one can tell. Her religious faith was unshakable. But she was surely disappointed with the public who for so many years had seemed to consider her God's darling, taintless and beyond reproach. She had been pulled down on the ground to fight, and got dirty.

Minnie, on the other hand, had started out cynical; the catastrophe of 1926 only made her a little more cynical, and conservative, and terribly weary. She was fifty-five years old. Her impulse was to trim the sails, focus on the Temple membership, and keep a low profile until Aimee had solidified public confidence.

Aimee's desire, predictably, was to use the new publicity to preach the Gospel. Like Barnum, she understood the principle that "there is no such thing as bad publicity." She had been well known before 1926, before her name appeared in headlines daily the world over. When she disappeared, only the Los Angeles papers reported the loss; but the whole world heralded her return. Now she was a celebrity, the most famous woman in America, with a stain upon her reputation she thought to erase by means of a transcontinental lecture tour. She would lecture, dramatically, on the "Story of My Life," with the added chapter about her kidnapping.

In this venture Aimee had the encouragement of Ralph Jordan, a former reporter for Hearst's *Los Angeles Examiner*. Jordan, a tall husky chain-smoker with curly red hair, had become indispensable to Aimee during the hearings. He had helped her deal with the press, intervening with Hearst on the evangelist's behalf. Aimee preferred Jordan's advice to her own chief counsel's, much to Minnie's dismay, because Minnie was paying several attorneys ten thousand dollars apiece to handle the defense. By January the fast-talking Jordan was on the Angelus Temple payroll as the personal road manager of Aimee's vindication tour.

"Get off the front pages," Minnie told her daughter.

Ignoring her mother's advice, Aimee left with her entourage on a three-month lecture tour beginning in January in Colorado, Nebraska, Kansas, Missouri, Illinois, and Ohio. Reporters followed her everywhere. Aimee answered whatever questions they put to her, frankly, wittily, and without inhibition. She talked about divorce, green bathing suits, morality—and as the clippings arrived in the mail at Angelus Temple, Minnie shook her head. The board of elders grew more and more distressed over their leader's shocking candor.

Minnie sent slender Gladwyn Nichols, an assisting minister and head of the music department, to catch up with Aimee's party in Lancaster, Pennsylvania. To keep him company, Minnie also sent little Churchilla Bartling, a smiling, round-faced nurse who often helped with invalids at church services. The idea was for these Temple officials to accompany Aimee's worldly, cigar-smoking, poker-playing entourage to Baltimore, Washington, and New York, and keep an eye on her *in loco parentis*.

In the anteroom of Aimee's hotel suite, Ralph Jordan and his assistant James Kendrick sat in their shirt-sleeves, playing cards and drinking whiskey with several reporters. These men took one look at sad Gladwyn Nichols and smiling Churchilla Bartling and told them to go away.

Nichols squared his narrow shoulders and told them where he had come from. And, as he later said to Minnie, "I walked through their midst like Moses through the Red Sea."

So he and nurse Bartling became a part of the Sister Aimee entourage that included Jordan, Kendrick, Emma Schaffer, Mae Waldron, and a woman called Bertha Daughter. Really, Aimee was safely chaperoned before the arrival of the nurse and the choirmaster, who made little impression upon the evangelist. She made an enormous impression upon *them*, however—Nichols and Bartling could not for the life of them get over the change they saw in Sister Aimee.

She had cut her hair. It was marcelled in tight curls around her face and done up in a peak high on her head. In her fine clothes she looked like a movie star, slender and artfully made up with lipstick, face powder, and mascara.

As they moved from hotel to hotel in Baltimore, Washington, and New York, the floating card game created a checkpoint outside Aimee's quarters. Nichols observed, with dismay, that clergy and friends from the old tent-meeting days were turned away from Aimee's chamber with the same brusque manners that had greeted him and nurse Bartling when they arrived from Los Angeles. A lot of cash was lying around.

When the good Nichols complained to Aimee that her new managers were worldly and had not accepted Jesus Christ as their savior, she listened. She said she had noticed they smoked, played poker, and drank bourbon in her anteroom, and did certain other things one might consider unfamiliar to a Christian atmosphere. Then she told Nichols that these men had helped her "when you people at the Temple couldn't." And there was not much he could say to that.

The tour received mixed notices, because the public did not really know what to make of it. Opinion about the evangelist was sharply divided already, and the way Jordan promoted Aimee only added to the confusion about her image. At first he booked her for a portion of ticket sales. When they failed to sell enough tickets, they threw open the doors and reverted to passing the plate. The problem was, she was not conducting a revival service. She was doing a one-woman show called "The Story of My Life," which climaxed in the kidnapping account and prayers for the deliverance of the modern world from kidnappers, district attorneys, and Darwin—all opponents of

old-time religion and the Good Book. (Aimee's popular autobiography *In the Service of the King*, Boni & Liveright, August
1927, is a literary version of her theater production.) The Boston
Ministerial Association voted to boycott this lecture, so Aimee
stayed out of Boston. In many cities she packed large theaters,
and moved people to tears and laughter with a narrative gift
similar to the stage magic of Lily Tomlin and Spalding Gray.

————

She arrived in New York on February 18, in a full-length fur
coat and a broad-brimmed slouch hat, a beaded bag on her arm.
Reporters surrounded her as she stepped from the train.

Removing the fur in the lobby of the Hotel McAlpin, she
revealed a yellow suit with buttons and collar of white fur, so
exquisitely tailored, it got its own note on the society pages.

"The world is wearing seven-league boots today," she told
The New York Times, "but the Church goes right on tripping
along in slippers. No wonder our young people are carried along
in the ever-churning whirlpool of this world's tawdry pleasures."

That night the crusader took the battle into enemy territory,
as she had done years before in Winnipeg when she toured the
dance halls and brothels, and in San Diego when she preached
in the boxing ring. Dressed in an evening gown and surrounded
by journalists flashing photographs as she stepped in and out of
her limousine, Sister Aimee visited the New York speakeasies.

On West 54th Street was the Three Hundred Club of Texas
Guinan, "queen of the nightclubs." This statuesque saloon
keeper, a brazen enemy of the Volstead Act, brought a flavor
of the Wild West and southern rebellion to the sophisticated
night life of the roaring twenties. Her long-legged chorus line
kicked and shimmied to hot jazz on a dance floor crowded by
tables. Mobsters rubbed elbows with politicians, athletes, and
captains of industry. As a local character Tex was as much
admired as "playboy" mayor Jimmy Walker, enjoying Tam-
many Hall's humorous indulgence.

Tex found Sister Aimee a good table amidst the revels, and
brought her a glass of water.

A reporter shouted in Tex's ear it might be a good idea to invite the famous woman to stand up and say a word to the patrons of the Three Hundred Club. And Tex nodded, agreeing it would be a good idea for both of them, for all of them.

Aimee, demure, dignified, stone sober, would be delighted to speak. She left her table and stood in the center of the dance floor, smiling until everyone was quiet.

> Behind all these beautiful clothes, behind these good times, in the midst of your lovely buildings and shops and pleasures, there is another life. There is something on the other side. "What shall it profit a man if he gain the whole world, and lose his own soul?" With all your getting and playing and good times, do not forget you have a Lord. Take Him into your hearts.

It was just that simple, short and sweet. There was a silence in which newsmen could scarce hear a glass clink, or the rattle of a bracelet. The revelers weighed the words and waited to see if Sister Aimee was finished. It was a strange moment, lifted out of time. They were not lost souls, mostly; they were just out for a few laughs, and the little evangelist had touched them somehow, caught them off guard. All at once they applauded, and Tex put her arm around Aimee. The clapping went on for much longer than her speech had taken.

Aimee got away with it for the same reason she had succeeded with the Klansmen, Gypsies, and the prize-fight crowd: because she did not judge them. In half a dozen sentences she broke through the flimsy barrier that separated them from her, from each other, and from the Lord. So for a precious moment He was among them, in the silence just before the applause. Then she sat down.

Aimee knew exactly what she was doing. This turned out to be one of the most effective publicity teasers of her career: The Evangelist in the Speakeasy. The newspapers played it for all it was worth, mentioning Aimee's call to the revelers, and her invitation to the whole city of New York, to come hear her at the Glad Tidings Tabernacle at 325 West 33rd Street.

She was beating the drum as she had in 1919. But this was

1927 and her image was slightly tarnished. What Aimee may not have anticipated was the backfire that worried Minnie, who read the clippings in Los Angeles. For every reader thrilled by the evangelist's great victory over the Devil, there was a reader thrilled by the Devil's little victory over Aimee. Rumors flew: that she had been all too comfortable in Tex's joint, that she had been smoking, drinking, dancing.

"Get off the front pages," said Minnie between her teeth.

What Ma Kennedy did not understand is that her daughter was entering the last phase of a ministry dedicated to tearing down the walls between religion and secular life, between lost souls and the redeemed. She was making way for a new spiritual possibility in the twentieth century. It was in the tradition of John Wesley and William Booth; emotional, combinative, head-butting missionary work. Aimee was doing essentially what she had done from the first. Folks were horrified she had cut her hair? Soon enough they would see that salvation is not a matter of *hair*. Folks were horrified she had gone to a *night club*? They should have seen Hong Kong in 1910. In 1927 Sister Aimee was living the paradox of the evangelist who is also a fundamentalist. A born evangelist, she knew that she must dress for the weather in order to save souls, dress sometimes at the expense of Scripture; and she knew this would shock and dismay the more parochial of her fundamentalist brethren.

The New York Times rhapsodized over her performance at the Glad Tidings Tabernacle:

> Her voice is a full-throated contralto and her enunciation in quick speech is excellent. No actress sounds more clearly the last letters or takes advantage of vowels and diphthongs with greater effect. She has a large expressive mouth, even teeth and brown eyes that flash or are luminous with tears at will . . .

Paxton Hibben of *The New Yorker* did not agree. The writer had loved the spectacle of Tex Guinan and Aimee Semple McPherson arm-in-arm on the Three Hundred Club dance floor. So the magazine sent their ace satirist around to the Glad Tidings Tabernacle to "send up" Sister Aimee in a short profile.

It was the perfect *New Yorker* assignment, the sort that would inflate the fledgling magazine's circulation among middle-brow sophisticates. Editor Harold Ross was sure the marcelled evangelist would be a perfect target for the arrows of Paxton Hibben's cynicism.

Hibben's essay, titled "Aimee and Tex," is an important projection from the prism of Aimee's persona in 1927. She meant different things to different people. To the hard-boiled readers of *The New Yorker*, she *had* to be a fraud; she was making too much money to be a fool. In "Aimee and Tex," one senses a genuine animus at work. Hibben says he "prefers Tex," but that hardly does justice to his feelings.

> Aimee's mouth is very large indeed, her nose long and bumpy, her eyes small and ever-shifting. She is generous-breasted and broad-hipped, though the middle-aged spread is hidden by the cape she wears. Her legs belong to the school known as piano.
>
> For three days crowds packed the narrow quarters of this ugly, out-of-the-way church of an obscure sect . . . Men and women stood ankle-deep in slush for hours, with rain and snow beating upon them, merely to hear Sister Aimee's piercing voice through amplifiers or to see her pass quickly in and out of her limousine. Pasty-faced young men wearing ushers' badges for once in their uneventful lives became individuals of high importance . . .
>
> The crowd in the Glad Tidings Tabernacle (or outside it) was nothing to her. She was after the newspaper men—with soft soap and honeyed words and her widest smile and "God bless them." And she got them. And never once, in prayer or sermon, did she for a single instant take her mind off the dear, dear friends in Radio Land . . .
>
> When the Rev. Robert A. Brown called upon his congregation "to go over the top" in providing funds to pay the expenses of Sister Aimee, she felt somehow that he was not doing that important job in quite the most effective way. So she took it away from him. It was Sister Aimee herself who exhibited the ten-dollar bill that the janitor of the church had slipped into her hand—and she did it just before the contribution baskets were passed.

And so it goes. Hibben is delighted when a news photographer's flash fails him at a critical moment. Aimee had struck a famous pose, one hand stretched toward Heaven, the other

clutching her bible to her bosom. Some sixth sense informed
her of the technical failure. So Aimee worked herself around
once more and, "clasping her bible to her ample bosom, faced
the balcony again with upraised arm. This time the flashlight
went off without a hitch."

The New Yorker has nothing to say about the kidnapping
debacle. By the spring of 1927 the "intellectual" press—H. L.
Mencken, Morrow Mayo, *The Nation*, and *The New Republic*
—stood shoulder to shoulder with the evangelist in her war
against the boosters of Los Angeles. It was considered unfash-
ionable to question her morals.

———

Mother Kennedy began preparing the Foursquare congregation
for the eventuality that their pastor might not return to her
pulpit.

"We have heard that she is finding work enough to do to
keep her busy indefinitely." This was true. Aimee was lecturing
to full houses in Florida and Texas, and she had bookings
enough to keep her on the road for years. Minnie might have
to continue without her. So before Aimee's return on March
31, after her tour of twenty-two cities in three months, Minnie
was taking the necessary steps.

Returning to the Temple, Aimee was met with hand-clapping
and hallelujahs. A review of the Sunday service in the *L.A.
Times* describes her as "the very epitome of success," indicating
that the newspaper had put aside the old scandal as she "sailed
down the runway with arms full of roses, her hair, with that
famous glint of gold-red, perfectly marcelled."

AIMEE VS. MINNIE, 1927

Four days later, Aimee moved out of the parsonage.

She took Rolf and Roberta, three secretaries, and two Filipino servants to stay at Mae Waldron's house at Ocean Park. The newspapers reported a quarrel. Minnie had conveyed to her daughter the congregation's concern over the pastor's hairdo, makeup, and new clothes; Aimee had in turn asked Minnie to hand over the checkbooks and Temple records to her and Ralph Jordan, and resign as business manager. Minnie thought that was a terrible idea, and said so.

Minnie had the support of Gladwyn Nichols, the choir, and several of the Temple's board. On her side Aimee had the force of her personality and the drawing power of her name.

One night, while Aimee was in the pulpit preaching, Minnie called the board together and urged them to curtail the pastor's authority. Aimee walked in on this scene. According to Rolf McPherson, his mother was so stunned that she fainted. After being revived, she announced to the board that she had no desire to fight with them. If they wanted her to step aside, she would. She would start over elsewhere, and let Minnie Kennedy keep the Temple.

As Aimee made for the door, several Church elders urged her to stay. At this point she issued the ultimatum: Either the board approved her conduct—past, present, and future—or she would retire from Angelus Temple's pulpit. Ballots were passed around the meeting room, asking: Did I do right in pursuing my case in court? Did I do right in making this tour and taking Ralph Jordan as manager? Will it be right for me to go on tour again and take him along?

Aimee won her vote of confidence. This confirmed Ralph Jordan's rule over Minnie Kennedy. When the board endorsed Jordan, Minnie stormed out of the meeting.

Gladwyn Nichols led the choir, the orchestra, and several hundred congregation members in a secession to start his own church one mile from the "changed" Temple.

"The God of the Gospels is being replaced at Angelus Temple by the God of materialism. When Mrs. McPherson bobbed her hair, she hurt her followers terribly. Bobbing of the hair is not according to the Scriptures," said the choirmaster.

As always, Minnie's concerns were more practical than doctrinal. She and Aimee were equal partners in the legal entity called the Echo Park Evangelistic Association, but she had arranged it so that much of the property was in her name and she had control of the funds. She announced:

> My daughter's like a fish on the beach when it comes to handling money. I don't believe if you put an ad in the newspapers you could find anybody dumber when it comes to business. All they got to do is let her have her way for a year, and she'll bankrupt the place, mark my words.

Her words were prophetic.

For the next three years Minnie Kennedy struggled to help her daughter while Aimee kept pushing her mother away, like a drowning woman fighting a lifeguard. When the choir walked out, Minnie did an about-face. She reaffirmed her loyalty to the embattled pastor. Before Aimee departed for the Midwest in May, she and Minnie had pulled the congregation together, and Minnie was again in control. But this renewed union lasted only a few months.

Minnie was prepared to resign, and Aimee wanted her out. The conflict over control ran much deeper than money. Aimee might have bought her mother's share of the Association very coolly and quietly; that is not the way it happened.

It was not enough that Minnie offered to resign, step down, go on a long-deserved vacation. Had she told Aimee behind closed doors that she would *never* abandon her daughter to the depredations of the likes of Ralph Jordan? Under the influence of Jordan, Aimee set the stage for a dramatic break. She did not want a tentative verbal separation in the summer of 1927; she wanted a legal divorce.

So she issued statements to the press:

> She is my mother and I love her. I have the greatest admiration for her and for all her invaluable services to me during the last eighteen long years. There is no trouble between us. My mother signified her intention of retiring long ago. She deserves a good rest, and she shall have one.

And then she permitted a series of "suggestions" to be issued by a committee of the Church board, as follows:

> 1. Mrs. Kennedy might remain with honor and respect as the evangelist's mother.
> 2. Mrs. Kennedy might tour the world at the expense of the Church, who would, we believe, contribute to the fund for a vacation so well deserved.
> 3. Mrs. Kennedy might permanently entertain work of her own in other fields as she has suggested.
> 4. Mrs. Kennedy might return to her wealthy husband, Mr. W. Whittebeck, who is a well-to-do engineer on a big Hudson River liner.

Like most of the Angelus Temple memorandums, this one got immediately into the newspapers.

Minnie blew up. Blind with rage, she was quoted as saying she would "break Sister, crush her, and drive her from every pulpit in America . . ." Aimee would have no cash and the Temple would go into the hands of a receiver. Minnie told the staff she would "drive Sister to her knees." She refused to comment on W. Whittebeck, knowing she had grounds for a libel action, having never married any steamboat engineer named Whittebeck. As for the other ultimatums, demanding that Minnie get far away from Angelus Temple and its ledgers, the evangelist's mother said:

> When my daughter gets ready to come to me and talk these things over, some thought will be given to them. But this so-called "com-

mittee," who never has had nor ever will have a legal position of authority in this temple, is not going to dictate my course.

She was right, as usual. Minnie owned half of everything they had built together, and any "divorce" would have to be worked out legally between them. She held on as long as she could, while the relationship deteriorated. From the pulpit Aimee announced that Minnie had neglected to sign the payroll checks (where Aimee was also a qualified signatory), implying that Minnie was spiteful or incompetent. Finally she said that doubt of the kidnapping story "was driving them both out of the Temple"; eventually she refused to see her mother except in the presence of an attorney.

No sooner would they enter a conference room with their lawyers than Aimee would call for a whole watermelon and a pitcher of lemonade. With a flourish she'd begin carving up the watermelon, and handing it around, and working away at removing the seeds with wonderful concentration. Now and then she would interrupt the absorbing business of eating the watermelon in order to drink a tumbler of lemonade, throwing back her head and gulping it as her neck muscles worked, then gasping and wiping her mouth daintily with a napkin. Minnie fumed, and the attorneys looked on admiringly.

"Watermelons and lemonade have broken up every conference we have ever had to settle this matter," wailed Minnie Kennedy.

On August 11, 1927 Minnie presented her resignation, and her claims. She insisted upon a fifty-fifty split of all property in return for quitting the Echo Park Association. The exact terms of the settlement were never to be disclosed. This was part of the "gag rule" that applied to the conflict between the women. Minnie received about a hundred thousand dollars in property and cash; Aimee received equal value in canceled checks representing the cost of her defense in the criminal case.

Ma Kennedy moved out of the parsonage. For a few months she rented an apartment on Le Moyne Street a half block away, on the other side of the Bible College, near enough so she could keep an eye on things.

———

On October 20, 1927, this obituary appeared in *The Woodstock Sentinel Review*:

> The death occurred this morning of a well-known resident of the Salford district in the person of James Kennedy, aged 85 years. The deceased had lived the greater part of his life in the Salford district, and for that reason was very widely known. His home was about one mile west of the village. He had been in poor health for some time. Two daughters, Mrs. Joseph Sabine and Mrs. McPherson, survive, the former residing at Fort Erie. The address of the latter could not be learned. The widow also survives.

Aimee had not seen her father in many years. Nowhere in her writing does she mention his death. She did not attend the funeral.

———

What Minnie saw, from her exile on Le Moyne Street, was her worst nightmare come true.

Aimee quickly reorganized the Church, with herself as the supreme authority over an eight-member "board of control," the heads of the Temple's seven departments. She was entirely in charge of the departments' financial affairs, while the board decided Church policy by majority vote. Thus the board became a shadow group, with less influence than a board of advisers, because she was paying them.

Ralph Jordan became Aimee's business manager.

Rolf McPherson and others argue that Aimee never initiated the harebrained business schemes that followed, almost bankrupting the Temple. Anxious to expand the work of the Church, she was pathetically gullible. Wouldn't it be wonderful if the Church had its own hotel to house out-of-town visitors? Wouldn't it be lovely to have a mountain retreat, so the Foursquare congregation could praise the Lord while vacationing together? And what about a beautiful memorial cemetery for the members the Lord was taking away, instead of burying

Foursquare members all over Southern California? The "wish list" continued to grow.

Promoters told Sister Aimee these dreams would come true if only she signed this paper, that paper. She trusted lawyers. Rolf recalls that the lawyers would shove folio-length contracts at her even as she stepped down, soaked with sweat, from the pulpit, full of the glory of the Holy Ghost and utterly defenseless. In that condition, Rolf argues, she signed things without reading them, just like signing an autograph. The Blessed Hope Memorial Park came to her when she was in such a state. The idea looked like one thing when realtors proposed it in hushed tones and half lighting—and like something entirely different, a gross exploitation of her name, when it appeared in garish brochures and display ads in the newspapers.

Minnie Kennedy called it "Aimee's boneyard." Somebody convinced Jordan and the pastor to purchase a fourteen-acre parcel of ground in a cemetery at Burbank. Aimee would build a magnificent crypt for her own family. A team of salesmen stood ready to hustle plots on commission. Members of the congregation were to purchase burial plots at prices that increased the closer they lay to Aimee's crypt, the nearest neighbors selling for $250. Salesmen worked the crowds in the Angelus Temple lobby, reciting the sales slogan: "Go up with Aimee!"

It was tasteless and expensive. Minnie could have told them it wouldn't work. Blessed Hope Cemetery was the first and one of the more embarrassing fiascos that led to the Temple's financial crisis in the mid-thirties.

The graveyard failed miserably, after Aimee advanced the money for the land, promotion, and real estate commissions, thousands of dollars she could not recover. Like a gambler desperate to make up for the loss, she became even more vulnerable to the next silly idea, and the next.

In July of 1928 she hoped to start a summer camp for her followers on donated land near Lake Tahoe. This in itself was not a bad idea, though the packaging, in brochures and ads that read "Vacation with Aimee," furthered the evangelist's image as a shameless self-promoter. The land was donated on the condition that Aimee build a tabernacle there that summer; a team of salesmen would sell adjacent lots to members of the congregation.

The camp, however, was too far from Los Angeles. Aimee's followers could not afford the railroad fare to vacation far from home. And the land was too expensive. Only a hundred people accepted invitations to go to the grand opening that summer, the ground-breaking for the tabernacle.

The real estate promoters hired caterers to feed seven thousand. It was the miracle of the loaves and fishes turned inside out: two tons of meat, seventy-five gallons of ice cream, and a thousand doughnuts were left rotting, melting, and hardening on the railroad station platform in Lake Tahoe.

Altogether Aimee sold seven lots. Failing to build the tabernacle, failing to sell enough land to pay off the realtors who had been advanced so many thousands of dollars, the promoters faced $70,000 worth of lawsuits for breach of contract and another $150,000 in a class action suit for "obtaining money from her congregation under false pretenses." Because the promoters were broke, Aimee was named in the lawsuit. She was in a bind, having committed to renting Royal Albert Hall for upcoming meetings in England at $1,000 per day. It was determined that returning dollar for dollar to creditors and complainants would actually cost $10,000. When the land developer agreed to settle out of court for that amount so Sister Aimee could clear her name and go ahead with her trip, she paid the money. "She was innocent of any willful dishonesty beyond a shadow of a doubt," agreed the attorneys. Still it was embarrassing.

And so unnecessary. Aimee was preaching magnificently twenty times a week. But as fast as the money poured into the collection plates, it leaked out again, into the pockets of land sharks and shyster lawyers, every crony of Ralph Jordan who came along with a sweet-sounding scheme to get rich quick, or with a sob story for a handout. And the payroll of Angelus Temple was now approaching seven thousand dollars a week.

At the same time Sister Aimee launched the ill-starred real estate projects, she was beginning a nationwide expansion of the Foursquare Church.

She had a vision, in the early months of 1928, that her Church would be transformed into a worldwide "Salvation Navy." Consecrated to the Salvation Army at birth, the swimming preacher was bound to hit upon the idea sooner or later. An architect's model of the new headquarters appeared in the Temple lobby. Rising from artificial rocks, the hundred-and-fifty-foot "lighthouse" would have a revolving beacon at the top for guiding lost souls to Salvation.

There are some funny pictures of Admiral Aimee and her staff and their children, dressed in Navy uniforms, with middie caps and blouses. But the crew squabbled over questions of rank, and some folks thought the outfits looked silly. At last the United States Navy complained to the L.A. district attorney that Aimee was abusing the Navy's uniform. So, when she had got all the publicity she could from it, she ordered everybody back into their civilian clothes.

But the lighthouse idea survived. During 1928, Foursquare lighthouses, with little towers and live beacons on the top, sprang up all over the country.

———

On board the S.S. *Aquitania* in New York Harbor, Aimee faced the reporters in September of 1928. She was bound for Cherbourg and Paris, for a little vacation before her campaign in England.

The journalists found her confident despite the months of public pressure she had endured. Her responses to their questions were quick and sometimes brilliant. This was the occasion of her famous comment on her religious appeal: "I bring consolation to the great middle class, leaving those below to the Salvation Army, and those above to themselves."

The reporters on deck were eager to hear Sister Aimee's opinion of Al Smith, the Catholic candidate for president. Fundamentalists were consolidating their anti-Catholic followers by bashing Al Smith, "the Pope's candidate." Robert Shuler, for one, had cast his lot with the Ku Klux Klan, and took every opportunity to malign or ridicule the Catholic who was running against Herbert Hoover. A sentence of anti-Smith sentiment from Aimee Semple McPherson would have been a banner headline. She would not stoop to it. Morrow Mayo applauds her restraint: during a crisis in her career, when she needed the support that would have come from attacking the Catholic, she would not do it. She was the *only* fundamentalist, said Mayo, who could resist that temptation, and did resist it.

"I am not against Al Smith," she said firmly. "I simply don't know him." She would be in England on election day. But if she were to vote, she said, she would cast her ballot for Hoover.

The English tour was a mixed success, reflecting the change in Aimee's image. While in Paris, she learned a movement was afoot across the Channel to exclude her as an undesirable alien. The home secretary considered and reconsidered, without acting to exclude her, which would be playing into the hands of press agents who had already reaped a bonanza over the controversy. This furor helped her to sell out Albert Hall, where she was both cheered and heckled.

Bea Lillie was in the audience, and Tallulah Bankhead, and other famous actresses who admired Sister Aimee's stage presence. Aimee had seen Tallulah's rehearsals for *This Year of Grace* as the actress's guest. Now, after her revival in Albert Hall, the actresses prevailed upon Aimee to ride with them in their car to Southampton, to attend a sailing party for Bea Lillie. This caused a scandal in the newspapers. They called it "Mrs. McPherson's all-night joy ride," to which she replied, sweetly: "I wanted to give a bible to Miss Lillie. She was ever so grateful."

In England, Aimee received word that a friend was in trouble at home. Judge Carlos Hardy had become the target of an impeachment probe. Hardy had been associated with Angelus Temple since the early twenties, when he was involved with the lawsuit against the Santa Ana church. The judge became a friend and confidant, lecturing at youth meetings and over the airwaves of KFSG, dispensing both legal and personal advice to Temple members. Hardy had turned the first spadeful of earth for the Bible College groundbreaking, and he advised Aimee during the grand jury proceedings of 1926.

Now he had fallen from political favor—and his impeachment would focus on his conduct during those proceedings.

Returning from England to Hardy's trial in California, Aimee would have to relive the ordeal of 1926. As one assemblyman declared during the impeachment debate, Judge Hardy's trial would be, in effect, the trial of Aimee Semple McPherson. Indeed, that case, dragging on through New Year's and the winter of 1929, must have seemed like a nightmare déjà vu, as the same old witnesses appeared and their testimony was sifted once more in the courtroom and the newspapers. This time the evidence was supposed to prove the judge's participation in the crimes of McPherson *et al.*; but since Aimee had been acquitted of wrongdoing, the impeachment was really just a pretext for trying the evangelist once again. It was one last chance to get even with the woman who had made a mockery of the California judicial system.

Judge Hardy was acquitted on all counts, but not before Sister Aimee suffered the same humiliation she had endured in 1926. Day after day she sat in the Sacramento courtroom, struggling to maintain her dignity and sense of humor as reporters, detectives, lawyers, and Temple officials argued about her hair, her legs, her morals. Printing the 1,378-page trial transcript cost the taxpayers $25,000. The entire cost of the impeachment, $50,000, might have been borne by the *L.A. Times* without making a noticeable dent in their profits from this story.

She returned from Sacramento legally unscathed, telling her congregation that her stay there had been a "vacation."

"I am back and ready to carry on my work. I have gone through fire ever since I started this work, and I suppose there is much more in store for me."

She was right. The Foursquare lighthouses were on the verge of revolt. The high-handed management of Cromwell Ormsby and his brother-in-law, auditor Frank Timpson, was more mercenary than that of Ralph Jordan and more abrasive than that of Minnie Kennedy.

Ormsby dismissed a Dr. Baker, who was writing a biography of the evangelist. When the offended author protested that he had an agreement, that Mrs. McPherson had told him he must stay on until his work was completed, Ormsby said a shocking thing. He declared, in the presence of several witnesses, that Aimee Semple McPherson would do just as he told her to do.

Stunning everyone within earshot, he swore that she would break with her church before she would break with him. Events would soon prove him wrong. But the fact that Ormsby said such a thing suggests that Aimee had led him to believe it.

We begin to discern a disturbing pattern. In desperation to find someone other than her mother to take charge of business matters, Aimee seems to have agreed, time and again, to surrender her will completely to any man who appeared fit for the job. There were Ralph Jordan and Cromwell Ormsby. Later there would be A. C. Winters and Giles Knight, before Rolf McPherson finally came to the rescue.

———

While lecturing in Des Moines in 1927, Sister Aimee had made a great impression on a Reverend John Goben. He followed her to Los Angeles in August of that year, joining her staff. She named Goben chief field agent, with the charge to organize Foursquare Gospel lighthouses—to take over existing churches and start new ones across the continent.

Goben began by dedicating his own tabernacle in Des Moines to the movement. Then he used his influence with other ministers around the country to bring them under the Foursquare banner. During the two years Goben was field secretary, he enlisted one hundred forty-eight branch churches, which became the backbone and limbs of what is now Foursquare International.

But Goben, Sister Aimee's wide-eyed admirer and devoted servant in 1927, became in 1929 her bitterest enemy. He had come to Los Angeles expecting to work with the inspired saint he had seen in the pulpit. But in the Angelus Temple business offices he saw a confused and desperate woman struggling to dig the Church out of debt.

He assured the branch churches they would retain their property and share the management of International Lighthouses. But in July of 1928, Ralph Jordan moved to put Aimee in control of that corporation. Goben, who enjoyed being treasurer, refused to give up his position. Thus began a feud which led to the defection of several dozen lighthouses and the firing of John Goben.

Goben's tactics were melodramatic, extreme. He hired two private investigators from the Nick Harris Detective Agency to follow Aimee and spy on her.

By September of 1929, everyone had heard the rumors that Sister Aimee was leading "a double life." A model Christian by day, she became at night a lewd hellion of the dance halls and opium dens. Rumor had it that Ormsby's chauffeur had barged into the pastor's bedroom one night drunk and pulled her out of bed and danced around the room with her! And everyone knew that she kept company with the notorious Mrs. Pantages, on trial for running over a Japanese gardener while driving under the influence. Someone heard that these women had been seen at a dance marathon, three or four nights in a row, watching the couples waltz to the point of exhaustion. When a couple looked as if they were fading, Aimee would walk out on the dance floor and toss dollars at them to buoy their spirits.

Everyone had heard about Aimee's double life, but no one could say they had actually seen any of the dark doings. Goben may have figured that the detectives would "get the goods" on Sister. Once he possessed sworn testimony of her wickedness, he would have the leverage he needed to oust Ormsby and Timpson. Then he could resume control of the Foursquare empire and the tithes he had labored so hard to multiply.

How many nights the Nick Harris "operatives" snooped on Sister Aimee, and how much it cost, is not known. They must have had a good laugh at Goben's expense, as a bonus for their futile labor. The lady preached, and then, most nights, she went to bed. She sat with the light on, typing till all hours of the morning. The detectives fell asleep in their car on Le Moyne Street.

Goben demanded affidavits describing Aimee's doings on the nights she did not go straight to bed, September 25 and 26. He had to get something for his money.

Goben apparently could not admit to himself that the affidavits were not worth what he had paid for them. They describe two visits to the Pantages' home, the first in the presence of Aimee's lawyer W. J. Ford. On the second night, in the company of Cromwell Ormsby, the evangelist realized they were being followed. On the way home to the parsonage at midnight they stopped at Ormsby's house, ran inside, switched off the lights, and looked out the window to see who was following them. Twenty minutes later they switched on the lights, and when they thought the coast was clear, Ormsby drove his employer home to the parsonage.

Perhaps Goben thought his fellow ministers would be so shocked that Aimee associated with the Pantages, a wicked theater family, and had actually been alone with Ormsby at one in the morning, they would unanimously censure the pastor, and she would dissolve in tears of remorse.

Then John Goben, heroic in his Christian magnanimity, might lift her from her knees and forgive her, on the condition that she fire those ungodly men Ormsby and Timpson and turn the Temple management over to him.

That is not the way it turned out.

Hearing that trouble was brewing, and that the ministers were planning a private council to question her character, the pastor called a meeting on the morning of October 2, 1929.

When they were assembled, Aimee asked anybody who had something to say against her to stand up and speak his mind. Nobody stood. There was a lot of whispering around the room.

Finally the wife of Goben's secretary got up and mumbled the story about the drunken chauffeur. This produced such an animated discussion, they could not get to the end of it. The meeting was adjourned till after the evening services, when the council reconvened on the roof of the Bible College.

There under the stars Aimee asked again for the ministers to come forward with any accusations against her. Goben had warned her, that afternoon, that he had affidavits, proof of her misconduct he would bring to light if she did not give in to his demands. He warned her, and she laughed at him.

Now, to his amazement, she asked Reverend Goben, with her head held high and eyes flashing, if *he* had anything to offer the discussion.

So he began reading the first affidavit "of E. B. Stavro and Paul Fruhling, first being duly sworn, etc. . . . operatives of the Nick Harris Detective Agency, etc. . . ." But before Goben got through the preliminaries, Sister turned pale; and before he reached the main passages of the affidavits, Aimee fainted dead away and rolled on the floor.

"You're killing Sister!" screamed Harriet Jordan.

And much to Goben's astonishment, the company turned against him—for doing the very thing so many of them had begged him to do. They had all wanted him to put Sister in a position where she would be forced to get rid of Ormsby and his cronies, and restore a fair government to the lighthouses, had they not?

When Aimee came to, she fired Goben. Whereupon he marched to the district attorney's office to force an investigation into the Temple's finances.

Hearing the news, Minnie Kennedy hurried home from Seattle, where she had been preaching. Wearily, she explained to her befuddled daughter that Reverend Goben was no better or worse than Cromwell Ormsby when it came to fighting for control of a business that grossed hundreds of thousands of dollars a year. When District Attorney Buron Fitts announced that the ledgers indeed should be placed before the grand jury, Aimee fired Ormsby. Later he sued her for $324,000 for breach of contract.

Aimee rehired Mae Waldron, who had told her all along that Ormsby was a bad egg.

And for a few months Minnie Kennedy brought order to the rebellious ranks of Angelus Temple.

————

To dwell on the sordid details of Temple politics and business disagreements is to slight the richness of Aimee's life in those years. She made a mess of things because she trusted the wrong people to manage practical affairs while her thoughts were elsewhere.

She was pioneering a religious theater. Thousands who saw the garden of Sister Aimee's inner life burst into blossom weekly in the illustrated sermons never considered what went into them. She worked, incessantly, obsessively, on her sermons. She scribbled songs and drafted scenarios. While detectives were peering into her bedroom windows at 2:00 A.M. trying to get a glimpse of her double life, she was typing the text of a sermon on Dr. Jekyll and Mr. Hyde, to be delivered in whiskers and wolf teeth.

The double life she was leading in those years was the double life of the performing artist, with its extremes of publicity and meditative privacy. When she was seen at all, she was seen by everybody. The rest of the time she was solitary, working, and did not want to be distracted by business appointments, meetings, banking matters, insurance, or lawsuits. Other people could take care of such things, which were "of the world," while the evangelist focused on the gifts that came to her from the Holy Spirit.

A million dollars' worth of lawsuits and a grand jury investigation into the Temple's finances did not interest her so much as the oratorio she was composing in the autumn of 1929. An action for a quarter of a million dollars in damages over her failure to build a hotel did not take up as much of her time, on any given day, as writing one of the twenty-one sermons she delivered weekly.

Minnie Kennedy took care of business for eight months of 1930, a very difficult year.

Her task between October and March was first to see that nobody filled the offices vacated by Cromwell Ormsby and John Goben. Better no management than corrupt management. All Aimee really needed was someone honest enough to count the money and make bank deposits while she preached and composed.

A number of lighthouses had withdrawn from the movement. While Aimee used her charm to woo them back, Minnie

assured the ministers that their property would be respected
and that the Foursquare organization was fiscally responsible.

The grand jury's auditors ran into a thicket of incomprehensible ledgers and bankbooks. At length they decided a thorough
investigation would not be worth the taxpayers' money. So the
district attorney failed to convict or absolve the Temple of any
wrongdoing. He gave up.

Minnie must have known her reconciliation with Aimee was
only temporary. While Aimee warmly informed the press that
her mother would be back in the work with her from now on,
Minnie qualified this: she would not be returning to the Temple
in any "official" capacity. Mother and daughter had been deeply
wounded by their last quarrel. Minnie was wise enough not to
put too much hope in the future.

THE CRASH

In March, 1930, Aimee led a group of pilgrims on a tour of the
Holy Land. The stock-market crash had decimated the party of
travelers who had promised $600 to $2,000 a head to be baptized by Aimee in the river Jordan. It was one more financial
failure, too late to cancel. Instead of chartering their own ocean
liner as planned, the Foursquare pilgrims would travel from
New York on the *George Washington*, with its cocktail lounge
and ballroom, in the company of voyagers bound for unholy
shrines.

She was glad to be free again, to feel the ocean breeze in her
hair. She was relieved to put behind her the Temple politics,
the spies, finances, and lawsuits, and reporters that haunted her
house day and night. Roberta, who accompanied her mother
on this voyage and many others, recalls that Aimee was a great

traveler, if somewhat manic. She wanted to see and do and try everything. She had a passion for detail in learning the names and histories of mountains, rivers, buildings, and every morsel of odd cuisine dropped on her plate. It was a voracious, intelligent appetite, the kind that might be expected of a woman just released from captivity—or condemned to die before her time.

She had a hard time coming home, though the welcome was as enthusiastic as ever. The band was there to greet her, and 4,000 of her followers, at the station when she returned to Los Angeles on June 20, 1930. Reporters jostled for closeups. Dispatches had come from Europe that Sister Aimee had had her face lifted. She denied it, and so does an examination of the photographs before and after.

The mayor sent his representative to extend the city's greeting. And Aimee's mother was there, looking youthful in her cloche hat, cotton print dress with pleats to midcalf, and matching boa. Rolf was there, too. Tall, dressed in white ducks and sport jacket, his satin tie jauntily askew and his thick hair parted in the middle and slicked back, he looks like a jazz-age model for an Arrow shirt advertisement. His smile mirrors Aimee's. The three of them posed for photographers at the station, Minnie and Rolf on either side of Aimee, her arm around his waist. Roberta was still in Ireland.

It is the last time Minnie and Aimee were photographed together.

The split between them this time would be violent. Whether or not it was physically violent was known only to the two women.

There are photographs of Minnie Kennedy in her hospital bed at Brentwood Sanitorium in August of 1930. She is smiling the sweet smile of martyrdom; a wing-shaped bandage covers her broken nose. It is true the nose was broken; true, also, that she had a wicked tongue when she got angry at Aimee. She had shown great skill before in using the media to fight back when Aimee drove her to it.

Later Minnie categorically denied the assault. Roberta, who

sided with Minnie in most disagreements with Aimee, dismisses
the nose-punching scandal with a wave of the hand. "What do
you think?"

MA SAYS AIMEE BROKE HER NOSE! screamed the headlines.

Minnie later explained that she "had fallen on the floor" while
engaged in a heated argument with her daughter, and slammed
her face.

More relevant is the little-known fact that Minnie had undergone plastic surgery on the eve of the fateful argument—probably to reduce the size of her beak. She may or may not have
broken it when she fell on the floor, but the surgeons certainly
had rearranged it before Aimee got to her.

The argument that led to Aimee's final conversation with her
mother began as a business dispute. Minnie despised Mae Waldron, the attractive, sloe-eyed stenographer. Unlike most of the
"inner circle," Waldron was married, though she used her
maiden name, to a well-to-do businessman. With a life apart
from the Temple, she was the most independent, modern, and
free-thinking of Aimee's associates. It was Waldron who had
alerted Minnie of the impending scandal over Ormiston's disappearance while Aimee was in Europe in 1926. And it was
Waldron's beach house to which Aimee escaped with the children when she had her falling out with Minnie in 1927.

A favorite story around the Temple was that Ma Kennedy
once got into a fury at a board meeting with Mae Waldron and
others. She began talking, probably rattling off a long list of
expenses from memory, and would not stop. Waldron covered
her ears; she rose from her chair and paced the room. At last,
driven to desperation by the rat-a-tat of Minnie's implacable
tongue, Waldron grabbed her, backed the yammering woman
into the closet, and locked her there. Despite this, Minnie went
right on talking through the closet door, without missing a
phrase or even a syllable, and making good sense in an argument
everyone else had wanted to avoid.

Minnie had agreed to return to Echo Park on the condition
that Mae Waldron leave the inner circle. At the time of Minnie's
recall, after the district attorney's investigation, Aimee had appointed Waldron vice president of the Evangelistic Association,

the Temple's legal corporation. Minnie needed to control the Association if she was really going to manage the Temple's affairs. And during her daughter's long absence she had seen far more of Mae Waldron, and of her influence, than she wanted.

For a month after Aimee's return, Minnie warned her daughter over and over that she would leave the Temple if Waldron stayed.

So Minnie knocked on the parsonage door on July 29 to tender her resignation. The house was full of people: Emma Schaffer, Harriet Jordan, Brother J. W. Arthur (an assistant pastor and sometime bookkeeper), and others.

Minnie told her daughter that she would be leaving town, since Mae Waldron was still vice president. Aimee asked her mother please to walk with her to the back patio, where they might have a word together in private.

There they stood in angry silence between the fieldstone fireplace and the goldfish pond, in the afternoon sunlight.

Aimee begged her mother to say what was *really* on her mind. Minnie's forthright answer is what brought on the fireworks. It came in a steady stream, Minnie's clear, staccato lambasting of Waldron and her influence, and Aimee must have understood immediately that the issue now was not money or even power. Waldron was honest, if not adept, in the handling of money.

Now the issue was Aimee's lifestyle, morals, and ultimately her theology. It all started with her hair. Was she or was she *not* a fundamentalist? Mae Waldron had been her lady's maid and confidante during the evangelist's makeover in 1927, dressing almost as stylishly as her mistress. Waldron was as comfortable with cigar-chewing newsmen as she was with a roomful of preachers. Waldron, devoted to Aimee's happiness and fulfillment, became her usher into the secular world of Los Angeles in the roaring twenties. She encouraged her to buy dresses, lingerie, and millinery at the best shops. She introduced her to the Pantageses and other theater people, who in turn introduced her to actors, artists, and writers, a society that trafficked in ideas and sensations forbidden to followers of the Foursquare Gospel.

These artists encouraged her to freshen the fountain of her creativity by listening to new music, by seeing the new plays and movies. They sent her books by Fitzgerald, Hemingway, and Lawrence, and slender volumes of poetry that did not rhyme or mention God.

Minnie Kennedy was born in Victoria's reign. Her mother was a "shouting Methodist." Minnie was no prude, but she knew what was expected of her daughter: Aimee had drawn her strength from a tradition that renounced secular art and learning as the Devil's work. Minnie told her daughter she must not go anywhere their followers were forbidden. She must not attend in private what she condemned in public.

And Aimee brooded.

What she said or did to her mother that afternoon on the patio behind the parsonage no one alive can remember. But that was the last conversation the two women would ever have, the last time they would ever see each other, except for a moment years later, a moment almost as violent and sad.

———

To anyone who has heard this much of her story it should come as no surprise that Aimee Semple McPherson suffered a complete mental and physical breakdown in August of 1930. Of the two women, Aimee suffered more. While Ma Kennedy ranted and railed at her daughter and the "unholy triumvirate of Waldron, Jordan, and Schaffer" in daily news headlines, Aimee took to her bed on August 5. Under heavy guard she lay in a darkened room, in a rented cottage at Malibu Beach.

For ten months she was absent from the pulpit. Her symptoms included insomnia, extreme agitation, acidosis, radical weight loss, and, at first, hysterical blindness. This last symptom comes with a load of symbolic cargo: she had failed to see herself or the practical dangers of her life. The blindness was most alarming to her followers, as Harriet Jordan reported day after day to the newspapers and the radio, and posted bulletins daily in the Temple lobby.

Doctors, hastening in and out of the Malibu cottage with their black bags, assured the public nothing was wrong with the pastor's eyesight. "Her vision may be a little blurred because of nervousness," said one physician, "but there is nothing organic . . . The only trouble with her is that she can't get a rest." Emma Schaffer explained that since Sister's return from Europe she had been busier than usual. In addition to her preaching schedule she had been working on two oratorios, writing a book, and taking screen tests for a film based on her life story, to be called *Clay in the Potter's Hand.* In order to slim down for the camera Aimee had been starving herself—she had lost twenty-eight pounds. (Before the year's end it would be forty pounds, a quarter of her body weight.)

The scenes around Angelus Temple from August 5 to 6 resembled the hysterical tableaus of 1926, when Sister Aimee was supposed to have drowned. Women gathered in clusters in the hallways, praying and keening, and on the sidewalks outside. Crowds gathered across the street, in Echo Park. For four days they continued their vigil, believing that Aimee was dying.

Late at night an ambulance stopped at the door of the Malibu cottage. Shielded from reporters by a cordon of secretaries, nurses, servants, and armed guards, Aimee was transported to a rented house in Santa Monica. Rolf rode with her. Roberta was returning from Ireland, where she had been visiting her grandparents.

The attending physician, Dr. Williams, a specialist in nervous disorders, said:

> We thought she would die. She had acute acidosis, would not take food or water. Her people didn't know it, but we had to resort to saline solution injections to pull her through.

On September 7, Rolf McPherson, seventeen years old, stood up to address a special meeting of the Foursquare Council. He smiled his mother's smile, but his eyes looked out with McPherson steadiness. The elders had known him as a boy playing with model airplanes in the alley next to the parsonage, or handing out programs in aisles of the Temple on Sundays. His mother's illness had sobered him, and now he looked like a man.

I hope I may be a great blessing to mother and help her. I surely appreciate the way you folks have taken care of her and helped her in every way. I believe mother is in good care with Dr. Williams.

Most of all we must trust in God to bear this load for us, and I am sure He will raise mother up and make her every whit whole in His own time. I appreciate the fact that you folks [the board members] are not rushing mother back, because I believe if she were rushed back, it would be only a short time till she would have another breakdown. We want her fully to recover and be raised up so that she will be able to go on in the strength of the Lord. We want the Lord to have His way. He will have His way whether we want Him to or not, and if we try to have our own way, it is not the best for us. Let us pray about mother that the Lord will have His own way . . .

It was a good speech for a seventeen-year-old, at once logical and mystical. His words naturally shaped themselves into a prayer that inspired confidence in all of them, and a sense of well-being.

This power to calm people and inspire confidence was to be his special gift as a leader. When he was a boy, the family's notoriety enforced on him a certain isolation from children his own age. Yet he had become a typical teenager, interested in girls and cars (his first independent publicity was for a speeding ticket). Rolf had no interest in pursuing a church career before his mother's illness—he wanted to study electrical engineering.

He recalls a 1930 conversation with his feeble mother—with wonder and resignation and humor. Somehow he knew it would be his fate to carry on her work. It has been agreeable, by and large. But in the autumn of 1930 it seemed a terrible responsibility; no less terrible because it came from within— his mother did not push him. He told her:

I am willing to work up from the bottom, run errands, do anything, let the Lord have His way. I do not know just what the Lord will plan for me, but whatever He plans is best . . .

And the philosophical young man and his mother prayed together. They prayed she would have ten more years to live, and that Rolf might get ten more years of preparation to take up the burden she would have to lay down sooner or later.

Roberta's commitment to Angelus Temple was more formal, dynastic. From the age of fourteen she had been groomed and promoted: Roberta Star Semple, her mother's "Star of Hope," delivered into the world to replace her father the martyred evangelist. And people said she was, almost from birth, as beautiful as the morning star. Roberta got the best of her parents' features, her mother's hair and brilliant smile and Robert Semple's blue wide-set eyes. Though she was short like her mother, Roberta had Semple's graceful proportions. From the time she could speak full sentences, it seemed, Roberta was taking her turn in the pulpit.

At many revivals Roberta led the children's service. In the 1920's she had her own radio program, and in *The Bridal Call* she wrote a column, "Aunt Birdie," full of jokes and puzzles and children's games. Roberta spoke with a slight lisp, but this seemed no hindrance to the young woman's career or to her confidence in front of an audience.

She never felt she had much choice in the matter. For the first six years of her life she was raised by her grandmother. By the time Roberta encountered her mother, Aimee had become such a heroic figure to the girl, she was overwhelmed; the bonding that allows give and take between mother and daughter did not develop easily.

Says Roberta Salter: "You did whatever was expected of you. You did not ask why, you did immediately the thing required." The two took delight in each other's company, traveling the world together several times. There was love between them as well as affection. But her mother's word was law—because Roberta, like Rolf, once she had her mother's attention, was desperate to please her. In an important way this relationship duplicated Minnie's domination of Aimee from Aimee's birth to middle age. Roberta, like Aimee, lived as the answer to her mother's prayers.

The shape of the future, as Aimee saw it from her sickbed in the autumn of 1930, was that Roberta would follow in her footsteps as pastor, while Rolf would provide the management needed to lead the Temple into the twenty-first century.

Half of this dream would come true.

————

Dr. Williams believed sea air would do Aimee good. In October she left for New Orleans, where she embarked on a United Fruit Company ship bound for the Caribbean.

Missionary Leeland Edwards recalls that Aimee visited his parents, also missionaries, in Panama in 1930. He remembers her as thin and sad but very charming. Edwards's father went to visit Aimee on the ship. She talked to him for a long time in private. Aimee told him she was terribly lonely and wanted to get married, if she could.

When the ship made port in New York, Aimee spoke briefly to reporters. A nurse held her by one arm, the ship's purser by the other. The journalists noted she kept clasping and unclasping her hands, and when one of them held out a news clipping to her, the hand that reached for it trembled violently.

A. C. Winters, the new Temple manager, met her in New York to accompany the pastor on the train across the continent. At the Continental Divide, Winters realized his folly: the northern route had been a stupid mistake. Sister Aimee, already frail, collapsed in the high altitude, unable to breathe.

On November 23, 1930 she arrived in Los Angeles unconscious. An ambulance delivered her to the parsonage, where the doctors waited.

"We hope that a few days' rest, at this lower altitude, will see an improvement," Winters announced.

But by now Aimee was such a controversial figure that even her illness was debated in the newspapers. Lawyers pursuing claims against the pastor cried she was bluffing, acting, playing possum: Aimee wasn't sick, she was just sick of courtrooms. These people—including counsels for Cromwell Ormsby, the scenarist Harvey Gates suing over the junked film project, and several disgruntled contractors—urged the D.A. to launch a grand jury investigation into her illness. It would be fun to have Sister Aimee back in court—they missed her.

Like so many grand jury investigations of her, this one never got off the ground. And she was incapacitated only for a year.

But the truth is, she never completely recovered. What the doctor called "the accumulated strain of four terrible, tempestuous years" was really the killing burden of an entire decade; it had destroyed her health. She would never again be healthy for more than a few months at a time. The achievements of her final years—the full flowering of her gifts as writer, actress, and reformer—were triumphs over perpetual pain, physical discomfort, and emotional distress.

The Caribbean cruise had not helped. But in January she secretly shipped out of San Francisco on another voyage, bound for China, with Roberta.

————

Roberta was twenty. She recalls that her mother gained strength as the ship put miles between them and Los Angeles. In Hong Kong they laid a wreath upon Robert Semple's grave.

Roberta fell in love with the ship's purser, a handsome American from Santa Helena only two years her senior. Aimee delighted in seeing them together. She encouraged the marriage, which took place March 4 in the Wesleyan church of Singapore. She smiled as she gave the bride away.

William Bradley Smythe was a young man with an adventuresome spirit and excellent manners. He was head-over-heels in love with the evangelist's gorgeous daughter. And he found his mother-in-law charming when not preoccupied (as she seemed to be much of the time) with some inner conversation, or rushing away on some errand of sudden importance.

The next morning in Los Angeles, reporters knocked at Minnie Kennedy's door. They found the proud grandmother propped up in bed raising a glass of orange juice to toast Roberta's photograph.

I was married when I was fifteen, and Aimee was married when she was seventeen; so Roberta waited three years longer. I hope she is happy! I practically raised Roberta, you know. She called me "Bonnie." I know *she* loves me still.

The bride and groom and the bride's mother made their way around the globe.

Aimee spent hours in her cabin, writing. In Shanghai she disembarked to preach in one of her own mission stations.

William Bradley Smythe soon wondered what he had got himself into. Every time they left the ship, reporters accosted them. Roberta had replaced Mae Waldron as vice president of the family holding company, to Minnie's delight. So now Smythe found himself on a "working" honeymoon with his bride; Roberta acted as Aimee's secretary, posting correspondence and handling the money, the itinerary, and the reporters. Taking care of the convalescing evangelist was a full-time job.

By the time they reached Marseilles, the bridegroom knew he would have to lay claim to his wife. Ever so politely, he did so. And as the honeymooners enjoyed more and more time alone, their joy reminded Aimee how lonely she was.

In Marseilles Aimee learned that Charlie Chaplin was vacationing discreetly with one of his mistresses. She desired greatly to meet him. It was rumored that Chaplin had been in the audience in Angelus Temple not once but several times, incognito. He admired her stage presence. But he did not want it known he attended a church whose faith was so removed from his own.

Chaplin, already silver-haired, had by 1931 achieved an eminence almost inconceivable for a Jew raised on the streets of London. A year older than Aimee, he had the physique of a welterweight; off-screen, his eyes and his smile were steely. For seven years he had produced his own films—no studio could afford him.

Now he was exhausted. Like Aimee, he had gone abroad to restore his nerves.

To say that Charles Spencer Chaplin lacked illusions does no credit to the romantic side of his nature. But compared to Sister Aimee, "the tramp" was as hard-boiled a cynic as she would ever come to admire. Between wives two and three, Lita Grey and Paulette Goddard, Chaplin was enjoying nights on the Riviera with May Reeves.

In Marseilles, he was settled in the royal suite of the Hotel Noailles, with Kono, his Asian manservant. These were the rooms occupied by the King of Spain as he passed through the French seaport—when Chaplin was not in residence.

One afternoon, while Chaplin was out on a long walk, Kono heard a knock at the door. It was Aimee Semple McPherson.

Kono did not have to ask who she was. Everyone who lived in Los Angeles knew the evangelist by sight. Though his profession had made Kono almost immune to astonishment, he was surprised to see Sister Aimee so far from home, and coming to visit the famous actor, without invitation, introduction, or so much as a phone call.

"I have always wished to meet Mr. Chaplin," she said with brilliant confidence. "This is the appointed time."

Kono resisted the impulse to dispute this. But Chaplin had been in a depression, partly the price of fame—he had grown weary of people's bizarre responses to him, the way they sought him out, assuming fawning or defensive attitudes in his presence. As politely as possible Kono tried to discourage the visit.

He explained that Chaplin had gone out and might not return for hours. He took long walks, alone. But Aimee stood like a rock in the foyer. When Kono gathered that the blond lady was not leaving, he invited her to stay for a cup of tea.

As they sipped their tea and Aimee talked, rapidly, in a high girlish voice, Kono quickly perceived that she was lonely. Her delight in Roberta's marriage had worn thin as the honeymooners left her too much alone. She was looking for someone to talk to in Marseilles. Naturally she thought of the other famous tourist, Charlie Chaplin of Los Angeles, a man she would never have approached in her home town: her followers would not approve of her associating with a notorious artist of the secular theater.

As the conversation continued, Kono was charmed, and soon enthralled. The woman had a peculiar radiance, he would later recall, a palpable magnetism. The servant was curious to see this at work upon his master.

At last the door opened, and Chaplin entered.

As he turned the corner, he stopped short at the sight of Aimee Semple McPherson drinking tea in his suite. He rose up on his toes like a dancer stopping suddenly at the edge of a puddle, and his face dropped. He looked at Kono in silent interrogation, then at the radiant face of Sister Aimee as Kono introduced her, a humorous formality. Chaplin could be bashful.

Now Kono saw that the master was utterly confounded that this "devil-pelter" had granted herself permission to enter his devilish presence. He gulped and recovered his composure, determined to make his demeanor cordial despite his discomfort. He could not imagine what Sister Aimee was doing here. Meanwhile she bubbled over with compliments and chit-chat about Marseilles, Kono's hospitality, and the pleasures of exile.

Chaplin raised an eyebrow. Aimee Semple McPherson was a fundamentalist. Surely she must know that he loathed fundamentalism in all its forms. Yet she smiled warmly at him, and he smiled back. He was handsome without his mustache.

He invited Aimee to dine with them. Meeting with polite resistance, he quickly prevailed on her.

Over dinner Chaplin began to tease her, good-naturedly, about her "audience." He would not call it "the congregation." Struck by his guest's intelligence, by her sense of humor, he was curious about an apparent incongruity: "Would you estimate," he wondered, wrinkling his forehead, "the mental age of your audience . . . to be above or below . . . fourteen?"

But Aimee was not to be patronized. She knew that Chaplin, too, had enormous appeal to the masses. She countered: Did Chaplin know the mental age of the audience for *The Gold Rush* (which she had parodied in Angelus Temple) or *City Lights*? Of course he did not know, any more than Aimee knew the age or intelligence or social backgrounds of the thousands who came to see her.

At this point Chaplin confessed that *he* must be counted as one of her audience.

"I've been to your Temple to hear you," he told her. "Half

your success is due to your magnetic appeal, half due to the props and lights."

Aimee smiled, proud to be praised by Charlie Chaplin, yet saddened that he understood her so narrowly.

Now he grew animated, enjoying his role as drama critic.

"Oh yes, whether you like it or not you're a great actress. You give to your drama-starved people, who absent themselves from the theater through fear, a theater which they can reconcile with their narrow beliefs. Don't you?"

Smiling still, she let him continue.

"Orthodox religion is based upon fear, fear of doing something on earth which will keep them out of heaven. My God, they miss out on all the glorious freedom of life in order to reach a mythical heaven where they can walk on golden streets and play a harp—a bait of pure boredom, if you ask me . . ."

She had not asked him. Now she looked a little shaken.

"Our worlds are different," she said softly. "Vastly different."

Whatever the difference, it did not discourage the conversation between the preacher and the actor. Chaplin composed the scores for his films; Aimee was composing an opera. They had plenty to talk about. The next night Chaplin informed Kono that he, Chaplin, would be escorting Mrs. McPherson to the colorful, rollicking Marseilles waterfront. And Kono recalls that the master returned from the excursion "gay, his mood of irritation with the world gone."

Next evening, Charlie Chaplin and Sister Aimee set out at twilight for a long walk about the city proper. Aimee's health was steadily improving. She had always been fond of walking. Precisely the same height, the silver-haired comedian in his dark suit and pearl-gray tie and the strawberry-blond fundamentalist fell into step together that evening, and the next. They strolled uphill and downhill every evening, in conversation and silence, until the morning came for Aimee to sail away. Neither of them would ever mention the other in public.

Walking the crooked cobblestone streets of the ancient port, these elegant tourists might have been mistaken for brother and sister when they smiled their famous smiles at once.

5

THE FINAL YEARS

ATTAR OF ROSES

Twenty thousand singing, cheering people jammed the Santa Fe railroad station yard on May 16, 1931 as the "Chief" chugged to a halt, screeching iron and hissing steam, bringing Sister Aimee home from her five months abroad.

On the rear platform of the train she stood, blond and slender in a green silk suit and white turban hat, next to Roberta and her astonished husband, William Smythe. No one could have prepared him. Charles Walkem, the music arranger, had joined Aimee in Marseilles to help her write an opera on the voyage back across the Atlantic; he was standing with Rolf McPherson, who had joined them in Chicago.

The fifty-piece Bible College band, arrayed on a float wrapped in red, white, and blue bunting, banged and honked and tootled. When these musicians paused, the Silver Band, seated below them, kept up the serenade.

Aimee led her family along an aisle formed by dozens of policemen linking arms, from the train to a flatcar on the siding. Amid a sea of palm branches, waving hats, flags, and Temple pompons in blue and gold, she mounted the platform. She signaled for silence. A city council member welcomed her home on behalf of Los Angeles. Then Aimee made a short speech thanking the crowd and the radio audience, saying how glad she was to be home again, and why she had needed to be away.

"I had been forgetting to rest, so God punished me. But I expect to be preaching for another twenty years."

This did not seem like too much to expect—she was youthful still. But she would get little more than half that number of years to pursue her ministry. Perhaps it was a clairvoyant sense of her abbreviated future that caused her to work so quickly.

———

Ten months after her breakdown, Aimee was back in the Temple.

Her homecoming sermon, called "Attar of Roses," was considered by many to have been the most moving of her career. The media and the general public rushed to Echo Park, unloading from special trolleys routed to Angelus Temple. When every inch of seating space had been filled in the Temple and in the College auditorium next door (where loudspeakers were set up), 10,000 people stood in the street to listen. The pressure of the crowd defied fire regulations—as Sister Aimee came down the runway from the mezzanine to the platform with her arms full of roses, people surged into the space behind her and sat in the ramp along the west wall.

"Attar of Roses" is the rare public exhibition of a private obsession, Aimee's study of the Song of Solomon. Scholars in the Temple archives discover a breathtaking legacy: in several files under the heading "Song of Songs" are *hundreds* of pages on the erotic Song of Solomon, sermons as delicate and different from one another as snowflakes. Like most of Aimee's sermons, these were not written for the Sunday night crowd; they were meant for smaller prayer services.

Journalists from the intellectual press—Sarah Comstock, H. L. Mencken, and others—attended only the illustrated sermons on Sundays, whose effects were overwhelmingly visual. These writers assumed that Sister Aimee's language was a primitive tool, fit only for slapstick or sentimental entertainment. Hundreds of stenographically recorded sermons correct this false impression. Mencken, who admired Aimee's intelligence, indeed sensed that Sister Aimee was playing down to her huge audience. What he did not know is that away from the footlights and the stage props she spoke another language, the discourse of Neoplatonic interpretation, meant for Bible students who hung on her every word, ten times a week.

In an early sermon on the Song of Songs she said she so loved this beautiful, impossible book of the Hellenized Hebrews, she could spend the rest of her life studying it and talking about it; indeed she would like to preach a sermon upon every verse of it from beginning to end. She probably did. Aimee was bold to celebrate the erotic dimension of the spiritual life, in public no less; and the Song of Songs was the ultimate expression of it, a simple mortal's passionate love for Christ's body, the Rose of Sharon.

As performance art, "Attar of Roses" is lyric theater at its best. The actor and the role merge in a poignant, intimate dramatic moment. Aimee arrived on the platform dressed in white satin, carrying an armful of red roses, her dark cape thrown back over her shoulders. She smiled her most endearing and vulnerable smile as the audience applauded her, the expression of the child within her she had somehow managed to preserve into middle age, for just such occasions. She led a song. When it was done, the crimson curtains opened to reveal a six-foot cross the stagelights made glow against a midnight-blue backdrop. Banked against the cross were sprays of red roses.

Picking up the white-bound bible, she read, in a simple voice a man in the second balcony heard as if she stood beside him: "I am the rose of Sharon, and the lily of the valleys."

"Rose of Sharon . . ." she mused. "What a beautiful name for the Lord! All of my life I have loved flowers—and I love Him, that fair, Eternal Flower."

Closing the book with tender care, she moved downstage in silence, approaching the audience to confide a secret:

> When I was a little girl, I used to go out gathering flowers in the woods. Sometimes from an armful of blossoms I would take one which was faded and throw it to the ground. Then my heart would be touched . . . and I would go back and hunt until I found that flower, and I would place it in the center of the bouquet, in the best place of all.

And the audience knew, because the actress felt it so strongly, that the flowers were more than flowers—each blossom, fresh or dim, was a human soul with immortal fragrance.

> Just a few weeks ago I was in Algiers. I went to the little places where merchants were sitting cross-legged in the street they call the Street of Perfumes. These men would pull long glass stoppers out of shining bottles and waving them would say, "Perfume, lady?

Perfume, lady?" And suddenly the most wonderful fragrance would fill the air—perhaps sandalwood, the Harlem perfume, or, most lovely and priceless of all, the Attar of Roses.

They say it takes three thousand pounds of rose petals to make just *one* pound of this matchless perfume—sweet, fragrant, velvet petals

she continued, her voice deepening with sensuality

must be crushed, bruised and beaten, that Attar of Roses might be given to the world.

As I thought upon this, the Lord began to speak to my heart about that Rose of Sharon that blooms for every one of us. Oh, what a rose He is!

Her attention slowly fixed on a cluster of roses at her pulpit. The stranger in the second balcony noticed that Aimee's full lips were a darker shade of red than the roses as she lifted her hand and gently took the thorned stem of one blossom in her long fingers.

First she spoke softly to the rose, like a mother to an infant:

First He was the rosebud yonder in the manger of Bethlehem . . . Cradled in the tender arms of His mother Mary, He began to grow. One by one the petals of His life unfolded . . .

And now Sister Aimee's voice played tricks on their eyes— was the rose suddenly, subtly opening as her voice grew firmer?

One by one, the petals of His life unfolded until at twelve years of age He was found there in the Temple, His wisdom confounding the wise . . .

From a voice full of a mother's pride the actress shifted, before anyone quite knew she had done it, to the tone of a maiden smitten at the first sight of her young lover:

Maturing, unfolding, increasing in favor with God and man, at last He, the Rose of Sharon, stood upon the banks of the River Jordan.

The rose she gazed upon at arm's length the audience now envisioned as a comely youth. In the auditorium's fourth row an unmarried stenographer could see two actions on the stage, superimposed: Sister Aimee reaching to finger the rose petals with breathless excitement, and a woman falling in love with a man so vivid in her mind's eye, he became visible to 5,000 spectators.

> For a time it was given the sons of men to behold—yea, and to touch—the glorious petals of the Rose of Sharon, the One altogether lovely . . .

As she caressed the petals, she named each one for a virtue: His wisdom, His humility, His piety.

> Into the stillness and fastness of the mountains He would ascend, and there He would lift His face unto the moonbeams and those silent stars, and pour out His soul unto the Father . . . There were other petals—divine healing that made crooked minds straight again, made twisted limbs firm and strong . . .

"The Rose of Sharon was in its glorious perfection," sang the evangelist. Then her hand flinched, and the audience saw the pain in her eyes: "But, ah . . . the Rose has a thorn . . . There is no crown unless there is first the burden of the Cross."

"Why?" she cried. "Why must it be so?" she wondered, pleading with the source of all mysteries for an answer to the age-old question of suffering.

She leaned toward the audience as if listening for an answer. "Why? Oh—" and she whispered:

> Do you not see? It is Attar of Roses in the making.
> The Scribes, high priests and Pharisees were jealous, and they began to strip the petals from Jesus. There came a terrible, agonizing stripping away of the petals of His reputation—

The last word rang in the ears of reporters down in front, the scribes who suddenly saw themselves caught up in the drama, the persecution of Christ and Aimee Semple McPherson, as the actress plucked a petal from the rose and cried out in anguish.

In her palm the scarlet petal she held high glowed in the stagelight like a drop of blood. She had stretched out her arm and thrown back her head as if the hand had been nailed in place, shuddering in pain.

Women gasped, and some cried out. One by one, Sister Aimee stripped petals from the rose as she told the story of Judas, and Pilate, and the soldiers.

> They whipped him—again and again and again the lash fell upon Him until His back was bruised and purple, and the blood flowed down.

The rose petals made a trail of blood across the stage.

Whispering, she told the story of the Crucifixion. The scene of suffering she evoked was so vivid and horrifying that men and women closed their eyes or turned away, trying to escape the inescapable vision. Children cried and screamed. Several women fainted and had to be carried out by ushers.

She intoned, her voice gathering strength and momentum:

> Then the winds began to swirl around that hill, thunders began to play in that fearful sky, the earth began to rock and sway and tremble. His form, first against the sapphire sky and then against the darkening clouds, had stood without a murmur, but one thing finished Him—His Father turned His back on Him.

"*Eli, Eli, lama Sabachthani?*" she cried at the top of her voice, expressing the agony of her own life. Why hast Thou forsaken me? Because the Rose must be thoroughly crushed to make Attar of Roses, essence of the Holy Spirit.

Now Sister Aimee's eyes shone with tears.

> Dear Rose, there is not much left of you now. The beautiful petals are gone, and there remaineth only the heart . . . such a message could come only from a heart that has known Golgotha and Calvary, a heart that has been crushed and broken, and crushed and broken again . . .

Perfume? Water and blood mingled, flowed forth—but, ah, over the hill, down the valley, over the minarets and towers, over Bethany, over Nazareth—

Standing on tiptoe, she flung wide her arms, crying in exultation:

> Away up through Rome and into France, it is on the breeze, it sweeps England, it is in America, the fragrance of the Rose of Sharon, borne by the missionaries upon their garments . . .

In human, sensual terms she sanctified an erotic realm by seeing Christ in the rosebud, as she had sanctified music and dancing by conducting them "in the Spirit." And she did this with such religious passion, not a man or woman in Angelus Temple stopped to question her. Slyly she was changing their way of thinking, and they were powerless to resist.

———

From May 1931 until October 1944 Sister Aimee worked toward two goals not always compatible: to create a living tradition of religious theater, and to lead a growing denomination of Fundamentalists into the twentieth century, into social action. Exasperating obstacles stood before the second of these goals: prejudice, narrow-mindedness, Church politics, and the theological bases of Fundamentalism itself, some of which she found repugnant. Charlie Chaplin considered that her intelligence must contradict what he thought was her religion. But Chaplin did not understand her religion. It was a new branch on an ancient tree, growing and in transition.

Nathaniel Van Cleave, now an important theologian, sat in Sister Aimee's class in the 1930's. He recalls her vast knowledge of Church history and doctrine. There are some fine anecdotes Van Cleave and others have preserved of her technique in the classroom—I will recount these presently—but for now it must be said that she understood the religious controversies of her time and would not waste a minute on academic trifles. She disagreed with half the Pentecostalists in America about where the Church was headed. While limiting her pronouncements to a few key issues like "sanctification," Aimee sought to lead by example rather than decree.

Her public example was a religious high-wire act.

By the 1930's a split had developed between her intellectual life and Church dogma. The "double life" people suspected was not what they suspected. It was not the double life of the body but the mind's double life, for the religious pioneer was working twenty-five years ahead of her congregation. One day she would be making a monkey of Darwin, to the delight of her creationist followers. And the very next day she would announce her betrothal to David Hutton, defying the Church prohibition against marriage while a former spouse was still alive.

Harold McPherson was still alive, a desk clerk in a Florida hotel. Somehow he had made peace with Aimee. Rolf went to visit him. The proud man had remarried, but was visibly struggling. He was grateful for the checks he received at the beginning of each month, without fail, from his first wife the celebrated evangelist.

Now the third marriage of Aimee Semple McPherson ought to be the subject of comedy—except that it caused her so much heartache. David Hutton Jr. was a short, hippopotamic baritone she hired to play the Pharaoh in her opera *The Iron Furnace*. He was a recovered victim of infantile paralysis. Aimee fell in love with the Pharaoh, in his stage whiskers and Egyptian headdress, as they rehearsed in the summer of 1931.

God knows she was lonely. Roberta married the purser in March, and Rolf married Lorna De Smith, a pretty Bible College student, in a regal ceremony on July 21, Aimee officiating. Minnie Kennedy had married that spring. Wedding bells were ringing for everybody but Aimee, who had confided to more than one colleague that she wished to have a husband.

"You have no idea how lonesome I have been . . . I have been seeing myself home every night with a trip-hammer in my throat."

But why did she choose the slovenly baritone?

It seems she did not really choose. She married Hutton because he was the one to ask her. Roberta Salter, compassionate in recalling her mother's loneliness, insists that the preacher, the celebrity, was virtually unmarriageable in the 1930's. "What kind of man," she asks, "would have married such a famous, independent, and driven woman in those days?" Carey McWilliams, a neighbor of Aimee's who wrote insightfully about the evangelist's personality, said that living with Sister Aimee must have been like being in a closed room with a radio going at full blast twenty-four hours a day. He also records a peculiar impression confirmed by the later photos: Aimee's powerful stage presence *suggested* sexuality, yet the woman herself, at forty, had little sexual appeal. The muscularity of her neck and shoulders, the athletic surety of her gestures, placed her ever-so-slightly upon the masculine side of conventional feminine allure.

Roberta Salter recalls an eerie incident that occurred that summer.

She was living with William Smythe in a small apartment off Wilshire Boulevard. Smythe had been offered a job in the Church administration; instead, he became an insurance salesman, hoping to distance himself from the emotional tempests of Angelus Temple.

A neighbor with an interest in spiritualism often had Roberta over for coffee. One morning Roberta arrived in the neighbor's kitchen to find a "spirit medium" holding forth, relaying messages from the world beyond.

As Roberta entered, the medium fixed her with a glassy stare. Roberta had never seen her before.

The medium announced: "Your father is about to leave home."

Now Roberta thought this was a bizarre statement, since her father, Robert Semple, had died before she was born. The medium explained that her father's spirit, nevertheless, had been watching over her, and over her mother and the whole family—but now he was about to give up on the family and "leave home."

Upon a good deal of reflection, Roberta understood this to mean (if it meant anything) that Semple's spirit could not endure the presence of David Hutton.

David Hutton would have been handsome if there had been less of him. He must have weighed three hundred pounds. He had good hair, dark, wide-set eyes, a dimpled chin, and a little gap between his front teeth. Smiling, he looked like a demented Herbert Hoover. When Hutton was not smiling, he resembled the sissyish tyrant of a boy scout troop. The idea that women found him attractive is supported by the lawsuits for "heart-balm" they filed against him, even after his marriage to the preacher.

The desperation and self-deception involved in Aimee's marrying the flaccid Pharaoh is pathetic. She wrote about it years later, saying:

> Few people know as I did what it is to be lonely in a crowd . . . Then David Hutton came across my path . . . Romance again would walk hand in hand with faith. At least, that was my silly womanly dream.
>
> I saw in David Hutton the promise of so many things I had missed in years gone by—the protection of a man, the thoughtfulness and tenderness and devotion of a good husband, and the helping hand of a sympathetic co-worker.

The night she got married, Rolf McPherson was with her. He and his new wife Lorna De were living in the parsonage with Aimee when the newspapers got wind of the preacher's romance. The parsonage filled with journalists drinking coffee, laughing, talking. He says it was the journalists' idea that Aimee elope with Hutton. What they proposed as a lark so appealed to the lonely woman, she went along with it. Incredible. A reporter kindly arranged for a plane to fly the family, and A. C. Winters, the business manager, and his wife, and Harriet Jordan, to Yuma, Arizona at 3:00 A.M. on September 13. Arizona did not require the three-day "cooling-off" period California did. And in Yuma she hoped to avoid publicity.

At dawn they landed in Yuma, where a sleepy county clerk issued a marriage license. Hutton was thirty, his bride ten years older.

The couple stood on the steps of the trimotor plane as Harriet

Jordan read the marriage service. There were kisses all around, and handshakes. Then the plane flew back to Los Angeles.

At eleven that morning the bride preached a sermon on the love story of Ruth and Boaz. She did not announce the marriage during that service. But when she returned to the parsonage, it was full of journalists.

"Was it love at first sight?" they asked Hutton, when Aimee left the room to freshen up.

"You figure that out for yourself," he advised.

Photographs of the newlyweds show the bride as ecstatic, starry-eyed, with her head on Hutton's lumpish shoulder. In Hutton's eyes, above his gap-toothed grin, one sees only dollar signs.

For years Aimee had followed the Church dogma that divorced persons must not remarry as long as both partners lived. Reporters attended the afternoon service, curious to see her followers' reaction to this reversal of policy.

The congregation invited Hutton to lead a hymn. When he chose "There Is Sunshine in My Soul Today," they clapped and cheered.

Then Brother Arthur, whom everybody trusted, spoke by right of seniority. "We elders approve of Sister's choice mightily," he declared.

It would not be that simple. But for the time being everyone was genuinely happy that Aimee was not going to be lonely anymore. Ma Kennedy wired her blessing. The newspapers devoted full-page spreads to the love match, and even the radio stations got in on the excitement. On Monday the 14th they set up a microphone next to Aimee's canopied bed in the parsonage, upon approval of the "man of the house." They interviewed Hutton in his bathrobe, and the bride in her negligee, smiling from a divan.

An ambitious performer, the Pharaoh was soon to learn the capriciousness of publicity.

That night, at the wedding supper, the reporter who had so kindly arranged the flight to Yuma casually remarked that a massage nurse was preparing to sue the bridegroom.

"Her name is Myrtle Hazel St. Pierre, and she says David promised to marry her and then broke her heart."

Hutton reddened, flustered; then he denied it.

On Tuesday morning a process server knocked at the back door of the parsonage with a summons. It was an action by the massage nurse, charging Hutton with breach of promise to marry. She wanted $200,000.

Sister Aimee got a few good months out of the marriage, more than anyone else expected, before her health failed, and Hutton's ambition proved greater than his love.

She so desperately wanted to be loved and protected that she projected upon the man and the marriage a dozen virtues they sadly lacked. She took his name. Newsreels show her clinging to him like a schoolgirl, blushing, head over heels in love: "This marriage of mine can never fail—never! I have all the longing of those empty years to give me realization of what this means . . . Now I have someone to shelter me, someone to lean on."

Too busy for a honeymoon, the newlyweds spent time at Elsinore, sixty miles southeast of Los Angeles. There a developer had built a bungalow for Sister Aimee, free, in order to lure home buyers. The bungalow attracted reporters by the carload because it looked like a castle through the camera lens, a symbol of sinful luxury. In fact the "castle" is four modest rooms strung out behind a minareted facade, no larger than a good-sized hotel suite. The house had a strong fence around it, and no telephone, so for many years Elsinore served as a safe retreat.

She would never again look as healthy and lovely as during those early months of the marriage.

Hutton's sense of humor, coarser than Aimee's, was a delight to her. The couple had fun traveling together that autumn. On September 18, less than a week after the wedding, Aimee was scheduled to begin an eight-day revival in Portland, Oregon. On the road they stopped in San Francisco so the pastor could comfort two former acquaintances serving terms in the San Quentin penitentiary.

The convicts were Asa Keyes, the district attorney who had labored so long and hard to put Aimee behind bars in 1926, and Cromwell Ormsby, her former attorney and business manager. He had nearly got her arrested for fraud. But there were no hard feelings that Hutton could see, as the convicts in their striped uniforms shook hands with Aimee, and gratefully accepted her prayers for their speedy deliverance. After all, she had little to do with their imprisonment. Keyes had accepted bribes in a case unrelated to Aimee's, and Ormsby was serving time on a conviction for jury tampering. Both men were pleased she remembered them in her prayers. Meanwhile Ormsby was suing her for a quarter of a million dollars for breach of contract.

In Portland she met the manager of Boston Garden, who had flown across the country to get Aimee's signature on a contract. They wanted her to preach for a week in Boston, in early October, in the 22,000-seat sports arena.

Flattered by the invitation to Boston, a Catholic stronghold where she had never been welcome, Aimee planned to preach on the text "Curfew Shall Not Ring Tonight." She would swing on the clapper of an enormous bell, out over the heads of the audience. To build her strength, she swam three and a half miles a day across Lake Elsinore, paced by Hutton in a rowboat. She looked better than she had in years.

At the nadir of the Depression, with the Unitarians, Episcopalians, and Catholics hostile to her, it seemed unlikely the evangelist would even cover her expenses in Boston. Remember the rioting she encountered in Hyde Park in 1916, and the Boston ministers' ban on her vindication tour in 1929? Now the Harvard students invited her to speak in Cambridge—and the administration canceled the event due to pressure from the school of divinity.

Yet the Boston revival turned out to be a surprise success which paved the way for her last national tours in 1933–34.

On October 4, Aimee Semple McPherson Hutton and "Dave," as the newspapers called him, faced the press as they boarded the train to Boston.

They say I'm going to Boston cold. But I'll guarantee you that I'm going in there red-hot, to turn that town upside-down with the biggest revival ever seen on the Atlantic seaboard!

Arriving in Boston, the Huttons called on the mayor at City Hall.

"This is my thirty-ninth birthday," Aimee gushed, her eyes shining. (She was forty-two.)

Mayor James Michael Curley was ready for her. He handed the evangelist a shillelagh, laughing. "If you are going to drive the devil out of the people who go to Boston Garden, you had better have this."

Then the Irish politician told them what a fine and honorable thing it would be if Sister Aimee would donate half the proceeds of her collections to the city's unemployed. These surrounded City Hall. The reporters looked at Aimee.

"I'll give it," she agreed, "if you will take up the collections."

At the opening meeting on Saturday night, fewer than 5,000 persons sat in the cavernous arena. Aimee threw herself into the sermon with enthusiasm. The swelling of the audience over the next seven days recalls her revivals in 1919. On Sunday she preached to 6,200 in the afternoon and 11,000 in the evening. She preached and she sang, and she swung on the bell clapper. She laid hands on invalids as Hutton stood by her side.

On Monday night, after the sermon, she invited journalists to join her on a tour of the night clubs.

"The parable of the lost sheep is on my mind," she said.

On Hutton's arm she left her hotel, dressed in black velvet with a white lace collar, a black Eugenie hat tipped over one eye, and wearing the jeweled necklace Hutton had given her for her birthday. In the speakeasies, where jazz bands inflamed the dancers, she seemed at ease. She loved dancing, loved to watch it. Invited to address the patrons, she kept it short: "The ninety and nine were safely in the fold at the Garden tonight. I hope you folks will come to fill up the top balcony."

They did. Row by row, tier by tier, the Boston Garden filled, until on the final Sunday night the arena was packed and hundreds of people were turned away.

THE COMMISSARY

Ask anyone who remembers the Depression in Los Angeles about Aimee Semple McPherson. They may or may not remember she was Pentecostal, or tinted her hair, or got "kidnapped." But everyone recalls that she kept tens of thousands of people from starving to death.

If Sister Aimee had done nothing else during the 1930's, her operation of the Foursquare Commissary and welfare programs would have kept her busy. Los Angeles was full of tradesmen, retirees, and former Midwestern farmers whose savings were wiped out by the Crash. And the city had no industry fit to carry them and their families through the hard times.

When the schools stopped feeding children free lunches, Aimee took over the program. When city welfare agencies staggered under the load of beggars, the women of Angelus Temple sewed quilts and baked loaves of bread by the thousands. When bread lines stretched for city blocks and "Brother Can You Spare a Dime?" was a hit song, when federal programs and the other charities faltered in a tangle of red tape, Angelus Temple was the only place *anyone* could get a meal, clothing, and blankets, no questions asked. Aimee's policy was "give first and investigate afterward." While this led to a certain amount of waste, it also alleviated suffering on an epic scale.

The Commissary had opened in August of 1927. The report for 1930, before the charity really got going, includes the following figures:

45,994	pieces of clothing given out (to individuals)
7,332	families clothed
6,126	families fed
20,562	people given food (individuals)
3,278	garments made for children

1,498   baby layettes supplied
1,400   baskets of food given at Christmas

This was before Los Angeles really felt the crunch, before November of 1931, when Aimee opened her first soup kitchen, serving stew, soup, coffee, and rolls to all comers. That year the numbers more than doubled. After Thanksgiving her Bible students made 30,000 Christmas wreaths and peddled them door to door, raising enough money to pay for 3,000 Christmas baskets with enough food to feed 15,000.

Aimee had a gift for making people give. Immediately she got the fire department and the police (who owed her so much) to assist in distributing the food and clothing to those who could not come to the Temple. She flattered and cajoled a dozen physicians and dentists into staffing a free clinic. This trained 500 nurses to treat children and old people suffering from malnutrition.

She coaxed or bullied the meat packers, millers, bakers, and grocers into donating supplies. She persuaded bankers and businessmen to make outright cash grants, and trucking companies to haul supplies out of the goodness of their hearts. Society women who would not set foot in Angelus Temple ransacked their mansion closets after getting a call from Aimee on the telephone. And so did their friends, and their friends' friends. She urged the federal government to reopen an abandoned Army cantonment east of Los Angeles, where 25,000 jobless men and women could be housed, and could farm the land for survival.

Quickly the Angelus Temple dining hall became too small for the crowds. Aimee persuaded J. A. Baldy, the president of the Yellow Cab Company, to donate a 120 × 200-foot building for a new soup kitchen. There 80,000 men, women, and children received meals the first month.

In the Temple hundreds of women worked day and night sewing quilts, baby clothing, and children's suits and dresses. They sat at rows of black sewing machines donated by the White Sewing Machine Company of Los Angeles.

The Commissary and soup kitchens were managed by David

Hutton and his parents, who had come to live in the parsonage with the newlyweds. Rolf McPherson, living there at the time with his wife, describes it as a full house—yet he seems to have got along well enough with Hutton. At the opening of the second soup kitchen, in January of 1932, someone took a picture of Hutton, his father, and Rolf McPherson. The Huttons are peeling carrots into a cauldron while Rolf, with an engineer's curiosity, inspects a soup strainer.

The telephone rang all day and night at the Commissary desk. On the wall hung the motto ANYBODY AND EVERYBODY IS SOMEBODY TO JESUS. The police department, the Juvenile Welfare Bureau, and a dozen other agencies called Angelus Temple for help.

> "Hello!"
> "Yes, this is Angelus Temple. Who is speaking, please?"
> "The police department? An emergency case? Family of five; no food, father ill; mother with baby; no furniture—to be dispossessed tomorrow—"

The operator nods and makes notes, repeating the officer's words for the journalist's benefit.

> "Yes? The family's only been in California three months, so the county cannot assist without a court order . . . food, clothing, rent, everything needed. Yes, I have the name and address. There will be a car on the way with supplies within fifteen minutes."

————

The scope and scale of business during these years staggers the mind. Yet Aimee's pursuit of funding, food, and human resources for the Commissary never interrupted her schedule at Angelus Temple—twenty or more services a week, including baptisms, healing services, prayer meetings, and the full-dress illustrated sermon Sunday night. Then there were the KFSG broadcasts. The evidence in the archives is incredible: she rarely repeated a sermon. There are thousands upon thousands of sermons stenographically recorded, and detailed notes for thousands more. She stayed up all night scripting sermons; there was no time to write them during the day.

These exertions, and the pressure of a dozen lawsuits, including Hutton's for breach of promise, led to another breakdown in March of 1932. Negotiations with the massage nurse had failed, and now the spurned woman demanded justice. The case was on the docket for mid-June.

In February the Huttons sailed on a rest cruise to Panama. They announced from the pier: "We are tired of being goldfish. We want to have a little privacy and do a lot of resting."

A week after her return, Aimee collapsed while preaching a Sunday sermon. She was rushed to the hospital for a blood transfusion. She was anemic. The anemia would eventually lead to a more dangerous blood disease. In March of 1931 she was plagued by carbuncles (boils) on her neck and trunk, which physicians now would probably diagnose as "shingles." She had suffered the same symptoms in the autumn of 1926.

A. C. Winters approached the illustrious minister Paul Rader with an offer to sell the Temple "should the condition of my [Aimee's] health reach the point where I cannot continue . . ." Nothing came of it except a furor in the newspapers and panic from Aimee's followers. But the offer was serious. It indicates the gravity of her illness. She recovered sufficiently to preach in Kansas City in April. After her nine-day Kansas campaign, Hutton took her on another sea voyage to Central America.

Doctors believed all Aimee needed was salt air and distance from her public.

She returned from the voyage in early June, and was carried from her railroad car on a stretcher. The traveler had contracted "tropical fever" in Guatemala. Her doctor reported to the newspapers that "frequent hemorrhages and the fever, with worry, have caused her condition to become serious." An ambulance delivered her to the retreat at Elsinore.

There, cut off from the radio, telephone, and newspapers, she recuperated while the two trials went forward: her scenarist's lawsuit for damages over the abandoned movie project, and Myrtle St. Pierre's action against David Hutton.

The Hutton–St. Pierre trial was sordid and silly beyond anything reporters had seen in the 1920's. Had the Pharaoh made love to the massage nurse or had he not? Soon it became clear that he had, but not before the attorneys paraded dozens of witnesses through the box in an effort to defame now Dave, now Myrtle. The trial assumed the tone of a bedroom farce. And though Aimee herself had no part in it, her invisible presence attracted the crowds that pushed and shoved into the courtroom galleries. Her unspoken name caused headlines as reporters rushed to press the newest details of the orgy: knee-kissing, nightgowns, gin bottles, Arabian rug dealers, ice cubes, midnight spankings, and "treatments, treatments, and treatments." That was the euphemistic code word for the massage nurse's professional attentions to Lotharios in spats, clients who did things with goldfish, canes, a three-legged duck.

"They're not trying Dave Hutton in this case," said the defendant, "they're trying poor Aimee, who lies flat on her back in the hospital."

From Elsinore she had been taken to a sanatorium at Palm Springs. A few days after the trial began she asked to see a newspaper. After much consideration the doctors decided they must accept the risk, brought the woman several newspapers, and watched as she read the accounts of both court actions, against herself and against her husband.

Aimee read the newspapers in silence. She lay still awhile before saying, gently, she was certain David would exonerate himself.

Then she asked that the news photographers, who had pursued her to the hospital and been kept at bay for weeks, be allowed into the room so they could do their work and go home. No photograph of Aimee had been published since her return from the Caribbean.

From that brief fusillade of flashbulbs emerges one essential portrait of the lady's head on the pillow. Sad eyes gaze from the oval of her face. She has somehow maintained that symmetry, the fullness of the lips despite the wasting of flesh over the high cheekbones, the perfect chin—a tragic beauty.

The scenarist's case against Sister Aimee came to trial, and the court found in Harvey Gates's favor, entering a judgment against Aimee for $10,000. But this was only a detail on the huge canvas.

From the desert sanatorium at Palm Springs she was further removed to a resort in the San Bernardino Mountains. Hutton had received a death threat, and a shadow outside her hospital window had thrown the nervous patient into hysterics. The doctors decided she would be better off in complete isolation.

Of much greater concern was a new scandal in the newspapers: a judge, addressing the Los Angeles Bar Association, charged that an agent of Angelus Temple had approached a political candidate, offering the endorsement of KFSG broadcasts in return for a "cash donation." The judge named Hutton's crony Roy Watkins, head of the Temple's Commissary department.

As the Hutton–St. Pierre trial drew to a close, Aimee returned to Elsinore. She was still hopeful that her husband would be vindicated. By mid-July the dreadful publicity had caused bitter discord at Angelus Temple. Crusaders were sick of David Hutton. A delegation of Foursquare members handed Myrtle St. Pierre several baskets of flowers as a token of support, as the massage nurse stood on the steps of the Hall of Justice.

Just after seven o'clock, on the Saturday evening after the trial, Aimee was resting on the sun deck at Elsinore. She heard a car pull into the driveway and turned to see it was her husband, with Roy Watkins.

She got up out of the steamer chair and called down over the railing to the men in the car.

"What is the verdict?"

Hutton shouted up to her. "It isn't so bad after all, Betty! It'll cost us only five thousand dollars!"

The nurse saw her sway, too late to reach the invalid as she fell and knocked her head soundly on the concrete. She was unconscious for forty-five minutes, while the doctor rushed from Los Angeles to Elsinore.

Aimee had fractured her skull.

————

That was pretty much the end of the marriage, though she would stubbornly cling to the ideal she had fabricated. She defended the marriage against her followers, the newspapers, and finally her rebellious husband himself.

The congregation and elders, who had welcomed Hutton into the fold as a brother, were now fed up with him. Foursquare churches in Ohio adopted a resolution deploring Sister Aimee's activities, especially her marriage. Thirty-two ministers in Minnesota and Iowa withdrew from the Lighthouse movement, citing "widespread publicity and policies of the international church, which have brought undue reproach on the work."

She must have known the marriage was over by September 13, 1932. That evening Rolf and Lorna De, David Hutton Sr. and his wife, and Mrs. Margaret Hutton, David's aunt, sat down with Aimee and her husband at a wedding anniversary dinner at the parsonage. Everyone smiles for the camera except David Hutton, who looks like a man reluctantly kept from another engagement.

The judge's charge that Roy Watkins had been working a political shakedown opened the door on a scandal in Angelus Temple's welfare program. The Los Angeles Social Service Commission ordered an investigation of the Commissary accounts. The bakeries and meat-packing houses cut off their donations while the investigation was pending.

The details are vaguely understood. Allegedly the police raided a still that was being used by Commissary workers to make brandy out of donated apricots. Allegedly the Commissary storerooms leaked sauerkraut and salad oil in the direction of a scowling grocer. Called to account at City Hall, Hutton and Watkins denied any wrongdoing. Nevertheless the examiners found violations of a city rule concerning the proper solicitation of charity. There were rumors of kickbacks to Temple officials for Commissary contracts.

The city briefly suspended the Commissary's permit to operate until Hutton "reorganized"—which simply meant firing Watkins. Nobody really wanted to interfere with the Temple's relief program. They just loved a good scandal, and once the press got going, the public would not be satisfied until there had been an investigation. If it wasn't the grand jury, City Hall would have to do.

Still recovering from her concussion, Aimee issued this statement:

> They have clashed loud their cymbals and blown their trumpets about a still and some sauerkraut, but although they speak with the tongues of angels, they have no charity. So long as suffering is in our midst, our work is still before us. I am sorry that things have not been altogether smooth down there. If anyone made a mistake, it is to be regretted, and if anybody abused his trust, it must not happen again.

With its simplicity and humor, that statement sums up the tragicomedy of her social ministry.

She left Elsinore in late August and returned to the parsonage alone. Hutton had gone east, "on Church business," she told reporters.

They photographed her at the typewriter, wearing a gingham jumper, looking well rested but gaunt and pale.

> I'm back to stay! My head is all healed up and my nerves calm as a mill pond when the wind has been turned off. I'll preach eighty-three sermons in the next ten weeks—eight a week and three thrown in for good measure . . .

It would take her a while to work into her regular schedule of twenty-one sermons a week.

———

Near Angelus Temple, Anthony Rudolph Oaxaka Quinn and his baby sister lived with their mother and grandmother in a tiny house without plumbing. Mother and grandmother were Mexican. The Irish-Mexican father, Francisco Quinn, had been killed outside their front door by an automobile. The family was dirt poor. The grandmother made day wages carrying water for a road crew.

One day Anthony Quinn came home from school to find

several strangers in his house, gathered around his grandmother's bed. A strong woman, she had developed some stomach disorder. The pain had grown so acute that for minutes at a time she could not inhale except in shallow breaths.

The men and women appeared very excited, some of them trembling, with their eyes closed as they held their hands on Quinn's grandmother and prayed. One was reading from a black bible while the others were making a strange gurgling noise in which the boy could make out the name "Jesus" but not much else.

Quinn had been going to Mass several times a week. He was studying with Father Anselmo, with a view of someday becoming a Catholic priest himself. At this point in his education the teenage boy suspected that anyone who was not Catholic might be the Devil's disciple.

So he shouted at these strangers, "Get out of my house, you're *evil!*" His grandmother groaned and shook her head.

A man held Tony's arms, explaining, "We're not doing anything wrong. We're praying to the same God, maybe in a different way . . . Your grandmother is going through great pain. She believes we can help her."

The old woman nodded in agreement.

"Grandma, I'll go to the church and have a Mass said for you. The priest will come and pray for you."

"Tony," she said, "I've heard these people can do miraculous things. I want them to stay."

The boy ran out the door, straight to the Catholic church. In breathless sentences he told Father Anselmo what he had seen. The "holy rollers" from Angelus Temple were practicing their heathen rites on his poor grandmother.

The priest looked very serious as he replied:

"Tony, I don't worship like the Protestants, but we mustn't be so narrow as to think they are devils. There are many ways to reach God. If your grandmother believes these people are the way, fine. Let them come."

Slowly the boy began to accept the Protestants coming and going in his house, as his grandmother's pain subsided under their ministrations.

"Now, Tony," said his grandmother. "I don't have the pains anymore. These people have helped me. We owe them something. I think we should both go and give thanks. I promised that if I got well, I'd give testimony."

That is how Anthony Quinn went to his first revival meeting, in the 500 Room of Angelus Temple.

Seated side by side were whites, blacks, and Mexican-Americans. Everyone felt at home, accepted.

"I had never seen five hundred people happy at the same time."

Watching his grandmother jump to her feet and give her testimony—about her son's death, her grandson's turmoil, and the miracle of her own healing—it seemed to Quinn that she was illuminated from within.

He had been an altar boy at the Catholic church. That Sunday he told Father Anselmo what the priest had known was coming: Tony would not be coming to Mass for a long while.

On Monday he took his saxophone to Angelus Temple. He told the musicians there he would be happy to play in their band. He played in the Temple. He played on street corners, where between songs he would preach to crowds in Spanish about the glories of Our Lord.

Until he was nineteen years old and his career in show business was well under way, Anthony Quinn's life centered on the Church of the Foursquare Gospel. From the great auditorium orchestra pit he witnessed the dramatic sermons, healing services, and the altar calls.

He writes:

> Years later, when I saw the great actresses at work, I would compare them to her. As magnificent as I would find Anna Magnani, Ingrid Bergman, Laurette Taylor, Katharine Hepburn, Greta Garbo, and Ethel Barrymore, they all fell short of that first electric shock Aimee Semple McPherson produced in me.

Anthony Quinn was so much in awe of the evangelist, he dared not look her in the eyes. She came to band rehearsals once in a while, and she had a big smile for everyone. But Quinn did not look Sister Aimee in the eyes because he was afraid she would be able to see into his soul.

One day he was blowing his saxophone at a rehearsal when he felt someone's eyes on the back of his neck. He knew it was Aimee. He resisted the impulse to turn around, until the pull overwhelmed him. During a pause in the music he looked over his shoulder.

She was sitting right behind him, smiling. Their eyes met.

Years later, the famous actor, seen by millions, would recall the joy of being seen by Sister Aimee: "I felt no fear, no embarrassment, no awe—just complete acceptance. She smiled as if to say, 'I know you. I like you.' It was so simple."

Other men and women recall a similar experience, standing in the unique light of those eyes. Perhaps she singled Quinn out because she saw in him so much of herself.

He was surprised that she knew his name.

"Tony, I understand you've played with the band the way I did when I was a young girl . . . I have the feeling that the Lord has singled you out to become a great preacher."

She told him she wanted to work with him next Saturday in the Mexican district.

When he arrived at the Temple to meet her that Saturday morning, Quinn saw a cavalcade of automobiles. She asked him to ride with her. He was fourteen years old.

"It was as if I'd been waiting an eternity for such an acceptance."

On the East Side, a huge crowd jammed the streets and surrounded the revival tent. Aimee kept Anthony Quinn close by her side as they made their way to the platform.

When the crowd was silent, she told them how happy she was to be among her Mexican brothers and sisters. And she was sorry she did not come more often, sorry she did not speak Spanish. But here, she announced, she had asked a young man she believed would one day become one of our great preachers, to translate her sermon into Spanish . . .

The boy was terrified.

"But she put her hand on my shoulder, and an electrical charge went through me. I spoke out loud and clear. I was her voice that night, the extension of that great power."

This was during the worst of the Depression. Most Mexicans in Los Angeles were illegal aliens. They were afraid to ask for county help no matter how urgent their need, because the civic authorities always asked embarrassing questions. Angelus Temple was a safe haven, a great source of comfort to the Mexican-Americans, because anyone could go there, day or night, and get help, no questions asked.

Thirty-five years later, the famous actor, star of classics like *Requiem for a Heavyweight* and *Zorba the Greek*, faced the television cameras and curiosity of Edwin Newman, the host of an NBC news program called "Speaking Freely."

Quinn blinked under the powerful lights, and his palms perspired. With all his experience as a performer and his verbal facility, he would never be at ease on live television.

Personal questions unsettled him. But when Edwin Newman broached the subject of the notorious Aimee Semple Mc-Pherson, asking if Quinn had *really* preached in her Temple, the actor felt a calm descend upon him. Anthony Quinn talked for five minutes on national television about his mentor, Sister Aimee, in a tribute that included much of the story just told, as well as the following.

I remember one Thanksgiving Day, actually and literally fainting on the street from hunger . . . and in those days if you called the government agency, you felt you could never recover your dignity from it. And the one human being that never asked what your nationality was, what you believed in and so forth, was Aimee Semple McPherson. All you had to do was pick up the phone and say "I'm hungry," and within an hour there'd be a food basket there for you.

She literally kept most of that Mexican community alive for many years. And for that I'm eternally grateful.

———

Aimee's return to the pulpit and welfare activities was wholehearted but short-lived. On December 30 she announced that

her health would not permit her to continue as pastor. She was
going to sail around the world and inspect the Foursquare
missions.

"I shall remain away as long as necessary to regain my health.
I don't know how long I will be gone."

She would travel with her nurse, Bernice Middleton. Her
husband would remain at home, minding the Temple.

"Mr. Hutton may join me on the French Riviera next fall."

But he would not meet her on the French Riviera, or anywhere else. As David Hutton came down the gangplank on
January 19, 1933, and the freighter cast off, bearing his sick wife
into the teeth of a gale, reporters observed that his eyes were
red from weeping. Had he grown to love her in spite of
himself? But now he knew the marriage was all but finished.

Hutton returned to the parsonage. There he took consolation
in the company of a friend from his theater days, a male dancer.
The male dancer came to live with David in the parsonage—
and something about him offended the sensibilities of the
church elders, always on guard against scandal. They told Hutton that the parsonage was no place for "such a person"—
people had begun to talk.

This put Hutton in a rage. So did the diminishment of his
authority at the Temple: before leaving, Aimee had given power
of attorney to act for her—in all official matters—to Harriet
Jordan and the lawyer Willedd Andrews. On the church records
Hutton was not even vice president anymore. He was merely
head of the music department.

Resigning from the music department, the baritone hired a
press agent/manager. He announced to the world that he was
returning to the stage.

The evangelist's daughter came home to live in the parsonage.
William Smythe, having done all he could do in America to put
distance between his marriage and the emotional storms of Angelus Temple, at last went back to sea. At the turn of the year
Roberta would bring an action for divorce. The complaint read:
"He humiliated her by speaking disparagingly of her mother
and of the religious purposes of the plaintiff," and that he had
"curbed the enthusiasm of the plaintiff about her mother, her

religious work, and her desire for church activities" by criti-
cizing the Church, its members and personnel.

Now Roberta was back in the fold. She took charge of the
Foursquare Bookstore.

From June of 1933 until Aimee's return in August, a dozen
telegrams passed between the baritone and the evangelist. Intimate, scurrilous, silly—somehow they all got into newspaper
headlines the day they were wired. It was a show-business press
agent's dream come true. The first cablegram, which arrived
from Paris on June 23 addressed to David Hutton at Angelus
Temple, was clearly a hoax: DARLING DAVE. NINE-POUND BOY.
DOING NICELY. UNDERSTAND PRESS INQUISITIVE BUT KEEPING
QUIET. ADORINGLY, WIFE. Anyone familiar with Aimee's medical
history (made public knowledge during the kidnapping episode)
knew that she lacked the organs of reproduction. But her lifelong business in the miraculous left room for speculation, controversy, and many column inches in the newspapers.

Hutton pretended the telegram had stunned him. His pleas
for confirmation, with Aimee's denials, led to a telegraphic
dialogue about their love and their marriage and whether he
would go to her or she would return to him.

For weeks this transatlantic opera was front-page news.

On the ship from Le Havre to Baltimore, Aimee got word
of Hutton's action for divorce. She refused to believe it. She
wired him: DAVID. SWEETHEART. REASSURE ME OF YOUR CON-
FIDENCE. To questions from the Associated Press she radioed
this simple message: "Never have I considered divorcing Mr.
Hutton. I still completely love him . . . With faith, and the
business tangles adjusted, the cloud will quickly pass and we
will live happily ever after."

Hutton faced his first paying audience in a vaudeville theater
in Long Beach. The curtains opened on the stout baritone in
white flannels and a blue blazer, leaning upon a distressed piano
and singing "Wanting You." He wore a flower in his lapel. He
sang love songs, and between songs he made jokes about his
marital difficulties.

His patter was interrupted one night on the Warner Theater

stage, when a woman in the second row pitched four raw eggs at the baritone, hitting him with three.

"Married life for me has been no bed of roses," said David Hutton.

Aimee's arrival in late July at the port of Baltimore attracted a swarm of newsmen and photographers. She received them in the captain's cabin, lying down. She wore a beige dress of woolen crepe and a scarf wrapped on her head like a turban.

Where her wedding band had been she wore a large aquamarine. A reporter observed: "Her lips were red, her cheeks were pink, her fingernails scarlet, and her face was an expressionless mask."

On August 1 she arrived in Los Angeles. She posed for newsreels with Rolf's baby daughter, born in her absence. Then a limousine drove her to the parsonage.

She wept when Hutton declined to meet her.

SHOW BUSINESS

In 1929 the Yale Puppeteers, led by Harry Burnett, created a marionette of Sister Aimee to play with figures of Gary Cooper, Helen Hayes, and Ramon Novarro in their celebrity review. Burnett persuaded the evangelist to be photographed with him, standing next to the dangling miniature of herself. Dressed in the same white dress and cape, holding the white bible in the same pose, the woman and the marionette create an eerie harmony.

Entering into the spirit of the photographic session, Aimee looks frighteningly like the puppet.

In these years she lived at the end of strings pulled by public opinion, adulation, reprehension, and obsessive curiosity. Her marriage had received astonishing press coverage. Now her divorce promised even more, as Hutton promoted his vaudeville career: "What's this latest report . . . ? David appearing in a film short carrying a nine-pound baby and the picture called 'Aimee's Tearful Eyeful!' He is merely getting this publicity because of my reputation!" said Aimee. This was true. But as vulgar as it was, the publicity was hers too, and she knew that *any* publicity was potentially bankable for the Church.

Hutton was booked at the Palace Theater in New York City as "Big Boy, the Baritone of Angelus Temple." The day after she returned from Europe, Aimee announced that her Church elders had approved plans for her to preach on the vaudeville circuit. She was playing a shrewd game with the promoters. Vaudeville managers had been knocking at her door with spectacular guarantees; every time she refused them, it made headlines, and then the promoters had to come back again and offer even more money.

Ma Kennedy, if Aimee had asked her opinion, would not have approved. "Get off the front page," was Minnie's advice in these situations, wherever Aimee tried to battle Satan in Satan's territory. But all of her instincts were telling Aimee to accept the money for the Church, and charge the enemy, in an arena where she would be most visible, controversial, and dramatic.

———

The headline in *The New York Times*, September 19, reads AIMEE M'PHERSON INVADES BROADWAY; the lead sentence features her guarantee—$5,000 per week.

A limousine took her to the Westbury Hotel on East 69th Street, where she talked to reporters and posed for photographs in the lobby. Mae Waldron and Bernice Middleton, her old New York City team, lent her support during the press conference.

"I am not on a vaudeville tour," she said. "I am going to preach at the Capitol Theater, coming on stage five times a day and preaching the Gospel for ten minutes."

The next day Major Edward Bowes hosted a celebrity luncheon. A hundred writers, artists, and actors showed up at the Hotel Gotham on Fifth Avenue. Aimee was guest of honor.

This time *The New Yorker* did not send Dorothy Parker to cut the evangelist down to size—Sister Aimee's welfare work had earned her a grudging respect even from that bastion of cynicism. Editor Ross dispatched the easygoing Morris Markey to follow Aimee from the celebrity luncheon to her performance at the Capitol.

Writes Markey:

> She is a gentle, conciliatory soul, tolerant of human frailty and willing to meet a sinner halfway. This was clearly demonstrated at her first public appearance on this visit . . . a luncheon affair . . . The hundred guests were perhaps surprised, certainly pleased, to find that their need for stimulant upon so awesome an occasion had been generously recognized. The Martinis were not distinguished, but plentiful.

Aimee arrived a bit late, neatly attired in a Paris street dress. Upon her entrance everyone sat down at table.

> During the meal she permitted herself to be gaily amused at the conversation of her immediate companions, and more than once her high, pleasant laughter rang above the hubbub of chatting voices.

After coffee, Major Bowes introduced her. Though he announced that no one but himself and the guest of honor would be addressing them, "it was hardly to be expected that Mr. Irvin Cobb and Mr. Charles Dillingham could take such an announcement seriously." The humorist Cobb began cracking jokes. "Most of the play of wit was upon the strange ways of the Lord . . . and that a good half of the assembled company were brought up in the Jewish faith."

At last Aimee rose to speak. All of her life, she said, she had worshiped from afar the distinguished names of the men and women who now sat before her at the table.

And now, when at last it is my privilege to greet you face to face, to see you and have you listen to my poor words, I feel humbled and meek. I am not clever. I am a simple country girl who happened to see the great light which shines so certainly upon the world.

She went on to tell her life story, in brief.
Writes Markey:

Four or five Broadway columnists later expressed regret that she did not go more deeply into her frequent romances and marriages, but she left such matters discreetly alone, and her final words were a benediction upon us all.

The next time the writer saw her, it was from a loge in the Capitol Theater. On the program Sister Aimee followed two acrobats, a midget, and the Radio Aces. As applause for the pop harmonists faded against the golden cupids of the proscenium arch, a hush fell on the auditorium. The lights dimmed to blue radiance; the curtains opened on a simple set.

Aimee wore a white satin robe which fell in graceful lines from the shoulder to the tips of her white satin shoes. She had on more clothing than all the other women in the review together. Her pale hair was pulled back tight; but the severity of her appearance was relieved by the black stole that draped her neck and fell below the waist.

She smiled at the clamor of applause.

"At this moment there are seventy thousand persons in the United States praying that God may give me courage and wisdom," she said.

Three of them were her managers, vaudeville agents Sam Lyons, Marvin Welt, and Al Weil, who were visualizing a healthy percentage split over $50,000, ten to twenty weeks in New York and another six weeks in Washington, D.C.

At his left, Markey heard a pale young woman murmur to her escort: "Gee, I don't wonder all them guys fell for her. She's got IT, and I don't mean maybe." The man said nothing; he lit a cigarette. The fumes drifted into a thin cloud of tobacco smoke that swirled in the strong beam of the spotlight.

The evangelist launched into the story of her life, as only she could tell it: childhood on the farm, Robert Semple's death in China, the building of the Temple, her faith in the white-bound bible she held in her hand. It was charming and simple, but the *New Yorker* writer knew perfectly well Sister Aimee was not going to shed much light upon the Great White Way.

He writes:

> In all truth, she was not preaching a belief to us, but giving us a glimpse of a celebrated person, giving us the tale of that person's checkered existence. It was precisely as if Admiral Byrd had been there, telling us how he licked the South Pole . . .
>
> And even then, it is the sad truth that in the end she let us down. She didn't get around to the divorces. Behind the cigarette smoke in the loges there was a good deal of murmuring at that.

She let them down. *She didn't get around to the divorces.* Reviewing her performance, *Variety* raved about her stage technique, calling her "a preceptress in the arts of projecting a personality over the footlights."

> Her poise in the face of sacrilegious titters is something to admire . . . She has perfect diction, a rapid flow of words, boundless self-assurance and a chummy personal intimacy. That Broadway refused to thaw out for her just proves what a stubborn bunch of sinners Broadwayites are.

The vaudeville agents Lyons & Lyons, Batchelor & Cargill, Marvin Welt and Al Weil—she let them down, too. The Capitol hit an all-time low for the week, with a gross of $17,600, of which Aimee got her guarantee of $5,000. They canceled her.

If they had only listened to her from the beginning, the agents would not have been so disappointed. Aimee had not been deceiving herself, and she certainly was not deceiving anyone else, when she told *The New York Times*, "I am not on a vaudeville tour." She knew exactly what she was doing. The week at the Capitol was a windfall, a bold breakthrough in public relations.

Newsweek (September 30, 1933) remarked:

It may seem incredible for so urbane and world-weary a New Yorker as Alexander Woollcott [*The Man Who Came to Dinner*] to become lyrical over a husky-voiced, sin-lashing evangelist who tells her audiences that a "gentleman cow" once said "boo" at her. But that is just what happened last week when the plump man of letters met blonde Sister Aimee at a luncheon in New York . . . This brought many of the city's intelligentsia to the Capitol Theater . . .

The promoters had spent 70,000 New York advertising dollars putting her name in lights and paid her $5,000 for a week's work. The press coverage and reviews had been generally favorable.

She was prepared for the cancellations in New York and Washington: within a week she was booked in auditoriums in Philadelphia and Boston. There she held full-scale revivals, traveling with a road crew of musicians, scene designers, and costumers. This was the beginning of her last national tour. Between September of 1933 and December 20, 1934 Sister Aimee would travel 15,000 miles, preaching in 21 states and 46 cities—336 sermons to more than two million people (which was about two percent of the population in 1934)—not counting the listeners reached by 45 radio stations.

Nearly everywhere she went, her picture took up three columns above the fold of the front page. Typical was the spread in *The Cleveland Plain Dealer*, December 16, where the headline linked her name with Mae West's.

"What do you think of Mae West, Mrs. McPherson?"

"I have never seen her and I don't think I'd care to say anything. That's a subject on which there are so many ins and outs . . ."

If Mae West saw the clipping, she must have been delighted—she could not have fed the evangelist a better gag line.

In 1932 Edith Barrett had co-starred with Texas Guinan and the child actress Helen Roland on Broadway in a dramatization of *Sister Aimee*, which was based on a biography by Nancy Barr Mavity. Two weeks after Aimee left New York, comedienne Helen Broderick was impersonating her in the hit musical *As Thousands Cheer* by Irving Berlin and Moss Hart. And after

Joseph Henry Steele's lengthy profile of Sister Aimee, "Bernhardt of the Sawdust Trail" in the March, 1933 issue of *Vanity Fair*, she became a mainstay of that most fashionable magazine—as an idol, a curiosity, a figure of fun. Painter and illustrator Constantin Alajalov drew an Aimee Semple McPherson-Hutton paper doll for that magazine, No. 2 in the notorious series called "Vanity Fair's Own Paper Dolls." Caricaturist Garetto included her in *Vanity Fair*'s "Great American Waxworks," drawing the preacher in a showcase with Babe Ruth, Max Baer, and Katharine Hepburn. Mae West is there, and Charles Lindbergh, Mickey Mouse, Herbert Hoover, and the Barrymores—only a few others. It is an intimate party.

In August of 1934 Aimee traveled to Bartlesville, Oklahoma to bring comfort to victims of the Dust Bowl drought. Staying at the new Hotel Maire, she wrote to a Miss Amanda Dye of Searcy, Arkansas. It is one of the few of Aimee's letters of any length that have survived. It speaks forcefully of her belief that her true vocation was a ministry of performance, particularly music.

August 1, 1934

Miss Amanda Dye
Searcy, Arkansas

Darling:

Your precious letter of the 22nd, with the first check toward my Musical Guild has been received, and has put new heart in me.

We are working here for God and Souls, and are sweltering at 112 in the shade. I have sent all the way to California for Charles Walkum to come and take down the music which God has poured into my soul.

Every day new expenses mount up, but somehow I do not care what I spend on the music, because I still maintain that when you and I are dead, the music will live on and on.

Honey, when we leave here to-nite, I am going to Pawhuska for two days. Then I'll be in Jefferson, Ohio, for a day and then back on the lecture platform, on clear up through Canada. You will always be able to reach me by letter in care of Harriet Jordon, or through Reverend Correll at Kenoshe.

I was so glad to hear of the children being at your home. I can just close my eyes now and see those swinging beds and imagine the baby tucked away in them.

We certainly should get together, as a church, and pray for rain. In every direction here, the corn is dead, simply burned up. I was entertained, yesterday at the home of Mr. Phillips, of the Phillips Petroleum Company here. Out here they are shooting their cattle and killing thousands of head, because there is no longer food or water. This is an awful situation, and collections are just nothing.

I must run now to my music, as Mr. Walkum is in the next room waiting.

Your appreciative
Sister

PS But I'm glad I know nice you. Hurry up and come somewhere I am, so's I kin sing you my new songs.

SHARING THE STAGE, L. A., 1935

Rheba Crawford had followed Sister Aimee's career with admiration verging on wonder since 1917. During that winter the young Salvation Army worker was driving through Florida when she saw Aimee wielding a maul, driving stakes for her revival tent. So impressed was Miss Crawford with Aimee's determination, she emptied her purse into the preacher's hand, said, "God bless you," then got back in her car and drove away.

Rheba's path lay north, to the Sodom and Gomorrah of New York City.

Pretty Rheba Crawford went on to become known as the "angel of Broadway." The heroine of Damon Runyon's *Guys and Dolls* is based on her. She made headlines by preaching in Times Square, tying up traffic while she saved souls.

In 1929 she arrived in Hollywood with a scheme to build a hotel as a shelter for the girls from small towns and farms who flocked to the film capital. The stock-market crash upset her financing. So she turned her attention to other ideas for helping victims of the Depression.

Dark-eyed, compact, with her strong Scottish profile, wide jaw, and square shoulders, Rheba was a dynamo, more like Sister Aimee than any other woman, but tougher, abrasive. She was less charismatic in front of a crowd, but still spell-binding; offstage she was far more persuasive. In that time of crisis she convinced Governor James Rolph to appoint her welfare director of the state.

Impatient with red tape and bureaucratic delay, she harried the legislature, making friends and enemies. She had grown up poor, an orphan. "I learned what it means to go hungry; hungry people can't wait." Months before FDR brought national resources to bear on the emergency in Los Angeles, Rheba Crawford jump-started California's relief program.

Her accomplishments in California caught Sister Aimee's eye.

Welfare work in Los Angeles brought them together, and their similar backgrounds provided a comfortable bond. Though the women would never become close friends, they quickly formed a working relationship. Aimee needed help with her preaching schedule, and her admiration for Rheba's prowess in the pulpit stopped just short of her finding it threatening— at first.

Shortly after Aimee's divorce, early in 1935, Rheba Crawford appeared at Angelus Temple as a substitute preacher.

Soon the newspapers reported that a contract existed between the two women, a curious contract. Later they confirmed it: Rheba would receive $600 a month from the Church. While Aimee was on the road, Rheba would occupy the pulpit and manage the radio station. When Aimee came home, Rheba would "go on tour," i.e., disengage herself from Temple affairs. The contract was controversial because Rheba was still a salaried employee of the state.

But for Aimee it looked liked an ideal setup. As she planned to sail for the Orient in January of 1935, she left the Temple

business management to Harriett Jordan and Roberta, and the
pulpit responsibilities to Rheba Crawford.

———

The split between Aimee's private life and her public persona
had been accomplished, at great personal expense, by 1930. One
proof of her labor to keep growing and changing as a free
intelligence is the remarkable book *Give Me My Own God*
(1936).

She had been dining with some college students in Boston,
in the autumn of 1934. They were trying to persuade the stylish
evangelist that "the teachings of the Nazarene have outlived
their usefulness; education and science have supplanted religion
and ancient legend; cold reasoning is the new savior of the
world."

Nothing she said could convince the students of the Scrip-
tural commonplace: "Blessed is the nation whose trust is in the
Lord."

"Piqued by their challenge," she writes in the opening of her
book, "I decided to find for the youth of today an incontro-
vertible answer. I went out and looked upon the world with
new eyes."

Accompanied by nurse Bernice Middleton, Aimee sailed for
Japan. It was a journey with a philosophical agenda, which
frames *Give Me My Own God*, a travel book with a simple
moral.

> I circled the globe, climbed the Himalayan foot-hills on frozen
> Tibetan borders, traversed the fiery deserts of Africa, penetrated
> the jungles of Zamboanga, and looked into the golden face of mod-
> ernized Tokyo.
>
> Travelling by junk and river schooner, by elephant and camel,
> bullock cart and donkey, tonga and dandy chair, I searched the
> world for first-hand information.
>
> I mounted endless worn stone steps and explored uncounted miles
> of pungent shrines, looked into the faces of Gods and men, children
> and beasts. I was the guest of statesman and reformer, of harem
> and zenana, of mansion and squalid beggar's hut. I talked to the

Foreign Minister of Japan, visited Mahatma Gandhi, listened to
Mussolini, and returned to America . . .

Using her celebrity status as a calling card, she interviewed
the rich and powerful; relying on her training as a missionary
and on her wayward audacity, she penetrated corners of society
off-limits to American tourists, forbidden to women. For this
dimension alone the book ought to be in print and available—
it is a detailed criticism of the world customs of 1935 by a bold
woman who is distressed by the universal subjection of women.

Setting out from Kowloon, Aimee visited the floating brothels on the Cantonese River, the infamous Flower Boats to which
impoverished fathers sold their blind daughters for food. She
also visited a harem and a leper colony. Her book contains many
images of women enslaved or victimized.

In Bombay, she received a telegram from Mahatma Gandhi
inviting her to visit him at his headquarters in Wardha.

Aimee's meeting with the ascetic sage in spectacles and loin-
cloth, the Oxford graduate known as the Soul of India, was the
only scene of her 1935 *Wanderjahr* to capture the attention of
the world press. The afternoon with Gandhi was briefly noted
as an amusing curiosity, somewhat like the meeting between
boxer Muhammad Ali and poet maid Marianne Moore forty
years later. *Vanity Fair* featured Gandhi and Sister Aimee in a
full-page cartoon: The evangelist is advising the great man how
they might prosper together by hitting the sawdust trail, as a
preaching duet. The caricature, like the brief press notices, is
an instructive example of image reduction and distortion—how
a story must be trimmed to play in the newspapers, and how
such reduction can completely belie the facts.

Aimee's eight-page account of meeting Gandhi and his famous companion Miss Slade presents a dialogue of substance.
She asks all the right questions—difficult questions—and records the Mahatma's answers fully and precisely.

Aimee, shocked by the squalor of the villages in the East,

probes Gandhi. Can they be improved? Gandhi tells her that nothing can be accomplished, materially, before India achieves home rule.

He continues:

> "Our villages have fallen prey to the very methods of production which have brought about your own Depression. Many industries, at one time our basis of wealth, have died out. Even occupations that cater to the everyday needs of the populace—clothing, shelter, food—have perished. Imports from abroad now supply the most primary needs. Thus we find in our land of today an eccentric maladjustment of commerce."
>
> "And you propose . . ."
>
> "If the economic conditions of the people are to be ameliorated, ways must be found to increase the number of occupations . . . We hope to stem the current of exodus from the village to the city, and reverse it."

Aimee comments that Gandhi's plan resembles Senator Johnson's "back to the soil" plan in America.

"Exactly," says Gandhi.

> As we sat and talked, his right hand busied itself with a small wooden spinning wheel. His left evolved a sturdy thread from a wad of cotton as mysteriously as an industrious spider spins gossamer for its web.
>
> I watched with fascination . . . the mechanism employed was the most simple . . . one which the poorest could easily afford.

When she leaves, Gandhi sends his secretary to guide her through the new schools, shops, and experimental stations.

And he gives her a white sari made of cloth his own slender hands have woven.

Aimee's conversation with Gandhi reveals a practical curiosity evident throughout *Give Me My Own God*. While the book's religious moral is the simple motto "Trust in God," Aimee's keen observations of communism, fascism, organized labor, and the Gandhian revolution reveal the careful refinement of a political point of view, independent and informed solely by field study.

Returning to America on the eve of the Second World War, Aimee led the American clergy in a violent denunciation of Hitler and Mussolini from the pulpit. And she was among the first to defend the establishment of a Jewish homeland in Palestine.

————

While Aimee was abroad, her daughter managed the affairs of the Temple with the help of Harriet Jordan.

Roberta, at twenty-four, an attractive dark-eyed divorcee, became a powerful new force in the Church, as vice president. Energetic, articulate, she showed every sign of realizing her mother's dream, following in Aimee's footsteps. What she lacked in experience she learned quickly under her grandmother's shrewd guidance. Minnie Kennedy, living comfortably in retirement at Hermosa Beach, kept in touch with the granddaughter she had raised. The two maintained the close bond that sometimes forms between child and grandparent, free of child-parent tensions. Now the independent young woman was very much Minnie's protégée—a modern Minnie, impeccably dressed, exquisitely refined.

Roberta Semple and her grandmother watched Rheba Crawford in the pulpit with growing concern. As the replacement for Sister Aimee, Rheba did a good job of filling the Temple on Sunday and keeping the collections moving. But too much of the preacher's success was owed to her attacks on the government. In fiery sermons from the Temple platform and over the airwaves of KFSG, the square-jawed preacher (still on the state payroll as welfare director) lambasted the mayor and city council for condoning gambling, prostitution, and drug traffic in Los Angeles. Reckless, explosive, Aimee's replacement was not afraid to call the alleged villains and collaborators by name.

It was a sure-fire way of getting attention, and Rheba got plenty. Evangeline Booth had once dismissed her from a Salvation Army position because the great Evangeline would not tolerate grandstanding by her subordinates. Aimee felt the same way. Furthermore, she would never have mounted this sort of sensational attack on the hometown lawmakers, or the police, with whom she had happily cooperated during a difficult decade.

On Aimee's return, Rheba gave up the pulpit, as agreed, then left Los Angeles on a speaking tour.

To celebrate her own homecoming, Aimee ascended the Temple dome. As photographers scrambled below, she dedicated a new seven-foot neon cross with a prayer, then came down to preach a sermon.

Her text was "Little Red Riding Hood." This was not her first sermon on a secular text; she had preached "Dr. Jekyll and Mr. Hyde" in 1929. But this comic illustration, in which she frolicked in a hooded cape, her enormous basket loaded with a cross, a bible, an oil cruse, grapes, Communion bread and wine, roast beef, and a crown (for the Second Coming), Sister's hilarious dialogue with a Bible student in a wolf's costume, was an instant hit. The skit was so successful, she followed it with a dozen fairy-tale sermons in the 1930's, including "Little Miss Muffet" (where the Devil, as spider, descended on piano wire to frighten little Aimee from the curds of Salvation), "Alice in Wonderland," and "Three Little Pigs."

Fairy tales and Mother Goose provided some relief from the horror story Aimee had brought home with her from Europe. She writes in *Give Me My Own God*:

> When I first saw him, Mussolini was standing on a flag-festooned platform in an open square in Rome, thundering terse, eloquent, war-inspiring words over a sea of black-shirts.
>
> Whether in Naples or Rome, Milan or Trieste, I was awakened at the crack of dawn by the tramp of military feet that passed beneath my window . . . Young boys in their earliest teens had been instructed to lay aside their bats and marbles and take up death-dealing arms. Young girls in uniform drilled industriously . . . War was in the air!

While Mussolini stirred up sentiment and looked for an excuse to invade Ethiopia, Aimee fought the calendar to prepare her book for publication in New York. It was all she could do: to cry out that disaster was imminent, a second world war that would make the first look like a medieval tournament.

Rolf McPherson recalls his mother working furiously that summer to finish *Give Me My Own God.* Day and night she toiled with a secretary, as if the book was the catharsis for her own dread, and perhaps also the handbook humankind might use to avoid destruction. This was the same woman who had been obsessed with the war in France in 1916–1917, building her ministry on sermons like "Peace Palace Parable" and "Modern Warfare," meditations that compare military action to the wars of the spirit.

Lacking the emotional center most of us find in marriage, family, and friendship, the evangelist was torn by a cosmic compassion, and scattered prayers to the four winds, wherever human need was most intense.

In Italy that spring she had experienced a vision of the coming holocaust. Inside her the war had already begun.

———

The working relationship with Rheba Crawford was a necessary paradox. To be an effective replacement for Sister Aimee, the associate pastor had to have her own appeal. Yet insofar as Rheba had an independent appeal, Aimee would find her threatening.

Roberta Salter remembers Rheba's powerful personality, that she was a women's rights activist, and that some Temple members found this repugnant. To people's horror or delight, Rheba went without a bra, and she had been seen dancing in public with her husband. When someone objected, she further alarmed everyone with the comment: "If I can sleep with him, I can dance with him."

In August, Aimee went on the road to preach in Atlantic City and in Rockford, Illinois, warming up for a two-month campaign of the Pacific Northwest and Canada. Rheba returned to the Angelus Temple pulpit.

She picked up right where she had left off. Over the radio she delivered a blistering denunciation of the city government, which, she said, was soft on the purveyors of vice. Finally she threatened, from the pulpit, to lead a recall movement against

the mayor and city council. At that point Aimee let it be known
she was not pleased by her associate pastor's sermons.

A jocular tension had existed for some time between the two
women. The Bible students recall a rare occasion when Aimee
and Rheba were on the Angelus Temple platform the same
night. Rheba had resisted every effort to get her into a Foursquare uniform. But on this particular night, as Rheba was
preaching, she overreached herself with a broad gesture, threw
open her arms while back-pedaling—and fell into the baptismal
font. The audience exploded in laughter as Aimee gave her
gasping and sputtering associate a hand up out of the water and
led her backstage.

In a few minutes Rheba emerged, escorted by smiling Aimee
and wearing, to everyone's delight, the Foursquare colors. This
evoked from the crowded auditorium a standing ovation. But
it was the first and last time Rheba was ever seen in a Foursquare
uniform.

By the beginning of the year 1936 this sort of good-natured
kidding between the two women was turning sour. Then came
the scandal over poor Vivian Denton. She was an owl-faced,
plump ex–chorus girl (from Tex Guinan's) who had been converted by Rheba. Rheba put the zany Vivian to work in the
Temple's publicity department. Whereupon Vivian began appearing, all too frequently, in the newspapers—promoting her
own career and Rheba Crawford's.

On February 10, 1936, Vivian Denton made the front page.
A neighbor had found her on the bathroom floor of her apartment, gasping for breath, saying that she had swallowed poison.

Vivian told the police and reporters she wanted to die because
of the way she had been treated by Aimee Semple McPherson.
She said that Sister had insulted her, fired her, and thrown her
down a flight of stairs.

> After I had gone through four hours of torture from Sister I came
> home and became moody. I paced the floor of my apartment until
> after midnight, and then all of a sudden I could restrain myself no
> longer. I walked into the bathroom and swallowed the poison while
> looking at my reflection in the mirror.

There had been witnesses with Aimee all day, and there was no flight of stairs, and these days she rarely talked to anyone for longer than twenty minutes, including her children.

Though Vivian Denton got nowhere with her case, she made news by suing Sister Aimee for slander, demanding $400,000 in damages.

All this happened while Rheba was in Glendale Sanatorium with "an intestinal malady" and Harriet Jordan spent many hours at her bedside. Aimee began to suspect that Rheba was masterminding a plot.

If Denton's action began to look to Aimee like the barb of a conspiracy, we can hardly blame her. She did not know whom to trust. And one should consider her overall state of mind, the emotional pressure she was under, which caused her to act as she did during the following months.

Her worst fears about Europe were quickly confirmed when Mussolini invaded Ethiopia in October of 1935. She was on tour in the Northwest, continually reaching for the newspapers, praying for the League of Nations. It had tried and failed to prevent aggression. Now Hitler felt encouraged to violate the Versailles Treaty by sending troops into the Rhineland.

A deepening tone of millennialism in her preaching reveals the evangelist's anguish over the impending catastrophe. The pressure mounting in Sister Aimee would soon be released in a series of prophecies made "in tongues," the first she had delivered in public since 1918.

In times of crisis Aimee threw herself into the routine of Angelus Temple, whose tremendous needs could totally absorb her. Returning from her autumn campaign in late November, she began writing sermons for the holiday season. Also, despite the efforts of Harriet Jordan and Roberta Semple, the Temple was mired in debt. Lacking an accounting system, the Commissary was plagued by rumors of graft. Moreover, while Aimee labored to control the Church and its dependencies under the holding company, that control was repeatedly challenged in time-consuming lawsuits.

Aimee had never abandoned the healing ministry; she had only tried to diffuse the public's interest in it. Ambulances continued to line up at the Temple doors on Wednesdays and Saturdays. Wheelchairs and stretchers still jammed the aisles and the altar rails. But Aimee would appear unannounced, when she did appear. Other ministers had the gift of healing, laid hands on the invalids, and prayed the same old prayers—with greater or lesser results. When Aimee did conduct a healing service, she worked side by side with them, so that less attention would be focused on her own peculiar endowment. Divine healing, above all, was a sacrament. It must not be perceived as a circus act or a clinic. She was not there to entertain journalists or demonstrate a technique to be reviewed by medical professors.

She wrote the divine healing sermons, one for each service she attended. She participated as an intercessor and a teacher. Most of the living eyewitness accounts we have of healings accomplished under Sister Aimee's ministry come from students who attended those services in the 1930's as a curriculum requirement. Aimee Semple McPherson was an authority on the spiritual dimension of healing; so her students went to take notes on the sermons, not to ogle "miracles." Yet what they witnessed, night after night, made their eyes bug out.

Fifteen of these students, now retired ministers, agreed to be interviewed in Hemet, California in 1991. Most of them were foreign missionaries. Now in their seventies and eighties, bright-eyed, ramrod-straight, they are an impressive sample of that generation. What most struck the interviewer was their universal good humor, and a no-nonsense style in giving information.

Questioned about the healings, they were grave at first, wanting the interviewer to understand that the subject was sacred. Then the accounts came: several had seen, with their own eyes, a goiter vanish on a man or woman's neck as if deflated by a pinprick; most had seen the blind and deaf healed; all had seen crippled men and women rise from wheelchairs after Sister Aimee's prayer, or toss away their crutches.

As the witnesses added story to story, the tone began to change from gravity to humor. Perhaps they had no other way to deal with such astounding memories of the awesome power of the Lord. As Pentecostal ministers they had seen people healed by the power of prayer throughout their long careers, but they had never seen anything like the drama of Sister Aimee's healings, the frequency and speed of the physical changes.

They began to recall the most humorous healings, because the ordinary blind, deaf, and lame now ran together in their memories.

There was a vain young woman who knelt at the altar. She looked like someone who ought to have praised God for her good health; yet she had come to get relief from the Great Physician because her dentures pained her. As she knelt before Sister Aimee, the young woman begged for a new set of teeth.

The evangelist looked quickly ahead at the line of invalids waiting at the rail, then into the young woman's eyes.

"Is that *really* what you want?" she asked.

"Oh yes, Sister, I am in such pain . . ."

Aimee shrugged, put one hand under the woman's jaw and the other behind her head, as you would to feed a pill to a dog. She held her for a moment and then passed on.

Weeks later, the woman returned, toothless and with a strange story. She had lost weight. One morning after Aimee had prayed for her, she could not get her dentures to fit in her mouth. She went to the dentist. After a thorough examination the amazed dentist told her that a new set of teeth was making its way through the inflamed gum tissue. For the time being, the false teeth were useless.

Then there was the woman whose right leg was two inches shorter than the left. She wore a lift in her right shoe so she could walk on the level. The woman walked proudly and gracefully to the altar so Aimee could lay hands on her and pray for her leg. Afterwards the hopeful subject got up from the rail, took a few limping steps, stumbled, and fell over—because Jesus had evened up the two legs, and now the orthopedic lift made her lopsided. Praise the Lord! She took off her shoes and walked naturally up the aisle of Angelus Temple, tears in her eyes.

As Italy completed the conquest of Ethiopia and Mussolini

backed the fascist Franco in Spain, Sister Aimee prayed for the
sick. She prayed for the Prince of Peace to bring sanity to world
leadership.

Meanwhile the bread lines lengthened in the streets of Los
Angeles. Aimee's Commissary hemorrhaged money. When reports reached her that the Temple's debt was approaching
$60,000, with the rumor that creditors would foreclose on
Temple properties, she moved to reorganize the accounting
department.

Desperate for the order the Temple had lacked since Minnie's
departure, Aimee looked around her for leadership. Her eyes
lit upon the Reverend Giles Knight as the bespectacled book-
keeper hunched over a ledger in the business office. A young
Foursquare minister who had studied law, Knight had been
Minnie's right-hand man in the early thirties, rising from di-
visional superintendent to Southern California field adviser of
Foursquare churches. Observing the stress on Sister Mc-
Pherson, Knight felt God calling him to help get the Temple
out of debt and put it on a firm foundation.

Tall and dignified, Giles Knight looked a little like Kenneth
Ormiston without any sense of humor—thin-lipped, hard-
working, holy-minded.

Aimee promoted Knight to the position of assistant business
manager (assistant to Harriet Jordan), with orders to reduce the
debt. This he began to do with grim diligence.

She left Los Angeles for a vacation in February of 1936. Emotionally and physically exhausted, she entrusted the Temple to
God for safekeeping. As far as she knew, Rheba Crawford,
Harriet Jordan, and a dozen lawyers and creditors were conspiring to take it all away from her.

———

Roberta Semple was in a curious and awkward position.

She understood why her mother might think Rheba Crawford and company were trying to take the Temple away from
her. But she knew it wasn't true. Roberta had spent a good deal
of time with Rheba, knew she was hotheaded, reckless, but not

treacherous. In the two years Rheba had been crusading against vice on Radio KFSG, the Angel of Broadway had made heavy-weight enemies both on the police force and in the Mob. These men would stop at nothing to see that Rheba Crawford found something to do other than talk about them on the radio.

Roberta recalls being invited to a meeting under a cloak of secrecy with two thugs who would not reveal their identities. They warned her that Rheba Crawford was conspiring to sell Angelus Temple to a rival church. They told Roberta they had seen Rheba talking to these ministers, making a deal with them—and that Roberta had best let her mother know it, so Aimee could act swiftly to dismiss Rheba Crawford before she had her way.

But Roberta knew the church leaders and the occasion in question, and understood it was altogether innocent. She knew these agents were lying, and that Aimee was under pressure by similar "informants" to dump Rheba Crawford before she succeeded in taking her place. Aimee's own lawyer, the beetle-browed Willedd Andrews, readily agreed Rheba was planning a coup.

Andrews had certain canine virtues—loyalty, obedience—which made him rather appealing beside his predecessor, Cromwell Ormsby. Unfortunately "he was *not* a good lawyer," in the understated judgment of Rolf McPherson. Rolf watched the bumbling Andrews, in an excess of zeal to protect his boss and his job, lay the groundwork for a family tragedy.

When Aimee left on vacation, Andrews was pressing for a new contract. He needed reassurance. She had given the Vivian Denton slander suit to a younger lawyer, Jacob Moidel. This handsome, red-haired bachelor was clever, fast-talking, intense. He had already charmed both Rheba and Roberta in his handling of the ugly lawsuit.

If Aimee had felt more secure about Temple politics, she might never have summoned another lawyer—but at the beginning of 1931 it seemed clear that Andrews did not have matters firmly in hand. On February 22, she wired the Temple from New Orleans. She was letting him go, canceling his re-

tainer. And on the way to visit the Grand Canyon, she sent
another wire, appointing Jacob Moidel to be the Temple's new
attorney.

Moidel's opinion was that stability in the affairs of Angelus
Temple would come only when the principal players all felt
secure in their roles. Rheba Crawford, whose own health had
been undermined by the pressures of serving people who dis-
trusted her, felt as if she had been cast as a conniving Lady
Macbeth. Harriet Jordan, who had served with unwavering
loyalty for fifteen years, now felt her future was threatened,
since Aimee suspected her of collusion with Rheba.

And Roberta, whom everyone still trusted, found herself in
the middle. Moidel, being a lawyer, thought what any employee
needed was a good contract; when he proposed this to Roberta,
it made perfect sense to her. She told her mother there was
urgent business to discuss, and Aimee agreed to meet her, Jordan, and Moidel in Phoenix on March 14, 1936.

What transpired in that hotel room in Phoenix between Aimee
and them became the crux of the last noteworthy courtroom
drama of her life—surely the saddest.

The facts are as follows: Moidel had four contracts in his
briefcase, one agreement apiece for himself, Roberta, Harriet
Jordan, and Rheba Crawford. These contracts guaranteed the
positions of the principals at a fair wage for a certain term:
Roberta as associate Temple business manager, Jordan as manager, Moidel as attorney, Crawford as associate pastor.

Aimee scowled at the sight of these documents. She did not
believe in written agreements for Church employees—Rheba's
case had been an exception. Harriet Jordan, for instance, had
never been under contract. Rolf McPherson confirms that his
mother thought contracts were superfluous in Church affairs.
He points out that to this day the Foursquare organization does
very well without them.

Roberta, Jordan, and Moidel explained to Aimee that without
such written agreements she would lose some if not all the
leaders of her organization; they would go elsewhere. And in
view of the debts and pending lawsuits, she needed all their
support if she was not to lose the Temple.

After a restless night's sleep, Aimee signed the contracts the next morning. They would be duly entered into the minutes of the Church corporation three weeks later. She signed them, and then became so busy that it would be six months before she got around to complaining she had been coerced.

Leaving Phoenix, everybody returned to Los Angeles to prepare for the thirtieth anniversary of the 1906 Azusa Street revival. The aged black veterans of that movement, from which modern Pentecostalism spread worldwide, had approached Sister Aimee, asking if they might use the Temple facilities for a one-week celebration.

She welcomed the opportunity.

"The revival spirit which had surged for years had waned by the spring of 1936. Attendances when I was not in the pulpit had dropped somewhat . . ." The multiracial Azusa Street celebration began as a one-week effort, but once the party got going, it went on for months.

> Conviction hung like a cloud over record audiences, and hundreds rushed to the altars in ever-recurrent waves crying, "God be merciful . . ." No less than three altar calls marked some of the services, especially the divine healing services . . . Deaf mutes commenced to speak and hear the Word of God, and lines of beds were carried out empty as joyous patients rose and walked. Moreover, hundreds of people at a time were sometimes slain under the power of God, many receiving the baptism with the Holy Ghost.

These spontaneous Holy Ghost rallies of April and May coincided with Aimee's sense of urgency that the world come to Christ quickly. It is the same millenarian anxiety that animates *Give Me My Own God*, and produces the first prophecy in tongues delivered in eighteen years.

> Affairs of the world are winding up to strike the twelfth hour, introducing the great Battle of Armageddon as told by John in Revelation 16:16.
>
> In the closing days of time before the coming of the Prince of Peace, allied evil powers are gathering together in war . . .
>
> The new line-up in Europe will carry all nations to a world war

so destructive and bitter as to make everyone forget the war just past some twenty years.

The prophetess, in her white uniform and the cape she had worn during the First World War, stood upon the stage of Angelus Temple and thundered. Hollow-eyed, inspired with a vision so awful, no voice but hers could convey it, she chanted prophecies on August 3, August 7, and September 28:

> Yea and I will not hold back My plague from this fair land . . . The Hand of God shall be lifted and the plagues of Satan shall be turned loose . . .

These were exactly the days Hitler was negotiating his pact with Mussolini, in which Germany would take eastern Europe as its sphere of expansion, leaving the Mediterranean to Italy.

———

While Sister Aimee preached and prophesied and laid hands on the sick, Rheba Crawford continued her attack on police and politicians over the radio. Though Aimee reassured the public she was getting along with her associate pastor, she allowed the Temple elders to call on Rheba to resign. When they denied Rheba the use of KFSG, she continued on an independent station. Jacob Moidel had to explain to the targets of her rhetoric that she did not represent the views of Angelus Temple.

From the pulpit in early July, Aimee said: "We are not in politics. Everybody talks too much. There is work to be done here. There is no time for bickering."

But the bickering made time for itself in the late summer and early autumn. The conflict between Rheba Crawford's friends and enemies battened on an argument over the Temple's finances. On July 10 Aimee had given Giles Knight orders to put the Temple "on a cash basis," to off-load the $60,000 debt— and let no one stop him.

Knight quickly reviewed the past and present difficulties. The Great Depression had taken its toll. The Temple had been split several times by visiting evangelists who, instead of leaving town after preaching, set up competing churches in the neighborhood, proselytizing Foursquare members. Knight recalled hearing how the settlement with Minnie Kennedy had cleaned out the financial reserves, and how Minnie still influenced her granddaughter Roberta. And, of course, it was well known that lawyer after lawyer had not only failed to protect Aimee from disastrous business deals—they actually had involved her in them.

It was evident to Knight that only the strictest control would restore fiscal stability. When he put everyone on a near-starvation budget—Harriet Jordan, Rheba Crawford, the Commissary, the radio station, Jacob Moidel—the crew mutinied.

Before this there was no requisition or purchasing system. It was like Molière's theater company: Whoever wanted money simply took what he needed from the treasury. The most honest of the Temple's leaders had grown so comfortable in the absence of standard accounting checks that Knight's new budget and purchase ledger seemed instruments of torture—of a financial inquisition.

On July 27, 1936, newsmen on the Temple beat were intrigued by the sight of a handyman unscrewing the light bulbs from the sign that spelled Rheba Crawford's name. It would be replaced by the words CONTINUOUS REVIVAL over the main entrance.

Roberta Semple, caught in the middle, wrote a letter of protest to her mother from Moidel's office (September 24):

> The powers he [Knight] demands as necessary to his employment are unreasonable and illegal. Legal action will be taken to protect the corporation from those who wish to create a dictatorship at Angelus Temple. As you know, I have no personal quarrel with you.

From Hermosa Beach, Minnie Kennedy announced she would fully support any action taken by her granddaughter.

To Knight and Aimee, the letter had the sound of an attorney. They suspected a convergence of familiar dangers: Rheba Crawford's ambition, Harriet Jordan's susceptibility to manipulation, and the strange power of the young lawyer who had won Roberta's trust. Moidel appeared to be gaining control over management. His securing of the four contracts had given him certain advantages, access to corporate records, the right to attend board meetings. Rolf McPherson, recalling Moidel's actions, says: "To Knight, it was unthinkable maneuvering. Something had to be done."

Aimee promptly fired Moidel and reinstated the faithful Willedd Andrews. She said the letter of September 24 did not sound like the language of her daughter. Nevertheless, on the same day that Aimee fired Moidel she issued a curious document to "Roberta's lawyer," which at once insisted that her daughter resign from all boards of directors and "assist me in publications, radio, platform and any such . . . business as I may ask," while guaranteeing "her contract shall be held valid and her salary retained," as well as her right to continue living at the parsonage.

It is a curious document, which gives with one hand what it takes away with the other—denying Roberta the responsibilities of an adult and guaranteeing her the rights of a child.

Late in the afternoon of Wednesday, September 28, Jacob Moidel escorted Roberta home to the parsonage. There ensued a shouting match between the attorney and his former boss. Knight, who stood between them, later signed a complaint to the California bar, requesting the disbarment of Moidel. In that complaint he claimed that Moidel had grabbed Sister Aimee by the arms and shaken her until she screamed.

Later, under oath, Aimee recalled that Moidel told Roberta to get her clothes, leave, and never come back.

"I begged my daughter to stay with me," said Aimee.

She wanted Roberta with her, but not in any official capacity.

Rolf was summoned to the offices in the parsonage after healing services on Thursday, October 1, for an emergency meeting of the trustees, which included him, his mother, and his sister. Roberta protested in writing that she was too ill to attend. Now Rolf, twenty-three, was in the middle—having issued a statement that his vote would be cast with his mother's.

While Knight, Andrews, and a recording secretary looked on, Rolf and Aimee voted a change in the bylaws of the Evangelistic Association: to allow two board members to constitute a quorum, and to make the president, Aimee Semple Mc-Pherson, and Rolf an executive committee to administer the Temple with all the powers of a full board. Their first act was to terminate the contract with Jacob Moidel.

Thus Roberta was disenfranchised.

It is a pity everyone did not go home then and go to sleep, having accomplished so much. But Andrews, flush with excitement at his reinstatement, could not contain his high spirits. In the presence of a reporter and Knight, the corporation's attorney issued this statement for immediate publication:

> Mrs. McPherson has been intimidated, threatened, and black-mailed for the last time. This time she is prepared to fight to the finish. While she regrets that the war will be sanguinary—with her own child—the only course ahead of her is protection of the organization which has consumed the best years of her life.

As Rolf McPherson puts it, smiling ironically, "Willedd Andrews was *not* a good lawyer. Now Joe Fainer, *there* was a good lawyer . . ."

Rolf's gentle irony politely guards a half-century of remorse. Willedd Andrews had blundered egregiously, and the damage was beyond recall. He should never have used the word *blackmail* so close to the reference to Roberta Semple.

Joseph Fainer was a brawny, good-humored Irishman with a mop of dark hair that swept his heavy eyebrows. He became Roberta's counsel when she decided to sue her mother's attorney for malicious slander.

———

Of all the catastrophes in Aimee's life, the falling out with Roberta is surely the most pitiful as well as the most difficult to understand. Roberta Salter is quick to remind us that she did not sue her mother, she sued her mother's attorney, Willedd Andrews. In the eyes of the public it quickly began to look like the same thing, a family quarrel dragged before a judge.

Battle lines were drawn, and as testimony appeared on either side of the blackmail question, tempers flared. Had Roberta Semple and Jacob Moidel blackmailed Aimee Semple McPherson in the Phoenix hotel room, or had they not? Did she sign the contracts willingly the morning after, or was she coerced the night before? On Roberta's side were ranged the high-principled Harriet Jordan, Jacob Moidel, and, for moral support, Minnie Kennedy. On Aimee's side were Willedd Andrews and that lengthening shadow, the Reverend Giles Knight—neither of whom had been present in Phoenix.

On Thanksgiving eve, Knight informed Rheba Crawford by letter that her contract was terminated. The cause: She had conspired to take the Temple away from Sister Aimee, she associated with gangsters, and she had engineered the removal of Willedd Andrews as chief counsel.

Lying in bed at Glendale Hospital, Rheba read and reread the letter from Knight, while Aimee, dressed as Priscilla Alden, was preaching her Thanksgiving Day sermon. The romantic heroine of "The Courtship of Miles Standish," dressed as a pilgrim, stood anachronistically at the wheel of the *Mayflower*, an emblem of free womanhood and the quest for religious liberty. Sister Aimee was at the helm, though mutiny raged below. She would keep the ship on course, whatever the cost.

$1,080,000 was the price of damages for which Rheba Crawford sued Aimee Semple McPherson, on eighteen counts of slander.

While there had never been any deep fellowship between Rheba and Roberta, their two lawsuits linked them in Aimee's mind. She convened a brief meeting at the parsonage, where she and Rolf, in the presence of Knight and Andrews, formally replaced Roberta on the board of the Evangelistic Association as well as the Bible College.

From her grandmother's house Roberta issued the following statement to the newspapers:

> When I was a very small child, I was told that I must prepare myself for membership on the board of directors of the Echo Park Evangelistic Association. I devoted my girlhood to the church, and was elected by the board . . . Now my mother has seen fit to oust

me from my lifework. I didn't believe she would allow herself to be so unfair. But if my own mother does not want me associated with her, I certainly do not intend to push myself into her affairs.

Roberta was not ambitious, she was devoted. From the day her mother expelled her from the board, she never once moved to regain her position as heir to the pastorate. Her thoughts dwelt on protecting her good name and salvaging the relationship with her mother.

But her mother was rewriting and rehearsing a full-length opera, the spectacular *Regeme Adorate* (Worship the King) with its double chorus, twenty-four soloists, and fifty-piece orchestra. It was a last cry for peace. In November, Hitler signed the Anti-Comintern Pact with Japan and Italy—the Rome-Berlin-Tokyo axis was born. What Aimee had failed to accomplish in *Give Me My Own God* and in her tongue-speaking prophecies, she might achieve in the spotlights and fanfare of an apocalyptic opera. Act I: the Creation and Fall of Man. Act II: the Annunciation and March of the Wise Men. Act III: the Adoration, in which all Nations worship together in peace.

An army of white-robed, haloed angels glided down an enormous glass staircase that joined the choir lofts and descended to the orchestra, while God's invisible footsteps were traced by strobes. At the finale, men and women dressed in costumes of all nations—German, Italian, French, Japanese—all touched by God's hand, gathered in peace to worship Christ in the city of David.

On the stage, in the warm tide of applause, there was a moment of peace, if there was none to be found anywhere else.

Depositions for the two lawsuits began in late February of 1937. At the final deposition, Aimee came face to face with Minnie Kennedy for the first time in seven years.

Aimee was already seated when her mother and daughter arrived together in the hearing room. She smiled, and they smiled back at her.

The testimony given at this last hearing was meager, inconsequential, a tying up of loose ends before the trial. As Aimee was on her way out the door, passing Roberta, she paused. Her daughter was seated at a conference table, behind her a shelf of legal volumes.

A newsman quick with his camera shot the last picture of Aimee Semple McPherson with her daughter. Aimee appears to be kneeling as she takes Roberta's small hand in her very large one, across a corner of the table. Aimee wears a white, crocheted tam that conceals her eyes, but the anguish in her profile is unconcealable. She is struggling to find a moment of intimacy in the crowded courtroom, whispering words hopeful of reconciliation. Roberta, her hair shining under a dark hat, looks down at her mother with a maternal solicitude that cannot be mistaken for anything but pity. Under these circumstances there can be no reconciliation. Later, it will be too late.

The trial of Willedd Andrews for slander opened in Department 19 of Superior Court on April 13, 1937.

Minnie Kennedy sat in the front row as Roberta took the witness stand, testifying sadly:

> Quite a few people stopped me on the street and asked me if it was true that I tried to blackmail my mother. I said "No," but they said it must be true or my mother wouldn't let Mr. Andrews say it.

Roberta's case was simple, requiring merely the newsman's oath that Andrews's blackmail statement had been meant for publication. Jacob Moidel then swore that Andrews had told him that it was "in Phoenix, Arizona" that Roberta had blackmailed her mother. In order to defend himself Andrews would have to prove that Aimee had been browbeaten in the Phoenix hotel—difficult, because it was her word against the sworn testimony of Moidel, Jordan, and her only daughter.

———

On April 14, 1937, Aimee Semple McPherson took the witness stand to defend her attorney against the charge of slander. Since early morning the superior court, from corridors to galleries, had been mobbed with people, so many that the bailiff had to call on six deputies to control them. This was to be Sister

Aimee's swan song, her farewell performance for the California judiciary.

She would be on the stand for two and a half days, center-stage in a drama doomed from the opening curtain to mar her dignity. In 1927 she had been magnificent, tragic, a heroine struggling to survive against the State, the Established Church, the Press, and an Antiquated Morality. Now, a decade later, she was ascending the witness stand to defend . . . her lawyer? Against her daughter?

Courthouse pundits and editorial writers naturally wondered aloud what Sister Aimee had to gain by it. To this day nobody knows. We may enumerate her motives, turn them over in the light. We may pick out the emotions that resonate in the stenographic record—anger at Roberta, fear that the Temple would be lost to creditors. Still, her decision to defend the jackstraw attorney is a mysterious exercise in futility.

Minnie Kennedy's pretrial view of the conflict is limited but valuable—because, like all of Minnie's perceptions, it comes to us direct, uncluttered by qualifications, subtleties, or manners of speaking.

> Aimee has done the same thing to Roberta that she did to me ten years ago. Ever since she left home at the age of seventeen, she has never been able to hold anyone close to her.

Harsh, and not exactly true—Rolf she would hold close to her forever—Minnie's observation hangs like a haunting family portrait, gloomily captioned.

> If my daughter continues so recklessly to separate herself from her devoted family, I prophesy she will chart her own course to ruin.

Seated in the witness chair, Aimee complained of thirst, stroking her throat. Handed a paper cup of water, she smiled and as politely as possible said that she couldn't drink from a paper cup. The reason soon became clear when two spectators who had squeezed out the door elbowed their way in again bearing a soda-water tumbler and a pitcher of ice water. As everyone in the courtroom watched Aimee, she downed the tumbler of water without coming up for air. Then she refilled the glass and lifted it again. She had a heroic thirst, did Sister Aimee, which could not be served by anything so humble as a paper cup. Testifying, she soon emptied a pitcher of water. So as not to slow the trial's progress, court attendants brought another pitcher, then another. Soon three pitchers and several tumblers of water stood in a row on the table beside the witness stand.

Aimee did not want to be in the courtroom; yet, having arrived, the incomparable actress would make the most of her appearance in what must be, at best, a third-rate melodrama of a mother spurned by a thankless child. She smiled and nodded to friends on both sides of the railing; she twisted her handkerchief. She told the story of being held prisoner in Phoenix almost an entire night. Her eyes filled with tears, and she dabbed at their corners with her lace handkerchief. She caressed her gardenia corsage. She drank more water and mumbled, while Ma Kennedy held her nose and Roberta stared in disbelief. The impish Moidel mocked the witness by aping her mournful expressions, grimacing and crossing his eyes until Aimee begged the judge to make him stop poking fun at her.

During the afternoon's questioning by Joseph Fainer, Aimee became so baffling and evasive that at last Fainer lost patience and asked her, point blank, if she was telling the truth. To which she responded that she was testifying to the very best of her memory. There were long pauses as she seemed unable to gather the meaning of simple questions; then she would ramble off on tangents and have to be reined in. Her voice, famous for its volume and range, would trail off into a whisper so small that nobody, bending toward her, could understand a word she said.

A newsman knelt to photograph Sister Aimee in her white double-breasted suit and tam as she shuffled out of the courtroom. She was literally held upright by Giles Knight on her left arm and Rolf McPherson on her right. Rolf's usual dignity, as he stares down the camera, is touched by a protective fury —he looks like a man who has had it up to his chin with foolishness. Aimee, her eyes shut, shuffles like a troubled sleep-walker in a nightmare.

Knight, realizing the inevitable outcome and his critical role in it, gazes abstractly into the middle distance of the evangelist's future.

After Harriet Jordan's testimony and proof that the notorious contracts were signed in the light of morning "after everybody had slept on the matter," the lawyers' summing up brought tears to Aimee's eyes. Sobbing uncontrollably, she was half led, half carried to an anteroom out of earshot of the verdict. As she lay on a couch, someone brought word the judge had awarded Roberta Semple $2,000 in damages and ordered Wil-ledd Andrews to pay all costs of litigation.

––––––––

Andrews had convinced Knight that Roberta Semple, Harriet Jordan, and Rheba Crawford were plotting to take over the Temple. Otherwise the reverend would never have supported Sister Aimee in a course so embarrassing, so tragic.

As business manager he had stepped into the breach left by Minnie Kennedy before Rolf McPherson was ready to take over. And this holy accountant, this stern penny pincher, had only the purest intentions. He was married and had two little boys. Knight's wife, a church worker, and the children were welcome guests at Aimee's new home in Silver Lake he had helped her build. They appear in photographs with her convivially seated around a table on the veranda. The whole family had a deep affection for their pastor, and Knight believed that his ministry, his special mission in 1937, was to rescue Angelus Temple and Sister Aimee from the forces of darkness.

He was her shining Knight. Though others would make dark puns at the mention of his name ("In Heaven there is no Knight"), in 1937 Sister Aimee saw in the tall, earnest book-keeper the embodiment of certain medieval virtues, a touch of chivalry. Giles Knight would see her through it, through the sniping of attorneys and reporters, the roar of the crowd, while Rolf McPherson stood by, keeping his own counsel.

"I feel that God placed Brother Knight here," Rolf said, "and called him just in time to save this Temple from bankruptcy."

Knight ascended the pulpit on April 18 to raise funds for the defense against Rheba Crawford's million-dollar slander suit. This was the first of dozens of such appeals that would weary the congregation in the course of reducing the Temple's staggering debt.

Fortunately Aimee did not need the money to pay the legal fees for Rheba's lawsuit: a delegation of church leaders and businessmen persuaded the litigants to settle out of court, for the cause of religion and the good of the community. Another lawsuit, by Jacob Moidel for salary due, had gone to court, occasioning a lurid review of the parsonage fracas of September 1936. At last the public had heard enough.

A *Los Angeles Times* editorial summed up the widespread feeling: "A news moratorium on the McPhersons et al. is the crying need of the day."

SANCTUARY

The Watch Night service had become a Los Angeles ritual. On New Year's Eve, after Sister Aimee's illustrated sermon featuring Father Time and the Infant Year, teetotalers flocked to Echo Park by the thousands, reveling, laughing, singing until daybreak.

At the turn of the new year 1939 they had something special to celebrate. Millions of candlepower from mobile floodlights bathed the facade of Angelus Temple, and the press turned out in force.

Sister Aimee ascended to the top of the dome, holding in her hand a sheaf of papers: mortgage notes for $66,505. Flanked by Rolf McPherson and Giles Knight, she approached a blazing brazier. As ten thousand clapped and cheered, she fed the mortgage notes to the flames, symbolizing the end of the Temple's debt.

On the parapet below, several white-robed girls with angel wings attached to their shoulders sounded their trumpets. Under the stars the girls danced a little ballet representing the triumph of faith over gold.

Putting Angelus Temple "in the black" had been the work of Knight as business manager, with Rolf in charge of the purchasing department. Before Knight took over the management, one news service counted up 45 lawsuits brought against Sister Aimee, demanding damages from a million dollars to $2.94. From 1926 to 1937 Aimee Semple McPherson's name may have graced the front page of the Los Angeles newspapers three times a week, appearing in the national press nearly as often, but much of the attention was unflattering. In the case of Roberta Semple against Aimee's attorney, the publicity was devastating.

The years of Aimee's life after 1938 have come under a cloud of mystery, pierced here and there by the floodlight of some carefully staged event, such as the burning of the mortgage notes on New Year's. The sentimental autobiographer, who had written thousands of pages about her rise to fame, devoted all of three pages to the years 1938–1944, as if she herself had grown weary of her story. *The Foursquare Crusader*, which for twenty years had chronicled Sister's life as the central subject of a religious epic, gradually shifted its focus away from Aimee, printing only her sermons. The Church was rapidly growing; the magazine was full of local news from the field supervisors of the national districts.

Aimee had made an agreement with Giles Knight. The exact details were known only to the two of them. But the survivors of the Knight era—Rolf McPherson, Roberta Salter, Nathaniel Van Cleave, Margery McCammon, and several other students—describe openly and bitterly the effects of that curious arrangement.

Giles Knight agreed to take over the management of the Echo Park Evangelistic Association and put the Temple "on a cash basis" provided Aimee granted him certain powers, some of them exceptional. One might expect that in an emergency such as Knight faced, the business manager and comptroller would request autonomy in budgeting, and accounting. Likewise one might expect that after the disgrace of the slander trial, he would insist upon control over the pastor's public image, limiting the press's access to the famous woman. Minnie had begged for it.

But from all accounts, it appears that Sister Aimee completely surrendered not only her public life but her personal life to the control of Reverend Giles Knight, from April of 1937 through February of 1944. During this period she was virtually under house arrest. She could not see anyone, even her children, without Knight's approval. She could not leave her house except to preach, or teach her classes at the College, without Knight's permission—and he routinely withheld it. She accepted no calls from the press.

The powers Knight assumed were extreme, penitential. Why he demanded such paternal control, and why the great woman granted it, is a matter of crucial interest, unresolved, mysterious. With his stern, ministerial bearing there is a look of compassion which warrants the man was not power-mad, not the sort of upstart who derives a perverse exhilaration by manipulating a celebrity in decline. Yet one cannot help but wonder. Rolf McPherson remains enigmatic on the subject of Giles Knight. He good-naturedly praises the late reverend for rescuing the Temple from litigants, newsmen, and creditors. Rolf Mc-Pherson may know more about this period than he cares to explain.

Rolf and De McPherson were on the "list" of those whom Giles Knight approved. This was a short list. It included Ella Nordine, the nurse and ex–Bible student who lived with the evangelist at Silver Lake and had accompanied her to the Orient. When Nordine returned to the East Coast to preach in 1940, another trained nurse, Angela Sid, took her place. Of course Mrs. Knight and her two sons were always welcome. So were artists Thompson Eade and Charles Walkem. But Roberta Salter was not on the roster of approved company.

Soon after the slander trial, a radio program called "Hobby Lobby" invited Roberta to come to New York, all expenses paid, to talk about her hobby of Biblical perfume. Roberta fell in love with the city, and the staff at NBC fell in love with her—particularly their music director, Harry Salter. He suggested she return to New York and look for a job. The $2,000 she had won from the slander suit paid for a "career hunt" in New York. Dave Elman, the producer of "Hobby Lobby," finally hired Roberta at the rich salary of $35 a week to research the hobbies of celebrities who appeared on the show. She married Harry Salter in December of 1941. Thereafter they worked as a team, as the bandleader created such shows as "Stop the Music" and "Name That Tune" on television.

Roberta could not reach her mother again, ever, by telephone or letter, try as she would.

Rolf McPherson's praise of Knight has firm support in the record. Knight rescued the Temple and vigilantly protected its pastor, forcing her to husband her energies. Despite Aimee's marked physical deterioration, she was amazingly productive during this period. Perhaps that was the sole reason for Knight's stern program and her submission to it.

Almost nothing has been written about these years, called a "blackout" by journalists and previous biographers. But there are many still living who knew Aimee and worked with her in the 1940's. From their recollections a portrait emerges of an artist and teacher in a culminating phase of self-development, an aging woman pausing at last to take a hard look at herself in the full-length mirror of solitude. She was joyful in Christ, when not oppressed by her mortal loneliness. If, before, she had found little opportunity to reflect on the meaning of her hectic life, now perhaps she had more time and silence than she could bear.

Charlie Chaplin would order his chauffeur to idle the limousine on Park Avenue by the rear door of the Temple. As the crowd poured out of the white building after a service, he would sit in the shadows of the back seat, waiting for Sister Aimee to appear. The chauffeur would drive to where she stood at the curb. Charlie would open the door and help her in.

He did not want to be seen in the Temple, and she did not

wish to be photographed with the unchristian comedian. So they sat in the limousine, parked between the parsonage and the Temple, and visited.

While she looked over his shoulder, Chaplin sketched a stage. He was showing her how to build the proscenium arch for Angelus Temple. He did not understand exactly what went on in there, but he knew it was theater of idiosyncratic genius. If she was going to continue creating in that space, he wanted to make sure she did it right.

Her life, what part of it was not spent in silent reflection, was passed in the theater and the classroom. Under the proscenium arch designed by Chaplin, the actress spent the most creative hours of her final years, redefining the boundary between secular and religious art. A few recordings have saved the rhythm of her voice from oblivion, preserved the complex orchestral accompaniments to some of the sermons. But conveying the scope and richness of 150 stage productions is impossible here —it is the proper work of a theater historian. How Aimee passed the hours after Giles Knight chased away the lawyers and journalists, building a wall around her, is evident from the stenographic record of the illustrated sermons, and from the staging notes filed in the Temple archives.

Here one finds the stage notes for a lost sermon, a comic production called "The Hoot Owl and the Music Box."

SCENE ONE: Night club showing revelry, drinking, card playing and featuring a girl in a cellophane dress. Swing-time music is playing throughout until a quarrel develops, and from a smoking gun a man is killed, and Police officers arrive as curtain closes. (Note: During this scene the music box plays discordant melodies on my right hand, and on my left the Owl rolls his eyes around and chatters happily, "Whoopey, whoopey!")

SCENE TWO: King Midas is shown seated at a table (which may easily be the same one used in the former scene), a pile of gold coin is piled up like a pyramid in front of him and golden images are set about the room. (Note: As to these golden images any cheap plaster paris statues, sprayed in advance with cheap gold liquid, will do. The actions of the music box and the hoot owl are similar to those in the first scene.)

SCENE THREE: The curtain opens on a glorified electric-lighted silk cross, from which filtered beams radiate from every angle. This cross should have a dark background. It is my intention to have about 7 young people dressed in civilian clothes come from the balcony and main floor in answer to my call and kneel at the foot of the cross, and the music box, plus the orchestra and choir, sing such songs as "Oh, the children of the Lord have a Right to Shout and Sing," and "My Cup Runneth Over With Joy." (Note: These songs are merely suggestions, to be worked out with Mrs. Esther Fricke Stewart and Mr. Boersma.) (Note: During this episode, the Owl looks very angry, cross-eyed, etc., and as his mouth opens, he says, "Hooey! Hooey!")

SCENE FOUR: The Aeolian Harp. If the Aeolian harp is not beautiful enough, or showy enough, we can borrow Mrs. Kohler's. Music notes should be strung here and there on invisible wires or thread. Said notes should be fluttered and glorified much like the snow-flakes originally made by Mr. Ratekin. I will want music at this time, as the harp will represent the baptism of the Holy Spirit.

The music box plays and the Owl shows his disdain.

Suggested songs: "Running over, running over, my cup's full and running over," "In My Heart There Rings a Melody," "It is Joy Unspeakable and Full of Glory!"

SCENE FIVE: Celestial Chorus of the Coronation Crown. As the curtain opens on this scene, a huge crown is revealed. It should be cut in a very elaborate and fanciful pattern, be-jeweled by crumpled cellophane and red and colored paper and colored electric lights. As this scene represents the hope of the Second Coming, such songs and music should be employed as, "We Will be Caught up to Meet Him in the Air," "When the Saints Go Marching In," "A Crown of Gold, a Mansion Fair." Actions of the music box and the hoot owl as in previous scene.

SCENE SIX: The Heavenly City. The Heavenly City is revealed as the eternal Four-square music box. This will be our heaven with the steps leading up thereto, with the cardboard angels kneeling on either side. The minarets, domes and towers of the Heavenly City should stand out one from the other in such a manner that colorful flood lights can be placed on the risers. Music for this scene will be comprised of such numbers as "Oh, I'm Climbing Up the Golden Stairs to Glory," "When They Ring Those Golden Bells for You and Me," "My Home is in Heaven," "On Jordan's Stormy Banks I Stand and Cast a Wistful Eye."

Without the text of the dialogue and sermon, one can only wonder what sort of resonance Aimee achieved in the above tableaus. We do know that the lighting, costumes, and sets in the 1940's were first-rate, and that Aimee traded heavily in comic irony. As bizarre as the stage effects may seem in the transcripts, they worked consistently at Angelus Temple, where there was never an empty seat on a Sunday night.

As Hollywood movies approached an apotheosis in the late 1930's, Aimee strived to keep up with secular entertainment. Kern and Hammerstein's operetta of Edna Ferber's *Show Boat*, first captured on film by Harry Pollard in 1929, had been a phenomenal success when it was remade in 1936, starring Paul Robeson and Irene Dunne. Movies like *Show Boat, Tale of Two Cities,* and *Wizard of Oz* became so much a part of the cultural mainstream that Aimee could be sure that her Fundamentalist brethren knew them. Since these secular images and stories lived in the memories of the congregation, why not reinterpret them in the light of the Gospel?

In the archives there is this letter from Aimee to her stage manager.

Mr. John Ratekin:

Dear Johnny:
    After having given a good deal of thought to the "Show Boat" for next Sunday night, I feel that the entire evening and sermon should be built with bright songful and colorful music and episodes.
    For instance . . . a boy should eat a large slice of watermelon in the old-fashioned way, clear to the ears.
    Period costumes should be worn . . .
    A local grocer, such as Bon Ton, might loan an entire bunch of bananas for which we would thank him, and they would be returned . . .
    You remember that Larry played three instruments at once and one other man, whose name I do not know, did likewise while Sorenson led them in a most unique manner. If this is followed

out, Sorenson should be notified immediately so someone else could preach in his place Sunday night.

Bales of cotton should be loaded upon the boat during the singing of "Old Man River."

A large fishing net might be draped somewhere as atmosphere if one could be loaned.

Larry, of Long Beach, could be well used with his mouth harp, but would need to be notified early. Dean Teaford no doubt will be able to contact him.

A gang-plank should be used. Pennants should flutter in the breeze and the entire ship should have an air of gaiety and activity. A ship's bell might also be employed to good use . . .

Kindly drop me a line as to all details you have worked on also, and such of these ideas as will be used.

Yours in the King's glad service,
Aimee Semple McPherson

The memo to Johnny Ratekin went out on a Wednesday, for a production four days later, Sunday evening. Aimee's request to "kindly drop me a line" suggests a leisure they surely did not have—the final stage notes indicate that for three days the Angelus Temple auditorium was a whirlwind of construction, costume fitting, and rehearsals, all supervised by Aimee herself.

The Boat is shown full side view . . . singers in groups, officers, deck hands . . . selected for size—small enough not to be out of keeping with the size of the boat. The singers both colored and white, in costumes of the period when Show Boat was in its heyday. Songs . . . "Roll Jordan Roll!" "Ole Man River" (with gospel words). A portion of the side of the ship should be made of scrim so painted as to represent the boat when unlighted. The scenes would be shown through the scrim during the sermon which would be accompanied by suitable songs from the Colored Choir.

The sermon was in two movements, which her notes refer to as "Satan's Show" and "The Gospel Show Boat."

As the audience settled in their seats, the gangplank slammed down onto the platform. Two little demons with trumpets appeared on either side, announcing the show, and the curtains opened behind Aimee at the lectern.

She announced Satan's first "showboat," the Garden of Eden.
She narrated the story of the temptation of Adam and Eve while
actors mimed it behind the scrim. As the scene faded, Satan's
mocking laughter echoed through the hall. The curtain closed.
It opened again on Belshazzar's Feast, with Satan in the midst,
urging the crowd on in its revelry. A crash indicated the fall of
the kingdom. A huge hand appeared and wrote upon the wall.
Again, as the scene faded out, Satan could be heard laughing
fiendishly.

Putting Satan's showboat aside, Sister Aimee welcomed two
angels who now appeared on either side of the gangplank, blowing their trumpets. What followed was a musical review of the
history of Pentecost, in ten scenes. First the Crucifixion, with
Christ on the Cross, thunder, lightning, and an earthquake; a
Roman soldier, the Virgin Mary, and John the Beloved, with
the choir singing, "Were you there when they crucified my
Lord?" The lights faded, coming up again on a group of saints
gathered as on the day of Pentecost.

Red paper flames streamed down on them as the choir sang
"Pentecostal Fire Is Falling."

Next, a set of painted flats descended to represent an ancient
street lined with sick men and women, crippled, maimed. As
Sister Aimee described "the Shadow of St. Peter," that Saint
walked down the lane of the afflicted, holding out his hands to
them. And the choir chanted, "Oh, my Lord's done just what
He said, He's healed the sick and raised the dead." Then Saint
Paul appeared at the bow of a crowded, wave-beaten ship,
illustrating "the Journeys of St. Paul" as the choir sang, "I could
climb the highest mountain."

Scene V was called "Apostasy" in Aimee's notes. Blue lights
came up on a cathedral covered with moss and icicles, and a
priest dressed in black robes sang dolefully, "How tedious and
tasteless the hours." This emotional valley of the drama gave
way to a rousing scene in which Luther, on an elevated pulpit,
addressed a group of reformers to the accompaniment of "Revive Us Again." John Wesley replaced Luther, then Charles G.
Finney followed Wesley, as a medley of Gospel tunes accompanied a living tableau of the Azusa Street tarrying service: black

and white praying and singing together with upstretched hands.

In the last scene, called "Dry Bones" in the production notes, footlights came up slowly on a corps de ballet of skeletons. By a clever rotation of dancers in and out of the wings, the skeletons put on flesh and sinew to become whole men, then crusaders marching with their flags and banners while the chorus sang, "Preach the Foursquare Gospel!"

The set for "Show Boat" went up on Sunday. Struck on Monday, it would never be used again. By midweek Aimee would be meeting with John Ratekin, Ernest Eade, and her musical director Esther Fricke Stuart, to plan new productions, equally elaborate: "The Lone Ranger" (1938), "Treasure Island" (1939), "The Wizard of Oz" (1939), "The Trojan Horse" (1940), "The Garden of Allah" (1941).

One of the most famous, "The Way of the Cross Leads Home," called for Eade to design a backdrop of blue sky and brown hillsides through which a real stream of water was sluiced. Center stage, a wooden cross pointed to Heaven as the way of salvation, while cardboard images of fallen bridges depicted mortal failures to reach Heaven without the Cross. Eade rigged up an electrical conveyor belt on the tilted cross; the belt transported little cardboard cutouts of men from earth to paradise.

A stagehand put some of these cardboard men on backward, which wasn't discovered until Aimee was in the middle of her sermon.

"She was always master of the situation," Eade recalls, laughing. "She said, 'Can you beat that? Some of those backsliders trying to get to heaven.' "

For Aimee's sermons Eade created a fully operational Trojan Horse, a Gold Rush town, a giant radio with a movable dial that caused Biblical scenes to change, and a twenty-foot-tall Easter lily from which Aimee preached in a gown the yellow of stamens. For her sermon "The Value of a Soul" he built an enormous pair of shining balances. On one pan was a pearl (a painted beach ball) depicting the human soul; on the other pan was a wad of money, toy cars, and other symbols of worldly wealth.

Shortly after the burning of the mortgage notes, Aimee sailed for Panama to attend a Foursquare convention. Again she stayed with the missionary family of Leeland Edwards. Edwards, nineteen then, recalls a woman spritely and good-humored despite her frail health, conversant in sports and current events as well as religion.

Aimee took Edwards downtown and bought him a new suit of clothes. She wanted him to look his best on stage when he interpreted her sermons into Spanish. He recalls her patience on a strenuous overnight journey by automobile into the interior. And she prayed for the sick. A Panamanian woman who did the housework had been diagnosed as having an inoperable tumor in her abdomen. Sister laid hands upon the tumor, there in the house. Next day she called for a doctor to examine the housekeeper—the tumor could not be found.

Panama was one of a growing number of Foursquare Missions, an empire whose dawning coincided with the eclipse of Sister Aimee's public life, and World War II.

She wrote:

> The outbreak of the war and America's subsequent involvement hindered several plans of the missionary department to spread the Word to untouched regions. But it also afforded us an opportunity to minister to thousands of servicemen who would pass through Los Angeles.
>
> Each Sunday hundreds of men in uniform attended services at Angelus Temple . . . Many of them had no religious affiliation and did not own Bibles. What a privilege it was to invite servicemen present in every Sunday night meeting to come to the platform, where I greeted them, gave each one a New Testament, and knelt in prayer with them for their spiritual needs and God's guidance and protection of their lives.

On June 21, 1942 Sister Aimee led her brass band and color guard to a bandstand in Pershing Square, downtown Los Angeles, to sell war bonds. This was the week of the gala Twentieth Anniversary Convention of Foursquare International. Ministers and members had come from all over the world to attend the convention, so Aimee had lots of support.

Dressed in a red-and-white gown and blue cape, and wearing a garrison cap, she stood at the microphone and rallied the crowd of 20,000. On her left knelt a Bible student dressed as Uncle Sam, on her right another student as Lady Liberty. Behind her the color guard waved ten American flags. Photographer Lucille Stewart captured the event on 16 mm color film, astonishingly vivid. Fifty-two-year-old Sister Aimee, clear-eyed, sharp-featured, her long golden hair braided close to her head, raises a fist to the imaginary enemy above the crowd. She spins, she throws her arms wide, then clasps them to her breast.

She sold $150,000 worth of war bonds in one hour.

Returning to the Temple at 2:30 that afternoon, she led the ordination service, and that night she preached a full illustrated sermon on the text "Behold He Cometh."

She preached several sermons that year for the Blood Bank. And "to dramatize pleas by national leaders that people use their automobiles sparingly in order to conserve on gasoline and tires," she drove to the Temple one Sunday night in a horse and buggy. In sermons like "Foursquaredom and Uncle Sam" (1942), "Remember Pearl Harbor" (1942), and "Praise the Lord and Pass the Ammunition" (1943) she spoke to the men in uniform of her commitment to military action in Europe and the Pacific. She saw it as long overdue.

Occasionally she made the national news wires with her famous curses upon Hitler and Tojo:

"How many of you would like to see Hitler covered with boils from head to foot?" she thundered.

The Army made Sister Aimee an honorary colonel. For her fund-raising and her use of Radio KFSG to teach the public about rationing, air-raid blackouts, etc., the U.S. Treasury and the Office of War Information issued her special citations for her "patriotic endeavors."

Under the Knight regime, her public image improved so dramatically that by mid-1939 her old enemy Robert Shuler commended the Foursquare vision in the *Christian Advocate*, saying that Aimee's missionary work was the envy of the Methodists. In 1943 a Los Angeles columnist saluted her on her birthday, on behalf of the city's working press: "She will live forever in the affection of every newspaperman who journeyed with her along life's rugged highway, when she established a world's record for sustained, countrywide news interest." Belated but sincere thanks for providing so many of them with jobs.

———

Under Giles Knight's restrictions Aimee rarely left the city to preach. In the summer of 1941 she ventured out on her last real tour: Yakima and Spokane, Washington; British Columbia; the Great Lakes area; Akron, DeKalb, Cedar Rapids; Wellington and Hutchinson, Kansas.

After Pearl Harbor the government curtailed domestic travel, which suited Knight, because this made it a little easier to keep Sister Aimee home. But she still broke out for a brief campaign beginning in Nashville, where she preached in Ryman Auditorium April 17–21, 1942.

Wrote Knight to *The Foursquare Crusader*:

Although drenching rains greeted us the opening night in Nashville, the natives of Tennessee's capital city were undaunted and jammed the auditorium to hear Sister preach. On the last night of the meetings we had to form a guard to protect Sister from the throng of admirers and well-wishers that if not restrained would have swept her off her feet.

Meetings in Joplin, Missouri one week later were a repeat of the successes in Nashville, as were those in Springfield, Ohio the week of May 14.

Returning from a tour of the Midwest, Aimee received a welcome as clamorous as ever: the Temple band played "California, Here I Come" as she passed beneath an arch of crossed flags, clutching an armload of American Beauty roses. With a cryptic smile she paused and held up for all to see the souvenir she had brought home with her—a songbird in a gilded cage.

"Giles Knight had convinced her that road evangelism was

not in her best interests," says Nathaniel Van Cleave. "But she chafed under Knight's regimen, and it may in fact have contributed to her death."

Late at night Aimee would seize the telephone. She would dial Harold Jeffries, one of the few Foursquare ministers in whom she felt she could confide. In the little girl's voice she used on the telephone she confessed: "I am lonely, so lonely. Dr. Knight won't let me go out, at all."

———

The L.I.F.E. College classrooms were large, whitewashed cinderblock rectangles with tall windows and brilliant overhead lights—austere, unforgiving, nowhere to hide. Men and women came from all over the world to study Scripture in these rooms, to learn history and theology and take turns preaching at the oaken lecterns.

In one of these lecture halls overlooking Le Moyne Street, students sat at attention, five minutes before the hour, reviewing the text of Acts 2. Their teacher, Sister Aimee, was strict in all things, but particularly in matters of attendance and punctuality. She would come through the door at exactly nine o'clock, knowing that every desk in the classroom would be occupied and that no one would dare interrupt the teacher by following her through the door once it closed behind her.

For years she had come and gone in the classrooms of the Bible College at will and as her schedule permitted. She appeared as a "special lecturer" but irregularly, which was probably as much due to her own restlessness (as a student she herself had been a terror in the classroom) as it was to the demands of her presidential schedule. She had only time enough to "take the temperature" of the classes, to see that the students were on the right track, safe from the heresies, ideologies, and emotional extravagances that constantly plagued the young revival.

Now she was in her fifties, and nothing was more important to her than educating a new generation of evangelists. She walked into the classroom with measured steps and military erectness, wearing a plain blouse of white silk without a wrinkle and a cream-colored pleated skirt that covered her ankles. She walked slowly because her legs hurt with arthritis. Her smile could not quite mask the pain.

"Won't you sit down, Sister?" Someone offered her a chair.

"No, thank you," she responded sweetly. "Once I sit down, it is so very hard to get up again."

Her strictness of bearing and speech, her precision in moving through dense theological discussions, reminded one of an aging prima ballerina who was passionate to convince the novices that triumph in their field was so much a matter of hard labor, honesty, and unwavering *attention*. This class in "evangelism" was a spiritual laboratory. Each student sat in his or her own circle of light, as under a microscope, with God and Sister Aimee taking turns looking down through the lens.

"The burden," says Nathaniel Van Cleave, "was that each student should be *evangelistically* trained"—that is, trained in the delicate art of winning souls from the world to Christ. Another student, Charles Duarte, insists that the practical training of evangelists was more important than the hours spent on more academic studies.

Though these Bible students would frown on the psychoanalytic model, for the secular observer there is nothing to which we can better compare the evangelist's training than to the training of the psychoanalyst: both must thoroughly know their own mental geography before they can venture safely as guides in foreign terrain. So did each of Sister Aimee's students have to discover his own relationship with Christ. Each had to open an independent dialogue, in a new language which concealed nothing personal, while surrendering to God the sum of his talents to serve.

They would sit and read together in turn; they would study separately at their desks, as Sister Aimee watched their faces.

> And when the day of Pentecost was fully come, they were all with one accord in one place. And suddenly there came a sound from heaven as of a rushing mighty wind, and it filled all the house where they were sitting. And there appeared unto them cloven tongues like as of fire, and it sat upon each of them. And they were all filled with the Holy Ghost, and began to talk with other tongues, as the Spirit gave them utterance. (Acts 2: 1–4)

She was not dramatic, by and large, in the classroom. She did not raise her voice to exhort or scold the students; she did not shock them or clown for them. She stood in the same spot and spoke softly, reading, rereading, or commenting on the combustible verses from the Acts of the Apostles, which she had seen shake the world during her lifetime. Having witnessed hundreds of thousands of conversions, she knew the power of the Word so well that her knowledge was dispersed in the close atmosphere of the classroom like attar of roses. She read the verses and watched the faces of thirty students as they prayed together, watched even more closely as they prayed separately, each moved in his or her own way by the Holy Spirit.

A young woman at a desk toward the back of the room was struggling. Aimee could see it in the quivering lips, the lines in the forehead. She could see it as a heavy shadow behind the closed eyes. So softly, the others hardly noticed, Aimee made her way down the aisle and stood above the young woman who sat, her hands folded in prayer, under an invisible cloud. Who knows what childhood trauma, adult remorse, or crisis of faith had darkened the medium of prayer? Perhaps Aimee knew because she had counseled the woman. But, then, Sister Aimee had "prayed through" so many a soul lost in the labyrinth of personality, that she had learned to read the soul's predicament as a diagnostician detects pathology by skin tone, posture, and subtle changes in eye color invisible to the layman.

Aimee whispered a few words, and the woman's face relaxed. Aimee placed her hands upon the student's shoulders and prayed with her—"Put your faith in *Him*"—until the cloud lifted and the woman's face as she prayed in a strong voice was transfused with light. She had received the good news.

This, above all, was evangelism, the spreading of the "good news," from the New Testament noun *euangélion*, which appears seventy-five times in the Gospels. But there were good and bad ways to spread the good news. In Sister Aimee Semple McPherson's class the future preachers were reminded, time and again, to STAY IN THE MIDDLE OF THE ROAD. In 1942 Aimee was as broad-minded as a Fundamentalist could be, but her insistence on the golden mean in the all-important business of

evangelism was paradoxically inflexible. On the one hand, denominational Christians tended to be timid, disengaged, emotionally and spiritually chilly. The Pentecostal revival which
Sister Aimee had pioneered, on the other hand, was prone to
emotional excess and a missionary aggressiveness that could do
more harm than good—by frightening away the herd.

STAY IN THE MIDDLE OF THE ROAD was not a catch phrase for
religious conservatism or even compromise. The motto had two
meanings for the student: first, be bold in standing in the traffic,
in the mainstream of life—don't be colonized by the secular
world; and second, be passionate in celebrating the gifts of the
Spirit, but never excessive. Don't intimidate the crowd. Again
and again she used the automobile metaphor to illustrate the
need for restraint in tongue-speaking and other "manifestations." The automobile with its top speed of eighty miles per
hour must not be driven full throttle on a city street. The power
was there, in reserve, to be meted out over a long journey in
the service of others.

This is why she was so calm in the classroom. Knowing the
power of the Holy Spirit, she understood it would fill them if
she gently opened their hearts. The students would do the same
thereafter in converting others. Charles Duarte, in her classes
from 1940 to 1943, recalls that her relationship with the students
was more maternal than professorial, "more like passing the
torch than merely imparting information." Sister Aimee admired a poem Duarte remembers as "The Bridge-Builder." As
he paraphrases the story, a man on a journey comes to a chasm
and miraculously leaps across it. With the fallen trees and rocks
he gathers on the far side he builds a bridge back to where he
started. And when someone asks why he built a bridge over a
chasm he had already crossed, the bridge-builder points and
explains: there is a young man back there who needs to get
over.

In a course called "Foursquare Fundamentals" Aimee dealt
with church history and theology. Van Cleave recalls her favorite authors in the course were John Wesley, leader of the
Methodist revivals and the inspiration of the nineteenth-century
Holiness movement; Dwight L. Moody, who stressed God's

love and mercy rather than hellfire; and the extraordinary Canadian revivalist Albert Benjamin Simpson, prophet of the "higher Christian Life," missionary and theological synthesizer.

Simpson's phrase "Fourfold Gospel" crystallized his belief in Christ as Savior, Sanctifier, Healer, and Coming King. It was Simpson's "restorationist" belief that church history since the Protestant Reformation would culminate in the days of the "latter rain," the outpouring of the Holy Spirit. He strongly opposed the dispensational notion that the gifts of the Spirit died with the Apostles. He pointed to Joel 2 and I Corinthians 12 as indications that the gifts of the Spirit would continue in the church until the Second Coming. Withal, Simpson was levelheaded and practical, chiding his missionaries for naively assuming they could rely on tongue-speaking as a substitute for hard language study.

It was Simpson above all who clarified the nature of sanctification for Sister Aimee, so that her firm position on the doctrine influenced the Assemblies of God and subsequently the entire charismatic movement. Simpson emphasized "the work of the cross," the idea that the work of attaining the Christian ideal was never ending. Perfection (if it could be called that) was progressive, a process of becoming. Wesley never claimed "sinless perfection" for himself, nor did Simpson, nor did Sister Aimee on the best day of her life. Even the Pope went regularly to confession. Conversion was an important step *toward* Christian perfection. The Baptism of the Holy Spirit, with the evidence of tongues, was not a sanctifying experience in the sense of delivering the Christian to a state of perfection, beyond sin. Simpson preferred to consider the baptism of the Holy Spirit as an "empowering experience," enabling the Christian to lead a more productive life, as a moral force and as a winner of souls.

Students read, with her, the journals of the eminent missionaries Hudson Taylor and Adonirom Judson. The class struggled with the ethics of self-sacrifice, the dangers of pride.

At the end of one class, which left the students wandering dazed in a forest of moral and religious riddles, Aimee gathered her books and left them to pray silently among themselves and adjourn at will.

One of the last to leave the classroom, keen-eyed Margery McCammon, noticed a peculiar thing. In a dark corner across from the staircase a gray shawl was dangling between an open door and the wall behind, scarcely visible. No one else saw it. Sister had made herself invisible under the shawl. She was watching students pass through the corridor, some going upstairs, some going down, talking and laughing. Only Margery McCammon saw her peering out of the shawl—and noticed the broom whose handle had fallen across the foot of the stairs. Everyone stepped over the broomstick until McCammon stooped to pick it up. Then Sister Aimee materialized from her hiding place to commend her. She had seen the broom and left it thus, curious to find out how many of her starry-eyed philosophers would step over the hazard before one bent to pick it up.

Aimee was intimate in the classroom, but not given to displays of emotion—at least not often. So Charles Duarte was surprised one afternoon to hear her voice break during a discussion of human weakness, the inevitable errors of judgment. She was using her own life as an example, telling of her marriage to David Hutton, how it had all been a terrible mistake and she had made it because she was so lonely. As she spoke of loneliness, she broke down and wept, until the students left their seats and moved to lay hands upon their beloved teacher, to comfort her as they had been taught.

———

The effort of these years should be measured by the index of Aimee's health. There are no medical records. Rolf McPherson admits, regretfully, that he was often misinformed or kept in the dark by his mother and her physicians, none of whom are now living. The actress grew stoical, and proficient at concealing frightful symptoms. Rolf says there was damage to her ureter as far back as the late 1930's. It was misdiagnosed because Giles Knight kept sending Sister to the wrong doctor, whose treatment over several years made things worse. The painful bladder condition caused raging fevers and was a constant annoyance as she continued to perform in public. This, and her agonizing arthritis, made her insomnia worse than ever, forcing increased dependency upon sedatives to capture the sleep she so desperately needed.

Margery McCammon, who lived awhile in the house on the hill at Silver Lake, grew alarmed because the lights never went out in Aimee's bedroom. Aimee was awake all night, writing, typing, and "calling aloud upon the Lord." Awakened by her cries, McCammon went to the bedroom door and pleaded with her to close her eyes and sleep. The evangelist replied that she was not going to let the devil take away from her the words and music that God had put in her heart.

The ministry of theater and music continued. The illustrated sermons during these years include the hilarious "Seven Sneezes of Shunem" (on phonograph record, 1943), "Snow White and the Seven Dwarfs," "All or Nothing at All," and "There Is No Death" (all 1944).

Lucille Stewart's film footage from 1942 and 1943 (discovered in a garage in 1990) shows the ailing woman in striking contrasts: in public performance and at small social gatherings. At a Bible College commencement or a war bond rally, she draws herself up to look tall and lean, moves gracefully and quickly, like someone half her age. At Camp Radford in the San Bernardino mountains where she has gone to share in a Church holiday, she leans heavily on the arm of Giles Knight. Bravely smiling, she has difficulty making it up and down the wooden steps of the camp headquarters, clinging to the railing. She sits on a bench, smoothing her flower-print dress, matronly, portly, preparing to cut the cake for her adoring students. They approach her as one approaches a deity. Daintily she slices the cake on her lap, smiling, handing it around, giggling as she licks a bit of icing from her fingers. It is the studied but wholly charming informality of a woman concealing acute pain. The camera captures every nuance as her expression shifts from kind attention to active interest. Head cocked, she listens. Gaily she responds, then shifts to a fierce absorption as she turns her thoughts inward, momentarily, staring into space, chewing the cake. Her oval face, under the golden braids wound close to her head, is still amazingly youthful. The eyes are riveting, their

vision sharpened on the grindstone of pain: whatever has weakened the body, the mind is as keen as ever.

On vacation in Mexico in the summer of 1943 she contracted
amoebic dysentery. She had been anemic for years before this.
According to Howard Courtney, who was called in to share
the pulpit with Aimee at the end of her life, the effect of the
primitive antibiotic treatment of the dysentery was to lower her
red corpuscle count. So during the last two years she had to
rely on frequent blood transfusions in order to keep working.
In conversation Courtney noticed that when she smiled broadly,
her gums were dead-white and so was her tongue. The "tropical
fever," as the press called it, eventually caused "perforation of
the intestine," so that medicines and nutrients were absorbed
erratically or not at all. She was continually dehydrated.

"And when she knelt at the altar," Courtney recalls sadly,
"her knees were so wasted with arthritis that they crackled like
parchment."

———————

Sometime during the end of 1943, Sister Aimee and her son
decided that Giles Knight had served his purpose, and God's,
at Angelus Temple. He had done a fine job. Without any evident
resistance or hard feelings, Knight resigned his executive positions in the Church.

On February 1, 1944, Aimee summoned reporters to her
home on the hill at 1982 Micheltorena Street for a brief press
conference. She introduced everyone to the new vice president
of the Church, her son Rolf McPherson. Rolf had taken over
the management and accounting duties from Knight. When the
journalists asked about her health, Aimee told them she was
good for another fifty years. Everybody laughed.

Her spirits were improved in 1944. Rolf McPherson, Nathaniel Van Cleave, Howard Courtney, and others who worked
with the evangelist agree that the end of the Knight era gave
Aimee a new lease on life. She was talking about going back
on the road and doing the thing she loved best, evangelizing in
tabernacles and auditoriums from coast to coast.

When the time came to dedicate a new church in Oakland,

she flew north with her son and an entourage that included her nurse, her music director, a tenor soloist, and a press agent. She loved airplanes. She was in high spirits when they landed in Oakland on Monday, September 25.

On her first full day in Oakland, Aimee decided to provide photo opportunities by driving a horse and buggy in a parade to the Oakland Auditorium. It was in Oakland, in July of 1922, that she had first had the vision of Lion, Ox, Eagle, and Man. So as 10,000 listened, she preached on the origins of the Foursquare Gospel, her vision and the living church. When she was finished, she announced that on the next night her topic would be "The Story of My Life," a sermon that had become a classic of religious oratory, an evangelistic "set piece."

This was wartime, and Oakland was under a blackout. In her darkened room at the Leamington Hotel, Aimee talked for some time with Rolf, in an effort to relax. The audience always excited her—at eleven o'clock she was still keyed up. Rolf recalls her standing at the open window, hearing an airplane roaring overhead and musing aloud: "I wonder, when we die, if we will be riding around in airplanes?"

Rolf kissed his mother good night and left her.

In her purse, Aimee carried a bottle of sleeping capsules. Rolf knew that his mother had been taking sedatives under Dr. Wilburn Smith's supervision. But these particular pills, containing a new barbiturate compound, bore no druggist's label on the bottle. The pills, legally classified as a "hypnotic sedative," had not been prescribed by Dr. Smith. It is not known where Aimee got them.

She shook several of the pills from the bottle, and then several more. She put the bottle back in her purse. She took some of the pills and got into bed. It was dark in the hotel room. She was not sure how many of the pills she would need in order to sleep, so she kept some on the pillow beside her. A few fell to the floor.

She lay in the bed and stared up into the darkness. Tomorrow would be a long day, and she could not do what she had to do without getting a few hours of sleep. She would be preaching "The Story of My Life," and it took a lot of energy, more energy as her life grew longer. She took some more of the pills, and forgot how many she had taken.

She had not seen her daughter or her mother in seven years.

Between waking and a restless trance that was not the sort of sleep she needed, Aimee drifted toward dawn, when she felt very sick. She was sweating heavily, her heart was racing, and she could not get her breath.

Not wanting to alarm Rolf by waking him, she picked up the telephone and called her doctor in Los Angeles. Dr. Smith was performing emergency surgery, so he could not respond. Aimee called another Los Angeles physician, who referred her to a Dr. Palmer in Oakland.

Before she was able to make the third call, she went into shock.

At ten o'clock Rolf went to wake his mother and found her lying in bed, unconscious, breathing hoarsely. On the pillow and on the floor were capsules of the barbiturate compound. Unable to revive her, he summoned medical assistance. But it was too late.

Sister Aimee was pronounced dead at 11:45 A.M. on September 27, 1944. She was 53.

The Angelus Temple chimes, programmed to ring at noon, mysteriously failed, hanging silent in the belfry.

———

Her body was flown back to Los Angeles. She lay in state on the Angelus Temple stage for three days and nights, in a bronze casket lined with quilted white satin. Dressed in a white gown with shield and cross stitched on the bosom, wrapped in her long blue cape, she clasped a white-bound bible. On her shoulders were gardenias and roses.

Sixty thousand mourners passed the bier. Lines formed around the Temple, four and six abreast. The comment most often heard was "There's the woman who led me to Jesus." Others came to thank Sister Aimee for the eyes they used to look upon her, the legs that carried them to the altar. The stage, orchestra pit, and choir loft were filled with flowers. And when the aisles were almost filled with roses, orchids, and gardenias, five carloads of flowers were turned away at the door. Florists said they had never seen the like; invoices totaled more than $50,000, $10,000 for the orchids alone.

The funeral was delayed to give Foursquare ministers from around the country time to get to Los Angeles. Wartime restrictions made travel difficult. Harold McPherson took a relay of buses from Ocala, Florida in order "to be with Rolf and comfort him in his sorrow."

Roberta and her infant daughter Victoria at last secured a plane ticket and flew out of New York. In Kansas City Roberta lost her seat to a military passenger, so she did not arrive in time for the funeral.

A motorcade of 600 automobiles escorted the hearse to Forest Lawn Memorial Park. Closed to the public, the cemetery admitted 2,000 made up of family and Church officials, and 1,700 ministers Aimee had ordained. These stood bearing American flags, forming an "Avenue of Sorrow" to the broad tomb on Sunrise Slope.

A photograph of the family approaching the tomb shows a grim-faced Rolf McPherson in the lead, his wife on his arm, her head down in sorrow; behind Rolf, his older daughter Kay, in adolescence the mirror image of her mother; the stoic profile of the hearty Harold McPherson with his arm around little Marlene, Rolf's younger daughter; behind them, Temple lawyer Joseph Fainer escorting a weeping Minnie Kennedy.

Sister Aimee was buried October 9, 1944, her birthday.

EPILOGUE

Rumors of suicide put a melodramatic spin on the climactic news story of Sister's career. Eulogies in the world press were lengthy, impassioned, and full of praise. In death, people did not hesitate to compare her to John Knox, John Wesley, Martin Luther, or Dwight Moody. Controversy over the cause of death was fed by an unusually lengthy inquest. The jury did not enter their verdict until October 13. They ruled out suicide. "Death was caused by shock (contributed to by adrenal hemorrhage) and respiratory failure, from an accidental overdose of barbital compound." There was no evidence of recent depression. Said Dr. Mary Ruth Oldt of Western Laboratories, assistant county pathologist in charge of the autopsy: "Mrs. McPherson was a very sick woman, with a bad kidney condition, which seriously damaged the liver, thus increasing the effect of the drug she took."

The cash value of Sister Aimee's estate was about $10,000. In her will dated March 27, 1944 she left $2,000 to Roberta and the rest to Rolf.

Minnie Kennedy died at her home in Hermosa Beach in November of 1947, of natural causes.

Like the Hebrew prophet who led his people to the borders of Canaan, Sister Aimee never enjoyed the Promised Land: the end of World War II, the exponential growth of the Foursquare Church under the leadership of her son.

When Rolf took over, there were 410 churches in North America, 200 mission stations and about 29,000 members. The church held assets of about $2,800,000.

As of this writing the balance sheet for the International Church of the Foursquare Gospel shows a total fund balance (assets minus liabilities) of $357,335,562. There are 25,577 Foursquare churches worldwide in 74 countries, with a total of almost a million and seven hundred thousand members. Rolf is semi-retired, but his example and the founder's are upheld in the leadership of President John Holland, Executive Secretary Charles Duarte, Vice President Roy Hicks, Jr., Secretaries John Bowers and Leita Mae Steward, and the Pastors of Angelus Temple, Harold Helms and his wife Winona.

NOTES

1. THE EARLY YEARS

MOUNT FOREST, ONTARIO, 1915

3–4 Aimee Semple McPherson, *In the Service of the King* (New York: Boni & Liveright, 1927), pp. 149–150.

AIMEE'S PARENTS

5 Roberta Salter, Interview, December 11, 1989.
6 Census of Lindsay, Ontario, 1881; Census of Salford, 1891.
6–7 Marriage license, record #183–5, Oct. 30, 1886, State of Michigan, County of St. Clair.
7–8 *This Is That* (Los Angeles: Echo Park Evangelistic Association, 1923, 3rd edition).
9 Ibid., p. 15.
9–10 Ibid.
11 Aimee Semple McPherson, *Aimee: Life Story of Aimee Semple McPherson* (Los Angeles: Foursquare Publications, 1979) pp. 9–10.
14 Salter, op. cit.

CHILDHOOD MEMORIES

15 *Aimee: Life Story*, pp. 10–11.
16 *In the Service of the King*, p. 64.
16–17 Ibid., p. 61.
18–19 *This Is That*, p. 23.

SCHOOL DAYS

20   *In the Service of the King*, pp. 64–66.

20–21 Ibid., p. 65.

21–22 *Aimee: Life Story*, pp. 14–15.

23   Ibid., p. 15.

23   *This Is That*, p. 26.

25   *Aimee: Life Story*, p. 12.

26   Ibid., p. 13.

28   Doug Carr, J. C. Herbert, Interviews in Salford, October 1989.

28   *This Is That*, p. 28.

REBELLION

29–30 Ibid., pp. 29–31.

30–32 *Aimee: Life Story*, p. 16.

33   *Family Herald and Weekly Star*, Wednesday, July 18, 1906.

34–35 *This Is That*, p. 31.

35   Ibid., p. 18.

35   *Aimee: Life Story*, p. 19.

36   Ibid., p. 20.

37   *This Is That*, p. 33.

38   *Aimee: Life Story*, p. 21.

39   Ibid., p. 22.

39   *Woodstock Sentinel Review*, August 31, 1907.

FIRST LOVE

41   *Aimee: Life Story*, pp. 22–24.

41–42 *This Is That*, p. 35.

42   Salter, Interview, December 5, 1990.

42–45 Stanley Burgess and Gary B. McGee, editors, *Dictionary of Pentecostal and Charismatic Movements* (Grand Rapids: Regency Reference Library, 1988), p. 850.

46   *This Is That*, p. 36.

47   Ibid.

CONVERSION

48   *This Is That*, p. 37.
48   Ibid., p. 38.
48   Ibid., p. 39.
49   *Aimee: Life Story*, p. 25.
49   *In the Service of the King*, p. 81.
49   *Aimee: Life Story*, p. 25.
50   *This Is That*, p. 42.
51   Ibid., p. 43.
52   *Aimee: Life Story*, p. 30.
53   Ibid., p. 30.
53   *This Is That*, pp. 44–45.
53   Ibid., p. 46.

MARRIAGE

54   *Sentinel Review*, August 13, 1908, p. 3, col. 3.
55   *Aimee: Life Story*, p. 34.
55   *This Is That*, p. 55.
56   *Aimee: Life Story*, p. 33.
56   Ibid., p. 36.
56   *This Is That*, p. 57.
57   Ibid., p. 58.
59   Ibid., p. 59.
59   Ibid., p. 60.
60   *Aimee: Life Story*, p. 37.
60   Ibid., p. 38.
61   Salter Interview, December 30, 1989.
62   *Aimee: Life Story*, pp. 44–47.
63   "Sermon: Lost and Restored," reprinted in *The Foursquare Gospel* (Los Angeles: Foursquare Publications, 1969).

CHINA

65   *Aimee: Life Story*, p. 54.
66   Ibid., pp. 56–57.
66   *In the Service of the King*, p. 121.
67   *This Is That*, p. 69.
69   *Aimee: Life Story*, p. 69.

69   *This Is That*, p. 72.
70   Marriage application and license #587845, issued in Cook County, State of Illinois. Aimee acquired U.S. citizenship by this marriage.
71   Rolf McPherson Interview, November 29, 1989.
71   *This Is That*, p. 73.
73   Ibid., pp. 74–76.
73   Ibid.
74   Ibid., p. 77.
75   Ibid., p. 77.
75   Ibid., p. 78.
75   Ibid., p. 79.

THE OLD-TIME POWER

76   *This Is That*, p. 82.
76   Ibid., p. 83.
77   Ibid., p. 82.
78   *This Is That*, 1st edition, p. 253.
78–79 *This Is That*, 1923, p. 86.

MOUNT FOREST, 1915

79   *Aimee: Life Story*, p. 81.
80   Robert Mapes Anderson, *Vision of the Disinherited: The Making of American Pentecostalism* (New York: Oxford University Press, 1979).
80   *Aimee: Life Story*, p. 81.
81   *In the Service of the King*, p. 151.
81–82 *Aimee: Life Story*, p. 98.
82–83 "Letter from Elizabeth Sharp," appendix to *This Is That*, 2nd edition, 1919, pp. 254–61.
84   *In the Service of the King*, p. 155.

TRIUMPH

86   *In the Service of the King*, p. 155.
87   Ibid., pp. 157–58.

88   "Letter from Elizabeth Sharp," p. 257.
88–91 Ibid., pp. 258–261.

2. HER RISE TO FAME

CORONA, NEW YORK, 1916

95–96 Salter, Interview, December 11, 1989.
97–98 *Aimee: Life Story*, p. 88.
99   Ibid., p. 90.
99   Ibid., p. 91.
100   Ibid.
101–3 "Testimony of Pastor W. K. Bouton," reprinted in appendix
       to *This Is That*, 2nd edition, 1919, pp. 261–64.
101   *In the Service of the King*, p. 170.
103–5 *This Is That*, pp. 94–96.

A MIRACULOUS HEALING

107   Rolf McPherson, Interview, December 1, 1989.
107   *In the Service of the King*, p. 173.
108   *Aimee: Life Story*, p. 92.
109   Ibid.
109   Ibid., pp. 92–93.
110   Ibid.
111   *In the Service of the King*, pp. 175–76.
114   Ibid, p. 176.

FAME

114   *Aimee: Life Story*, p. 94.
115   *This Is That*, pp. 98–99.
115   *In the Service of the King*, pp. 180–82.
116   Salter, Interview, December 30, 1989.

117   *In the Service of the King*, pp. 183–87.

117   Ibid., p. 189.

118   Ibid.

118–19 *Aimee: Life Story*, pp. 95–96.

119   Ambrose Worrall, *The Gift of Healing* (New York: Harper & Row, 1965), pp. 234–38.

120   *In the Service of the King*, p. 193.

120   *This Is That*, p. 102.

121   *In the Service of the King*, p. 196.

121   Salter, Unpublished memoir, n.d.

122   *This Is That*, p. 105.

123   Ibid., p. 107.

124   Ibid., p. 109.

124   Ibid., p. 108.

125   Ibid., p. 111.

THE GYPSY LIFE

126   *This Is That*, pp. 112–13.

127   Ibid., p. 113.

127   McPherson, Interview, November 29, 1989.

128   *The Bridal Call*, January 1918, pp. 13–14.

128   *This Is That*, pp. 116–18.

129   Salter, Interview, October 5, 1991.

130   Salter, Unpublished memoir, n.d.

130   *The Bridal Call*, May 1918, pp. 2–3.

131   Ibid., p. 6.

131   *This Is That*, p. 120.

132–33 McPherson, Interview, November 29, 1989.

133–34 *This Is That*, pp. 126–27.

PHILADELPHIA, 1918

135   *The Bridal Call*, August 1918.

137   Ibid., p. 14.

138   Ibid., July 1918, p. 1.

139 ff. Ibid., September, 1918.

143   *This Is That*, p. 141.

144   *The Bridal Call*, March 1922, p. 8.
145   *This Is That*, pp. 142–143.

CALIFORNIA

146–47 *This Is That*, p. 129.
147 ff. Salter, Interview, December 30, 1989.
148   *This Is That*, p. 151.
149   Ibid., p. 154.
151   *The Los Angeles Times*, April 18, 1906.
152   Frank Bartleman, *Azusa Street* (South Plainfield, Bridge Publishing, Inc., 1980 reprint of 1925 ed.), pp. 13–66.
152   Ibid., p. 54.
152–53 *This Is That*, pp. 160–62.
153   Ibid., pp. 163–64.
154   *This Is That*, p. 166.

BALTIMORE, 1919

154–55 *The Bridal Call*, February 1919, p. 2.
157 ff. *The Baltimore Sun*, Saturday Morning, December 6, 1919.
160 ff. *The Baltimore Star*, December 9, 1919, Evening edition, p. 9.
160 ff. *The Baltimore News*, December 6–9, 1919.
161   *The Bridal Call*, January, 1920.
162–66 *The Baltimore Star*, Ibid.
166 ff. Descriptions of healings from the point of view of the invalids is necessarily impressionistic. All are based upon eyewitness accounts.
168 ff. *The Baltimore Star*, December 12, 1919, p. 7.
170   *This Is That*, p. 175.
171   Ibid., p. 178.
173   *The Bridal Call*, March 1920, p. 14.
173   *This Is That*, pp. 192–95.

3. THE HEALING TOUCH

WASHINGTON, D.C., 1920

177 ff. *The Washington Times*, April 9, 1920.
183   Ibid., Monday, April 12, 1920.

THE RISING TIDE

184–85 McPherson, Interview, December 30, 1989.
186   *This Is That*, p. 214.
187 ff. Ibid., pp. 201–214.
187–95 *The Dayton Journal*, May 14, 1920; *The Dayton Times*, May
        14–24, 1920.
195 ff. *This Is That*, pp. 218–23.
196 ff. *The Alton Times*, June 24–July 12, 1920.
197   *The Bridal Call*, April, 1920, p. 10.
198   *This Is That*, p. 223.
199   Ibid., p. 227.
199   Ibid., p. 228.
200   *The Public Ledger*, Frederick Norcross, October 29, 1920.
200   *The Evening Bulletin*, October 29, 1920.
200   *The Philadephia Inquirer*, October 29, 1920.
201   *This Is That*, p. 229.

CALIFORNIA, 1921

201   Salter, Interview, December 30, 1989.
203 ff. *Aimee: Life Story*, p. 118.
203 ff. *In the Service of the King*, pp. 246–48.
203 ff. *This Is That*, pp. 528–33.
204   Ibid., p. 530.
205   *Aimee: Life Story*, p. 121.
206 ff. *This Is That*, pp. 250–53.

207   Ibid., p. 269.

208   Ibid., p. 268.

208   Ibid., p. 276.

209   *The Los Angeles Times*, January 27, 1921.

209 ff. *In the Service of the King*, pp. 221–29.

209 ff. *This Is That*, pp. 277–93.

212   Ibid., pp. 311–12.

212   *The St. Louis Globe Democrat*, April 25, 1921.

213   *This Is That*, pp. 317–35.

THE GREAT CAMPAIGNS

217   *The Bridal Call*, September, 1921, pp. 11–14.

217   Salter, Interview, May 19, 1990.

218   Lately Thomas, *Storming Heaven* (New York: William Morrow and Company, Inc., 1970), p. 37.

218 ff. *The Bridal Call*, October 1921, p. 6.

218   *The San Jose Mercury*, August 7, 1921.

219   Ibid.

220 ff. Ibid., August 9, 1921. All quotes from files of *The San Jose Mercury*, issues August 7–September 7.

223   Aimee Semple McPherson, *Divine Healing Sermons* (Los Angeles, Echo Park Evangelistic Association, n.d.), p. 46.

224   Ibid., pp. 107–8.

225   *The San Jose Mercury*, August 11, 1921.

226   *The San Francisco Chronicle*, August 12, 1921.

227 ff. Ibid., August 21, 1921.

232   *The San Jose Mercury*, August 22–28, 1921.

233   Ibid., August 30, 1921.

234   Ibid., September 6, 1921.

234   Robert Middleton, "Fresno Staff Reporter Writes," reprinted in *The Bridal Call*, March, 1922, pp. 11–12.

235   *This Is That*, p. 423.

235   *Aimee: Life Story*, p. 121.

236   Middleton, op. cit.

237 ff. *The Bridal Call*, August, 1921.

237 ff. *This Is That*, pp. 336–72.

238   Frances Wayne, *The Denver Post*, July 13, 1921.

239   *This Is That*, pp. 442–51.

240   *The Daily Press*, Arkansas City, May 29, 1922, reprinted in *This Is That*, pp. 404–5.

THE FIRST ABDUCTION

241 ff. Frances Wayne, *The Denver Post*, June 18, 1922.
243   Salter, Interview, December 30, 1989.
243   Ibid.
243   *This Is That*, p. 495.
244   Ibid., p. 503.

4. THE TEMPLE

NEW YEAR'S, 1923

247   *This Is That*, p. 539.
248   *The New York Times*, January 2, 1923.
249   *In the Service of the King*, p. 250.
250   John and Laree Caughey, *Los Angeles: Biography of a City* (Berkeley: University of California Press, 1976), pp. 255–59.
251   Morrow Mayo, *Los Angeles* (New York: Alfred Knopf, 1933), pp. 252–53.
251   Leo Rosten, *The Movie Makers* (New York: Harcourt Brace, 1941), p. 21.
253 ff. Salter, Interviews, December 11 and 30, 1989.
257   According to Salter the bird disappeared after the first profanity. Accounts differ.
258   A. B. Teffetteller, Interview, January 26, 1991.
258   Elmer and Margery McCammon, op. cit.
259   Salter, Interview, December 30, 1989.

AT HOME IN LOS ANGELES, 1924

259 ff. Salter, Interview, December 30, 1989.
261–63 Roberta Salter, Unpublished memoir, n.d.

264   *Aimee: Life Story*, pp. 127–28.

264   Lately Thomas, *The Vanishing Evangelist*, pp. 28–29.

264   *Aimee: Life Story*, pp. 111–12.

265   According to Rolf McPherson, after Elim's contact with ASM, their name was changed to Elim Foursquare Gospel Alliance.

265   *The Bridal Call*, October, 1922.

266 ff.   Alma Whitaker, *The Los Angeles Times*, March 23, 1924.

273–74 Lately Thomas, *Storming Heaven* (New York: William Morrow & Co., 1970), pp. 33–34.

275   *The Bridal Call*, January, 1924.

276 ff.   Salter, Unpublished memoir, n.d.

278 ff.   Salter, Interview, December 30, 1989.

280–82 McPherson, Interview, December 1, 1989.

SCANDAL

282   *The Los Angeles Times*, October 15–28, 1925.

282   Nancy Barr Mavity, *Sister Aimee* (New York: Doubleday, Doran and Company, 1931), p. 63.

283   Gerald Johnson, *The American Mercury*, July, 1924, Vol. II, #7, p. 366.

284   Morrow Mayo, *Los Angeles*, p. 275.

285   Harold Ellens, *Models of Religious Broadcasting* (Grand Rapids, Michigan: Eerdmans, 1974).

286 ff.   Minnie Kennedy, Interview with William Parker of the Hearst Service, July 16, 1928, reprinted in Mavity, p. 87.

288   *The Los Angeles Times*, August 30, 1925.

288   Thomas, *Storming Heaven*, p. 40.

288   Thomas, *The Vanishing Evangelist*, p. 325.

289   Raymond Cox, *The Verdict Is In* (Los Angeles: The Research Press, 1983), pp. 110–11.

290 ff.   *Aimee: Life Story*, pp. 137–43.

291   Mavity, p. 80.

292   *In the Service of the King*, p. 263.

293   Transcript of the grand jury, pp. 809ff.

294 ff.   Files of *The Los Angeles Times* and *Examiner* from May 19, 1926 through January 11, 1927 contain extensive daily coverage of the disappearance, reappearance, and trial of ASM. Unless

otherwise noted, dates, quotes, and details refer to news reports confirmed by two or more sources.
295   Salter, Interview, May 19, 1990.

KIDNAPPED

299   Cox, pp. 230–31.
301   Mayo, p. 285.
301   *The Vanishing Evangelist*, pp. 181–84.
301   *Storming Heaven*, p. 60.
302   Mayo, p. 286.
302   Ibid., p. 288.
303   *The Vanishing Evangelist*, pp. 121ff.
304ff. Grand jury testimony, Transcript, pp. 570–74.
306   Mavity, p. 213.
308   *The New Republic*, November, 1926, p. 291.
308–9 *In the Service of the King*, p. 274.
309   *The Vanishing Evangelist*, p. 253.
309ff. Transcript quoted by Cox, pp. 112–15.
312   *Storming Heaven*, pp. 61–62.
314   H. L. Mencken, *The Baltimore Evening Sun*, December 13, 1926.

VINDICATION

315   *Storming Heaven*, pp. 61–62.
316   Ibid., p. 65.
317   Ibid.
318   *The New York Times*, February 19, 1927.
319   Ibid., February 20, 1927, p. 12.
321   *The New Yorker*, Vol. 3, March 5, 1927, pp. 65–67.
322   *Storming Heaven*, p. 67.
322   *The Los Angeles Times*, April 3, 1927.

AIMEE VS. MINNIE, 1927

323   *Storming Heaven*, p. 71.
323   Rolf McPherson, Correspondence, May 1992.
324   *Aimee: Life Story*, p. 225.
325ff. *Storming Heaven*, p. 74.

325   McPherson, Interviews, January 24–25, 1991.

326   *Storming Heaven*, pp. 87–88.

327   *Sentinel Review*, Woodstock, Ontario, Thursday, October 20, 1927.

327   *Storming Heaven*, p. 91.

327   McPherson, Interview, January 23, 1991.

328 ff.   McPherson, Correspondence, May, 1992.

328–29 Mavity, pp. 340–45.

330   *Storming Heaven*, p. 92.

330   Ibid., p. 114.

330   Ibid.

331   *The Baltimore Sun*, October 18, 1928.

332   *Storming Heaven*, pp. 116–22.

332   Ibid., p. 125.

333   John Goben, *Aimee—The Gospel Gold Digger!* (Los Angeles, 1932), p. 36.

333   *Storming Heaven*, p. 393.

334 ff.   Goben, Ibid., p. 40.

336   Ibid., p. 42.

THE CRASH

339   *The Los Angeles Times*, August 1930.

340   *Storming Heaven*, p. 155.

341 ff.   Goben, pp. 45–50.

342   *The Bridal Call*, December 1930, pp. 12–15.

343   *Storming Heaven*, pp. 162–63.

344   *Aimee: Life Story*, p. 229.

344   McPherson, Interview, November 29, 1989.

346   Leeland Edwards, Interview, January 24, 1991.

346   Mavity, p. 353.

347   *Storming Heaven*, p. 173.

347   *The Los Angeles Times*, March 5, 1931.

347 ff.   Salter, Interview, May 19, 1990.

348 ff.   Gerith von Ulm, *Charlie Chaplin, King of Tragedy* (Caldwell, Idaho: The Caxton Printers, Ltd., 1940), pp. 328–31.

5. THE FINAL YEARS

ATTAR OF ROSES

355   *Storming Heaven*, pp. 178–79.

355   Ibid.

357 ff. *The Bridal Call*, June 1931, pp. 9–10, 33.

361   Nathaniel Van Cleave, Interview, January 25, 1991.

362   McPherson, Interview, January 24, 1991.

362   *Storming Heaven*, p. 210.

362   Salter, Interview, October 5, 1991.

363   Carey McWilliams, "Aimee Semple McPherson: 'Sunshine in My Soul,' " from *The Aspirin Age*, ed. Isabel Leighton (New York: Simon & Schuster, 1949).

363   Salter, Interview, December 30, 1989.

364   *Aimee: Life Story*, pp. 233–34.

364   McPherson, Interview, January 22, 1991.

365–66 *Storming Heaven*, pp. 206–7.

367   *Aimee: Life Story*, p. 235.

367–68 *Storming Heaven*, pp. 214–18.

368   *The Boston Herald*, October 10–18.

THE COMMISSARY

369   Report: To the Honorable Board of Equalization/County of Los Angeles/Hall of Justice/Los Angeles, California, June 1936.

370 ff. *Storming Heaven*, pp. 219–20.

371   *The Bridal Call*, February 1932, pp. 16–17.

372 ff. *Storming Heaven*, pp. 222–36.

375 ff. Ibid., pp. 238–42.

376 ff. Anthony Quinn, *The Original Sin* (Boston: Little Brown Co., 1972), pp. 123–30.

380   Transcript of "Speaking Freely" on NBC News, host Edwin Newman, taped November 12, 1968, aired November 30.

381   *The Los Angeles Times*, December 30, 1932.

381   *Storming Heaven*, pp. 254–55.

382   *Newsweek*, July 1, 1933, p. 18. According to Roberta Salter, the "baby telegram" was a reference to a running family joke about the couple having children.

382   *Storming Heaven*, p. 260.

383   Ibid., pp. 261–65.

SHOW BUSINESS

383   Forman Brown, *Small Wonder: The Story of the Yale Puppeteers and the Turnabout Theatre* (Metuchen, New Jersey: Scarecrow, 1974), pp. 110–12.

384   *Storming Heaven*, p. 262.

384   *The New York Times*, September 19, 1933, p. 23.

385 ff. *The New Yorker*, vol. 9, September 30, 1933, pp. 30–34.

387   *Variety*, September 26, 1933, p. 12.

387   Ibid., October 4, 1944.

388   *Newsweek*, September 30, 1933.

388   *The Cleveland Plain Dealer*, December 16, 1933.

389   *Variety*, October 3, 1933, p. 50.

389   *Vanity Fair*, March 1933.

SHARING THE STAGE, LOS ANGELES, 1935

390   *Storming Heaven*, p. 17.

391   Ibid., pp. 275–78.

392   Aimee Semple McPherson, *Give Me My Own God* (N.Y.: Kinsey & Co., Inc., 1936), p. 1.

392   Ibid., pp. 2–3.

393 ff. Ibid., pp. 169–73.

395 ff. Salter, Interview, May 19, 1990.

396   *Give Me My Own God*, p. 301.

398   Teffetteller, McCammon, Baker, et al., Interviews, January 26, 1991.

398–99 *The Los Angeles Times*, February 10–12, 1936.

400   Mary Young, A. B. and Modena Teffetteller, Edythe G. Dorrance, Elmer and Margery McCammon, Ruth Baker, Edyth Campbell, Interviews, January 26, 1991.

401   Ibid.
402   McPherson, Correspondence, May 1992.
403   Salter, Interview, May 19, 1990.
404   McPherson, Interview, January 25, 1991.
405   *Aimee: Life Story*, pp. 245–46.
405–6   *Foursquare Crusader*, August 5, 1936, p. 3.
406   *Storming Heaven*, p. 290.
407   McPherson, Correspondence, May, 1992.
407   *Storming Heaven*, p. 291.
408 ff. McPherson, Interview, January 25, 1991.
409 ff. *Storming Heaven*, p. 295.
410   Ibid., p. 296.
410–11 Ibid., p. 301.
411   *Regem Adorate*, Program notes.
411   *Foursquare Crusader*, December, 1936.
412   *Storming Heaven*, p. 310.
412 ff. *The Los Angeles Times, The Los Angeles Herald*; files from April
        13–27, 1937 contain extensive daily coverage of the slander
        trial. Unless otherwise noted, all quotes and details refer to
        news articles. See also Lately Thomas's *Storming Heaven*,
        pp. 303–24.
415   *Aimee: Life Story*, p. 245.

SANCTUARY

416   *Aimee: Life Story*, p. 248.
417   *Storming Heaven*, p. 310.
418   Interviews with Salter, McPherson, Nathaniel Van Cleave,
        Margery McCammon, et al.
418–19 Salter, Interview, May 19, 1990.
419   McPherson, Interview, December 1, 1989.
426   Leeland Edwards, Interview, January 24, 1991.
426 ff. *Aimee: Life Story*, p. 249.
427   Ibid., p. 251.
428   *Foursquare Crusader*, September, 1941.
429   Nathaniel Van Cleave, Interview, January 25, 1991.
429 ff. Teffettellers, McCammons, Baker, et al., Interviews, January
        26, 1991.
430   Van Cleave, op. cit.
431   Margery McCammon, Interview, January 26, 1991.

431 Teffettellers, McCammons, et al.

432 Charles Duarte, Interview, November 30, 1989.

432 ff. Van Cleave, op. cit.

434 Margery McCammon, op. cit.

434 McPherson, Interview, January 25, 1991.

435 Margery McCammon, op. cit.

437 Various wire service and news accounts, including *The Oakland Tribune*, September 27, 1944.

438 McPherson, Correspondence, May 1992.

438 *The Los Angeles Times*, October 9, 1944.

440 Certificate of death of Aimee Semple McPherson, State of California Department of Public Health, 10-13-44, #44-061113, Coroner's Register-Inquest #7986, Mark L. Emerson, M.D., Coroner.

440 Financial information supplied by Foursquare International.

440 Rolf and Roberta, living on opposite sides of the continent, keep in touch and get together at the annual convention of the Church.

BIBLIOGRAPHY

BOOKS ABOUT SISTER AIMEE

Bahr, Robert, *Least of All Saints*. Englewood Cliffs, N.J.: Prentice-Hall, Inc., 1979.

Brown, Forman G. *Small Wonder: The Story of the Yale Puppeteers and the Turnabout Theatre*. Metuchen, N.J.: Scarecrow, 1980.

Coletta, Paolo E. "Political Puritan," in *William Jennings Byran*. Lincoln: University of Nebraska Press, 1969.

Cox, Raymond. *The Verdict Is In*. Los Angeles: Research Publishers, 1983.

Douglas, George H. *Women of the 20's*. Dallas: Saybrook, 1986.

Ellens, J. Harold. *Models of Religious Broadcasting*. Grand Rapids, Mich.: Eerdmans, 1974.

Handlin, Oscar. *This Was America*. New York: Harper & Row, 1949.

Goben, John D., Rev. *Aimee the Gospel Gold Digger*. Los Angeles: Peoples Publishing Co., 1932.

Highet, Gilbert. *Explorations*. New York: Oxford University Press, 1971.

Jones, Charles J. *A Guide to the Study of the Pentecostal Movement*. ATLA Bibliography Series, No. 6. 2 Vols. Metuchen, N.J.: Scarecrow, 1983.

Kershner, John J. *The Disappearance of Aimee Semple McPherson; with a Scientific Analysis of Her Teaching, Activities, and Emotions*. Published by Author, 1926.

Mavity, Nancy Barr, *Sister Aimee*. Garden City: Doubleday, Doran and Co., Inc., 1931.

Mayo, Morrow. *Los Angeles*. New York: Alfred Knopf, 1933.

McPherson, Aimee Semple. *Aimee: Life Story.* Waco, Texas: Word, 1973.

————, *Divine Healing Sermons.* Los Angeles: Echo Park Evangelistic Assn., n.d.

————, *Fire from on High.* California: Heritage Committee, 1969.

————, *The Foursquare Gospel*, comp. Dr. Raymond L. Cox, California: Heritage Committee, 1969.

————, *Give Me My Own God.* New York: H. C. Kinsey, 1936.

————, *In the Service of the King.* New York: Boni and Liveright, 1927.

————, *Lost and Restored.* Los Angeles: Foursquare Publications, n.d.

————, *The Story of My Life.* Hollywood: International Correspondents' Pubn., 1951.

————, *This Is That.* Los Angeles: Bridal Call Publishing Co., 1919. 2nd Edition: Los Angeles: Echo Park Evangelistic Assn., Inc., 1923.

McWilliams Carey. "Sunlight in My Soul," *The Aspirin Age*, ed. Isabelle Leighton. New York: Simon & Schuster, 1949.

Mencken, H. L. *The New Mencken Letters.* New York: Dial, 1977.

Nichols, Beverly. "Christ in Vaudeville," *The Star Spangled Manner.* New York: Doubleday, 1930.

Quinn, Anthony. *The Original Sin.* Boston: Little Brown, 1972.

Ross, Isabel. *Charmers and Cranks.* New York: Harper & Row, 1965.

Shorer, Mark. *Sinclair Lewis: An American Life.* New York: McGraw, 1961.

Sherrill, John L. *They Speak in Tongues.* Westwood, N.J.: Spire Books, 1964.

Shuler, Rev. R. P. (Bob). *McPhersonism.* Los Angeles, 1924.

Steele, Robert V. P. (pseud. Lately Thomas). *Storming Heaven; the Lives and Turmoils of Minnie Kennedy and Aimee Semple McPherson.* New York: Morrow, 1970.

————, *The Vanishing Evangelist.* New York: Viking, 1959.

Toller, E. "Man and Masses in the United States," *This Was America*. New York: Harper & Row, 1949.

Von Ulm, Gerith. *King of Tragedy, A Charlie Chaplin Biography*. Caldwell, Idaho: The Caxton Printers Ltd, 1940.

Williams, Ben, and Williams, Charles. *The Story of Aimee McPherson: Was She Kidnapped? Not an Attack—Not a Defense*. Los Angeles: Williams and Williams, 1926.

BOOKS ON RELATED TOPICS

Anderson, Robert Mapes. *The Vision of the Disinherited: The Making of American Pentecostalism*. New York: Oxford University Press, 1979.

Bartleman, Frank. *Azusa Street*. South Plainfield: Bridge Publishing, Inc., 1980.

Burgess, Stanley, and McGee, Gary, eds. *Dictionary of Pentecostal and Charismatic Movements*. Grand Rapids: Regency, 1988.

Caughey, John and Laree. *Los Angeles: Biography of a City*. Berkeley: University of California Press, 1976.

Cranston, Ruth. *The Miracle of Lourdes*. New York: Image Books, 1988.

Goodman, Felicitas D. *How about Demons? Possession and Exorcism in the Modern World*. Bloomington, Ind.: Indiana University Press, 1988.

Loud, Grover C. *Evangelized America*. New York: Dial, 1928.

McLoughlin, William G. *Revivals, Awakenings, and Reform: An Essay on Religion and Social Change in America, 1607–1977*. Chicago: University of Chicago Press, 1978.

Melton, J. Gordon. *The Encyclopedia of American Religions*. Detroit: Gale Research Co., 1987.

Rooney, Theodore W. *The Arthritis Handbook*. New York: W. C. Brown, Publisher, 1985.

Rosten, Leo. *The Movie Makers*. New York: Harcourt Brace, 1941.

Worrall, Ambrose. *The Gift of Healing*. New York: Harper & Row, 1965.

ARTICLES ABOUT SISTER AIMEE

Aikman, Duncan. "Savonarola in Los Angeles." *American Mercury*, 22 (1930), 423–30.

"Aimee MacPherson Death Rings Down the Curtain on Glamour Gospel Career." *Variety* (October 4, 1944), 2.

"Aimee Overflows Denver's Main Street—24,000 Drawn by Her." *Variety* (January 19, 1927), 2.

"Aimee Semple McPherson." *Liberty*, 69 (Winter 1974), 37–39.

"Aimee Semple McPherson." *Life*, 17 (October 30, 1944), 85–88.

"Aimee Semple McPherson." *Newsweek*, 6 (August 24, 1935), 30.

"Aimee Semple McPherson." *Time*, 9 (February 28, 1927), 20.

"Aimee Semple McPherson." *Time*, 12 (September 17, 1928), 48.

"Aimee Semple McPherson." *Time*, 15 (June 23, 1930), 34.

"Aimee Semple McPherson." *Time*, 15 (March 3, 1930), 36.

"Aimee Semple McPherson." *Time*, 15 (April 7, 1930), 40.

"Aimee Semple McPherson." *Time*, 15 (April 21, 1930), 54.

"Aimee Semple McPherson—People in the News." *Time*, 12 (September 17, 1928), 48.

"Aimee's Foursquare behind the War." *Newsweek*, 22 (July 19, 1943), 64.

"Aimee's 'Jayhawk Hitler.' " *Newsweek*, 12 (November 28, 1939), 30.

"Aimee Soft-Pedals Her Way Into New York." *Variety* (February 23, 1927), 24.

"Aimee's Rival." *The Literary Digest*, 123 (March 20, 1937), 32.

Alajalov. "Vanity Fair's Own Paper Dolls no. 2—Aimee MacPherson Hutton—Caricature." *Vanity Fair*, vol. 41 no. 3 (November 1933), 38.

"All Charged Up." *Time*, 9 (February 28, 1927), 20.

Asbury, Herbert. Review of *In the Service of the King* by Aimee Semple McPherson. *The Outlook*, 149 (August 29, 1928), 712.

Bliven, B. "Sister Aimee." *The New Republic*, 48 (November 3, 1926), 289–91.

Bissell, Shelton. "Vaudeville at Angelus Temple." *Outlook*, 149 (May 23, 1928), 126.

Bretherton, C. H. "A Prophetess at Large." *The North American Review*, 226 (December 1928), 641–44.

Budlong, Julia N. "Aimee Semple McPherson." *The Nation*, 128 (June 19, 1929), 737–39.

"California Evangelist, A" (signed J.A.S.). *The New Statesman*, 28 (November 13, 1926): 134–38.

Christiansen, Larry D. "Henceforth and Forever Aimee and Douglas." *Cochise Quarterly*, vol. 8 nos. 3–4, vol. 9 no. 1 (1979), 62.

"Christ in Vaudeville." *The New Statesman*, 31 (October 6, 1928): 785–86.

Clark, David L. "Miracles for a Dime: From Chatauqua Tent to Radio Station with Aimee Semple McPherson." *California History*, 57 (Winter 1978/1979), 354–63.

Collins, Michael. "Sister Aimee." *The Beaver*, 69:3 (June/July 1989), 28–32.

Comstock, Sarah. "Aimee Semple McPherson: Prima Donna of Revivalism." *Harpers*, 156 (December 1927), 11–19.

Covarrubias, Miguel. "Imaginary Interview No. 1, Aimee Semple McPherson vs. Mahatma Gandhi." *Vanity Fair*, vol. 37 no. 4 (December 1931), 56.

—————. "Peck's Bad Boys and Girls of the Arts." *Vanity Fair*, vol. 34 no. 5 (July 1930), 30.

Ebeling, Harry. "Aimee S. McPherson: Evangelist of the City." *Western Speech*, vol. 21 no. 3 (Summer 1957), 153–59.

Faulder, Carolyn. "The Sad Passion of Sister Aimee." *Nova* (June/July 1969), 52–55.

"Foursquare." *Time*, 40 (February 16, 1948), 71–72.

Garretto. "Vanity Fair's Great American Waxworks—The Chamber of Heroes." *Vanity Fair*, vol. 43 no. 6 (August 1934), 28–29.

"Groceries vs. Evangelism." *Time*, 44 (October 9, 1944), 58.

"Has Sister Aimee Been Deposed?" *Christian Century*, 50 (February 15, 1933), 232.

Heller, E. "Criticisms of Mrs. McPherson." *Promise*, 1 (March 1922), 17–18.

Hibben, Paxton. "Aimee and Tex." *The New Yorker*, 3 (March 5, 1927), 65–67.

Holtby, Winifred. "The Psychology of Revivalism: The Failure of Aimee Semple McPherson." *The Realist*, 1 (April 1929), 54–63.

"Hutton as Opposish to Aimee Likely in Chi." *Variety* (October 3, 1933), 45.

Johnson, Gerald W. "Saving Souls." *The American Mercury* (July 1924), 364.

Johnson, Kenneth M. "The Impeachment of Judge Carlos S. Hardy." *Journal of the West*, 10 (October 1971), 726–33.

"Law-Filed: by Aimee Semple McPherson." *Newsweek*, 2 (December 30, 1933), 26.

Lothrup, Gloria. "West of Eden: Pioneer Evangelist Aimee Semple McPherson in Los Angeles." *Journal of the West*, 27 (April 1988), 50–59.

Lynd, R. "Hot Gospel." *The New Statesman*, 32 (October 13, 1928), 8–9.

Markey, Morris. "Manifestation." *The New Yorker*, 9 (September 30, 1933), 30–34.

Mayo, Morrow. "Aimee Rises from the Sea." *The New Republic*, 61 (December 25, 1929), 136–40.

McLoughlin, William. "Aimee Semple McPherson: Your Sister in the King's Glad Service." *Journal of Popular Culture*, 1 (Winter 1968), 193–217.

Mencken, H. L. Review of *In the Service of the King* by Aimee Semple McPherson. *The American Mercury*, 13 (April 1928), 506–8.

—————. "Sister Aimee." *The Baltimore Evening Sun* (December 13, 1926).

"McPherson v. Voliva." *Time*, 14 (September 16, 1929), 34.

"Milestones—Sued." *Time*, 19 (March 7, 1932), 40.

Morris, B. G. "The Revivals of Aimee Semple McPherson." *Pacific Christian Advocate*, 70 (October 5, 1921), 4.

Parker, Dorothy. "Our Lady of the Loud Speaker." *The New Yorker*, 4 (February 25, 1928), 79–81.

Pearson, Edmund. "What Happened Afterward." *Vanity Fair*, vol. 43 no. 6 (February 1935), 54.

Plowman, Edward E. "Foursquare Anniversary: In Love with Aimee." *Christianity Today*, 17 (March 30, 1973), 50–51.

Russell, Francis. "Billy and Aimee." *National Review*, 23 (June 29, 1971), 716.

Ryder, David Warren. "Aimee Semple McPherson." *The Nation*, 123 (July 28, 1926), 81–82.

Setta, Susan. "Patriarchy and Feminism in Conflict: The Life and Thought of Aimee Semple McPherson." *Anima*, 9 (Spring 1983), 128–37.

Sherman, Richard. "Sophisticate, 1933." *Vanity Fair*, vol. 43 no. 2 (October 1933), 27.

"Sister Aimee." *The Christian Century*, 61 (October 11, 1944), 1959–1960.

"Sister Aimee $5,000 Flop at Cap; 'Harmony' $60,000; M. H. $86,000; 'Jones' Wow 37 ½ G., 'Woman' 32 G." *Variety* (September 26, 1933), 9.

"Sisters v. Satan." *Time*, 29 (January 18, 1937), 32.

Sinclair, Upton. "The Evangelist Drowns." *The New Republic*, 47 (June 30, 1926), 171.

Smith, R. L. "Has Sister Aimee Been Deposed?" *Christian Century*, 50 (February 15, 1933), 232.

Steele, Joseph Henry. "Sister Aimee: Bernhardt of the Sawdust Trail." *Vanity Fair*, vol. 40 no. 1 (March 1933), 42.

"Story of My Life." *Time*, 44 (October 9, 1944), 58.

"Tex and Aimee." *Variety* (February 23, 1927), 33.

"Theatrical Note—News in Brief." *Newsweek*, 2 (September 9, 1933), 8.

"Transition—Aimee Semple McPherson." *Newsweek*, 6 (August 24, 1935), 30.

"Transition—Arrived: Aimee Semple McPherson." *Newsweek*, 5 (June 22, 1935), 24.

"Transition—Arrived: Aimee Semple McPherson." *Newsweek*, 5 (February 23, 1935), 27.

"Transition—Exaggerated." *Newsweek* Headliners, 1 (July 1, 1933), 18.

Worthington, W. "Healing at Angelus Temple." *Christian Century*, 46 (April 24, 1929), 549–52.

Young, Stark. "Variegated Hits—Review of *As Thousands Cheer* by Irving Berlin." *The New Republic*, 76 (October 18, 1933), 279.

ARTICLES ON RELATED TOPICS

Ausubel, D. P. "Causes and Types of Narcotic Addiction: A Psychological View." *Psychiatric Quarterly*, 35 (1961), 523–31.

Coakley, J. H., Smith, P.E.M., et al. "Myositis Ossifications Non-Progressiva-Riverside Muscle Calcification in Polymyostis." *British Journal of Rheumatology*, vol. 28 no. 5 (October 1989), 443–45.

Colligan, Douglas. "A Dose of Mother Teresa." *Omni*, 10 (October 1987), 125.

Drobyski, William R., and Qazi, Raman. "Spontaneous Regression in Non-Hodgkin's Lymphoma. Clinical and Pathogenetic Considerations." *American Journal of Hematology*, vol. 31 no. 2 (June 1989), 138–41.

Holzman, David. "Chasing Answers to Miracle Cures." *Insight*, 5 (February 20, 1989), 52–54.

"How Cataracts Form." *Science News*, 119 (May 9, 1981), 296.

Hutchinson, Thomas B. "Cataracts." *Harvard Medical School Health Letter*, vol. 13 no. 6 (April 1988), 6.

Ichikawa, Motoki, Yanagisawa, Mitsuhiko, et al. "Spontaneous Improvement of Juvenile Rheumatoid Arthritis after Lymphocytosis with Suppressor Phenotype and Function." *Journal of Clinical and Laboratory Immunology*, vol. 27 no. 4 (December 1988), 197–201.

McIlwaine, G. G., Fielder, A. R., and Brittain, G. P. "Spontaneous Recovery of Vision Following an Orbital Haemorrhage." *British Journal of Ophthalmology*, vol. 73 no. 11 (November 1989), 926–27.

O'Regan, Brendan. "Healing, Remission and Miracle Cures." *Whole Earth Review* (Winter 1989), 126–36.

Straus, Hal. "The Lazarus File: When the 'Spontaneous' Cure Comes from Within (Spontaneous Remission of Illnesses)." *American Health* (May 1989), 67–74.

Sutton, Horace. "Way Back When: Frisky, Risky Birth of the Auto Age." *Smithsonian*, 11 (September 1980), 135–48.

DISSERTATIONS

Lacour, Lawrence Leland. "A Study of the Revival Method in America: 1920–1955, with Special Reference to Billy Sunday, Aimee Semple McPherson and Billy Graham." Ph.D. diss., Northwestern University, 1956.

McLoughlin, William G. "Aimee Semple McPherson: "Your Sister in the King's Glad Service." Providence: Brown University, Winter 1967.

Ross, Shelley Helene. "A Comparison of the Angelus Temple Commissionary to Other Welfare Agencies in Los Angeles During 1923–1929." Unpublished thesis, 1975.

Shanks, Kenneth Howard. "An Historical and Critical Study of the Preaching Career of Aimee Semple McPherson." Ph.D. diss., University of Southern California, 1960.

Tibbetts, Joel Whitney. "Women Who Were Called: A Study of the Contributions to American Christianity of Ann Lee, Jemima Wilkerson, Mary Baker Eddy, and Aimee Semple McPherson." Ph.D. diss., Vanderbilt, 1976.

INTERVIEWS

Baker, Ruth, January 26, 1991, Hemet, California

Campbell, Edyth, January 26, 1991, Hemet

Carr, Douglas, October 12, 1989, Salford, Ontario

Courtney, Howard, January, 1991, by telephone

Davis, Alice, November 28, 1989, Los Angeles

Davis, Marc, November 28, 1989, Los Angeles

Dorrance, Edythe G., January 26, 1991, Hemet

Duarte, Charles, November 30, 1989, Los Angeles

Edwards, Leeland, January 24, 1991, Los Angeles

Gulick, Jean, January 22, 1991, Los Angeles

Herbert, J. C., October 12, 1989, Salford

McCammon, Elmer, January 26, 1991, Hemet

McCammon, Margery, January 26, 1991, Hemet

McPherson, Rolf, November 28, 29, December 1, 1989 and January 21–25, 1991, Los Angeles

Salter, Roberta (née Semple) December 11 and 30, 1989, May 19, 1990, New York; October 5, 1991, Baltimore

Van Cleave, Nathaniel, January 25, 1991, Los Angeles

Wilson, Everett, October 12, 1989, Salford

Young, Mary, January 26, 1991, Hemet

UNPUBLISHED MEMOIRS

Roberta Salter, "The Living Church," 1956 and "Memories of Harold McPherson," n.d.

McPherson, Aimee Semple, "True Details and Facts of My Connection with Anthony Jacob Moidel," n.d.

Iris Cowie Brinkman, "Divine Healing Testimony," June 20, 1991

CORRESPONDENCE

To Daniel Mark Epstein
from Rolf McPherson, November 14, 1989
   September 28, 1990
   October 2, 1990
   May 15, 1991
   May 22, 1991
   April 13, 1992
   April 29, 1992
   June 1, 1992
   June 18, 1992

from Roberta Salter, March 19, 1991

from Everett Wilson, January 28, 1990
   February 10, 1990
   January 5, 1991
   February 10, 1991

To Amanda Dye
from Aimee Semple McPherson, August 1, 1934

INDEX OF BIBLICAL
PASSAGES AND REFERENCES

OLD TESTAMENT

NEW TESTAMENT

CHRONOLOGY OF
AIMEE SEMPLE McPHERSON

October 9, 1890	Born in Salford, Ontario
September, 1896	Enrolled at No. 3 Dereham Public School
1902	Wins gold medal in public speaking contest sponsored by Woman's Christian Temperance Union
September, 1905	Enters Ingersoll Collegiate Institute (high school)
July 18, 1906	Publishes letter concerning evolution in *Family Herald and Weekly Star*
December, 1907	Meets evangelist Robert Semple
February, 1908	Is converted, receives baptism in the Spirit and speaks in tongues
August 12, 1908	Marries Robert Semple in Salford
March, 1910	Gives first sermon in Victoria and Albert Hall, London
June, 1910	Arrives in Hong Kong
August 17, 1910	Robert Semple dies in Hong Kong
September 17, 1910	Roberta Star born in Hong Kong
November 1910	Returns to New York

February 28, 1912	Marries Harold McPherson in Chicago
March 23, 1913	Rolf McPherson born in Providence, R.I.
August, 1915	Holds first independent revival meeting in Mount Forest, Ontario
Winter, 1916–1917	First preaching tour of Florida
June 1, 1917	Begins publication of *The Bridal Call*
Summer of 1917	Preaches in Long Branch, Long Island and Boston
Winter, 1917–1918	Second Florida tour: Miami, Key West
July 21, 1918	Nationwide camp meeting, Philadelphia
October 23, 1918	Begins first transcontinental tour
December 23, 1918	Arrives in Los Angeles
October 1919	Publishes *This Is That*
December 8–21, 1919	The Baltimore revival
Spring of 1920	Washington, D.C. and Dayton, Ohio revivals
January, 1921	The San Diego revival
February, 1921	Groundbreaking for Angelus Temple
March 27, 1921	Ordained by First Baptist Church of San Jose
New Year's, 1923	Angelus Temple dedicated
February, 1924	Radio KFSG started
December 7, 1925	Opening of L.I.F.E. Bible College
May 18, 1926	Reported missing after swim at Ocean Park
June 23, 1926	Walks in from desert at Agua Prieta and tells story of kidnapping

September 16, 1926	With Minnie Kennedy, Lorraine Wiseman, and Kenneth Ormiston, charged with corruption of morals and obstruction of justice
January 10, 1927	All charges dismissed
January–March, 1927	Her "Vindication Tour"
August, 1927	Opening of Angelus Temple Commissary
October 20, 1927	James Kennedy dies
October, 1927	Publishes *In the Service of the King*
October 7–18, 1928	English tour
December, 1929	Premiere of her opera *Regem Adorate*
Spring, 1930	Tour of the Holy Land
August, 1930	Nervous breakdown
September 13, 1931	Marries David Hutton
November, 1931	Opens first soup kitchen
Summer, 1932	Contracts tropical fever
April, 1933	Produces opera, *The Crimson Road*
September, 1933–December, 1934	Last national tour
January, 1935	Divorces David Hutton
1936	*Give Me My Own God* published
December, 1936	Revival of her opera *Regem Adorate*
April 13, 1937	Her attorney sued for slander by Roberta Star
Summer, 1941	Tours Tennessee, Missouri, Ohio
September 27, 1944	Dies in Oakland
October 9, 1944	Buried in Los Angeles